UNDER HIS VERY WINDOWS

SUSAN ZUCCOTTI

Under His Very Windows

THE VATICAN AND THE HOLOCAUST IN ITALY

YALE UNIVERSITY PRESS   NEW HAVEN & LONDON

Designed by Rebecca Gibb. Set in Scala type by dix!, Syracuse, New York. Printed in the United States of America by R. R. Donnelley & Sons, Harrisonburg, Virginia.

Library of Congress Cataloging-in-Publication Data
Zuccotti, Susan, 1940–
Under his very windows : the Vatican and the Holocaust in Italy / Susan Zuccotti.
p. cm.
Includes bibliographical references (p.) and index.
ISBN 0-300-08487-0 (alk. paper)
1. Jews—Persecutions—Italy.   2. Holocaust, Jewish (1939–1945)—Italy.   3. World War, 1939–1945—Religious aspects—Catholic Church.   4. Catholic Church—Relations—Judaism.   5. Judaism—Relations—Catholic Church.   6. Pius XII, Pope, 1876–1958—Relations with Jews.   7. Antisemitism—Italy.   8. Italy—History—1914–1945.   I. Title.

DS135.I8 Z87 2000
940.53'18'0945—dc21
00-043307

10 9 8 7 6 5 4 3 2

*This book is dedicated to John E. Zuccotti, who made it possible,
and to our children Gianna, Andrew and Margaret, and Milena*

We feel we owe no greater debt to Our office and to Our time than to testify to the truth with Apostolic firmness: "to give testimony to the truth." In the fulfilment of this, Our duty, we shall not let Ourselves be influenced by earthly considerations nor be held back by mistrust or opposition, by rebuffs or lack of appreciation of Our words, nor yet by fear of misconceptions and misinterpretations.

Pope Pius XII
Summi pontificatus
Papal encyclical, October 20, 1939

I can confirm the reaction of the Vatican to the removal of Jews from Rome. . . . The Curia is dumbfounded, particularly as the action took place under the very windows of the pope, as it were.

Ernst von Weizsäcker
German ambassador to the Holy See
Report to his government
October 17, 1943, one day after the German roundup of 1,259 Jews in Rome and one day before most of them were deported to Auschwitz

By all accounts, the pope, although harassed from various quarters, has not allowed himself to be stampeded into making any demonstrative pronouncement against the removal of the Jews from Rome.

Ernst von Weizsäcker
Report to his government
October 28, 1943

Contents

Acknowledgments

Historians are often asked to give freely of their time and accumulated knowledge. Most do so, to an extent not always recognized or appreciated. But even within a generous profession, five people have been exceptionally good to me. Temporarily putting aside their own extensive commitments and responsibilities, Liliana Picciotto Fargion and Michele Sarfatti at the Centro di documentazione ebraica contemporanea in Milan patiently answered my many questions and recommended sources during the course of my several visits. Alberto Cavaglion welcomed me in Turin and introduced me to some of Italy's finest historical scholars. Klaus Voigt read part of the manuscript and saved me from several errors. And Giovanni Miccoli in Trieste shared his vast knowledge of Church history not only in conversations but in a continuing correspondence. These five are among the best in their field. Their work is cited throughout this text. Their kindness and generosity astonished and deeply moved me. I am more grateful than I can ever say.

So many others—survivors, rescuers, priests, historians, archivists, friends—gave me information, anecdotes, suggestions, and source recommendations. It is impossible to mention them all. Some of them will be pleased with this book. Others may not welcome an association with it, but their generosity and charity in meeting with me despite basic disagreements are all the more impressive. Needless to say, those who do not agree with me are in no way responsible for my conclusions.

Let me, then, express my most sincere gratitude to the following: Renato

J. Almansi, Giorgina Arian Levi, Don Carlo Badala, Father Maria Benedetto, Don Bruno Bertoli, Bruna Bocchini Camaiani, Silva Bon Gherardi, Sister Lodovica Bonatti, Sister Bernadette Brumelot with Sisters Dora, Filomena, and Luisa, Don Aldo Brunacci, Tullia Catalan, Furio Colombo, Walter Crivellin, Lea Di Nola, Albert Feldman, Eugene Fisher, Renza Fozzati, Saul Friedländer, Monsignor Pier Francesco Fumagalli, Bartolo Gariglio, Ivo Herzer, Robert Katz, Hans Kirchhoff, Rabbi Leon Klenicki, Lia Levi, Guenter Lewy, Gigliola Lopez, Gadi Luzzatto Voghera, Riccardo Marchis, Michael Marrus, Father Fedele Merelli, Meir Michaelis, Bice Migliau, Father John Morley, Luisella Mortara Ottolenghi, Emanuele Pacifici, Mordecai Paldiel, Lisa Palmieri, Don Battista Angelo Pansa, Michael Phayer, Don Fabrizio Poli, Father Thomas J. Reese, Teresa, Vittoria, and Anna Repetto, Gerhart Riegner, Joseph Rochlitz, Charles Roman, Miriam Rotondo Michelini, Renata Segre, Mother Maria Serena, Denise Siekierski, Alexander Stille, Michael Tagliacozzo, Harold H. Tittmann III, Andrea Tournoud, Monsignor Giuseppe Tuninetti, Giovanni Battista Varnier, Giorgio Vecchio, Monsignor Elio Venier, Giovanni Vian, Monsignor Giulio Villani, Graziella Viterbi, David S. Wyman, Tullia Zevi, and Giovanna and Andreina Zuccotti.

Librarians and archivists whose names I often did not even know also made an indispensable contribution to this book. I want to thank the dedicated staff at the many archives and research centers in Italy, France, and the United States mentioned in the list of abbreviations, as well as personnel at the New York Public Library and the libraries of Columbia University. I am also grateful to my editor, Heidi Downey, for her careful attention to detail.

Finally, I thank my family—my husband, John, and our children Gianna, Andrew and his wife, Margaret, and Milena—for their continuing patience and understanding. This book is dedicated to them.

Introduction

PIUS XII, the head of the Roman Catholic Church during the Second World War, did not speak out publicly against the destruction of the Jews. This fact is rarely contested, nor can it be. Evidence of a public protest, if it existed, would be easy to produce. It does not exist. The pope publicly referred to people who were dying because of their national or ethnic origins on just two occasions. At the end of his long Christmas message of 1942, he briefly mentioned that humanity must struggle to restore a just society. He continued, "We owe it to the innumerable dead . . . to the suffering groups of mothers, widows, and orphans . . . to the innumerable exiles . . . to the hundreds of thousands who, without personal guilt, are doomed to death or to a progressive deterioration of their condition, sometimes for no other reason than their nationality or descent [*stirpe*] . . . to the many thousands of non-combatants whom the air war has [harmed]." [1] Then in an address to the Sacred College of Cardinals on June 2, 1943, he spoke of his compassion for "those who have turned an anxiously imploring eye to Us, tormented as they are, for reasons of their nationality or descent [stirpe], by major misfortunes and by more acute and grave suffering, and destined sometimes, even without guilt on their part, to exterminatory measures." [2] In these two wartime speeches, Pius XII never used the words Jew, anti-Semitism, or race. [3] Nor did he denounce the "exterminatory measures" he mentioned on June 2, or name their perpetrators.

The pope frequently expressed in general terms his sorrow for the sufferings of innocent civilians, but again, he never directly mentioned Jews. Indirectly, there were just two references. Ten days after the roundup of 1,259 Jews in Rome on October 16, 1943, the Vatican newspaper *L'Osservatore Romano* mentioned the pope's compassion and charity, which did not "pause before boundaries of nationality, religion, or descent [stirpe]."[4] Late in the war, on June 2, 1944, the pope referred to Jews by implication when he told the assembled cardinals that his compassion and charity extended to all "without distinction of nationality or descent [stirpe]."[5] Neither reference mentioned that victims were dying. Finally, *L'Osservatore Romano* actually used the word "Jews" in two articles published in December 1943 to protest not the deportations and destruction of European Jewry at the hands of the Nazis but an Italian measure ordering Italian police to arrest Jews and intern them within the country.[6] But that was all. It was very little.

With increasing frequency over the years scholars have addressed the issue of the papal silence and attempted to understand it. Motivating factors include the pope's desire to remain neutral in order to negotiate an eventual peace; his belief that a public condemnation of Nazi policies would make matters worse for Jews and Catholics alike yet help no one; his concern that German Catholics, including the clergy, would reject his protest and leave the Church; and his fear that Fascists and Nazis who surrounded the Vatican City would invade and prevent it from functioning.[7] More hostile critics focus on several alleged personal attitudes of the pope himself, including anti-Semitism, indifference to Jewish suffering, fear of begin kidnapped, admiration for Germany, and fanatic hatred of Bolshevism. Since these and other explanations have been examined in great detail elsewhere I discuss them only briefly in the conclusion of this book.[8] On the other hand, papal defenders also explain the silence by stressing Pius XII's desire to protect and facilitate the manifold efforts of Vatican diplomats working behind the scenes to save Jews in immediate danger of death. Those efforts, they continue, were often effective, saving thousands, indeed tens or hundreds of thousands, of Jews. Had the pope enraged Hitler by speaking out, all such interventions on behalf of Jews and other victims of the war would have been jeopardized.[9]

The argument is not persuasive. Interventions by diplomats of the Holy See were naturally most likely to be fruitful in German-occupied countries where local government officials were Catholics. In addition to Italy after September 8, 1943, these countries included occupied France, Croatia, and much of Belgium. Poland may be excluded from the list because German occupiers gave Polish elites little opportunity to collaborate in local administration.

Other countries where papal efforts might have had some influence were those in which German control was limited and local policies toward Jews could sometimes determine events. Such conditions prevailed for various periods in Italy, southern France, Slovakia, Romania, and Hungary, to mention only those areas where papal apologists claim some success. Yet in all these countries, diplomatic interventions by the Holy See on behalf of the Jews were too few, too cautious, and too late to obtain meaningful results.[10] Jews generally survived there not because of the efforts of the Holy See but because of decisions reached by indigenous government officials for other reasons. Especially in France and Belgium, Jews also survived because of self-help organizations, aided and abetted by sympathetic non-Jews, often Catholics.[11]

Many scholars who admit all this insist on one exception. In Italy, they claim, Pius XII *was* able to save Jews. He allegedly did so in many ways, demonstrating his deep sympathy and concern. When Benito Mussolini issued his version of the anti-Jewish Nuremberg laws in 1938 and 1939, they maintain, Pius XII's predecessor Pius XI, who died in 1939, protested publicly, vehemently, and continually. When thousands of Italian and foreign Jews scrambled to emigrate from Italy before the war, Vatican officials helped them obtain the necessary documents and funds. When thousands of other foreign Jews were interned throughout the country after Italy entered the war on the side of the Germans in June 1940, a Vatican envoy visited them to ensure that they would be treated humanely. When Mussolini contemplated turning over Jews in Italian-occupied areas of Croatia and southern France to the Germans in 1942 and 1943, diplomats of the Holy See persuaded him to change his mind. But the most important papal contribution, it is argued, came after September 8, 1943, when Marshal Pietro Badoglio, head of government after Mussolini's removal by King Vittorio Emanuele III in July 1943, announced an armistice with the Allies that would take Italy out of the war. The Germans immediately occupied Italy, reinstated Mussolini as a puppet ruler, and proceeded to round up and deport Jews. At that point, the pope allegedly opened Church institutions throughout the country to Jewish fugitives, saving thousands from certain death.[12]

Claims of Vatican achievements in Italy appear to constitute the strongest justification for the papal silence. Papal defenders argue that if Pius XII had alienated the Axis powers at any time during the war by publicly criticizing their Jewish policies, his interventions for Jews in Italy would have been fruitless. Mussolini would not have listened to his appeals for them at home or in the Italian-occupied territories. The Germans, once in Italy, would have had no reason to refrain from raiding convents and monasteries—no more need to be cautious and correct in order to ensure continuation of the papal silence. Thousands of Jews sheltered in Church institutions would have been deported. More than one Jewish fugitive has agreed with Michael Tagliacozzo, a Roman Jew hidden for several months at the Seminario Romano near the Basilica of San Giovanni in Laterano, who approved of the papal silence that enabled him and many others to survive.[13]

How valid are these claims of successful papal intervention? Pius XI *did* protest some aspects of the Italian racial legislation, but did those objections extend beyond laws regarding marriage between Jews and Catholics, Jewish converts to Catholicism, and Jews in mixed marriages? Some Jewish refugees subsequently claimed that Vatican officials helped them to emigrate, but was that help given to all Jews, or limited to Jews who had become Catholics? Monsignor Francesco Borgongini Duca, the papal nuncio accredited to the Italian state, *did* visit Jews interned at Ferramonti Tarsia and elsewhere between 1940 and 1943, but he did so in the course of visits to most prisoner-of-war and internment camps in the country. Was he interested in succoring all prisoners, or was he mostly concerned with those who were or might become Catholics? Borgongini Duca and other Vatican envoys *did* petition Italian authorities on behalf of foreign Jews in the occupied territories, and those Jews were ultimately not handed over to the Germans, but was there a causal connection between those two facts? And while thousands of Jews did indeed hide in convents, monasteries, Catholic schools, and even, in some cases, Vatican properties, did Pius XII have anything to do with the hospitality? Did he even approve of it?

In this book I address these and other questions regarding papal efforts to help Jews in Italy during the Second World War. The matter is of the utmost importance to the Vatican's record during the Holocaust. It is, in every sense of the word, its last bastion of defense. The approximately 33,350 Jews in German-controlled Italy in autumn 1943 were few in number compared with Jewish populations in most other occupied countries, but the nation of their birth was the same as that of the pope and of most Vatican officials.[14] In addition, about 10,000 of Italy's Jews resided in the Eternal City itself. A large portion of these Roman Jews lived, so to speak, under the pope's very windows. They resided in the ancient neighborhood of Trastevere, which nearly abuts the massive walls of the Vatican City. Jews had lived and worked there, on the banks of the Tiber, before Jesus was born. Other Roman Jews lived just across the river from Trastevere, in the vicinity of the old ghetto where former popes had forced Jews to reside from 1555 until as recently as 1870. Italian Jews, then, were not only the compatriots but also the neighbors of most Vatican officials. If those prelates did not demonstrate concern for Italy's Jews, how could they claim to have cared for any others?

There was, also, considerably more that Vatican officials could do for Italian Jews than for those in other countries, including predominantly Catholic ones. The pope was, by virtue of his office, bishop of Rome and primate, or primary bishop, of Italy. As such, he enjoyed special influence within the Church locally and nationally that exceeded even his international authority. He knew personally far more priests and prelates in Italy than elsewhere, and he understood them better. He shared their language, culture, and educational background, and grasped the problems they faced in their dioceses. He could, if he wished, call on them readily for help and advice.

In addition to his enhanced role within the Italian Church, the pope and the independent Vatican City State in general enjoyed a special relationship with Italy itself, created by ties of geography, history, and personality. The relationship was not always amicable. Priests and prelates could never quite forget that the Italian state had seized the Papal States, including Rome, during the national unification process, depriving the Vatican of its temporal power. Italian government officials remembered that Pius IX, pope from 1848 to 1878, had responded with rage and bitterness, declaring himself a prisoner in the Vatican and forbidding practicing Italian Catholics from participating in national politics and even from voting. Yet through it all, and increasingly as tensions eased in the 1920s and were finally (at least formally) resolved by the Lateran Accords in 1929, a love-hate relationship endured.[15] It took many forms. Of greatest relevance here, Vatican diplomats just before and during the Second World War assumed a right to intervene with Italian government officials, making suggestions as well as requests, to a much greater extent than with representatives of other nations. They were assured that they would be received and respected, if nothing else. For the most part, they were correct.

In explaining the special relationship, the immense importance of the fact that most members of the Vatican hierarchy during the war were Italians by birth should not be overlooked. In addition to Popes Pius XI and XII, Vatican officials who were Italians included the secretary of state and his two chief assistants; all but one of the twenty-two cardinals in the Roman Curia; virtually all papal nuncios, apostolic delegates, and other papal representatives abroad; and most lower officials and staff.[16] These men were linked to Italy's political, economic, and social elites by language and culture, as well as religion. Bureaucrats from both church and state came mostly from the same social class and the same schools. They knew each other. They were connected through networks of family, friends, and colleagues. They read the same newspapers and books. They vacationed in the same mountains. If Pius XII and his officials could not take advantage of their special geopolitical and personal connections in Italy to help Jews, they could not help them anywhere. Even more serious, from the Vatican's point of view, if the Jews of Italy were destroyed, the pope's lack of compassion and influence would be demonstrated to the entire world, while accusations of indifference would circulate, grow, and perhaps prevail.

A word about sources is in order here. As is well known, Vatican archival documents dating from the past eight decades are essentially unavailable to scholars. The cutoff date is 1922, the year of the death of Pope Benedict XV and the election of Pius XI. Coincidentally, 1922 is also the year in which Mussolini came to power in Italy. In the early 1960s, however, a small group of historians, all priests of different nationalities who enjoyed the confidence of Pope Paul VI (1963–1978), were assigned the task of selecting for publication relevant wartime diplomatic documents from the vast Vatican collection. The project grew out of the worldwide controversy sparked by Rolf Hochhuth's play *Der Stellvertreter* in 1963, which attacked Pius XII's silence about the Holocaust.[17] The result of the effort was the *Actes et Documents du Saint Siège relatif à la seconde guerre mondiale,* eleven volumes of original documents published in the language in which they were written, with historical background, summaries, careful cross-references, and commentary in French.[18] For the most part, the documents concern correspondence between high officials at the Vatican Secretariat of State and their diplomats or bishops abroad. Only a portion of the documents involve Jews. The rest indicate papal efforts to prevent or end the war, protect Rome and other cities from physical destruction, and assist prisoners of war, hostages, refugees, and civilians in general.

The publication project necessarily involved extensive selection of documents. It was, furthermore, basically defensive in nature, intending to show the best of Vatican efforts, to refute charges of indifference and inaction. As a result, many scholars are dissatisfied. They argue that the flaws of Vatican policies may have been covered up and that independent verification of the total picture is impossible. The concern, of course, is valid. The eleven volumes do not facilitate analysis of policy formation and behind-the-scenes maneuvering among Vatican officials. It is rarely possible to use them to pinpoint prelates who may have pressured Pius XII to remain uninvolved in Jewish assistance and rescue. Readers cannot even separate the pope's policy input from that of his secretary of state, Cardinal Luigi Maglione, and Maglione's two chief deputies, Monsignors Giovanni Battista Montini and Domenico Tardini, respectively secretaries of the Sections for Ordinary Ecclesiastical Affairs and for Extraordinary Ecclesiastical Affairs.[19] The most that can be said in that regard is that Pius XII was known to have read all incoming diplomatic reports, involved himself intimately in all aspects of policy formation, and made all final decisions himself. As two of his most ardent defenders put it in their book: "Throughout the war Pope Pius reserved all major and many minor diplomatic matters to himself, and he frequently kept his own counsel. When requiring advice or information he turned to a handful of trusted priests: his confidential aide, Father Robert Leiber, the cardinal secretary of state, Luigi Maglione, or the latter's two under-secretaries, Domenico Tardini and Giovanni Montini. Even the members of this inner circle were often ignorant of important policy initiatives."[20] To say more would require unrestricted access to the archives of the Vatican Secretariat of State and the pope himself.

This book, however, is not concerned primarily with policy formation or opportunities not taken. It is not exclusively about Popes Pius XI and XII. It is not intended to release demons or to reveal venomous anti-Semitic skeletons in the closet. The purpose of this book is to separate fact from fiction, reality from myth, about what the two popes and their principal officials at the Secretariat of State actually *did* to help Jews in Italy, the country where they enjoyed the greatest opportunity to be useful. For that purpose, the *Actes et Documents du Saint Siège* are more than adequate. Although much that is unfavorable may have been omitted, it is reasonable to assume that all that is favorable was included. The task then becomes one of evaluating the evidence of Vatican assistance to Jews to determine whether it was as extensive as Vatican apologists have maintained or as limited as more hostile scholars claim. The eleven volumes, supplemented by archival material from local dioceses, Church institutions that helped Jews, Jewish documentation centers, and the Italian government, as well as by newspapers and journals, published memoirs, and personal interviews, reveal a fascinating story.

CHAPTER ONE

The Vatican and Anti-Semitism

ON APRIL 2, 1928, the Vatican's Holy Office published a decree declaring that "the Catholic Church has always prayed for the Jewish people, depositories, until the coming of Jesus Christ, of the divine promise, regardless of their subsequent blindness, or rather, precisely because of it. Moved by that spirit of charity, the Apostolic See has protected this same people against unjust vexations, and just as it reproves all hatreds and animosities between people, so it especially condemns hatred against the people elected by God, a hatred that today is vulgarly called 'anti-Semitism.' " [1]

Despite the uncomplimentary reference to Jewish blindness, this condemnation of anti-Semitism was by far the strongest, most unequivocal, and most public statement on the subject to emerge from the Vatican during the interwar period. Adolf Hitler's rise to power in January 1933 evoked no papal admonition of the Nazis' vicious anti-Semitic program. On the contrary, as the new Führer imposed his initial anti-Jewish measures during that first spring and summer, Vatican representatives led by Eugenio Pacelli, the future Pope Pius XII, successfully negotiated a concordat between the Holy See and Germany. When the Nazis announced comprehensive anti-Jewish measures at Nuremberg in September 1935, Pius XI expressed no disapproval. Eighteen months later, the pope did issue an encyclical, *Mit brennender Sorge,* criticizing German violations of the concordat and, to a lesser extent, racism. As will be seen in detail below, however, he never mentioned anti-Semitism or Jews. The dreadful year 1938 witnessed the German absorption of Austria and the immediate public humiliations of Jews in Catholic Vienna, the first anti-Jewish laws in Mussolini's Italy, and Kristallnacht and the ensuing murders of about ninety Jews and the imprisonment of some thirty thousand others in Germany. Yet nothing prompted a papal denunciation of anti-Semitism even remotely approaching the clarity of the Vatican declaration of 1928. Nor, for that matter, was there a similar papal statement during the Holocaust itself.

In its original context, however, the condemnation of 1928 was not so clear at all. It constituted part of an official Vatican announcement that the Holy Office had examined the Friends of Israel, a Catholic society devoted to demonstrating good will to Jews and praying for their conversion, and decided on its abolition. The original announcement stated only that "over time, the society . . . has adopted a manner of operating and speaking alien to the sense of the Church."[2] But a better explanation was forthcoming. On May 19, 1928, an unidentified author in the Jesuit journal *La Civiltà Cattolica* informed readers that members of the Friends of Israel, while admirable in their dedication to Jewish conversion, erred, perhaps inadvertently, when they "covered up not only [the Jews'] defects but also their historic crimes, and attenuated the traditional [Church] language and even that used in the sacred liturgy."[3] Apparently members were too friendly toward Jews and lost sight of the Church's teachings about their misdeeds. In any case, the society was dissolved and the Holy Office's condemnation of anti-Semitism soon forgotten.

In fact, the same unsigned article in *La Civiltà Cattolica* on May 19, elaborating on the original condemnation of anti-Semitism, seemed deliberately designed to weaken it. The Jews should surely be the subjects of Christians' prayers, it said, "since prayers are so much more necessary and urgent when the sinners seem blinded or hardened in their guilt." Animosity toward Jews must especially be condemned because they are "more exposed to hatred than other people because of their own misdeeds." After paying lip service to the Holy Office's denunciation of anti-Semitism the article carefully explained that it had been directed only against anti-Semitism "in its anti-Christian form and spirit, as interpreted and applied by . . . [individuals] alien to genuine Catholicism and sometimes even to every practice of Christian life: adversaries of the Jews because of allegiance to political parties or nationality, for material interests, jealousies and competition regarding commerce or money, and similar reasons, none of them morally and religiously justified."[4]

Was some other form of anti-Semitism, then, "morally and religiously

justified"? The article did not answer directly but continued, "In fact Liberalism has removed the Jews from the special condition that [formerly] distinguished them from the rest of the nation and confined them, more for preventive caution than as a punitive measure, in a collection of their own
houses, that is, in the ghetto: [Liberalism] has rendered them bold and powerful, creating for them, under the pretext of equality, an ever more preponderant condition of privilege, especially economic, in modern society."[5]
Nevertheless, the Church would continue to protect "even its most relentless
enemies and persecutors, who are the Jews." And not only would it protect
them, but it would labor to procure for them "the greatest possible good, individual conversion and eternal salvation."[6]

The lengthy article went on to emphasize the decisive role of Jews in the
triumph of Bolshevism in Russia, as well as their control of international
banking, finance, and politics. Theirs was an influence far out of proportion
to their numbers. It was rather "the result of their hidden meddling and the
undue power thus acquired . . . contrary . . . to reason and the common
good." Jews thus bore a terrible responsibility for all the ills of modern society.
"It is they who have prepared and sometimes even unleashed . . . religious
persecution against Catholics and the clergy, and the anti-Christian struggle
that is the sorry end product of the entire Liberal and Masonic movement."[7]

All the elements of the Church's traditional position regarding the Jews
are here. The Jews are in error, and profoundly guilty. Despite being dangerous enemies of the Church, they merit charity and attempts at conversion.
They must be punished for their spiritual offenses but not persecuted for political or nationalistic reasons. But the article did not hesitate to inject its own
political content: Liberals have abolished the traditional separation of Jews
from Christians, unleashing the Jews' power to dominate the economy and
the society itself. The results? All the ills of the day: Bolshevism, capitalist exploitation, and, apparently worst of all, persecution of the clergy, a reference
to the efforts by Liberal governments to separate Church and state that flourished and succeeded in most of Western Europe around the turn of the century. Anti-Semitism and politics, it seems, are not so easily separated after all.

In 1928, just five years before Hitler's rise to power and the onset of Jewish persecutions in Germany, the Church is revealed here to be deeply trou-
bled by the presence of Jews in predominantly Christian societies. Whether
that attitude can be labeled anti-Semitic is in part a matter of definition. Since
the word "Semite" has broad racial connotations, the term "anti-Semitic" is
sometimes equated with racism or with dislike of Jews (and other Semitic

peoples) on racial grounds. In this sense, the official Church has rarely been anti-Semitic, for it has generally regarded all Catholics as equal regardless of their race.[8] Using this definition, Vatican spokesmen in the 1920s and 1930s could, and very occasionally did, condemn anti-Semitism. But in defiance of its etymology, the word "anti-Semitism" is often viewed as synonymous with anti-Judaism, a hostility or prejudice toward Jews because of their religion, culture, or some twisted behavioral stereotype.[9] According to this definition, the Catholic Church is much more vulnerable. To call Jews "relentless enemies and persecutors" of the Church, justify their ghettoization as "preventive caution," define emancipation from the ghetto as a "condition of privilege" with evil consequences, and find Jews responsible for all contemporary ills, is to be profoundly anti-Jewish indeed.

Can so much be learned about attitudes within the Vatican from one article in La Civiltà Cattolica? The bimonthly publication was produced by the conservative Jesuit leadership in Rome, but readers of the day would have recognized it as a faithful reflection of Vatican opinion. This status had developed over time. The Jesuits founded La Civiltà Cattolica in 1850, by order of Pope Pius IX (1846–78) and with papal funding. That same pope then proceeded to dismiss its first editor in 1875. Pius IX's successor, Leo XIII (1878–1903), further strengthened the Vatican-Jesuit relationship. During the papacy of Pius X (1903–14), the editor of La Civiltà Cattolica began to be appointed by the pope or with his direct approval. Of the journal in the 1920s and 1930s, one prominent Church historian has written that it was "extremely authoritative . . . because of its tight ties with the [Vatican] secretary of state."[10] Another respected scholar has observed, "As always, the views of Civiltà Cattolica [in 1938] were in accord with those of the Pontiff."[11] A third historian adds that slightly later, during the papacy of Pius XII, an official from the Secretariat of State reviewed all articles before publication.[12]

La Civiltà Cattolica printed major papal speeches and messages in full, along with significant news items from the Vatican. It also carried some unsigned pieces by non-Jesuits, including the pope himself. Most articles, however, were by a small number of regular writers, all Jesuits. Their continued publication depended on acceptance at the Vatican. As another indication of Vatican involvement, many articles from La Civiltà Cattolica, including those about Jews, were reprinted with attribution or merely summarized in L'Osservatore Romano, the Vatican's daily (except Sunday) evening newspaper. Vatican opinion was obviously never monolithic, and no single individual, not even a pope, could impose his views on the entire Church hierarchy.

But the attitudes toward Jews expressed in *La Civiltà Cattolica* from at least the 1890s until the outbreak of the Second World War remained consistent, and they were never challenged within its pages.[13]

As Hitler implemented ever more severe anti-Jewish policies in the 1930s, *La Civiltà Cattolica*, far from downplaying its particular variant of anti-Judaism, repeated it more often. In 1934, for example, the Jesuit Father Enrico Rosa, a regular contributor to the journal, wrote two reviews of a notorious German anti-Semitic manual, *Handbuch der Judenfrage*. "We do not deny," Father Rosa explained, "that [the German authors of the manual] could be pardoned, and perhaps even found worthy of praise, if their political opposition were contained within the limits of a tolerable resistance to the maneuverings of Jewish parties and organizations."[14] The German authors, then, were guilty only of exaggeration. The Jesuit praised references in the manual to "Jewish Marxist theory—which has given substance to the new Socialism and Communism, and even to Bolshevism, which was in great part a Jewish creation." He also applauded the equation of Freemasons with Jews. He concluded by reminding his readers that the Jews "have always been and are still . . . the relentless and irreconcilable enemies of Christ and of Christianity, particularly of integral and pure Christianity, the Catholicism of the Roman Church."[15]

Two years later an unidentified book reviewer articulated similar anti-Jewish themes in *La Civiltà Cattolica*. "The two facts of capitalist financial predominance and revolutionary Communism remain clear and proven," the reviewer wrote in approval of a particular book, "if not among the entire Jewish people, certainly among the most visible part. Thus, if not all, still not a few Jews constitute a grave and permanent danger to society."[16] The reviewer went on to address the book's three proposed solutions to the "Jewish problem": assimilation, Zionism, and ghettoization. He declared that none were feasible and suggested that God must have reasons for placing Jews in Christian society.

Less than a year later, in June 1937, another unidentified book reviewer in *La Civiltà Cattolica* returned to the theme, so ominous in retrospect, of solutions to the "Jewish problem." The English Catholic writer Hilaire Belloc, the Jesuit explained, had used the word "elimination" in his book, *The Jews*, first published in 1922 but translated and printed in Italian in 1934 in *Vita e Pensiero*, the journal of the Catholic University of Milan. Accurately summarizing Belloc's position, the reviewer wrote, "The solution [to the Jewish problem] can only come about through two ways: elimination or segregation.

Elimination can be achieved through three methods: one clearly hostile, that is through destruction; or, still hostile but less cruel, through expulsion; or in a friendly and gentle manner, through absorption." [17] The reviewer was quick to declare that Belloc himself dismissed the alternative of destruction. He wrote, describing Belloc's position, "Of these three methods [for elimination], the first two are contrary to Christian charity and the natural law; the third has been shown to be historically unachievable." [18] He and Belloc were clear enough, but, in light of subsequent events, the merest mention of destruction is chilling. Furthermore, the idea of the need for a solution to a "Jewish problem" was firmly planted in the pages of a Jesuit journal—and in the minds of its readers.

Belloc himself settled on the solution of "friendly segregation," which he defined as a recognition by Jews and non-Jews alike of a separate Jewish nationality. According to his Jesuit reviewer, he favored a "civil and charitable accommodation . . . the only practical and effective means to the solution of the Jewish question." [19] The reviewer never disagreed. Advocacy of friendly segregation and a mutual recognition of a separate Jewish nationality may seem relatively innocuous, of course, but their unavoidable consequence is the denial to Jews of full rights as citizens in the countries where they live, including the right to participate with non-Jews in the broader society. These were precisely the denials imposed by Mussolini in his anti-Jewish laws in 1938.

Elaborating on what "friendly segregation" could entail, the same Jesuit reviewer went on to discuss a second book, *Israel, son passé, son avenir,* by H. De Vries de Heekelingen. That author considered Zionism an effective solution to the "problem" of Jews living in Christian societies. His position, as his reviewer described it, was: "Those who want to retain Jewish nationality . . . must be provided with a Jewish passport and treated like all other foreigners in the State where they reside; thus they may not serve in public offices, the army, the judiciary, the Government, etc. Those who do not wish Jewish nationality . . . each State may dispose of these as it believes best. The undesirables: revolutionaries, usurers, etc., will be considered as belonging to the Jewish State and expelled." [20]

At this point, the Jesuit reviewer finally objected, but not for humanitarian reasons. "Jews, who are comfortable where they are," he wrote, "will never be induced to go to Palestine, a sterile land whose inhabitants are not hospitable." He continued, somewhat inconsistently, "Once the Zionist State is achieved, will the Jews abandon their messianic aspirations to dominate the world and to exert their double preponderance, capitalistic and revolutionary? Won't a Zionist State perhaps be a new and stronger stimulus and a support for that innate messianic aspiration and double preponderance?"[21] By rejecting Zionism, the Jesuit reviewer implicitly left readers with Belloc's friendly segregation of those who had a "separate Jewish nationality" as the only "solution." Imposing segregation, of course, was precisely what Hitler was doing in Germany, and what Mussolini would do a year later.

Two more articles on the "Jewish question" followed within a few weeks.[22] Both were by an author who was unidentified but was surely the same as the reviewer previously mentioned. The wording was the same, and the Jews' "double preponderance, capitalistic and revolutionary" was regularly invoked. The new articles dealt with Catholic conversion efforts—the need, recommended procedures, and past success rates. Interestingly, the final article, after repeating yet again the stereotypical description of Jews, concluded with a warning. "Every form of anti-Semitism is condemned by the Church," the author declared, apparently referring to the association of particular characteristics with race or blood.[23] Profound anti-Judaism on the basis of religion or culture was evidently acceptable.

This brief survey of anti-Jewish articles in La Civiltà Cattolica reveals a surprising absence of condemnation on traditional religious grounds. Jews are rarely subjected to the centuries-old accusations of killing Jesus and rejecting his teachings. Instead, the charges are political, social, and economic. Jews are deeply involved in, if not solely responsible for, all the major challenges to traditional society: atheism, rationalism, Liberalism, democracy, constitutionalism, capitalist exploitation, excessive nationalism, Socialism, Communism, and revolution. Those challenges to traditional society, of course, also represented challenges to the Catholic Church. The French Revolution and the ultimate triumph of Liberalism in Western Europe in the nineteenth century entailed, in many countries, the expropriation of Church properties, the separation of Church and state, and the end of the Church's control of education and family law. Also, the triumph of Italian nationalism resulted in the gradual seizure of the Papal States, that huge area of central Italy that included, along with Rome and the region of Latium, most of Romagna, Umbria, and the Marches.[24] The Church's losses were staggering, and as late as the 1930s and 1940s, still profoundly lamented by many. Priests and prelates in their late seventies in 1938, for example, might have witnessed the entry of the Italian army into papal Rome in 1870. They could remember when Jews were required to live in the ghetto on the Tiber. Younger clergymen would have heard first-hand accounts of the ancien regime from their parents, teachers, and priests. To many, and especially to the older priestly diplomats and bureaucrats who had made their careers in the Vatican and were in positions of authority during the years of Fascism and the Second World War, a restoration of that ideal world appeared as a desirable and perhaps even possible objective.

While the rejection of modernity by many men and women of the Church is not difficult to understand under the circumstances, their linking of Jews with unwelcome change may seem puzzling. The same Liberals who had rescinded the rights and privileges of the Church, however, had also emancipated the Jews, beginning with those in countries affected by the French Revolution. Grateful new Jewish citizens had responded with understandable patriotism and devotion to Liberal governments, constitutions, and modern principles of liberty, equality, and fraternity. And with their traditions of education, family ties, and self-help organizations Jews were able to benefit from newly available political and economic opportunities. As a result they were clearly present and visible, though not predominant, among those perceived as "enemies" of the Church.

Churchmen looking for a scapegoat for modern challenges found it easier to blame outsiders, in this case Jews, than to target countrymen of their own religion. Conditioned by their Church's traditional anti-Judaism for religious reasons, they thought of Jews almost instinctively when searching for an economic, social, and political enemy as well. Conveniently enough, they found a receptive audience among certain groups of disaffected Catholics who were less well educated than many Jews and less able to take advantage of new opportunities. It was a recipe for disaster.

While the Jesuit editors of La Civiltà Cattolica espoused anti-Jewish attitudes, they viewed racism very differently. The distinction was absolutely clear to them. Jews were defined by their religion and culture. Their faults— messianism, excessiveness, a desire to dominate—resulted from their religious and cultural education, never from their race or blood. Jews who converted were freed of tendencies toward excess and dominance and were Christians, pure and simple. All Christians, or more precisely, all Catholics, were equal, regardless of their race. No individual race could be superior to others. The fundamental difference from Nazi ideology, which glorified "Aryans" at the expense of all others and regarded Jews as an inferior race, regardless of their religion, is obvious.

The official Catholic Church also disagreed profoundly with Fascists and

Nazis on issues regarding nationalism and citizens' obligations to the state. For the Church, patriotism and loyalty to one's country were valid, but an excessive nationalism that defined one country and nationality as superior to others was unacceptable. Furthermore, citizens' obligations of obedience to their rulers were limited by an overriding obligation to adhere to God's laws, as defined by the Church. In case of conflict, the Church had precedence. Clashes between the Vatican and the governments of Italy and Germany throughout the 1930s revolved around issues of race and government powers but did not focus on anti-Judaism at all. A careful reading of statements by Jesuits and Vatican officials, including the pope himself, makes this clear.

On February 3, 1934, the Jesuit Father M. Barbera reviewed Alfred Rosenberg's *Der Mythus des 20.Jahrhunderts* (*The Myth of the Twentieth Century*) for *La Civiltà Cattolica*. The book, published in Germany in 1930, had strongly endorsed Article 24 of the Nazi Party Program of 1920, which said that the party "stands for a new 'positive Christianity.' " This new cult would abolish the "Jewish" Old Testament, purge the New Testament of humanitarian and pacifist themes, and create a German church anchored in blood, race, and soil. The party program and the book itself constituted a direct challenge to Catholics and Protestants alike, and Father Barbera was not delicate in his response. Because of the book's emphasis on the superiority of the pure "Aryan" race and its distortions of Christian history and teachings, he unequivocally rejected it as a "subversion of the very foundations of Religion and the Christian State." [25] He did not mention Rosenberg's anti-Semitism.

A few weeks later another Jesuit wrote an article condemning the German law of July 14, 1933, which made sterilization mandatory for individuals with hereditary diseases. The author opposed any "defense of the race" or "improvement of descent [stirpe]" if the methods used were contrary to natural, divine, or ecclesiastic law.[26] In a continuation of the article in the next issue the author roundly condemned German assertions that "Aryan blood is the supreme good, the maximum exponent of society," and that "the custodian of [the purity of] the race is the State." [27] The implication was that laws contrary to the teachings of the Church should not be obeyed. The author reminded readers that Pope Leo XIII had declared in his encyclical *Rerum novarum* in 1891 that "the individual has precedence over the State." He added that the current pope, Pius XI, had written in his own encyclical, *Casti connubii*, in 1930, "The family is more sacred than the State."

The Jesuits did not direct their criticism only against Nazi Germany. An article in *La Civiltà Cattolica* in 1937 examined the work of the American

Jesuit Father John LaFarge among African Americans. It praised his efforts but concluded that "the movement favorable to complete justice for Blacks has made little progress, and there still endure unjust exclusions from schools and especially from civil provisions common to all citizens." [28] The "unjust exclusions" of Jews from Italian schools and from other "civil provisions" were less than a year away. We shall see that the Jesuits of *La Civiltà Cattolica* who rightly protested injustices to African Americans in the South did not object when they concerned Jews in Italy.

Fully as much as *La Civiltà Cattolica,* Pope Pius XI made his objections to German racism and statism known. That opposition, however, was far from apparent at the onset of his papacy in 1922. Achille Ratti, born in 1857 and the son of a Lombard silk manufacturer, became pope in the same year that Benito Mussolini was appointed head of the Italian government. Earlier in his career, after studies in Milan and at the Jesuit-run Gregorian University in Rome, he had headed the Ambrosian Library in Milan and then served as a vice-prefect of the Vatican Libraries in the Eternal City. In 1918, Pope Benedict XV (1914–22) sent him to Poland as an apostolic visitor. His title was changed to papal nuncio a year later. He was recalled to Italy in 1921 to become a cardinal and the archbishop of Milan. But his time in Poland had decisively influenced his views. After witnessing the Soviet army approach Warsaw in 1920 and struggling to trace thousands of Polish and Lithuanian Catholics deported to Siberia, he acquired a powerful aversion and mistrust of Communism. His dislike of Fascism was not nearly so strong.

Like many other Italian Catholic conservatives, Pius XI regarded a stable Fascist regime in Italy as a far more effective bulwark against Communism than democratic governments with their ever-changing coalitions could ever be. He perceived that Mussolini could also be used to eliminate Liberals and Socialists hostile to Church interests. Under Mussolini, then, Church and state might work together. But a barrier to such collaboration existed in the form of the thorny "Roman Question," the break in diplomatic relations that had occurred in 1870 when the Italian army had seized papal Rome. As seen, the pope at the time, Pius IX, had retreated behind the Vatican walls and declared himself a prisoner there, to communicate no more with the secular state that surrounded him.

Fifty years later a normalization of relations made far more sense to Pius XI than a brooding over past injustices. Furthermore, it was apparent that the moment was at hand—that the Church could obtain more from a single authoritarian ruler than from the anti-clerical Liberals and Socialists who had preceded him. Mussolini, eager to cloak himself in the mantle of Catholic respectability and gain prestige both at home and abroad, was ready to negotiate. From the very beginnings of their regimes, both leaders maneuvered delicately toward a mutual understanding.

Among his first acts in office, Mussolini restored the large cross in the Coliseum and the crucifix in the law courts. He declared blasphemy to be a penal offense, and he made other friendly overtures to the Church. Vatican officials, in turn, remained silent when two Fascist thugs beat the priest Giovanni Minzoni to death near the town of Argenta, in the Province of Ferrara, in August 1923. Don Minzoni had won a silver medal for valor during his service as a military chaplain in the First World War.[29] After the war he became an enthusiastic member of the Catholic Partito Popolare Italiano (PPI) and a devoted advocate of social programs for the poor. Unlike his Vatican superiors he was also an outspoken opponent of Fascism. His criticism cost him his life.

The PPI was itself a barrier to Church-state understanding by 1923. It had been founded just four years previously by a priest, Don Luigi Sturzo, with Vatican authorization. Sturzo and his associates saw the party as a Christian, non-Marxist popular movement, independent of Vatican control, that would defend and promote the interests of peasants and workers. Catholic conservatives regarded it as a necessary and temporary expedient to defeating Socialism during the ferment immediately following the war. The Vatican began withdrawing support from the PPI well before 1923, but many of the party's priests and laymen persisted in opposing Fascism and contesting elections. They were occasionally embarrassingly successful. In elections in Brianza in 1924, for example, the Popolari won 24,000 votes and the Fascists 12,000.[30]

From the beginning of his papacy Pius XI was demonstrably unsympathetic to the PPI, less because of its social advocacy than because of its institutional independence and hostility to Fascism. Vatican pressure forced Sturzo to resign as party secretary in July 1923. The pope forbade priests from belonging to political parties in February 1924, and he enjoined Catholics from supporting the Aventine opposition to the government after Fascist assassins murdered the Reform Socialist Deputy Giacomo Matteotti in June 1924. Pius finally dissolved the Popolari in 1926, taking yet another step toward an understanding with the Duce.[31]

On February 11, 1929, after prolonged and difficult negotiations, Pius

XI's dream of an official accommodation with the Italian government was achieved. For the first time since 1870, relations between Italy and the Holy See were normalized by treaty. The Lateran Accords included a diplomatic treaty, a religious concordat, and a financial convention, as well as specific agreements on mail, currency, physical access, and all the other technical details essential to the existence of a tiny independent state entirely surrounded by a large one. Italy recognized the inviolability of the 108.7 acres of the Vatican City State, adjacent to St. Peter's Basilica and, for the most part, separated from the city of Rome by a massive wall. It also granted extraterritorial status to an additional fifty-two acres owned by the Vatican outside its walls, three basilicas, eight large buildings (*palazzi*), a hospital, and the papal country retreat at Castel Gandolfo. The Lateran Accords "placed under guarantee" about a dozen other Vatican properties in Rome that lacked formal extraterritorial privileges, and acknowledged Vatican ownership of many others without granting them any special status. These scattered properties were remnants of the centuries of papal control of the entire Eternal City. The financial convention provided compensation for other Vatican properties permanently lost to the Italian state.

In addition to the property settlement, the Italian government defined Roman Catholicism as the official religion of the nation. It agreed to recognize and register all marriages performed in accordance with canon law, grant freedom to Catholic Action as long as it refrained from political involvement, and make religious education compulsory for Catholic pupils in the public primary and secondary schools. In turn, the Holy See recognized the Italian state with Rome as its capital. It agreed that groups identified with Catholic Action would not engage in politics. It promised, finally, to remain neutral in any international conflicts.[32] After nearly sixty years, the Roman Question was settled.

The Lateran Accords eased tensions between Church and state in Italy but did not resolve all disagreements. Broad differences regarding nationalism and the power of the secular state remained. While not referring specifically to Mussolini, Pius XI raised the former issue briefly in his Christmas message of 1930. He called for "the peace of Christ" throughout the world but added, "It is more difficult, if not impossible, that peace should endure between peoples and between States, if in place of a true and genuine love of country there should reign and rage an egotistical and hardened nationalism."[33] This was a theme that he would repeat over and over again in the years to come.

Equally aggravating was the issue of arbitrary state interference with the Church. Soon after the ratification of the Lateran Accords on June 7, 1929, and in flagrant violation of them, Fascist attacks on Catholic Action intensified. Founded by Pius XI and especially dear to him, Catholic Action was a coordinating body for the Church's many charitable, social, educational, spiritual, and apostolic organizations for laypersons. Its youth groups were especially active, rivaling those being established by the Fascists. Mussolini, it seemed, did not relish competitors.

In response to Fascist attacks Pius XI issued the encyclical *Non abbiamo bisogno* on June 29, 1931. Despite claims to the contrary, the pronouncement cannot be glorified as a sweeping and courageous condemnation of Fascism. Although the pope referred to "many acts of brutality and violence" and "many insults in the press," as well as to "the participation of members of a political party, some of whom were in uniform," he never uttered the word "Fascist." Near the encyclical's conclusion, he added, clearly enough, "we have not said that we wish to condemn the party as such." [34] Nor can *Non abbiamo bisogno* be described as an appeal for democratization and civil rights for the Italian people, for it was primarily concerned with the interests of the Church. The acts of brutality and violence and the insults in the press that Pius XI protested were almost exclusively those directed against the Church and its lay organizations.

Non abbiamo bisogno did raise the broader issue of state versus Church authority, however. Without using the word "Fascist," Pius described Italy's ruling caste as "a party and a regime based on an ideology which clearly resolves itself into a true, a real pagan worship of the State." He declared that any oath of unreserved loyalty and total obedience to the orders of a secular authority was unlawful, for in case of conflict between the demands of government and those of natural law as defined by the Church, the latter had priority. He suggested that the difficulty could be overcome if individuals who had already taken or were required to take the oath made a mental reservation "before God, in their own consciences" to recognize that priority. [35] In fact, Pius XI demonstrated in his encyclical that the Church could and would speak out on issues it considered important.

Adolf Hitler's rise to power in Germany in January 1933 created new challenges for the pope, who was again eager to regularize diplomatic relations. Pius XI believed that the interests of the Church could be best protected through treaties with foreign governments rather than through Christian Democratic political parties. Preceded by treaties between the Vatican and

Serbia, Italy, Austria, and several German states (Bavaria, Prussia, and Baden), a concordat between the Holy See and the Third Reich was officially signed on July 20, 1933.[36] As with Italy, however, conflicts and grievances remained, fanned by Nazi radicals hostile to religion and eager to attack all who disagreed with them. During the years following the concordat, priests in Germany were attacked, churches desecrated, Catholic schools closed, observance discouraged, and religion in general ridiculed in the press.

One result of Nazi violations of the German concordat was yet another papal encyclical, *Mit brennender Sorge,* issued on March 14, 1937. The letter was written under the guidance of, if not actually by, Cardinal Eugenio Pacelli, the Vatican secretary of state who would be elected to succeed Pius XI just two years later. Secretary of state since February 9, 1930, Pacelli was exceptionally well qualified to prepare an encyclical about the Third Reich. He had served as papal nuncio in Munich and then in Berlin from 1917 to 1929, years that he later remembered with great fondness. During that period he had acquired fluency in the German language, many friends and associates, and a profound sympathy for the German people and culture.

Addressed "To the Venerable Brethren the Archbishops and Bishops of Germany and other Ordinaries in Peace and Communion with the Apostolic See" and smuggled into the Third Reich, *Mit brennender Sorge* was read from the pulpit in all German Catholic churches on Palm Sunday, March 21. Since it is often cited, like *Non abbiamo bisogno,* as evidence of Pius XI's courageous stand against Fascist and Nazi regimes and in favor of human rights and justice, a careful examination of its contents is in order.[37]

Mit brennender Sorge began with a protest against violations of the treaty of 1933 by "the other contracting party," meaning Germany.[38] It never used the words "National Socialist," and it rarely even referred to the Reich government as such. The two specific violations mentioned concerned the concordat's provisions guaranteeing confessional schools and the freedom of parents to choose Catholic educations for their children. After declaring that protests against specific violations were not its chief purpose, however, the encyclical proceeded to attack in strong language many teachings and policies current in Germany regarding religion. Among these were the definition of a pantheistic or a national God, efforts to found a national German church that would not recognize the primacy of the bishop of Rome (the pope), the pressuring of citizens to leave the Church, and the requiring of young people to leave religiously oriented youth groups and join government-created secular ones (unstated, the *Hitlerjugend*). In an unspecified but unmistakable jibe at Hitler, the encyclical declared, "Should any man dare, in sacrilegious disregard of the essential differences between God and His creature, between the God-man and the children of man, to place a mortal, were he the greatest of all times, by the side of, or over, or against, Christ, he would deserve to be called prophet of nothingness." [39]

Mit brennender Sorge was undeniably outspoken. It was again proof that the Church could and would object when it judged issues to be necessary and important. Unfortunately, however, the issues so judged in this case concerned, with two brief exceptions, only the interests of the Church and Catholics.

The first exception involved the much quoted paragraph 8, which read: "Whoever exalts race, or the people, or the State, or a particular form of State, or the depositories of power, or any other fundamental value of the human community—however necessary and honorable be their function in worldly things—whoever raises these notions above their standard value and divinizes them to an idolatrous level, distorts and perverts an order of the world planned and created by God." [40] Here at last was an unequivocal condemnation of German racism as well as statism. Although limited to a single sentence in a document of forty-three paragraphs and not specifically naming the Nazi regime, it was nonetheless clear enough and wholly consistent with Church teachings before and throughout the Second World War—and long before, and long after. It might be noted, however, that this sentence referred to race but never mentioned Jews. Because the Church regarded Jews as a people to be deprecated because of their religion and culture rather than their race, it is unlikely that any reference to observant Jews was intended.

The second exception involves the encyclical's insistence that the Old Testament not be excised from Christian teachings in school and churches, as many Nazis wished to do. The wording, however, while it concerned Jews as well as Christians, was hardly flattering to Jews:

> The sacred books of the Old Testament are exclusively the word of God, and constitute a substantial part of his revelation; they are penetrated by a subdued light, harmonizing with the slow development of revelation the dawn of the bright day of the redemption. As should be expected in historical and didactic books, they reflect in many particulars the imperfection, the weakness and sinfulness of man. But side by side with innumerable touches of greatness and nobleness, they also record the story of the chosen

people, bearers of the Revelation and the Promise, repeatedly
straying from God and turning to the world. . . . It is precisely in
the twilight of this background that one perceives the striking
perspective of the divine tutorship of salvation, as it warms,
admonishes, strikes, raises and beautifies its elect.[41]

The Old Testament, then, must be taught because it is a credit to Christians
rather than to the Jews who wrote it. Those who remain religious Jews after
the crucifixion of Jesus may be seen as weak and sinful, not among the elect
who are "raised and beautified." Even their religion may be dismissed because, as the encyclical said elsewhere, "No faith in God can for long survive
pure and unalloyed without the support of faith in Christ."[42] This, then,
was the extent of papal support for the Jews, after four long years of Nazi
persecution.

Just five days after *Mit brennender Sorge* was issued and two days before it
was actually read in Germany, Pius XI issued another encyclical. *Divini Redemptoris* was an explicit text that attacked every aspect of "atheistic Communism" with all the sweeping general phrases that were missing in the
encyclical to the German bishops. Purporting to provide a "brief synthesis of
the principles of atheistic Communism," it labeled the system a "satanic
scourge," a "false messianic idea," a "pseudo-ideal," and a "plague." Communism was "absolutely contrary to the natural law itself." Wherever it is tri-
umphant, it subverts the social order and eradicates every vestige of the
Christian religion "with a hatred and a savage barbarity one would not have
believed possible in our age."[43] The encyclical spoke of hundreds of atrocities
against the Church in the Soviet Union, Mexico, and Spain. Pius XI did not,
in this case, mince words.

Even though papal condemnations of Communism were not at all new,
La Civiltà Cattolica printed *Divini Redemptoris* in full, in two successive issues,
along with two lengthy articles on the subject.[44] It subsequently printed *Mit
brennender Sorge* in a single issue, along with one article of comment.[45] The
author of the latter article pointed out that the two encyclicals in the course of
a single week had the same goal, to defend the religious patrimony of the
Christian West, "threatened with ruin as much by the godless Reds as by the
neo-pagan currents of National Socialism."[46] The equation was well taken,
but Vatican attacks on Communism remained far more sweeping, precise,
frequent, and better publicized than those on Nazism.

From the point of view of the Catholic clergy, the later years of the 1930s were bleak indeed. Threatened, as they thought, by the "godless Reds" in the Soviet Union and "neo-pagan currents of National Socialism" in the Third Reich and its rapidly expanding zone of influence, they also distrusted Liberal democracies such as France, not to mention Protestant strongholds like Great Britain and the United States. The Church seemed to be a fortress under siege, surrounded by enemies. Modern challenges that had been eating away at its foundations since the French Revolution now seemed about to overwhelm it. Never had the term "Fortress Church" seemed more apt. Under these circumstances, many Vatican officials became more suspicious, timid, and inflexible than ever. Their activities became equally narrow and defensive, directed exclusively toward their own constituency. There was little room for concern about the poverty, oppression, or violations of the human rights of non-Catholics, who were, by definition, enemies of the Church.

Frozen within their narrow ecclesiastical world, Vatican officials under the leadership of Popes Pius XI and XII focused primarily on Church centralization and standardization, control over the appointments of bishops, and Catholic education and youth groups. These objectives could be achieved by means of treaties with individual countries. With the Soviet Union, unfortunately, treaties were impossible, but they could be arranged with countries with conservative or National Socialist governments. Furthermore, many churchmen in the 1930s believed that while the Communists would remain in power for generations, Hitler and his Nazi followers were a temporary phenomenon. They expected that with time, the Germans would produce a more moderate regime, perhaps like Italy's, which would be more amenable to the Church. Hence, they viewed right-wing governments as regimes to be cultivated and cajoled. Communism could only be stubbornly confronted.

In the year and a half between the two encyclicals of 1937 and the declaration of the Italian anti-Jewish laws, storm clouds darkened over Europe. Already in October 1935, the Italian army had invaded Abyssinia and greatly antagonized the British and French with whom Mussolini might otherwise have found common ground in opposition to German expansionism. Since July 1936, Italian and German political leaders had grown more friendly while supporting Franco's cause in the Spanish Civil War. In November 1937, Italy joined the Anti-Comintern Pact, initiated the previous year by Germany and Japan. The following month, she withdrew from the League of Nations. When the German army marched into Austria to proclaim *Anschluss* in March 1938, the Italian government that had opposed such a step in 1934 remained silent. As the German-Italian alliance solidified, expressions of racial hatred of Jews and Africans appeared in the Fascist press, and then flourished. A law prohibiting "relations of a conjugal nature," meaning cohabitation, between Italian citizens and "subjects" in the African colonies was promulgated early in 1937.[47] By the spring of 1938 the future of Italian race policy was not difficult to foresee.

Vatican responses to the frightening events leading to war are beyond the scope of this book. Only responses to Jewish issues will be considered here, and, on the eve of the Italian anti-Jewish laws, those were few and far between. An article in *L'Osservatore Romano* on June 10, 1938, however, may be cited as representative of the Vatican position toward the Jews. In the article, the Jesuit priest Enrico Rosa who wrote so often for *La Civiltà Cattolica* discussed, among other matters, the ever more violent anti-Semitism and expulsions of Jews from Austria since it had become part of the German Reich in March. He wrote:

> Above all it is an error to say without any limitations or reserve . . . that the hunt for Jews is 'a holy enterprise,' that it 'was already in the designs of divine Providence.' . . . Nor are the usual reasons [for the hunting of Jews] that we repeatedly hear of any value: the Jews are merely guests of other nations; they reside there as foreigners; but although they are foreigners, they conduct themselves so as to usurp the best positions in every field, and not always by legitimate means; thus the enormous disproportion and the privations that come from their small numbers and the suffering of the immense majority of the native populations. *We admit all these inconveniences, and others still more grave,* such as the hatred and the constant struggle of the Jews against the Christian religion, and against the Catholic clergy, the religious, the papacy; the favor given to Freemasons and to other subversive groups. . . . However we maintain that all these [Jewish] confrontations and crimes can and should induce the authorities to look for a remedy, to repress abuses, to contain within just limits the undue invasion or interference, even to punish individuals when it is appropriate; but *they do not justify . . . the unjust and violent hunting down of everyone together,* guilty and innocent. Nor in this brutal process, *without legal status,* can we recognize an *equable and lasting solution to the formidable Jewish problem.*[48]

This article is perfectly consistent with others cited in this chapter. Like Hilaire Belloc cited above, Father Rosa believed that the Jews constituted a separate nationality, abused the hospitality of the nations where they resided, and participated disproportionately in the broader society, causing immense damage. Violence was to be condemned, but in pointing to the need for "an equable and lasting solution to the formidable Jewish problem" while mentioning "legal status," Father Rosa was virtually calling for the very anti-Jewish laws that Mussolini, for his own reasons, was considering at the time.

Nor was Rosa's readership insignificant in number. Because *L'Osservatore Romano* was a Vatican, and therefore a foreign, publication, it was not subject to Italian censorship. Before and during the Second World War it was often the only nonclandestine newspaper easily available to Italians that did not present the Fascist point of view. Its popularity consequently soared. Its circulation of about 20,000 at the beginning of the 1930s has been estimated to have grown to at least 80,000 by October 1939 and 150,000 by May 1940.[49]

But still more needs to be said here. Pope Pius XI did not just miss an opportunity to condemn the persecution of Jews at the time of the Anschluss. He also, at that critical moment, allowed his institution to endorse clear anti-Jewish prejudices. For if anti-Judaism consists of imputing highly unfavorable characteristics to Jews as a group and calling for a solution to the problem they allegedly created, then Father Rosa and the Vatican newspaper for which he wrote must be called profoundly anti-Jewish. To have written such words in mid-1938, after Jews on their hands and knees in Catholic Vienna had been forced to clean the sidewalks with toothbrushes, was to be not only anti-Jewish but blind and deaf to the implications of current events in Europe. With these attitudes and prejudices, Vatican bureaucrats including the pope were about to deal with the Italian anti-Jewish laws, Kristallnacht, and, in a little more than a year, the onset of the Holocaust itself.

CHAPTER TWO

The Vatican and Anti-Semitism in Italy

IN AN official news bulletin on February 16, 1938, Benito Mussolini explicitly denied the existence of a Jewish problem in Italy. Such a difficulty, he explained, was impossible in a country with only 50,000 to 60,000 Jews among a general population of 44 million. His government, therefore, was not considering special measures against the Jews, and opposed pressure for their assimilation. Existing laws regulating the life of the Jewish Community would remain unaltered. But the Duce concluded with the more ominous words, "The Fascist government will keep a vigilant eye on the activities of Jews recently arrived in our country and will ensure that the role of the Jews in the comprehensive life of the nation does not become disproportionate to the intrinsic merits of individuals and to the numerical importance of their community."[1] This statement, carried in the major Italian newspapers of the day, has been regarded as a hint of anti-Jewish measures to come. Mussolini, it is argued, was beginning to consider the possibility of tailoring the participation of Jews in the society to their proportion of the overall population.[2]

Almost exactly four months later, on July 14, a pseudo-scientific document entitled *Manifesto of the Racial Scientists* was published with much fanfare in the mass-circulation daily *Giornale d'Italia* and most other Italian newspapers. The manifesto was identified as the creation of a group of Fascist scholars affiliated with Italian universities but working temporarily with the Ministry of Popular Culture. The scholars claimed that their position represented "the position of Fascism regarding problems of race."[3]

The manifesto was an ideological rather than a programmatic statement, designed to introduce racism into Italy. In ten jumbled points it declared that human races existed, that the racial composition of different nations varied, that there was a pure Italian race of "Aryan" origin, and that Jews did not belong to the Italian race. It stated clearly, "To say that human races exist does not mean a priori that superior or inferior races exist, but only that different human races exist." With a more sinister flourish, however, it declared that "it is time that Italians proclaim themselves to be frankly racist." In a general but clear allusion to marriage between non-Jewish Italians and members of other "races," it concluded, "The purely European physical and psychological characteristics of the Italians must not be altered by any means. Union is admissible only in the context of the European races." [4]

The manifesto had, in fact, two slightly different themes and purposes. It intended, first of all, to place Italians solidly in the Western European or "Aryan" racial mainstream—a position frequently denied them by German race theorists who asserted that the blood of Mediterranean or Latin peoples was mixed with that of Semitic, Hamitic, and black North Africans. On the contrary, the manifesto declared, "Theories that assert the African origin of some European peoples and include in a common Mediterranean race even Semitic and Hamitic populations, establishing absolutely inadmissible relationships and ideological sympathies, are dangerous." [5] The document's second theme, of course, was the definition of Jews as a separate, non-European race. As it said, "The Jews represent the only population that has never assimilated in Italy because they are constituted from non-European racial elements, absolutely different from the elements from which Italians originated." [6]

In the weeks following publication of the manifesto, anti-Semitic rhetoric throughout the country grew to startling proportions. Newspapers such as *Il Tevere, Quadrivio,* and *Il Regime fascista* paved the way. Telesio Interlandi's new, viciously anti-Semitic newspaper *La Difesa della razza* joined them on August 5. That same day, another government news bulletin called for "a strong sentiment, a strong pride, a clear, omnipresent consciousness of race," and it denounced the "creation of a bastard race, neither European, nor African" in Italy's new empire. It also criticized the Jews for being too numerous, separatist, and favorable to Bolshevists and Freemasons. It announced that "to discriminate does not mean to persecute" and concluded that "the time is ripe for Italian racism." [7] After such an announcement, the anti-Jewish measures of September and November could hardly have come as a surprise.

In analyzing the responses of Pope Pius XI to the escalating danger of anti-Jewish legislation in Italy, it is useful to keep a chronology clearly in mind. Between Mussolini's denial of a Jewish problem but simultaneous reference to a possibly "disproportionate" Jewish presence in Italy in February 1938 and the Manifesto of the Racial Scientists on July 14, a pending government anti-Jewish program was explicitly rejected but vaguely implied. Between the manifesto in July and the actual anti-Jewish decrees of September and November, however, such a program was obviously in preparation. What did Pope Pius XI and officials at the Vatican Secretariat of State do and say during these two critical periods, as they became more and more conscious of Mussolini's intentions?

Papal speeches and articles in *L'Osservatore Romano* and *La Civiltà Cattolica* in late 1937 and early 1938 continued to criticize the Third Reich for its persecution of Catholics and glorification of the "Aryan" race. To cite just one example, Pius XI spoke at length on the subject to the College of Cardinals on Christmas Eve 1937. He stood solidly behind his message as articulated in *Mit brennender Sorge,* demonstrating that he was not about to back down. He insisted that the Church was concerned with religion, not politics, but that citizens had to adjust their civic obligations to the laws of God. He was clear but not specific.[8]

There is no indication of papal objections during this same period to the possible introduction of anti-Jewish measures in Italy. Often cited as evidence to the contrary is a letter sent by the Vatican Congregation of Seminaries and Universities to the rectors of Catholic institutions of higher education on April 13, 1938.[9] The letter asked Catholic educators to oppose eight errors of Nazi doctrine involving race. Roughly summarized, the errors included beliefs that the various human races were very different; that purity of blood must be maintained by every means; that intellectual and moral qualities arise from the blood; that the essential purpose of education is to develop pride in race; that the law of race prevails over religion; that race determines the juridical order; that there is only the cosmos or universe; and that individuals exist only for the state. The letter to the educators never mentioned anti-Semitism or Jews.

The Vatican letter received little publicity at the time, for it was not published in *L'Osservatore Romano*. It appeared in *La Civiltà Cattolica* three months later. It was nevertheless important, as it represented a continuation of Pius XI's explicit condemnations of German racism. It was reinforced by an admirable article objecting to German race theory in *L'Osservatore Romano* on April 30, which concluded with a reference to "the brotherhood of peoples, the equality of their dignity and thus their reciprocal esteem: the basis, that is, and the necessary conditions of cooperation and peace between Nations." [10] The Church was doing what it had always done and what it was supposed to do: defending the rights of all God's children to equality of treatment on racial grounds. In so doing, it was antagonizing Hitler. Relations between the Holy See and the Third Reich became so strained that the Führer refused to seek a papal audience when he was in Rome in early May to visit the king and Mussolini. The pope responded by withdrawing to his summer retreat at Castel Gandolfo and closing the Vatican museums. *L'Osservatore Romano* printed a long article about Pius XI's departure, explaining rather ambiguously that it did not constitute "petty diplomacy" but occurred because "the air of Castel Gandolfo makes him feel good, while that [in Rome] makes him feel bad." It did not mention Hitler's presence. [11] The feud simmered, and Pius XI acted courageously. He was not, however, defending the rights of religious and cultural Jews to equality before the law.

The best way to understand the content and limitations of the Vatican's condemnations of racism during this period is to compare them to its simultaneous statements and articles specifically about Jews. One such article, about anti-Semitism in Austria, was published in *L'Osservatore Romano* on June 10, 1938, and quoted at the end of the previous chapter. In the article, the Jesuit Father Enrico Rosa condemned violence and brutality against the Jews but agreed that the Jews "usurp the best positions in every field, and not always by legitimate means," cause "the suffering of the immense majority of the native populations," hate and struggle against the Christian religion, and favor Freemasons and other subversive groups. As seen, he urged "an equable and lasting solution to the formidable Jewish problem" but called for legal means.

About a month later, and just two days after the publication of the Manifesto of the Racial Scientists, a lengthy article entitled "The Jewish Question in Hungary" appeared in *La Civiltà Cattolica*. [12] The Jesuit author provided statistics to show that Jews, 5 percent of the Hungarian population, constituted 47 percent of the lawyers in Budapest, 62 percent of the veterinarians, 37 percent of the pharmacists, 40 percent of the engineers, 67 percent of the journalists, and equally large proportions of bankers, businessmen, and landowners. Here, clearly demonstrated, was the threatening Jewish "preponderance" against which Jesuit authors had so often warned, described at the very time that Mussolini was concerning himself with "proportions" of Jews in Italy. The author went on to declare that "all or almost all the Jews in the intellectual and ruling class are not believers [in Judaism], but free thinkers, or revolutionaries, or Freemasons and organizers of Freemasons: anti-Christians in their moral and intellectual life; capitalists in their economic life, they are Socialists or philo-Socialists in their social life, maintaining connections with Socialist trade unions and their leaders; in a word, the law of their life (and their practical moral law) is success in the world by whatever means." [13]

In such a situation, Catholic anti-Judaism in Hungary could not be seen as vulgar fanaticism or racism but as a "movement in defense of national traditions and of the true liberty and independence of the Magyar people." [14] Some 250,000 men in Catholic Action in Hungary were therefore asking their government to halt Jewish immigration and expel all who had entered the country illegally. The article then called for the defense of the nation against the present danger of an invasion of Jews escaping from Germany, Austria, and Romania. It declared that the only "law for that defense" currently in effect was one that limited the enrollment of Jews in the universities to 5 percent, their proportion of the population. Laws restricting Jewish participation in other fields were being considered, however—measures that, "without persecution," might encourage Jews to leave Hungary. The author concluded by saying, "We do not enter into the particulars of this proposed legislation; we only note that it is inspired by the noble Magyar traditions of chivalrous and loyal hospitality, restricting itself only to what is absolutely necessary, which many believe to be insufficient." [15] Surprisingly, he did not even object to the Hungarian definition of Jews that rejected conversions that had occurred after August 1, 1919. He explained that many believed that such a rejection would discourage insincere and opportunistic conversions in the future.

It is hard to escape the conclusion that by printing such an article at a time when Mussolini was considering what proportion of Jewish participation in Italian life was acceptable, the editors of La Civiltà Cattolica were advocating restrictions similar to those being proposed in Hungary. These were not necessarily the precise views of Pius XI, but they are an indication of the pressures being leveled on him. Nor would they have been printed if the editors of the Jesuit journal had expected that the pope would strongly object.

Other indications of both the pope's thinking and the pressures on him are revealed by the strange story of the "hidden encyclical." Years after the death of Pius XI, on February 10, 1939, evidence that he had been planning a major encyclical on racism was unearthed. At the end of June 1938, just two weeks before the publication of the Manifesto of the Racial Scientists, he asked three Jesuit priests to prepare a document condemning racism in all its forms and elaborating on the theme of the unity of the human race. The procedure was unorthodox, not only because it was unusually secretive, but because it bypassed the Father General of the Jesuit order, Vladimir Ledóchowski. A rough draft of the encyclical was nevertheless ready in September, but it promptly disappeared within the labyrinthine corridors of the Jesuit and Vatican bureaucracies. Pius XI, preoccupied by then with the Munich crisis, the Italian anti-Jewish laws, and his own ill health and growing weakness, was unable to ensure the survival of the document he had himself requested. Conspiracy theories regarding the disappearance abound: Ledóchowski deliberately held it up; opponents of the encyclical convinced Pius XI to change his plans by playing upon his fears of Communism; it was stolen from the pope's bedtable on the evening he died; Pius XII deliberately sabotaged it.[16]

The story of the hidden encyclical sheds light upon the inner workings of the Vatican bureaucracy. Above all, it reminds us that however authoritarian it may be, the Vatican administration remains heterogeneous. Vatican policies cannot be determined by a single individual, even if that individual is the pope. The story is probably not, however, an indication of a lost opportunity. A draft of the encyclical, recovered years later with great effort, contains admirable sections on the unity of the human race and the inadmissibility of racism. While it condemns anti-Semitism explicitly and at length, however, which was more than any Vatican spokesman had done since 1928, it continues to describe the "Jewish question" in terms that had not altered for centuries. The Jews are the people chosen by God to receive the Messiah; the blindness of their leaders has condemned them to ceaseless suffering; they can be redeemed by repentance and acceptance of Jesus; and it is the mission of the Church to facilitate the process. Meanwhile, in dealing with the Jews, the Church is not blind "to the spiritual dangers to which contact with Jews can expose souls, or . . . unaware of the need to safeguard her children against spiritual contagion." The Church has a clear "need for energetic measures to preserve both the faith and morals of her members and society itself against the corrupting influence of error." Anti-Semitism is unacceptable because it is ineffective in protecting society and in facilitating the conversion of the Jews. Persecution is unacceptable because "instead of obliterating or lessening the harmful or anti-social traits of a persecuted group, [it] merely intensifies the tendencies that gave rise to them." [17]

It seems unlikely that Pius XI would have significantly altered the sections on Jews. Indeed, as will be seen, he confronted the Italian anti-Jewish laws in the autumn of 1938 in a manner totally consistent with them. He accepted the separation of Jews from the rest of society without a public word, apparently agreeing with Mussolini's opinion that it was "discrimination, not persecution."

A Dutch Jesuit scholar who managed to see a version of the draft of the hidden encyclical in the early 1970s wrote that the references to Jews and to anti-Semitism were mediocre and deplorable. He added that anyone who read the text in the context of the German racial legislation of the period would see it as embarrassingly inadequate and say to himself, "God be praised that this draft remained only a draft!" [18] He was correct. The text remains as testimony to the tragic inability even of churchmen of good will to recognize the inherent evil of anti-Jewish legislation and the terrible, inexorable link between separation and elimination.

On July 15, 1938, one day after the publication of the Manifesto of the Racial Scientists, Pius XI addressed a large group of nuns at an assembly of the Sisters of Notre-Dame du Cenacle. [19] Since his speech has been described as evidence of his opposition to pending anti-Jewish measures in Italy, it deserves examination. [20] In a conventional introduction, Pius spoke warmly of the nuns' mission. He then broadened his remarks to discuss what he called "that curse that is exaggerated nationalism" that produces a "sterile apostolate. . . , that prevents the health of souls, that raises barriers between peoples, that is contrary, not only to the law of the good God, but to the faith itself." The word "catholic" means universal, he continued; the Catholic Church means the universal Church, and therefore "the contrast between exaggerated nationalism and Catholic doctrine is evident." [21]

Pius XI did not mention specific people or countries, and he never used the word "racism." He did, however, refer briefly to the manifesto. He declared that he had learned that very morning of "something very grave: it deals with a form of real apostasy. It is no longer merely one or another erroneous idea; it is the entire spirit of the doctrine that is contrary to the Faith of Christ." [22] The allusion was obscure but probably clear to his listeners. The condemnation of Fascist racism was unmistakable. But there was no mention of anti-Semitism or the Jews.

The following day, *L'Osservatore Romano* mentioned the manifesto directly but expressed none of the pope's regrets. An article of three short paragraphs on the newspaper's second page summarized the manifesto's contents briefly and accurately. It then concluded, in its usual ponderous and obscure style: "Newspaper comments tend to underline the difference between these 'objective scientific remarks' and any philosophical theory usually defined as 'racism.' There is no lack of those who affirm still more explicitly that to the biological concept of race there is added and prevails among us [Italians] that spiritual [concept] upon which is based the just repudiation of any distinction between different races as superior and inferior." [23] There was no criticism of either the manifesto or anti-Semitism here. On the contrary, despite Pius XI's words the previous day, the tone is one of vague approval of a document that did not make value judgments about the various races. A Jesuit priest named Father A. Brucculeri went still further. On July 17, in an article in the Roman newspaper *L'Avvenire,* he wrote, "About racism the Italian scholars have taken a clear and precise position with which, from a philosophic position, there is nothing to object." [24]

Nevertheless, Pius XI was clearly not happy with the manifesto. On July 21, six days after his speech to the nuns and in contrast with it, he used the word "racism" in a public forum. During an audience with 150 Church-appointed assistants working with Catholic Action, he said, "Catholic means universal, not racist, nationalistic, separatist. . . . It is necessary to say, in fact, that there is something particularly detestable, this spirit of separatism, of exaggerated nationalism, that precisely because it is not Christian, not religious, ends by being not even human." [25] This was brief, with the emphasis still on nationalist divisions rather than racial ones, but his audience and readers would have associated the reference to "racism" with the manifesto. And the pope would do much better seven days later. On July 28, in a speech to students at the Collegio di Propaganda Fide, he at last spoke eloquently and from the heart. Over and over he repeated the same theme: "In the human type [*genere*] there is one single great universal catholic human race, one single great, universal human family, and with that, in that, diverse variations." The students of the Collegio, from thirty-seven nations, represented a "true and just and sane practice of a racism corresponding to human dignity and reality; because human reality is to be men and not beasts . . . human dignity is to be one single great family, the human type, the human race." [26]

Pius XI's disapproval of the new Italian version of racism that divided the "single great universal human family" into subgroups was now absolutely clear. One specific paragraph among many general ones made the allusion unmistakable. "We can then ask ourselves how, unfortunately, Italy has felt the need to go and imitate Germany. . . . The Latins never used to speak of race, or of anything similar. Our old Italians used other more beautiful, pleasant words." [27] The pope was associating nascent Italian racism with the German version in a way that L'Osservatore Romano on July 16 had failed to do. Yet even here, when he seemed most ready to challenge Mussolini, he did not refer to anti-Semitism or Jews.

The Duce was infuriated nevertheless. Always sensitive to the charge of imitating Germany, he issued public denials on several occasions—although he was hard pressed to explain his own originality. [28] His government ordered local Catholic publications not to print the pope's speech, and few did. [29] In his diary on July 30, Foreign Minister Count Galeazzo Ciano called the speech "violently anti-racist." He added that he had promptly summoned Francesco Borgongini Duca, the papal nuncio to Italy, to warn him that "if [the Vatican] continues on this path, a clash is inevitable because the Duce, since the conquest of the Empire, regards the racial question as fundamental." Ciano continued, "I spoke very clearly to Borgoncini [sic]: I explained the assumptions and goals of our racism. He seemed quite convinced to me. And I will add that he showed himself to be personally very anti-Semitic. Tomorrow he will confer with the Holy Father." [30]

Borgongini Duca may have delivered Ciano's warning to the pope, but the Holy Father did not immediately back down. On August 6 an article appeared in La Civiltà Cattolica that directly contradicted part of the manifesto, and on August 13 the same piece was printed in L'Osservatore Romano. The Jesuit author of the article denied the very existence of pure races, which the manifesto had described. He added that nations did not consist of a single race but were mixed—"neither race, nor language, nor religion, nor territory constitute the essence of the nation." [31] The disagreement with Mussolini, then, continued, but it concerned nascent Italian racism rather than anti-Judaism.

Interestingly enough, the same August 6 issue of La Civiltà Cattolica carried another, very different reference to the manifesto that sounded like near

approval. The mention occurred in its news section, "Cronaca contemporanea," covering the dates July 7 to 26, a standard span for this section. After
printing the text of the manifesto in full the author declared that its difference
from "intrinsically and explicitly materialistic and anti-Christian Nazism or
German racism" was apparent to all.[32] He did not object to the content of the
manifesto, but only to its lack of precise terminology, which might open the
door to a more German-style racism in the future. Considering the pope's reference to Italy imitating Germany just a few days before, this appraisal suggests significant disagreements within the Vatican.

August 6, 1938, represented the high point of Vatican criticism of Italian
racist rhetoric. The Fascist government's official news bulletin of August 5,
with its unfavorable descriptions of Jews and its announcements that "to discriminate does not mean to persecute" and "the time is ripe for Italian
racism," evoked a tortured, confused, and ultimately meaningless response
in L'Osservatore Romano two days later.[33] The article described part of the contents of the news bulletin but omitted the deprecating remarks about Jews
and quoted the phrase "to discriminate does not mean to persecute" as if it
was intended to apply to the African colonies. Then on August 8, after another meeting with Papal Nuncio Borgongini Duca, Foreign Minister Ciano
wrote that "as for the race problem, the pope, now that he understands what it
is really about, is beginning to disarm."[34] The following day Ciano noted a
conversation with the Jesuit Father Pietro Tacchi Venturi, an unofficial but
frequent intermediary between the pope and Mussolini since 1929, when he
had helped with negotiations for the Lateran Accords. According to Ciano's
account, Italian racism was not even discussed. Instead, the talk focused on
recent incidents demonstrating Fascist hostility to the always vulnerable
Catholic Action. Ciano wrote, "We agreed on the usefulness of carrying out
direct action to avoid a conflict between the Holy See and Fascism. There is
no reason to refuse. Friction with Catholic Action is of little importance and
easy to limit, if there is good will on both sides."[35] Why were Italian race policies not also mentioned as a potential cause of friction? Had Ciano implied to
Tacchi Venturi that the Fascists would leave Catholic Action alone if the pope
would refrain from criticizing the imminent anti-Jewish laws?[36]

There exists still another possible explanation for the apparent easing of
Church-state tensions in early August. Soon after the publication of the Manifesto of the Racial Scientists on July 14, with its statement that marriage was
"admissible only in the context of the European races," Cardinal Eugenio

Pacelli, then the Vatican secretary of state, met with Count Pignatti Morano di Custoza, the Italian ambassador to the Holy See. Pacelli had learned of the possibility that the new anti-Jewish laws might prohibit marriages between Italian citizens and members of other races, even if Catholic. As will be explained in detail in the next chapter, such a prohibition would constitute a grave violation of the religious concordat, part of the Lateran Accords of 1929, which gave the Church the sole right to regulate marriages between Catholics. Pacelli reminded the ambassador of that fact, and the ambassador promised to convey his position to the Italian government.[37] "Conflict between the Holy See and Fascism," as Ciano had described it, could only have been avoided if the Italian government promised not to prohibit inter-racial marriages between Catholics. Could Ciano have hinted that it might do so, to quiet both Tacchi Venturi and Pacelli? If so, he deliberately deceived them.

For whatever reason, Pius XI was backing away from confrontation. On August 12 an article about his speech of July 28 in L'Osservatore Romano denied that he had referred to Italian racial measures as copies of German laws.[38] The pope, it explained, was speaking of spiritual, not political, matters. Wherever Judaism was a force of egoism, domination, and persecution of others, he would warn against it, but when Judaism represented misery, pain, and a target of persecution, he would defend it. In the context of the times, this was indeed a lukewarm defense of the Jews.

Vatican-Italian reconciliation at Jewish expense continued on August 14, when L'Osservatore Romano published a remarkable article describing all the good things that past popes had done for Jews in the former Papal States— "not that the Jews, as such, had deserved such exquisite sentiments of pontifical paternity. On the contrary." Nevertheless, popes had offered hospitality and sanctuary to Jews throughout history. They had prevented Christians from forcing the Jews to convert, and from disturbing their synagogues, their Sabbath, and their holy days. At the same time, popes and secular rulers alike had shared "an interest in preventing their nations from being invaded by Jewish elements, risking loss of the direction of society." Therefore, "Jews had been prevented from holding any public positions, civil or military, and that prohibition was also extended to the sons of converted Jews. The precautions applied to the exercise of the professions, teaching and even commerce."[39]

With considerable distortion of the truth, the author proceeded to provide a history of the exceptional benevolence of Pius IX, whose papacy had extended from 1846 to 1878. To show his good will, that particular pope had ordered the destruction of the walls of "that ghetto [in Rome] formerly regarded as [the Jews'] little paradise on earth because, removed from frequent popular reprisals, the Jews lived there together, around their synagogue, in conformity to their laws, under the authority of their leaders and with full liberty of religion." Yet for that magnanimity and much more, the author asserted, the Jews proved themselves profoundly ungrateful. They were the first to defame the Church when government troops seized Rome in 1870 and united it to Italy.[40]

As the editors of *L'Osservatore Romano* certainly knew, this article was a travesty of the truth. Far from being a paradise, the ghetto in Rome in the nineteenth century had been overcrowded, impoverished, and unsanitary. As part of a short-lived reform period soon after his election, Pius IX did order the gates removed, but ghetto residents still could not reside or own property outside the area without special permission. They were excluded from the professions and subjected to onerous financial tributes. They enjoyed nothing even approaching equal civil rights. Under certain circumstances, Jewish children could even be secretly baptized by Catholic household servants and then, because they were "Christians," forcibly taken from their own families. Such a tragedy happened to six-year-old Edgardo Mortara in Bologna, in the Papal States, as late as 1858. Despite protests from around the world, Pius IX never returned the boy to his parents.[41] Except for a brief revolutionary period in 1848 and 1849 when Pius IX was temporarily removed from power, these conditions endured in Rome until Italian troops seized the city in 1870. The Jews were emancipated only when papal rule ended.

The primitive distortions in *L'Osservatore Romano*, however, are not the point. The relevant and terrible point here is that the author of this article expressed no disapproval of past restrictions on Jews' rights to hold positions in the public service, professions, teaching, and even commerce. These were, in fact, the very restrictions being considered at the time for Mussolini's new anti-Jewish laws. How could this article have been interpreted, other than as an expression of approval for almost everything that Mussolini was doing?

Two days later, on August 16, Mussolini approved a private note to the Vatican, discussing his future anti-Jewish measures and suggesting a resolution of the conflict over racism. It read, in part:

> The Jews, in a word, can be sure that they will not be subject to worse treatment than that applied to them for centuries by the popes who hosted them in the Eternal City and in the lands of [the Church's] temporal domain. On that premise, it is the urgent desire

of the Honorable Head of Government that the Catholic press, preachers, lecturers and so forth abstain from treating this matter in public; the Holy See, the Supreme Pontiff himself does not lack ways of expressing himself directly to Mussolini through private channels and of proposing to him those observations that are believed opportune for the best solution of this delicate problem.[42]

With its references to past treatment of Jews by earlier popes, this sounds like a direct response to the Vatican article of two days previously.

Pius XI made one more speech critical of current developments on August 21, but, significantly, he did not mention racism. At the conclusion of a weeklong conference on Catholic missions held at the Collegio di Propaganda in Castel Gandolfo, he offered eloquent advice to missionaries: "Be especially on guard against exaggerated nationalism, because there is nationalism and nationalism. . . . Thus there is a place for a just, moderate, temperate nationalism associated with all the virtues. But guard against 'exaggerated nationalism' as against a real curse. It seems to us that all events unfortunately show us to be right when we say 'a real curse' because it is a curse of divisions, of contrasts with a risk of war."[43] Although Pius seemed determined to stand behind his earlier warnings against national rivalries and hatred, he was now willing to avoid the issue of racism altogether.

La Civiltà Cattolica, however, picked up the racial theme one more time before the anti-Jewish decrees of September 5 and 7 altered the terms of discussion. In its September 3 issue, after informing its readers that Fascist policymakers were considering measures to address the "defense of the race" and the "Jewish problem," the unidentified author noted his journal's consistent condemnation of the "materialistic evolutionism" of Charles Darwin, exploited by "the Jew Karl Marx." He expressed gratitude to the Fascist government for "the guarding and improvement of the physical and moral health of the Italian people." But he then added, "This . . . is not an argument in favor, and much less in justification, of the errors current today in Germany, of false exultation or even divination of the race, errors that a rash interpretation of the ten propositions of the group of 'Fascist scholars' [authors of the Manifesto of the Racial Scientists] might unknowingly introduce even among ourselves."[44] And so the debate continued. La Civiltà Cattolica, in insisting on the resemblance of some Fascist race theory to that of the Nazis, seemed to remain close to the thought of Pius XI. But again, the debate did not involve anti-Jewish measures. And the pope himself, for a time, said little.

Careful readers of Pius XI's speeches in the summer of 1938 may argue that too much has been made in these pages of the difference between racism and anti-Judaism. Everyone at the time understood that the pope's words were directed against Nazi racism, and Nazi racism in the 1930s and early 1940s meant the persecution of the Jews. The Holy Father did not have to spell it out. Jews and their defenders throughout the world understood, or thought they understood, and were grateful.

It is true that Jews were grateful. They interpreted Pius's words subjectively. They heard what they wanted to hear, and they grieved when Pius died. It is also true that some of the papal statements, if read out of context, could be interpreted as supportive of Jews, even though they were never specifically mentioned. A condemnation of racism, after all, includes a condemnation of the persecution of Jews on purely racial grounds. But the pope's speeches cannot be read out of context. At the same time that they were being delivered, L'Osservatore Romano was publishing articles, cited above, about the "Jewish question" in Austria and Hungary, on June 10 and July 16, and about Jews in the former Papal States, on August 14. These and other articles repeated all the old anti-Jewish stereotypes: Jews usurp the best positions in every field, support revolution, cause suffering, hate and threaten Christians, are ungrateful for all that Christians do for them. The implication was always that Jewish influence should be limited, and those who were Jews by religion or culture should be separated from the rest of society.

Whether Pius XI personally shared these views is not relevant. What matters is that he did not publicly challenge them. There was a good reason why he did not use the words "anti-Semitism" or "anti-Judaism." The men who ran the Vatican were nothing if not intelligent. If they did not use the words, it was because they chose not to. The difference between racism and anti-Judaism was clear to them. They chose occasionally to condemn racism that penalized Jews because of their blood. They did not condemn other types of anti-Jewish attitudes, which rejected Jews because of their religion and culture. The terrible truth was that they wanted the Jews to be put in their place.

By the end of the summer of 1938, world leaders were focusing on the imminent confrontation between the Third Reich and Czechoslovakia over the Sudetenland. The pope had less time or strength for issues of racism or anti-Judaism. Eighty-one years old and already ill for several months, he was losing influence and control over those within the Vatican who wanted above all else to avoid a rupture with the Italian government in such perilous times. Mussolini, while also eager to avoid a break, had made it clear that he would not back away from his racial program. The pope, never firmly opposed to anti-Jewish measures, quietly retreated from opposition to racism as well. But a worse confrontation lay just ahead.

CHAPTER THREE

Italian Anti-Jewish Laws During the Papacy of Pius XI

JEWISH survivors of the Holocaust in Italy often recall that, prior to the German occupation, the most devastating moment of the Fascist persecutions occurred when they learned that they or their children could no longer attend the public schools. On September 5, 1938, as children all over Italy were returning from vacations and gathering up their books for the new school year, a decree entitled "Provisions for the defense of the race in the Fascist school" was promulgated with little warning. Jewish students were suddenly banned from public elementary and secondary schools. Those already enrolled in universities were allowed to finish, but no new Jewish students could register. Jewish teachers were to be immediately dismissed. The law was to apply to all individuals with "two parents of the Jewish race," regardless of their religion. Thus, the children of two converts were affected, although the offspring of mixed marriages were not.[1] This decree was instantly and thoroughly enforced. School administrators were required to locate all Jews in the system, and they complied with a vengeance.[2]

Two days later, another decree affected most foreign-born Jews in Italy. Jews who were not citizens could no longer maintain legal residence in Italy, Libya, or the Dodecanese Islands. Still worse, Jews who had been naturalized after January 1, 1919, lost their citizenship and were declared foreigners. They became stateless. The decree specified that all Jews who had immigrated after January 1, 1919, must leave the country within six months. Those remaining in March 1939 were to be expelled. The definition of Jewishness was the same as that for the education decree, so again conversion to Catholicism offered no protection.[3]

About ten days later Mussolini made it clear that restrictions on foreign Jews and on Jews in the schools were to be only the tip of the iceberg. In a speech to a huge crowd in Trieste on September 18, he announced his commitment to a broad policy of separation while promising that "Jews of Italian citizenship who have undeniable military or civilian merit with regard to Italy and the Regime will find understanding and justice."[4] Two weeks later, on the night of October 6–7, details of his new policy became known when he presented his "Declaration on Race" to the Fascist Grand Council for its approval.[5] The declaration outlined the anti-Jewish measures soon to be drafted into law. Included were a prohibition of marriage between Italian "Aryans" and other races, a repetition of measures against foreign Jews, definitions of Jewishness, categories of "merit" entitling Italian Jews to some exemptions, and a list of the restrictions about to be imposed.

The comprehensive anti-Jewish decrees of November 17, then, virtually unchanged from the Declaration on Race, came as no surprise.[6] Entitled "Provisions for the Defense of the Italian Race," the first article repeated the proscriptions on marriage. While this prohibition applied to "Aryan" Italians and all other "races," the other decrees were aimed only at Jews. These victims were banned from employment in the public sector, including the national, provincial, and municipal civil service and the military. They were to be dismissed from positions in "banks of national interest," private insurance companies, and the Fascist Party. They were prohibited from owning land, factories, or businesses over a certain value, as well as any enterprise involved in national defense. They could not employ "Aryan" domestics. Overnight, thousands of people lost their jobs. Expropriation of property took a little longer, but it too was eventually enforced with devastating effectiveness.[7]

Crucial to the new decrees was its definition of Jewishness. That definition would determine who would be subjected not only to the new prohibitions, but to the September measures on education and foreigners as well. Declared legally Jewish were those with two parents "of the Jewish race," regardless of religion; those with one parent "of the Jewish race" and one "of foreign nationality"; those with a Jewish mother and an unknown father; and those with at least one Jewish parent who themselves "belong to the Jewish religion, . . . or have been inscribed in a Jewish Community, or have demonstrated, in any other manner, manifestations of Jewishness." Not to be considered Jewish was "anyone with two Italian parents of whom only one was

Jewish, who, on the date of October 1, 1938, . . . belonged to a religion other than the Jewish one." In other words, to be declared non-Jewish the offspring of mixed marriages were required to produce proof of prior baptism.[8] The Catholic offspring of two Jewish parents who had both converted to Catholicism, however, were to be considered Jewish. As will be seen, this provision, along with the restrictions on marriages, created serious dilemmas for the Church.

The decrees also defined categories of merit that entitled individual Jews to apply for, but not necessarily receive, exemptions from some restrictions and prohibitions. Categories included the families of those killed in recent wars or for the Fascist cause; wounded veterans, volunteers, or medal winners from the same wars or cause; those who had joined the Fascist Party between 1919 and 1922 or in the second half of 1924; those who had served in Fiume in 1919 and 1920; and individuals of an undefined "exceptional merit." Prohibitions subject to exemption included military service (until later rescinded), ownership or management of large properties, and employment in private insurance companies. Prohibitions concerning education and public sector jobs were not subject to exemption. Again, these measures were thoroughly enforced.

In the months following November 1938 the government issued a host of new proscriptions against Jews. By a law of June 29, 1939, Jewish professionals such as physicians, pharmacists, veterinarians, lawyers, judges, accountants, engineers, architects, chemists, agronomists, and mathematicians could practice only within their own community, unless they received special exemptions. Jewish journalists could not practice at all without exemptions. Jewish notaries could never practice or receive exemptions. Administrative circulars during the same months prevented Jews from owning radios, placing advertisements or death notices in newspapers, publishing books, holding public conferences, listing their names and numbers in telephone directories, frequenting popular vacation spots, and much more.[9] Separation in the public sphere was virtually complete. Only in housing were Jews allowed to remain side by side with non-Jewish Italians.

Following the original decrees regarding education and foreign Jews on September 5 and 7, Mussolini's critics might still have hoped to influence him and deter further anti-Jewish measures. After the Declaration on Race informed members of the Fascist Grand Council on October 6 of measures yet to come, however, that hope waned. The possibility of influencing and altering specific proposals before they became law nevertheless remained until they were promulgated in November. How did Vatican officials respond to these shifting possibilities throughout the autumn of 1938?

Pope Pius XI must have been deeply upset by the original education decree on September 5, for the following day he spoke more favorably and frankly about the Jews than he had ever done before or would ever do again. In an audience with a group of 120 pilgrims from the Belgian Catholic Radio on September 6, he evoked the reference in the Holy Mass to the sacrifice of Abraham and continued, apparently spontaneously:

> Listen carefully: Abraham is defined as our patriarch, our ancestor. Anti-Semitism is not compatible with the sublime thought and reality evoked in this text. Anti-Semitism is a hateful movement, with which we Christians must have nothing to do. . . . Through Christ and in Christ we are the spiritual descendants of Abraham. No, it is not licit for Christians to take part in manifestations of anti-Semitism. We recognize the right of all to defend themselves and to adopt measures to protect themselves against those who threaten their legitimate interests. But anti-Semitism is unacceptable. Spiritually, we are all Semites.[10]

The reference to "the right of all to defend themselves" was regrettable, but the remainder of the passage was deeply moving. One can only lament and speculate about why such words were not uttered more often. Pius's advisors must have been startled, for he had never mentioned anti-Semitism in his earlier speeches. In fact, as seen, he had mentioned racism only a few times. In the previous two weeks, also, he had seemed to be backing away from confrontation with Mussolini.

Some advisors must have been more than just startled, for the pope's words were never printed in Italy. The article in *L'Osservatore Romano* reporting the audience with the Belgians omitted any mention of the pope's reference to Jews.[11] At the pope's specific request, the speech was published in *La Libre Belgique* on September 14 by a Monsignor Picard, head of the Belgian Catholic Radio, who had accompanied the pilgrims to Rome. It subsequently appeared in France in *La Croix* on September 17, and in *La Documentation Catholique* in its volume for 1938. It became known in Italy only slowly and indirectly.[12] This suggestion of a coverup of Pius XI's "spiritually, we are all Semites" speech again indicates dissension within the Vatican on the issue of anti-Semitism.

Pius XI's anguished but unreported statement was in fact his only public protest against Mussolini's emerging anti-Jewish policies in the month of September. *L'Osservatore Romano* did not describe the measures prohibiting Jews in the public schools and depriving foreign Jews of their citizenship and expelling them. On the contrary, on September 8 it reported yet another papal discourse, in which Pius XI seemed to be saying that his speeches on July 21 and 28 had been misunderstood and distorted by the press. The pope did not want to speak about racism, the article continued, but simply "of human variety, praising those who want to . . . participate in the treasures of our civilization, our Christian, Catholic civilization, the only true civilization capable of doing good for all mankind." [13] The timing of such words was inappropriate, to say the least.

La Civiltà Cattolica reported the new decrees without comment on September 17.[14] Then, instead of focusing on ways to prevent or mitigate future anti-Jewish measures before it was too late, the Jesuits allowed the Fascist daily *Il Regime fascista* to provoke them into defending a series of three articles on "The Jewish Question in Europe" that had appeared in *La Civiltà Cattolica* as long ago as 1890. In so doing, they proved that their views had not changed in nearly half a century.

The incident began when a reporter for *Il Regime fascista* drew attention to the forty-eight-year-old anti-Jewish articles and commented gleefully, on August 30, that there was "much to learn from the Fathers of the Company of Jesus." The reporter continued, "Fascism is quite inferior, both in its propositions and in their execution, to the rigor of *La Civiltà Cattolica*." [15] The original articles in the Jesuit journal had indeed been explicit.[16] They had argued that the Jews were invading public life, and that the Talmud taught Jews to hate all non-Jews, especially Christians, and to oppress and despoil nations that offer them hospitality. Laws granting equality were a grave error, for the Jews planned to profit from emancipation to infiltrate cities, gain power, and corrupt and conquer the world.

And what remedies for the "Jewish question" did *La Civiltà Cattolica* propose in 1890? Banishment (or, in twentieth-century terms, deportation) was deserved but not practical, for where could 8 million Jews go? In addition, banishment was contrary to the laws of God.[17] A less drastic remedy could include a confiscation or nationalization of Jewish possessions, robbed in any case from Christians. Such a step, however, must be performed in a "Christian manner" and according to law, for "not all Jews are thieves, swindlers, cheats, usurers, Freemasons, blackguards and corrupters of customs." [18]

Laws should be passed declaring all Jews to be foreigners, denying them civic equality, regulating their participation in capitalist ventures, and prohibiting them from owning land. As long as governments remained faithful to the principles of the French Revolution, the author pointed out in 1890, they would suffer under the Jewish yoke.[19]

The first response to the attack from *Il Regime fascista* was printed in *L'Osservatore Romano* on September 7, 1938, the very day of the government's decree regarding foreign Jews.[20] A short article explained that Church measures regarding Jews in the past had had nothing to do with racism but were intended to protect the faith and civilization. They were aimed, that is, against Judaism, as they might have been against Islam, Protestantism, sectarianism, or Communism.

La Civiltà Cattolica responded somewhat later, and at greater length, with two articles.[21] While the authors could lament that the writings of 1890 were quoted incorrectly, selectively, and out of context, however, there was little to add or deny. Recognizing that fact, they confirmed most of the original assertions. As in 1890, they denounced the pernicious teachings of the Talmud.[22] They repeated the fantasy that Roman Jews had been grateful for the protection of the ghetto and had considered the city a paradise.[23] They claimed again that emancipation had enabled Jews to rise above Christians in power and wealth, and to become, with the Freemasons, persecutors of the Church.[24] As if that were not enough, the Jesuit writers even threw in new charges, impossible in 1890, that the Communists owed their successful revolution largely to Jews.[25] To soften these views, they could only stress that Jews who converted should always be encouraged and welcomed, innocents protected, and "justice" preserved. Nothing should be done for reasons of vengeance. The repeal of emancipation must be effected through changes in the law.

Repeal of emancipation through changes in the law was exactly what Mussolini was contemplating at the time.

While the editors of *La Civiltà Cattolica* were implicitly approving anti-Jewish legal measures in Italy, however, they continued to oppose German racism. Again the distinction was absolutely clear to them. In the September 17 issue, the same one that carried the first justification of the anti-Jewish series of 1890, an article condemned current German race-purification policies, including forced sterilization, differing categories of citizenship, restrictions on marriage, and the glorification of "Aryanism."[26] German statism and absolutism, the author stated flatly, were as intransigent as in the Soviet Union. When government racial policies reduced human beings to the level of flesh and nerves, the author concluded, one is "not in the presence of a true civilization, but of a perversion, an inversion, that is a sign of supreme decadence. In this case a people has only one mission, to reconstruct its public life according to the demands of a true and genuine civilization, and to return to obedience of the insuppressible laws of human nature." [27] This was strong language, verging on a call for civil disobedience. But it was not directed toward the anti-Jewish laws.

On October 5 the Fascist government prohibited Catholic publications from printing articles on racism, including German racism.[28] *La Civiltà Cattolica*, published in Italy, was effectively silenced on the subject. *L'Osservatore Romano*, issued from the independent Vatican State and not subject to Italian censorship, would continue the campaign throughout November and beyond.

On October 7, the day after Mussolini presented the Declaration of Race to the Fascist Grand Council and thus made his specific intentions for future anti-Jewish legislation known, the Italian ambassador to the Holy See informed Foreign Minister Galeazzo Ciano of the Vatican's reaction. "They point out some good aspects of the [Fascist Grand Council's] deliberations," he reported, "while they cannot hide their concern about the marriage provisions." He added that the proposal to prohibit marriages between non-Jewish Catholics and converts from Judaism "is the only point of the racist proclamation of the Grand Council to which the Church would formulate objections." [29] *L'Osservatore Romano* confirmed this assessment on October 8, publishing the Declaration on Race in full and commenting only that "The news . . . cannot exclude worries on our part especially regarding the principles and matrimonial discipline of the Church." [30] The Vatican newspaper expressed no worries about the other anti-Jewish measures.

The marriage clause, in fact, struck hard and deep at one of the Church's most cherished privileges. In 1929, article 34 of the religious concordat of the Lateran Accords had guaranteed that, with a few specific exceptions, all marriages performed by the Church would be registered and considered valid by the civil authorities.[31] Under canon law, the Church permitted and blessed marriages between the races, as long as both parties were Catholics. It also occasionally sanctioned marriages between Catholics and persons of a different religion as long as the latter promised not to interfere with the religious practice of the former and the Catholic upbringing of the children. The new Fascist proposal prohibiting marriage between Italian "Aryans" and "non-

Aryans" denied the Church's right to determine which couples might marry. It was unacceptable to the Vatican, which viewed it rightly as a treaty violation. The pope immediately attempted to persuade Mussolini to withdraw it.

A series of tangled communications ensued. On October 24, Pius XI approved a memorandum to Mussolini addressing the issue of mixed marriages and suggesting solutions to the emerging conflict.[32] According to the document, the Church rarely authorized mixed marriages. To ensure the continuation of that policy, the pope himself promised to examine the merits of all future requests. The implication was that special dispensations allowing Catholics to marry Jews who had not converted would cease.[33] By the term "mixed marriages," however, churchmen meant couples with different religions, not different races. The pope was not really addressing Mussolini's prohibition of marriage between "Aryans" and "non-Aryans." Ignoring that reality, Pius nevertheless asked that in exchange for his promise to reduce mixed marriages as he defined them, the Italian government agree to register all marriages sanctioned by the Church. He pointed out that penalizing those whose marriages were sanctioned by the Church would constitute "a grave offense against religious sentiment and natural law." [34]

Bypassing normal diplomatic channels, as often happened, Father Pietro Tacchi Venturi sought an audience with Mussolini to present this memorandum. On the evening of October 25 the Duce refused to receive him, demanding that he submit his request in writing instead. The priest did so the following day, but Mussolini simply passed his communication along to Guido Buffarini Guidi, in effect his minister of the interior (the Duce in fact held the portfolio). Two days later, Borgongini Duca, the papal nuncio to Italy, officially delivered the same memorandum to the same minister.[35] Both Tacchi Venturi and Borgongini Duca subsequently met several times with Buffarini Guidi.

In early drafts of the legislation that followed the Italian government seemed prepared to agree to register and recognize some Church-sanctioned mixed marriages performed "on the brink of death" or to render offspring legitimate. At the same time, however, it threatened to include a clause severely punishing couples married in religious ceremonies who proceeded to live together without civil registration.[36] Encouraged by the possible concessions but distressed by the new threat regarding what the government called "concubinage," the Church insisted that the law be modified to include civil registration of all religious marriages between individuals of the same Catholic faith. The demand was understandable, because the Church could not, according to canon law and assuming that all other standards were met, refuse to perform such marriages.

Desperate to circumvent the pending violation of the religious concordat, Pius XI wrote to Mussolini on November 4 and to King Vittorio Emanuele III the following day.[37] The first brief letter repeated that some of the proposed constraints on marriage were contrary to the concordat, and it asked that they be withdrawn. Mussolini did not deign to reply. The pope's letter to the king pointed out that while Mussolini had agreed to register marriages to legitimize offspring, he had not conceded in all cases of marriages between Catholic individuals who were "racially diverse." The letter to the king was politely acknowledged, but nothing changed. Late on November 9, the eve of the meeting in which the Council of Ministers was to approve the new racial measures, Father Tacchi Venturi made one last desperate attempt. Writing to Mussolini late at night because, as he explained, the pending conflict between Church and state upset him so much that he could not sleep, he declared:

> If you consider the small number of Italian citizens of the Semitic race and the aversion that most Jews feel toward marriage with Christians and that most Christians feel toward Jews, an aversion that will without doubt increase as a result of the new laws, I do not hesitate to assert that marriages between an Aryan spouse and one of the Jewish race professing the Catholic religion will not amount to even a hundred in the course of a year. A real drop in the bucket! Is it necessary to violate, for so little, a solemn pact that forms one of your most magnificent glories, causing immense bitterness to the Father of all Christendom?[38]

Tacchi Venturi pleaded with Mussolini to consider the "unmeasureable gravity of a break with the Church at this anxious historical moment." But even with this undisguised threat of a break, he obtained little. The final legislation approved by the Council of Ministers did not include the "concubinage" clause, but it also failed to mention registration of religious marriages performed on the brink of death or to legitimize offspring. The defeat for the Church was total and humiliating.

While Vatican representatives were concerned above all with the marriage provisions of the anti-Jewish laws, they were also uncomfortable with definitions of Jews that included converts. As the Italian ambassador to the Holy See reported, they were grateful that the offspring of mixed marriages who were baptized before October 1, 1938, would not be considered legally Jewish.[39] However, as the papal nuncio to Italy observed in a memorandum to Mussolini on October 21, churchmen failed to understand why there was a cutoff date for baptism. Since every convert had broken ties with the Jewish Community, "it would be unjust to send him back among those who consider him a deserter and an apostate, and expose him to reprisals." Furthermore, the nuncio asked, how could the children of Jewish parents who had converted be required to attend Jewish schools and learn about the "mosaic religion, that their parents had happily abandoned"? "It is necessary," he concluded, "that converts to Catholicism not be confused with the Jews."[40]

Borgongini Duca apparently did not know that the Italian government had already agreed to allow the children of converts to attend private Catholic, but not public, schools.[41] But he also did not yet realize that there would be no other concessions. After November 1938 and throughout the war years, the children of mixed marriages who were baptized before October 1 or at birth were regarded as non-Jews, but the offspring of two Jews who had converted to Catholicism were treated as Jews and persecuted along with their parents. After the objections registered in the autumn of 1938, the Church protested this fact very little. Yet hundreds, if not thousands, of Jews were baptized after that date, in the mistaken belief that conversion would help them avoid persecution.[42]

Examination of the Vatican reaction to the marriage provisions of the Italian anti-Jewish laws reveals that Church diplomats and negotiators were capable of vigorous protest in defense of their most cherished principles. On at least one occasion the pope even violated established procedure and risked Mussolini's wrath by appealing directly to the king without first clearing the communication through diplomatic channels. These actions reveal deep concern, anxiety, and even anguish. Throughout the coming Holocaust, Vatican officials would never protest as strongly again. It is clear, however, that their concern in September 1938 was less about the principle of unrestricted marriage between Catholics regardless of race than about the fact that a prohibition of such marriages would violate and perhaps invalidate the existing treaty between Italy and the Holy See. The Church did not protest similar laws against interracial marriage in the Third Reich or, for that matter, in the United States, where legal prohibitions of marriage and cohabitation across racial lines were on the books in many southern states until the federal Supreme Court declared them unconstitutional in 1966.

With the exception of the measures against interracial marriage and converts to Catholicism, there is no evidence that Vatican spokesmen objected to the principal Italian anti-Jewish laws. On the contrary, as the Italian ambassador to the Holy See had written in another report on October 10, 1938, "the recent deliberations of the Grand Council [approving the Declaration on Race] have not found, overall, an unfavorable welcome at the Vatican."[43] Far from editorializing against the new laws, L'Osservatore Romano never even fully described their content. On November 14–15 it referred only to the marriage provisions, explaining the Church's position and expressing the hope that they still might be amended.[44] On November 16 it confided in a single paragraph that the pope had written to the king of his wish to remedy the wound inflicted on the religious concordat, and that the king had responded courteously.[45] During the next two weeks a number of articles reported the sufferings of Jews in the Third Reich after Kristallnacht and deliberations in the United States and Britain to revise Jewish immigration policies.[46] Another article reported an important speech by Cardinal Ildefonso Schuster, archbishop of Milan, in his cathedral on Sunday, November 13, vehemently condemning what he called the "Nordic racial myth" and insisting that there are no distinctions of race within the Church. Schuster even congratulated the Italian government for "holding far from our country this new Nordic heresy that depresses us."[47] But about the Italian anti-Jewish laws, there was nothing.

The Lateran Accords remained in effect despite Mussolini's unilateral rescinding of the marriage clauses. Diplomats of the Holy See presented a formal note of protest of the violation on November 13. In his message to the assembled cardinals on Christmas Eve, Pius XI referred to it again publicly in the context of the approaching tenth anniversary of the Accords. He mentioned no other facet of the anti-Jewish laws.[48] In the weeks preceding Pius's death in February 1939, Vatican officials tried to reopen discussions with Mussolini on the marriage law, to no avail. The Church swallowed a major diplomatic affront, and life went on. Priests continued to perform marriages between Catholics and converts whom the law regarded as Jewish, but the religious unions had no legal validity in Italy.

Strangely enough, L'Osservatore Romano, which had not commented on the major anti-Jewish legislation in November, objected to a minor incident of harassment in December. On their own initiative, some theaters were attempting to terminate subscriptions taken out by Jews. Such action, the Vatican newspaper complained, was not consistent with the content of the Manifesto of the Racial Scientists, which "excludes the existence of inferior and superior races; excludes all and any absurd imitations"—the latter a pointed reference to Nazi race policy. Nor were the theaters' efforts consistent with a recent speech by the minister of education, who described the Italian anti-Jewish laws as measures of distinction and separation, but not of persecution. Furthermore, the efforts were unenforceable, for "neither Jews nor anyone else in this world goes about with the faith of their birth pinned to their buttonholes." What, furthermore, were Jews with special exemptions from the anti-Jewish laws expected to do? Should they go to the box offices with the death certificates of those they had lost in past wars? The policy would only lead to more hatred and pain for no purpose. The article concluded that it was time for "civic solidarity, Christian charity: the conception of humanity and life according to the 'sense of Christ.' " [49]

Italian Jews at the time may have been grateful for this small expression of support. However, when Jews throughout the country were losing jobs, property, and the right to attend public schools, it seems strange that the Vatican newspaper chose theater subscriptions as the sole target of its criticism on humanitarian grounds. Were churchmen simply insensitive to the deeper material hardships and psychological pain the anti-Jewish laws were causing?

There is, of course, a better explanation of the article. Even as late as December 1938, Vatican officials were reluctant to oppose the government's anti-Jewish policies because they still hoped to obtain a modification of the marriage law and enlarged rights for converts. A real confrontation with Mussolini would not only prevent future concessions on those special issues but might endanger other privileges obtained by the Lateran Accords, especially the existence of Catholic Action. Cancellation of Jewish theater subscriptions, however, was a private initiative rather than a government policy, and it could be criticized with relative impunity. Opposition to it allowed the Church to plea for moderation and take a moral and humanitarian stand with little risk to its primary objectives and responsibilities.

The priority placed on institutional obligations in 1938 was realistic. Mussolini would probably not have modified the anti-Jewish laws, no matter how vigorously the pope had protested. In fact, he made no alterations even to the marriage law, despite vehement papal objections. But in acting as he did, Pius XI lost an opportunity of providing moral leadership in Italy and throughout the world on the issue of anti-Judaism. And each delay or postponement made it more difficult to speak out the next time—for how could the previous silences be explained? The papal silence also made a fatal impression on Hitler. The Vatican, it now appeared, would not interfere on Jewish issues as long as Catholics were not directly affected. That policy, and the priority placed on institutional obligations to Catholics, continued throughout the Holocaust, as Pope Pius XII later remained silent to preserve the inviolability of the Holy See in German-occupied Italy and to protect and retain the loyalties of German Catholics.

There is a second, still less flattering explanation for the Vatican's silence in the face of Mussolini's anti-Jewish policies. Many Church spokesmen did not oppose the Italian laws in 1938 simply because they did not disagree with them. Analysis of past articles in *L'Osservatore Romano* and *La Civiltà Cattolica* has revealed the support among many Catholic writers for traditional forms of legalized separation between Christians and Jews. Also described above was the report to Ciano from the Italian ambassador to the Holy See, who wrote on October 7, 1938, of the reaction of Vatican officials to Mussolini's Declaration on Race and declared, "They point out some good aspects of the [Fascist Grand Council's] deliberations [regarding the anti-Jewish laws]."

Additional suggestions of approval of some aspects of anti-Jewish policies abound. On January 15, 1939, for example, *L'Osservatore Romano* printed a long homily delivered for Epiphany by Bishop Giovanni Cazzani of Cremona.[50] The decision to publish the words of a lower-level prelate indicated that many Vatican officials, if not the pope himself, approved of them. The article stated that the bishop had evoked "the horrendous deicide, the odious Jewish persecution against the Messiah, his apostles and disciples, and the nascent Church." It then went on to quote him at length. Cazzani said, among much else:

> The Church has always regarded living side by side with Jews, as
> long as they remain Jews, as dangerous to the faith and tranquility
> of Christian people. It is for this reason that you find an old and
> long tradition of ecclesiastical legislation and discipline, intended to
> brake and limit the action and influence of the Jews in the midst of
> Christians, and the contact of Christians with them, isolating the
> Jews and not allowing them the exercise of those offices and
> professions in which they could dominate or influence the spirit,
> the education, the customs of Christians.

Bishop Cazzani informed his listeners that the Church "has always done everything, and continues to do everything, to prevent mixed marriages," by which he meant unions between Catholics and Jews who had not converted. "It is a fact," he declared, "that almost all mixed marriages with unconverted Jews have always been purely civil." He continued, "Also, Catholics obedient to the directives of the Church at present do not take on or accept Jewish domestic servants, or put themselves in the service of Jews when they must live with the family; and still less do they entrust their babies to Jewish wet nurses, or their children to be instructed or educated by Jewish teachers. If in our schools, until recently, Jewish teachers were not few, it was not because of the work of the Church." He reminded his flock that Catholics prayed for the conversion of the Jews, that converts were the equal of all other Catholics, and that excessive punitive measures against the Jews were unacceptable. But the tenor of the homily was that the Church was comfortable with the recent Fascist measures against the Jews, and Italian Catholics should be also.

Additional evidence emerged when the French head of state Marshal Philippe Pétain asked Léon Bérard, his ambassador to the Holy See, on August 7, 1941, to inform him of the Vatican's attitude toward the new anti-Jewish decrees in France. For the most part, the measures, issued primarily on October 3, 1940, and June 2, 1941, resembled the Italian laws. The major difference was that intermarriage was never prohibited in France. Bérard replied with a long description of the writings of St. Thomas Aquinas, who, according to Bérard, had advocated a special badge for Jews in the Middle Ages, as well as their partial or complete removal from government service and the professions. Bérard then added, "As an authorized person at the Vatican informed me, [officials there] have no intention of quarreling with us over the Jewish statute." The Vatican, the French ambassador continued, had only two requests: "That no provisions on marriage be added to the law on the Jews," and "that the precepts of justice and charity be considered in the application of the law." [51]

When they learned of Bérard's report, some Vatican officials described it as exaggerated and simplistic.[52] Cardinal Luigi Maglione, the Vatican secretary of state, also called the French anti-Jewish laws unfortunate.[53] He never denied the report, however, or declared that it was inaccurate. On the contrary, he informed the papal nuncio to France that Bérard had conferred with both Monsignor Domenico Tardini and Monsignor Giovanni Battista Montini, Maglione's two closest deputies at the Vatican Secretariat of State.[54] The Bérard report, of course, is not evidence of Vatican approval of the entire content of the French anti-Jewish legislation. But neither was there any public expression of dissatisfaction. Vichy authorities successfully avoided a direct confrontation with the Vatican, for their anti-Jewish legislation never prohibited intermarriage.

A still more revealing indication of Vatican attitudes to the Italian anti-Jewish laws came a full two years later. In July 1943, as the Allies were landing in Sicily, Mussolini was removed from power and replaced by Marshal Pietro Badoglio. Italy remained in the war on the side of the Germans, while Italian diplomats secretly attempted to negotiate a separate peace. Their success and the announcement of the armistice on September 8 inadvertently led to the German occupation of Italy and the onset of Jewish deportations from that country to Auschwitz. During the strange forty-five-day interlude, however, Italians naturally expected that the most repressive measures of the Fascist regime, including the anti-Jewish laws, would be revoked. Thus, Father Tacchi Venturi met with the new Italian minister of the interior to propose changes in the laws to benefit Jewish converts to Catholicism. In his report of the meeting to Cardinal Maglione on August 29, Tacchi Venturi carefully explained that he had not "alluded in any way to the total abrogation of laws which, according to the principles and tradition of the Catholic Church, have some dispositions that should be abrogated but contain others worthy of confirmation." [55] By August 1943, millions of European Jews had been murdered in the Soviet Union and in Poland. As will be seen, Vatican officials were perfectly aware of that fact. Yet still they approved of the denial of full civil rights to Jews and their legal separation from Christians.

There should be no implication here that Vatican officials also approved of anti-Jewish violence and the destruction of human life. Physical violence had never constituted part of official Catholic rhetoric against the Jews, and it did not do so during the Holocaust. Indeed, the Church had taught that the Jews should be permitted to live, separately but safely, within Christian society, as a reminder of the sin of rejection of Jesus Christ and as a challenge to Catholics to show charity and work for their conversion. The Vatican's blindness with regard to the laws against the Jews was not the result of a desire for their destruction. It was, rather, a consequence of the failure to understand the direct relationship between the civil rights of all human beings in modern secular societies and the right of those same human beings to life itself.

One of the more disastrous effects of anti-Jewish laws throughout Europe in the 1930s was that they accustomed people to regard Jews as second-class citizens, without full legal rights. That attitude facilitated each of the several next steps leading to destruction. Few churchmen applauded the destruction. They simply did not understand, until it was too late, the potentially lethal consequences of what was for them simply a return to the "good old days."

The making of the myth of papal benevolence toward the Jews in Italy began early. In August 1939, for example, the United Jewish Appeal of the United States donated $125,000 to the Vatican, in memory of the deceased Pope Pius XI. The reasons for the gift cannot be examined in detail here, but they involved the rather exaggerated impressions of American Jews regarding Pius XI's stand against racism, as well as the understandable hope that his successor would do even more. Contributors also hoped that their gift would reach those in need and improve Christian-Jewish relations. The money was to be used to assist refugees regardless of race or religion.

The mythology is linked not to the gift itself but to the letter of thanks written on behalf of the Vatican by the auxiliary bishop of Chicago, Monsignor Bernard Sheil. On December 29 the bishop wrote: "No man in our day or generation fought more vigorously or courageously the fanaticism of intolerant racialism than Pius XI. When cruel and tyrannical laws were enacted against your people, his fearless voice was raised in indignant protest. He denounced racial intolerance and hatred as contrary to the laws of God, to the dictates of right reason and to the welfare of civilization." [56] Monsignor Sheil may well have believed what he wrote. Pius XI did indeed protest "racialism." He did not, however, raise his voice "in indignant protest" against the "cruel and tyrannical laws" imposed upon Jews in Italy or anywhere else. With regard to laws levied against those who were Jewish by religion or culture, he remained silent.

CHAPTER FOUR

Italian Anti-Jewish Laws During the Papacy of Pius XII

ON MARCH 2, 1939, his sixty-third birthday, Cardinal Eugenio Pacelli was elected pope by the sixty-two cardinals responsible for the selection. The decision came on only the third round of voting, in one of the shortest papal conclaves in Church history.[1] The first Roman to become pope since Innocent XIII in 1721, Pacelli was from a staunchly conservative Catholic family whose men had served the Vatican for nearly a century.[2] He had been selected by Pius XI on February 9, 1930, to be secretary of state, the Vatican's second-highest office. During his nine full years in that position, during which he acted as a kind of prime minister and foreign minister rolled into one, Pacelli was extremely active. He negotiated the concordat with Germany in 1933, met American President Franklin Delano Roosevelt during an official visit to the United States in 1936, traveled in South America, drafted much of the papal encyclical *Mit brennender Sorge* in 1937, and associated himself in every respect with Pius XI's policies. Pacelli was in fact Pius's choice as successor.[3] In honor of his mentor, he chose the papal name of Pius XII.

Pius XII's diplomatic skills, fondness for Germany, and abhorrence of Bolshevism are among the best-known facts about him. All three characteristics became evident early in his career. Eugenio Pacelli prepared for the priesthood in Rome's most elite Catholic institutions and was ordained in 1899.[4] He never, however, served in a full-time pastoral capacity. Two years after ordination, while a postgraduate student in canon law, he accepted a position in the Section of Extraordinary Ecclesiastical Affairs in the Vatican Secretariat of State. His section, one of the two that constitute the Secretariat, has been described as charged with foreign relations, although its difference from the Section of Ordinary Ecclesiastical Affairs is difficult to define. Pacelli became undersecretary of the Section of Extraordinary Ecclesiastical Affairs in 1911, and secretary of the section in 1914, at the age of only thirty-eight.

In the spring of 1917, Eugenio Pacelli was made a bishop and appointed papal nuncio to Bavaria. During the chaos of revolution following the First World War, Bolshevik militiamen invaded his residence in Munich and apparently threatened his life. The incident left an indelible impression on the papal diplomat. But Pacelli remained in Germany, moving to Berlin when a Vatican post was established in that capital city in 1920. He served there until Pius XI made him a cardinal and returned him to Rome at the end of 1929. A few months later he was appointed secretary of state.

During his twelve years in Germany, Pacelli learned to speak the language fluently and acquired numerous German friends and acquaintances. He subsequently referred often to his happy years among the German people. Throughout his entire papacy his private secretary and closest advisor was a German Jesuit, Father Robert Leiber, whom he had known in Berlin. A rival to Leiber for the pope's affection was another German priest, Monsignor Ludwig Kaas, a former president of the German Catholic Center Party who also served as a secretary. Pacelli's personal confessor from 1945 until his death in 1958 was a German Jesuit, Cardinal Augustin Bea. His housekeeper for forty-one years, Sister Pasqualina Lehnert, was a German Franciscan nun whom he had met during his service in Munich. Her two assistants were also German nuns.

While the events of Eugenio Pacelli's career are clear, his character and personality are less so. Those who knew and worked with him stress, above all, his delicate sensibilities. In 1963, for example, just before his election as Pope Paul VI, Cardinal Giovanni Battista Montini described him as a man of "exquisite sensibility and the most delicate human sympathies." But, Montini added, "the frail and gentle exterior of Pius XII, and the sustained refinement and moderation of his language, concealed—if they did not, rather, reveal—a noble and virile character capable of taking very firm decisions and of adopting, fearlessly, positions that entailed considerable risk." Pacelli was also a hands-on administrator, Montini contended, for "it was his constant desire to be informed of everything."[5] During the war Montini had served under Cardinal Luigi Maglione, Pius XII's secretary of state, as secretary of the Section for Ordinary Ecclesiastical Affairs. In that capacity he knew the pope both personally and officially.

Others who worked closely with the pope during the war have recorded how deeply affected he was by the sufferings of victims and by his responsibilities to them. Wladimir d'Ormesson, for example, the French ambassador to the Holy See from May to October 1941, was impressed by the pope's spiritual grandeur, simplicity, kindness, and "anxiety . . . for all of Europe and for the future of Christian civilization."[6] Albrecht von Kessel, aide to Ernst von Weiszäcker, German ambassador to the Holy See during the German occupation of Rome, agreed. Kessel recalled Pius XII as a "tremendous figure . . . [who] almost broke down under the conflicts of conscience. I know that he prayed, day by day, week by week, month by month for the answer [to the question of whether he should act on his knowledge of the Holocaust]."[7] Finally, Sir d'Arcy Osborne, British minister to the Holy See, a Protestant, later wrote:

> So far from being a cool . . . diplomatist, Pius XII was the most
> warmly humane, kind, generous, sympathetic (and, incidentally,
> saintly) character that it has been my privilege to meet in the course
> of a long life. I know that his sensitive nature was acutely and
> incessantly alive to the tragic volume of human suffering caused by
> the war and, without the slightest doubt, he would have been ready
> and glad to give his life to redeem humanity from its consequences.
> And this quite irrespective of nationality or faith.[8]

Monsignor Domenico Tardini, secretary of the Section for Extraordinary Ecclesiastical Affairs in the Secretariat of State during the war, confirmed d'Ormesson, Kessel, and Osborne's descriptions of a pope who suffered from his knowledge of the agonies caused by the war. He also emphasized Pius's ascetic nature, claiming that he refused to heat his private apartment and that he fasted during the war as a kind of personal atonement. He added that Pius XII was "by natural temperament, mild and rather shy. He was not born to be a fighter." Tardini described him as humble and concluded, "His great goodness encouraged him to please everyone and to not aggravate anyone; to prefer the ways of sweetness to those of severity, persuasion to command." But Tardini hinted at another characteristic when he quoted the pope as once having said, "I do not want collaborators, but people who will carry out my orders."[9]

A representative of the Catholic Information Bureau in the United States named Father Morleon also knew Pius XII well. He seemed to disagree with Tardini's view when he described the pope as a "kind-hearted man, deeply affected and disturbed by the slaughter let loose in Europe, but intimidated by his entourage and by the rules of protocol. In any public diplomatic act . . . he would be influenced by the inner circle of his advisers." [10] The French Cardinal Eugène Tisserant, the only non-Italian cardinal in the Curia, shared that opinion. At the time of the papal conclave that elected Pacelli, he made it clear that he considered him too weak and indecisive to be pope. [11] Also in 1939, Heinrich Brüning, a former German chancellor and head of the Catholic Center Party, expressed his conviction that Pacelli was politically naïve, for he seemed to believe that Germany and Italy could be dealt with rationally. [12] However, Ernst von Weiszäcker, the German ambassador to the Holy See, was not so sure. He described the pope as a political realist. "My general impression was that I met more a man of religious devotion than a politician," he wrote in July 1943 after meeting him again after fifteen years, "yet he is a politician to a high degree." [13]

Father Robert Leiber also described his friend Pius XII as a political realist. He wrote, "We would say that the dominant character trait of the . . . pontiff was a sober matter-of-factness." Leiber added that the pope had a "formidable, steel-like will to work" and that "he also pondered things for a long time before saying yes or no." He was a deeply religious man, Leiber insisted, but his asceticism and spiritual mysticism had been greatly exaggerated. He was aloof and solitary but "captivatingly charming." [14]

If witnesses who knew Pius XII disagreed slightly about his character, second-hand accounts differed radically. One critic of the papal silence, for example, called the pope a "superman type," in marked contrast to Tardini's description of him as "mild and rather shy." [15] Rolf Hochhuth, in a hostile portrait in his play The Deputy, stressed the pope's cold aristocratic hauteur. [16] A colleague of Cardinal Bea's but not of Pius XII's maintained that the pope demanded "submission, unquestioning service, and distance" from those around him. He strongly disagreed both with Morleon's belief that the pope was intimidated and influenced by his entourage and with Tardini's statement that he preferred persuasion to command. Instead, he evoked his "authoritarian and disdainful treatment" of the prelates and priests who worked with him. [17]

A historian of the Catholic Church and Nazi Germany noted, more objectively, that "all biographers agree that Pius XII, in contrast to his predecessor, was unemotional and dispassionate, as well as a master in the language of diplomatic ambiguity." [18] This contradicts descriptions of a pope who wept and fasted. It does, however, point to what another historian called Pius XII's "unrivalled diplomatic skill and his grasp of the political realities of the world scene." He continued, "The British ambassador . . . described the Pacelli of the Berlin days as the most capable diplomat in the whole Berlin corps. He spoke seven languages fluently." [19] Still a third specialist has pointed to Pacelli's highly centralized decisionmaking, declaring that a "great part of the work of the Vatican ended up in the hands of the pope, who bore the ultimate responsibility for the grand design, but also for minute decisions." [20] But another historian is less impressed. He considered the pope to be isolated and unworldly. "He carried the idea of a cultic pope, a sacred personage, to its extreme point, whence it was impossible to come out at the world," he wrote. He believed the pope to be a man who postponed controversial decisions, explaining that "he grew up in a nineteenth-century tradition of Vatican circumlocution, fitted it naturally, and carried it to the extreme." [21]

From these and other often conflicting accounts and observations it is possible to draw a few conclusions relevant to this book. Pius XII does indeed seem to have had a genuine religious calling. But if he was spiritual, or even mystical, by temperament, he was a diplomat by training and experience. He had climbed his personal career ladder by avoiding confrontation and displeasing no one. It was a talent he would continue to display in the Chair of St. Peter. In addition, he was a priest almost totally without pastoral experience. His worldview was that of a diplomat and aristocrat who had spent his adult life behind ecclesiastical walls. He had never come face to face with the unpleasant physical realities of human suffering and misery. He may have found it difficult to imagine mass extermination when called upon to respond to the destruction of European Jewry.

The new Pope Pius XII was to enjoy no gradual transition into office in 1939. Three days after the papal coronation on March 12, the German army entered Prague and seized the remaining Czech lands, in flagrant violation of the Munich agreements of the preceding September. On Good Friday, April 7, the Italians bombed Tirana and occupied Albania. The pope spoke of peace in general terms at his first Easter Pontifical Mass two days later, but he said nothing specific about these two most recent acts of naked aggression. As Hitler turned greedy eyes toward Danzig during the spring and summer of 1939, papal envoys tried to persuade him and Mussolini on the one hand, and the French and the Poles on the other, to settle their differences amicably. The efforts, of course, failed.

The new pope's most public act for peace occurred on the evening of August 24, three days after the German announcement of the nonaggression pact with the Soviet Union. As the world awaited an expected German invasion of Poland, Pius called on all national leaders to seek peaceful solutions to international problems. He was thus firmly on the record as calling for peace, but he had given no hint that any single leader or nation was responsible for war.[22] It was a pattern that he would repeat throughout the war years, condemning atrocities committed against civilians without naming names—without mentioning the perpetrators of such deeds.

On October 20, 1939, about eight weeks after the outbreak of war, Pius XII issued his first encyclical. Entitled *Summi pontificatus,* it was intended as a kind of introduction to his papacy. In light of his subsequent silence in the face of appalling horrors, some of his declarations take on a cruelly ironic tinge. "We feel We owe no greater debt to Our office and to Our time than to testify to the truth with Apostolic firmness: 'to give testimony to the truth,' " he wrote. "In the fulfillment of this, Our duty, we shall not let Ourselves be influenced by earthly considerations nor be held back by mistrust or opposition, by rebuffs or lack of appreciation of Our words, nor yet by fear of misconceptions and misinterpretations." One may wonder whether he ever understood how dismally he failed to fulfill that promise. But much of the encyclical addressed what he referred to as the "unity of all mankind," the "unity of the human race," or the "human race in the unity of one common origin in God." He described a "mutual love and a lively sense of charity [that] unite all the sons of the same Father." The message has often been seen as Pius XII's version of the "hidden encyclical" of his predecessor, and in its calls for love and respect for the "particular characteristics which each people, with jealous and intelligible pride, cherishes and retains as a precious heritage," it was not unworthy.[23] It did not mention that one particular party in the current war was a vicious advocate of racial distinctions. It was not confrontational in the way that Pius XI's encyclicals had been. But it made a valuable statement.

The encyclical never mentioned Jews. Indeed, despite references to the unity of the human race, it seemed to single out Christians, or perhaps Catholics, for special consideration. Is it overly critical to direct attention to sentences such as "All [human societies] that in such usages and customs [are] not inseparably bound up with religious errors will always be subject to kindly consideration and, when it is found possible, will be sponsored and developed"? Or, again, to point to the phrase, "Those who enter the Church, whatever be their origin or their speech, must know that they have equal rights as children in the House of the Lord, where the law of Christ and the peace of Christ prevail"?[24] The pope went on to describe his continuing efforts to achieve greater racial diversity among the Catholic clergy and bishops. That was an admirable goal and not to be deprecated, but neither can it be depicted as a campaign against anti-Judaism.

Closer to home, the new pope immediately found himself obliged, as Pius XI had been, to deal with Mussolini on the subject of the anti-Jewish laws. Like his predecessor, he focused entirely on the needs of Jews who had converted, but his actual interventions were even more limited. On March 28, Father Pietro Tacchi Venturi, the Vatican's unofficial liaison with Mussolini, reported that he had met with the Duce and presented five requests for slight alterations in the laws. He had asked that all offspring of mixed marriages, if baptized at birth and raised as Christians, be recognized as "Aryans," even when the "Aryan" parent was a foreigner; that such offspring be considered Christians not only if they had been baptized at birth or before October 1, 1938, but also if they had been enrolled before that date in catechism classes in preparation for baptism; that mixed families have the right to employ Christian household servants; that Jewish teachers who had converted be permitted to teach in private schools; and that couples engaged to be married before the prohibition of mixed marriages be allowed to marry.[25] Tacchi Venturi had focused on narrow, possibly negotiable legal points, but he never questioned the laws themselves.

The five demands were in fact responses to specific pleas for help from individual converts. The request that instruction in the catechism prior to October 1, 1938, be considered entitlement to Christian status, for example, was linked to the case of a Professor Ettore Debenedetti of Asti, who was baptized only on October 10 but who long had been preparing for the sacrament.[26] As Cardinal Luigi Maglione, the Vatican secretary of state, put it, the Church needed to answer the appeals of individual converts, even if negatively, "to provide them with yet another proof of the concerned interest of the Holy See on their behalf."[27] Needless to say, the answers were almost always negative.

Along similar lines Cardinal Maglione wrote to Papal Nuncio Francesco Borgongini Duca on May 5 of the difficulties about to be imposed on converts by pending legislation denying Jews the right to practice their professions except among their coreligionists. Converts, he pointed out, would be legally denied a practice among Christians and personally rejected by Jews.[28] At Maglione's request, Borgongini Duca petitioned Italian bureaucrats for a modification of the measure, to no effect.[29] But Maglione was so concerned about the issue that he twice asked Tacchi Venturi also to intervene for a change.[30] The Jesuit was equally unsuccessful. Borgongini Duca had better luck, however, when he inquired about the right of Jewish children baptized after the official cutoff date of October 1, 1938, to attend Catholic schools. Here, at least, he received the positive reply that the Italian government envisioned no prohibition at that time.[31]

Efforts to obtain small alterations in the laws for the benefit of converts continued until at least the end of 1942. Maglione's office sent a poignant appeal on February 25, 1940, to the Italian Embassy to the Holy See, describing the hardships suffered by an estimated 2,500 mixed families because of the anti-Jewish laws.[32] "One of the two parents," the document lamented, "considered to be of the Jewish race, finds himself in a state of inferiority in comparison to the other members of the family."[33] Could a representative from the embassy try to obtain some modification of the law? After all, "the fact of a Jew's having celebrated a regular mixed marriage [early enough to be] not suspected [of trying to avoid the anti-Jewish laws], raised his offspring in the Christian faith, and been himself baptized, in many cases, must have a great weight in his favor."[34] The appeal stressed that the economic measures directed against a Jewish father caused suffering for the entire family, all of whom were "Aryan." The Church had adopted Fascist racial terminology.

Mussolini granted no modifications, but Maglione's hopes were continually raised by rumors. The laws *might* eventually be amended to grant exemptions from the anti-Jewish laws to Jewish fathers in mixed marriages. All baptized offspring of mixed marriages *might* be granted Christian status regardless of the date they actually received the sacrament.[35] Although Maglione suspected by the summer of 1941 that such changes would not occur until after the war, he continued to urge his diplomats to keep the issues alive.[36]

In 1972, in their introduction to volume VI of the Vatican wartime diplomatic documents, the editors wrote, "To tell the truth, the result [of Father Tacchi Venturi's appeals to Mussolini about the anti-Jewish laws] did not always correspond to the efforts deployed, but it remains true that the influence of the Father moderated the racial politics of the Fascist government."[37] There is no evidence to confirm such a statement. The editors were more truthful when they declared simply, "It is impossible to establish in detail the actual result of these interventions of the Holy See, but one can affirm without risk of error that they made an impression."[38] That, without doubt, they did. Vatican requests for modifications in the anti-Jewish laws were not merely perfunctory. But they were limited to laws affecting Jews who were involved with Catholicism, and they changed nothing.

In the same introduction, the editors also claimed that in 1939 and 1940 the Holy See had intervened for some 2,000 individual Jews. "In general," they admitted, "it was a question of Jews who had become Christians or of half-Jews." They explained that most cases concerned residents in Italy who hoped to obtain exemption from anti-Jewish measures. They stated that interventions were "frequently crowned with success."[39] In a later volume the same editors repeated the claim, writing that "in the course of the first years of the war, the Holy See was able to obtain rather broad concessions from the government in Rome, in favor of Italians and foreigners affected by the anti-Semitic legislation from before the war. These concessions involved several types: [among them] . . . exemption from every restriction."[40] There is little doubt that such interventions were made, mostly, on the Vatican's own admission, for Jews who were involved with Catholics in one way or another. However, claims of frequent success and of exemptions from every restriction must be treated with caution.

As seen in the previous chapter, the anti-Jewish laws defined a policy of possible limited exemptions for individuals with specific merit, upon application to a special government commission. The award was not automatic, and decisions were often arbitrary. Vatican officials could and did write requests and recommendations for applicants, which might have helped but would rarely have been decisive. A typical example occurred in May 1941, when Tacchi Venturi, at Maglione's request, intervened at the highest levels of the Ministry of the Interior in support of exemption status for an individual whom he called a "non-Aryan Catholic." Tacchi Venturi was told that an exemption was impossible because that individual did not qualify under any of criteria carefully defined by law.[41] His intervention had made no difference. There was no recourse.

In addition, the Vatican editors' claim to have obtained "exemption from every restriction" was inaccurate. No one who was legally Jewish, for example, was exempted from the educational proscriptions. Vatican editors writing after the war may have been unaware of that fact and written of exemptions in good faith, but they erred.

The only Jews legally released from every restriction were those defined by law as "Aryans." This condition could be achieved in two ways. First, as seen in the previous chapter, offspring of mixed marriages were considered "Aryan" if they had been baptized before October 1, 1938, or, if born after that date, immediately at birth. Baptismal certificates had to be produced, not only for the individual in question but also for his or her allegedly non-Jewish parent. Many cases became extremely complicated, and priests often produced backdated certificates, usually but not always for those they knew to be practicing Catholics. It is doubtful that Vatican officials actually recommended this illegal procedure, but they may well have referred supplicants to priests and then looked the other way.

The second method of obtaining "non-Aryan" status was less palatable. On July 13, 1939, a program was introduced by which a specially constituted commission could declare that an individual was "Aryan" rather than Jewish because he or she had a biological parent who differed from the legally registered parent. Beneficiaries of this program were generally Catholics or alleged Catholics whose birth certificates indicated that they had two Jewish parents, but who successfully claimed that those certificates were mistaken. False or backdated baptismal certificates could play a role here as well, and well-intentioned clergymen may have occasionally provided them. Chicanery and bribery seem to have been more useful in convincing the commission, however. In any case, the numbers involved in this program remained small. Some 163 requests for "Aryanization" had been made by October 1942, of which 104 had been approved and 43 refused.[42]

Papal defenders have also claimed that the Vatican helped Jews by offering them professional positions that the anti-Jewish laws denied them in 1938 and 1939. Joseph Lichten, for example, wrote without evidence that "many Jewish citizens, expelled from government, scientific, and teaching positions, were invited to the Vatican; the president and two professors from the University of Rome and a famous geographer, all Jews ousted by the Fascists, received important positions in Vatican City."[43] Certainly it was within the power of the Vatican, a foreign country, after all, to offer such positions. Evidence on this point is scarce, but it seems likely that a few such invitations were extended and accepted. It seems equally likely that most of the beneficiaries were converts rather than observant Jews. Regarding Lichten's specific claim, the former president of the University of Rome, if not the others, was a convert to Catholicism.

Far from granting modifications or concessions, Mussolini imposed yet another anti-Jewish measure in 1942, and the Vatican was again asked to respond. On May 6, an Italian administrative circular ordered all Jews between the ages of eighteen and fifty-five to register for obligatory labor service. Unlike earlier anti-Jewish measures, this one was clearly unpopular with the Italian public, and it was poorly enforced. Some 15,517 Jews duly registered, but only 2,038 had actually worked by July 1943.[44] But among those working was a group of Jewish men digging and reinforcing earthworks along the banks of the Tiber River in Rome, in the very shadow of the Vatican. A photograph in *Il Messaggero* on June 7, 1942, of Jewish laborers stripped to the waist and wielding shovels and pickaxes so enraged Harold Tittmann, the American chargé d'affaires at the Vatican, that he wrote to Monsignor Giovanni Battista Montini three days later. Tittmann angrily declared:

> I cannot begin to tell you how degrading I consider the situation which this photograph represents. It seems all the more appalling to me that it could exist within the shadow of St. Peter's, the fountain of Christian charity.
>
> I feel certain that the Holy See must have already approached the appropriate authorities with a view to eliminating this shameful persecution, if not from Italy, at least from the precincts of the sacred Eternal City.[45]

It is not clear how the pope could have protested Jewish forced labor "in the precincts of the sacred Eternal City," as Tittmann wrote, but not in the country as a whole. But the American diplomat was correct in another sense. On behalf of the Holy See, Father Tacchi Venturi had already discussed the general issue of forced labor with Guido Buffarini Guidi, Italy's acting minister of the interior. Tittmann would probably have been surprised, however, had he known the content of those talks. As with earlier anti-Jewish laws, the Vatican representative had merely sought slight modifications. He requested a complete separation of converts from other Jews at the work sites and then urged that individuals of the "cultivated classes" not be required to perform manual labor for which they lacked the necessary strength and abilities.[46] He never protested the use of Jewish forced laborers in Rome, much less the principle of compulsory labor itself. Yet, it might be recalled, such labor went well beyond the treatment of Jews considered acceptable by the Church—separation, denial of civil equality, and deprivation of property.

Only twice in the many documents concerning the Italian anti-Jewish laws selected for publication by Vatican archivists is there an expression of concern for Jews in general, as opposed to Jews who had converted. In the first case Maglione noted on June 11, 1942, that he had asked the Italian ambassador to the Holy See "to intercede for these poor Jews [recruited for forced labor]." [47] The note was clearly a response to Tittmann's protest to Montini. In the second case, five months later, Borgongini Duca informed Maglione on November 10, 1942, that during the course of a long meeting with Buffarini Guidi he had asked if an eventual improvement in the situation of the Jews could be expected. The minister was evasive. [48]

With these two exceptions, Vatican officials wrote as if they took it for granted that their role was to intercede only for converts. To some extent this attitude was a product of the times. As one distinguished Catholic historian has observed, "up to the time of Pius XII, it was not considered self-evident that the Catholic Church should champion the rights of those outside its fold—Jews, Protestants, and others were 'overlooked.' " [49] One might add that the attitude endured throughout the papacy of that same Pius XII. The pope and the prelates around him felt threatened by a hostile, liberalizing, and atheistic world. They conceived of no transcending moral mission, no broad crusade for human rights and justice. This was true despite their knowledge, by the summer of 1942, that hundreds of thousands, if not millions, of Jewish men, women, and children were being murdered. [50] They defended their constituency, men and women of the Catholic faith, just as personnel in embassies throughout the world protect their own compatriots. They were diplomats before they were moral leaders.

CHAPTER FIVE

Refugees and Emigration

1939–1942

ON JANUARY 31, 1943, Papal Nuncio Francesco Borgongini Duca sent a report to Cardinal Luigi Maglione, the Vatican secretary of state, describing his office's work for refugees during the previous three years. Regarding Jewish refugees in Italy he wrote, in part:

> The state of war has brought a hardening of the racial question. Many Jews have fled from territories occupied by Germany, preferring to come to Italy, even running the risk of internment. Here they have involved this Apostolic Nunciature in securing the possibility of going abroad, especially to America. Through our intervention, many have obtained the necessary visas from various consulates, also for transit, and the Holy Father, in his inexhaustible charity, has provided many with the considerable expenses for the voyage.
>
> The Nunciature has even succeeded, but in only a few cases, in obtaining from [Minister of Foreign Affairs] Count Ciano visas for entrance into the kingdom [of Italy] for Jews who were in danger of being deported.[1]

Was this report entirely forthright?

Let us address the second paragraph first. Foreign Jews granted "visas for entrance into the kingdom [of Italy]" by the Ministry of Foreign Affairs during the war and allowed to reside there freely were virtually nonexistent. Klaus

Voigt, a specialist on wartime refugees in the country, has found evidence of only one such individual.[2] If there were others, documents concerning them remain unavailable. In one other *apparent* exception, 74 Jewish youngsters stranded without parents mostly in Croatia were admitted to Slovenia, then technically part of Italy, and transferred in July 1942 and April 1943 to reside relatively freely at the Villa Emma in Nonantola, in the province of Modena. They did not enter Italy with visas from the Ministry of Foreign Affairs, however, but with special permits from the Ministry of the Interior granting them special status and the right to reside together without internment. Their sponsor, furthermore, was Delasem, an Italian Jewish refugee assistance organization that will be discussed below. There is no evidence of an intervention by the Holy See on their behalf.[3]

On the other hand, many foreign Jews were permitted to enter Italy without visas after the outbreak of war, but they were immediately interned or placed in supervised residence under the jurisdiction of the Ministry of the Interior. Few of these, also, owed their entry into Italy to the Vatican. The largest group included 494 Jewish survivors from the *Pentcho,* a decrepit riverboat that left Bratislava in April 1940, tottered down the Danube, and finally sank in the Aegean in October. Interned initially in the Italian colony of Rhodes, the refugees were transferred to the Ferramonti internment camp in southern Italy without extra clothing, blankets, or money in February and March 1942.[4] There is no reliable evidence that Vatican officials were responsible for the transfer. Claims to the contrary apparently originated with Pinchas Lapide, who visited Ferramonti with a Palestinian unit of the British Eighth Army after the camp's liberation. There he was told that a man from the *Pentcho* had escaped from Rhodes to Italy when the other passengers were still interned on the island. The escapee had allegedly obtained an audience with the pope and persuaded him to intervene. Lapide recounted the unlikely story in a book about Pope Pius XII and the Jews, and other authors repeated it.[5] But there is no confirming evidence in the *Actes et Documents du Saint Siège,* the eleven volumes of Vatican archival documents from the war years selected for publication. Nor did the Jesuit Fathers Pierre Blet and Robert Graham, both editors of those volumes with access to the entire archival collection, ever mention a Vatican intervention for the *Pentcho* Jews in their own writings on papal efforts to assist the Jews.[6] Had such an intervention occurred there would surely have been a document on the subject, and that document would surely have been published.

In addition to the survivors of the *Pentcho,* some other foreign Jews were admitted to Italy without visas in 1941 and were immediately interned or placed in supervised residence. Nearly all were from Italian-annexed or Italian-occupied areas of the former Yugoslavia. Among them, apparently, was a group of Jewish refugees who had fled first from Croatia to Slovenia. This group did receive Vatican help. Assisted by the Jesuit Father Pietro Tacchi Venturi, an unofficial liaison with Mussolini, they were admitted to Ferramonti in October. The relevant Vatican documents, however, indicate that the bishop of Lubliana, the cardinal secretary of state, and Tacchi Venturi were almost exclusively concerned to help those Jews in Slovenia who had converted to Catholicism.[7] In any case, Borgongini Duca was not referring to these individuals in his report to Cardinal Maglione on January 31, 1943, for he wrote of entrance visas obtained through the Ministry of Foreign Affairs.

Rather than succeeding in obtaining visas for entrance and free residence in Italy for "Jews who were in danger of being deported," as Borgongini Duca had put it in his report, Vatican efforts usually failed. In a report to Maglione on December 17, 1941, Tacchi Venturi described just such a failure in a case involving two elderly Viennese women, the eighty-year-old grandmother and the mother of a formerly Jewish woman who had converted to Catholicism and was living in Bolzano. The two women wanted to move to Italy to live with the daughter because they were, as he described it, "on the point of being sent from Vienna to die in a concentration camp in Poland." Tacchi Venturi had petitioned Mussolini's private secretary for permission for the daughter to receive them in Bolzano and had been refused. In his report to Maglione he concluded, "Things being as they are, I am of the opinion that it makes no sense for us to expose ourselves any more to similar refusals."[8]

Tacchi Venturi's report would suggest that if the Vatican had some slight success in bringing individuals into Italy before December 1941, it had none after that date. The claim in the second paragraph of Borgongini Duca's report on January 31, 1943, then, is highly misleading.

The claim in the first paragraph, concerning problems of emigration, is still more complex. Borgongini Duca used the word "many" when referring to the obtaining of visas for foreign Jews for transit through Italy on the way to other countries. With its diplomatic envoys abroad, and especially in Catholic countries in Latin America, the Vatican was particularly well placed to help refugees. How successful was it, and who were the beneficiaries? Were they "many"? And were they in fact Jews by religion and culture, as Borgongini Duca implied, or were they mostly Jewish converts?

Pius XII seems to have made only one major effort to facilitate Jewish emigration on a general rather than an individual basis. The initiative, however, originated elsewhere, and the beneficiaries were clearly intended to be exclusively German Jews who had converted to Catholicism. Just a few weeks after his consecration the pope received letters from leaders of the German Catholic Church begging him to help secure 3,000 special Brazilian visas for "German non-Aryan Catholics" in the Third Reich.[9] On April 5, Maglione asked the papal nuncio in Brazil to request the visas from President Getulio Vargas.[10] To everyone's surprise, the request was granted two months later.[11] The special visas were to be distributed by the Brazilian embassy in Berlin to candidates selected and prepared by the Opera di San Raffaele (Sankt-Raphaels-Verein), a German Catholic organization in Hamburg dedicated to facilitating the emigration of Jewish converts.

The Brazilian government, however, was not as eager to receive refugees as Vargas's initial response suggested, and the visas were soon encumbered with conditions. Converted German Jews were to deposit a minimum of 20,000 lire with the Bank of Brazil and then promise to work in agriculture or industry in Brazil rather than in business, commerce, or the professions. These terms imposed real difficulties, for many potential immigrants lacked the financial resources. German laws not only restricted the funds they could transfer abroad but imposed highly unfavorable exchange rates. Furthermore, German Jewish converts were generally less qualified in agricultural and industrial work than in the sectors of the economy forbidden to them.

German bishops, priests active with the Opera di San Raffaele, and the papal nuncio in Berlin sent many messages to the pope asking him to request mitigation of the constraints. Some of these letters have a decidedly anti-Jewish tone. One from the secretary general of the Opera di San Raffaele in Hamburg, for example, pointed out that the candidates for emigration to Brazil were converts of long standing who "have no relationship with the synagogue or the Jews." The writer continued, "They have absolutely no intention of conducting business in the large Brazilian cities and damaging, in this way, the businessmen of the country, [like the] damage that the Jews cause."[12] Even among priests dedicated to helping former Jews who had become Catholics, anti-Judaism festered.

Vatican officials nevertheless tried to obtain changes in the financial terms to facilitate emigration to Brazil.[13] In early January 1940 and again the following August the Brazilian government seemed to agree to waive the requirements in some cases.[14] But apparent progress simply led to other hurdles. Who was entitled to financial waivers, and who would grant them? How were trips from the German Reich to Brazil to be financed? Would Brazil accept families in which one parent was not Catholic? What about converts whose German citizenship had been revoked? What proofs of conversion would be required? The papal nuncio in Berlin, Monsignor Cesare Orsenigo, never known for imagination or daring, lamented, "I foresee that only with great difficulty will I be able to dismantle all these obstacles."[15]

In March 1940 officials of the Brazilian Embassy to the Holy See further complicated matters by suggesting that 1,000 of the 3,000 visas go to German converts already outside the Reich.[16] As a result, 600 visas were finally allocated to Italy and 100 each to Switzerland, Holland, Belgium, and France. The latter four countries had not imposed racial laws on their Jews, nor had the latter three yet been occupied by the Germans. In March 1940, Jews in all five countries were in far less desperate straits than were those in the German Reich.

Also in the spring of 1940, Brazilian officials ruled that candidates for the remaining 2,000 visas available in Germany would need the recommendation of the Opera di San Raffaele or the papal nuncio in Berlin. Those outside Germany could be recommended by Vatican officials. All candidates must have proof of baptism before 1933.[17] The Vatican secretary of state agreed to these terms while suggesting gently that Brazil might eventually augment the number of visas available in Germany and update the year required for baptism.[18]

In the months that followed, Vatican officials, as well as priests and monks with the Opera di San Raffaele, tried to resolve old problems and confront new ones: charges of corruption, bribery, and the issuance of false visas; the necessity of transit visas through Spain and Portugal; allegations of false conversions; and much more. According to Vatican sources but unconfirmed elsewhere, all but 80 of the 1,000 visas available to German converts already outside the Reich, including the 600 allotted to Italy, were issued.[19] Klaus Voigt, however, has found that only 112 people left Italy under the Brazilian visa program.[20]

The Brazilian ambassador in Berlin, meanwhile, refused to grant any of the 2,000 special visas at his disposition, claiming that the financial terms for immigration into his country still had not been clarified and that he had no authorization to distribute them. The exasperated secretary general of the Opera di San Raffaele in Berlin became so desperate that he actually described the ambassador, in a private letter to Orsenigo, as "having anti-

Semitic inclinations."[21] Finally on September 3, 1940, the Brazilian Embassy suspended the special visa program, pending clarification of the financial and employment constraints.[22] Haggling over terms and efforts to secure Portuguese transit permits nevertheless continued until the Brazilians officially revoked the 2,000 visas allocated to converts in the German Reich in November 1941.[23] Vatican officials briefly considered asking Brazilian diplomats if the eighty remaining visas available for German converts already outside the Reich could still be filled, but they decided against it on the grounds that the answer would almost certainly be negative. The decision was consistent with the Vatican's tendency to make requests only when affirmative responses were expected. On December 2 the official response from the Holy See to the Brazilian ambassador simply expressed the pious hope that the revocation of the visas would be reconsidered in the future.[24]

As late as mid-July 1942, Cardinal Maglione was still trying, gently and politely, to revive the Brazilian visa offer.[25] As he certainly knew, however, the German converts who would have benefited were rapidly disappearing into the inferno of Eastern Europe.[26] By the end of 1942, 100,516 Jews had been deported from Germany. Another 19,417 disappeared during the first three months of 1943. By April 1943, only 31,910 Jews not in mixed marriages and therefore eligible for deportation remained.[27]

Between Italy's entry into the war in May 1940 and the end of 1942, other Vatican efforts to facilitate emigration were lukewarm at best. Catholic and Jewish organizations continued to struggle—the Opera di San Raffaele tried especially to help German converts reach safety abroad, while an Italian Jewish organization called Delegazione per l'assistenza agli emigranti, or Delasem, assisted Jewish refugees in Italy.[28] In one report Delasem claimed to have directly enabled 647 foreign Jews to emigrate during the short period between June 1 and November 30, 1940, and it published the names of the beneficiaries. It helped another 150 indirectly.[29] On the other hand, Father Anton Weber, *procuratore generale* of the Palatine Order and director of the Opera since 1942, informed Pius XII after the liberation of Rome that his organization, working with the Vatican, had enabled 2,000 people to emigrate from Italy throughout the war years. About 1,500, Weber claimed, were Jews.[30] There is no available evidence to confirm this figure, and many historians believe that it is greatly exaggerated.[31] But given the Vatican's resources and diplomatic access to Catholic countries, even the number 1,500 seems rather small.

By early 1941 the Portuguese and Spanish governments were obstruct-
ing the granting of all refugee transit visas, and representatives of both the
Opera di San Raffaele and Delasem wrote to the pope for help. Father Franz
X. Hecht, director of the Opera di San Raffaele at the time, wrote in February
on behalf of some 150 German converts already out of the Reich and on their
way to Brazil with some of the 1,000 visas made available to the Vatican for
distribution. Father Hecht added with annoyance that "[helping converts] is
also a question of prestige, because the Jewish organization HICEM in Lisbon is obtaining transit visas for Jews with great ease."[32] The request was relayed by telegraph to the papal nuncios in Lisbon and Madrid on March 4, but
apparently nothing changed, for in May, Delasem officials asked the pope for
the same help for Jews in general.[33] There is no evidence of a papal response
to the Delasem request, but another petition from the Opera di San Raffaele
in June prompted a second Vatican cable to the papal nuncio in Lisbon on
July 1. On October 1, eight months after the first request for help, the Portuguese government agreed to grant transit visas more readily.[34]

If a papal petition in Lisbon ultimately resulted in the easing of Portuguese transit visa policies, one wonders why it was not made earlier, and on
Vatican initiative rather than at the request of another organization. One may
ask, also, why Vatican officials did not more insistently press other nations,
especially those whose populations were predominantly Catholic, to accept
Jewish refugees, or, at the very least, Jewish converts to Catholicism. They apparently did make some polite requests for converts on an individual basis,
but with little success. As an unidentified official at the Vatican Secretariat
of State admitted on January 2, 1941, "only with great difficulty have some
representatives of the Holy See in Central and South America succeeded in
obtaining some visas for special cases (with the exception, naturally, of
Brazil)."[35] Regarding Jewish refugee problems before and in the early years
of the war, Vatican officials were no more or less concerned than the leaders
of other Western European nations. But from the spiritual leader of Chris-
tendom, one might expect more.

As seen, Borgongini Duca's 1943 report on his efforts to aid Jewish
refugees also declared that the "Holy Father, in his inexhaustible charity, has
provided many [Jewish emigrants] with the considerable expenses for the
voyage [abroad]." What evidence exists for this claim? The Vatican seems not
to have maintained a special fund for refugee assistance.[36] In the autumn of
1939, however, the United Jewish Appeal (UJA), an American organization,

placed $125,000 at the pope's disposal, in honor of Pope Pius XI. The funds, to be used to assist "refugees of every race, faith and color," were ultimately divided among several groups.[37] Fifty thousand dollars went to two American committees, one founded by President Franklin Roosevelt in April 1938 to aid political refugees of all religious persuasions and the other established by the American Catholic hierarchy to favor the immigration of Catholic refugees into the United States. An additional $30,000 went to the Opera di San Raffaele in Hamburg, to support its activities on behalf of German Jews who had converted to Catholicism. The remaining $45,000 was deposited in a Vatican fund for future distribution. Of this latter amount, about $7,000 went to the archbishop of Utrecht, who had asked for funds to help Jewish refugees in the Netherlands, and $3,000 was sent to a charitable organization in Switzerland.[38]

Vatican officials expressed a strong preference for using most of the remaining $35,000 to subsidize transportation from Europe to North and South America for Jews "without distinction of religion."[39] Some 45,000 lire was duly sent to Cardinal Pietro Boetto, the archbishop of Genoa, for assistance to Jewish refugees and, especially, for payment of their sea passage from that city to Rio de Janeiro.[40] The remaining funds seem to have been used elsewhere for a similar purpose, and Pius XII added at least an additional $10,000 from his own resources when they were exhausted.[41] But it is apparent that the $35,000 portion of the UJA gift constituted the main source of what Borgongini Duca described in his 1943 report as the pope's generous contribution to the "considerable expenses for the voyage [of Jewish refugees in Italy to countries abroad]." The money made a considerable difference in the lives of those fortunate enough to secure passage, but most of the papal donation that Borgongini Duca praised so effusively did not originate with Pius XII.

The issue of financial aid from the Vatican for emigration evokes the broader question of charitable contributions for refugees in general. In contrast to the Catholic Church in many other countries, the Church in Italy during the war maintained no nationwide agency specifically to aid refugees, be they Jews or non-Jews. Furthermore, on only a few exceptional occasions did the Vatican make special funds available to help refugees. In his report in January 1943, Borgongini Duca mentioned donations to refugees in Italy of 625,816 lire to Poles and 307,705 lire to all others, including Greeks, Slovenes, Croatians, Serbs, and repatriated Italians.[42] Some Jews may have been included among these categories, but he alluded to them only once. Many destitute Polish women and girls, as he described them, found housing at the convent of the Orsoline del Cuore Agonizzante in the Via di Villa Ricotti near Via Nomentana. The same nuns, he added in a subsequent paragraph, provided continual religious instruction to the women they sheltered, and several Jews were converted.[43]

For the most part, Catholic refugees, like all others passing through Italy on temporary transit visas, were obliged to apply to local soup kitchens or other social services provided on the parish level for the poor in general. After the intensification of Allied bombing raids on northern Italian cities in the autumn of 1942, they could also find local committees for the recently homeless. These various services were sometimes run by Catholics, but they were local rather than national, and they were directed toward all those in need rather than just toward refugees. Alternatively, needy foreigners could turn to refugee assistance organizations operated by non-Catholics, such as Delasem, the Quakers, the Salvation Army, or the Red Cross. During the period preceding the German occupation of Italy in September 1943 the Italian Catholic Church seems to have made only modest donations to local Catholic aid committees, and none at all to other refugee organizations.[44]

The situation sometimes became embarrassing. On July 25, 1941, for example, a Delasem representative in Genoa informed the papal nuncio that since the American Friends Service Committee (the Quakers) had been forced to close its doors for lack of funds, Catholic refugees were almost totally deprived of any assistance. Delasem itself, the informant continued, had been helping Catholics as well as Jews but did not have the resources to continue doing so. Could Borgongini Duca provide the name of an assistance agency to which Catholic refugees could be referred?[45] Twelve days later, the nuncio replied that his office had been helping Polish refugees of all religions, and had also provided a "great many Jews" with the price of a voyage abroad.[46] We have already seen that those Jews were almost entirely Catholic converts.

The Vatican's policies toward Jewish emigration and assistance between 1939 and early 1942 can be criticized on two counts. The almost exclusive focus on Jewish refugees who were converts was lamentable. Equally so was the failure to help significant numbers even of converts. In considering these realities, however, it should be recalled that the full meaning of the Final Solution was barely suspected at the time. Until the summer of 1942 it was not clear that the Jews who could not escape from German-occupied Western and Central Europe would almost certainly be killed by the Nazis. Many German, Austrian, and Czech Jews were deported "to the east" in 1941, but they were usually not immediately murdered there. Their fate was deeply troubling but largely unknown. The systematic gassing of Polish Jews, as opposed to their ghettoization and death by starvation, disease, and occasional murder, began at Chelmno in December 1941 but also remained unknown outside of Poland for several months. Concerned observers had some knowledge of Nazi massacres of Jews in the Soviet Union after the German invasion at the end of June 1941. But even the best informed did not understand that the mass destruction of all European Jews would become German policy until in fact it did, at the Wannsee Conference in January 1942 and in the course of the deportations in the spring and early summer of 1942.

Jews in German-occupied countries were, of course, subject to intense persecution long before that. They lost their property and civil rights, and could usually be killed with impunity. In an early horrifying instance, known as Kristallnacht, 91 German Jews were murdered on the night of November 9–10, 1938, and some 30,000 others were imprisoned. It was a warning of things to come that often went unheeded. Then in late 1941, as deportations from the Greater German Reich (Germany, Austria, and the Sudetenland) intensified, terrified Jews there began to ask themselves whether the frailest among them could survive the rigors of life in Eastern European ghettos. But those Jews who sought help from the Vatican and other institutions before 1942 rarely understood that they all would soon be threatened with murder. In their poverty, desperation, and fear they should have received far more help than they did. The issue was emigration or severe suffering. But it did not yet appear to be one of emigration or death.

The second consideration relates to the Vatican's exclusive focus on Jews who had converted to Catholicism. As seen in earlier chapters, the attitude was, for better or for worse, a historic characteristic of the Church, magnified since the French Revolution by a growing siege mentality, a result of the challenge of secular modernity. Vatican diplomats defined no real moral mission for themselves but invariably acted as if their primary function was to defend their constituency. In addition, many churchmen held exaggerated views of the resources and influence of international Jewish organizations able to help their own people. They also felt not only a genuine sympathy for Jews who

had chosen to convert but a special responsibility as well. Often denied the social services of the increasingly impoverished community they had left, converts had every right to expect support from their new coreligionists.

The attitude expressed by the papal nuncio to Italy with regard to converts subject to the anti-Jewish laws was prevalent among officials of the
Church, and bears repeating in this broader context. "It would be unjust,"
Borgongini Duca wrote, "to send a convert back among those who consider
him a deserter and an apostate, and expose him to reprisals." [47] While injustice and reprisals were not really at stake, it certainly would have been an em-
barrassment to see converts to Catholicism turning to Protestant or Jewish
refugee assistance agencies.

These observations are intended not as excuses but as partial explanations. But the basic fact remains. Vatican officials failed to provide significant
help even to those Jewish refugees who arrived under their very windows, so
to speak, in Italy itself. Committed to a bureaucratic career track that did not
reward initiative or risk, and punished failure, they acted with extreme caution. They were clearly unwilling to offend Mussolini's Fascists or his Nazi
partner in the ongoing war. Refugees, after all, in fleeing the German Reich
and its occupied territories, were making a political statement and displaying
their disapproval of Hitler to all the world. Facilitating their transit to North or
South America was not inconsistent with Italian government policy, especially since most foreign Jews had been required to leave by the anti-Jewish
law of September 1938. Providing help was, however, a public indication of
sympathy. From this point of view, supporting refugees while they remained
in Italy was equally controversial.

Nevertheless, it surely should have been possible to offer more food and
shelter to refugees. Delasem, with far fewer resources and no national prestige, was sustaining Jewish refugees, and, less frequently, converts to Catholicism as well. Here again the Catholic Church hierarchy failed to reveal a
human dimension, leaving the initiative for acts of charity almost entirely to a
handful of parish priests, monks, nuns, and Catholic laypersons. It was a pattern that would continue into the years of German occupation.

Equally disturbing is the fundamental dishonesty of claims from ostensibly reputable sources that the Vatican helped refugees far more than in fact
it did. The claims have a long history. At the end of December 1941, for example, soon after the Brazilian project was ended, Vatican Secretary of State
Maglione sent a self-serving message to the German bishop who had originally asked for the visas. He was less than honest, and certainly not charitable,

when he wrote, "As you have certainly been informed . . . many emigrants have departed [under this program, from outside the German Reich only] and—I am sorry to say—from what I have been told, a good part of them, by their incorrect conduct and demands, have not corresponded to the concern that the Holy See has shown on their behalf." [48] It was, in other words, the converts' own fault that the visa program had been canceled.

Borgongini Duca's report, seen at the beginning of this chapter, followed about a year later. "Through our intervention, many have obtained the necessary visas from various consulates," he wrote rather deceptively, and "the Holy Father, in his inexhaustible charity, has provided many with the considerable expenses for the voyage." Veracity here depends on the definition of "many," while the self-congratulatory tone remains unjustified. But the mythology continued. In 1961, German Jesuit Father Robert Leiber, Pius XII's private secretary during his entire papacy and his staunch defender after his death in 1958, wrote, "Brazil . . . put 3,000 'visas' solely for Catholic Jews at the disposition of the pope." [49] Leiber surely knew that fewer than 1,000 of these were actually used, but he never said so.

Two years later, Joseph Lichten, head of the Intercultural Affairs Department of the Anti-Defamation League of B'nai B'rith, added to the mythology with a profoundly inaccurate description of Vatican involvement with the Opera di San Raffaele—claims that Leiber and, somewhat later, the editors of the Vatican documents, never even remotely made. "The papal Ministry of State made innumerable requests of foreign governments for exit and entry papers," he wrote, "with more than fair success." He continued, "The government of Brazil . . . supplied 3,000 entry visas at first intended for Jewish converts to Catholicism, but that they were used by practicing Jews is undisputed." Not only were they not used by "practicing Jews," but fewer than 1,000 were used at all. Lichten added that "the first source [of the money needed for emigration] was the Vatican itself." [50] He never mentioned that the Vatican contribution came largely from the UJA.

In 1967, Israeli diplomat Pinchas Lapide continued to feed the legend. Lapide claimed that the Brazil project began at the initiative of the pope rather than at the request of leaders of the Church in Germany. He added that all 3,000 visas were filled, and that the Opera di San Raffaele helped 4,000 to 6,000 Jews with emigration problems. [51] Even the most cursory examination of the published Vatican documents shows these statements to be false. Yet the mythology persists. [52]

CHAPTER SIX

Foreign Jews in Italian Internment Camps

1940–1943

THE FOREIGN Jewish community in Italy on the eve of the war was small and impoverished. Just 2,000 or 3,000 remained from the roughly 11,000 present in September 1938, when an anti-Jewish decree had ordered the emigration of foreign Jews. For the most part they represented the exceptions provided for by the law—immigrant Jews who had been naturalized before January 1, 1919, or foreign Jews over the age of sixty-five or married to Italian citizens before October 1, 1938. They were subjected to the other provisions of the anti-Jewish laws, and if not naturalized, they could not hold jobs in Italy. But they could remain.

About 3,800 others were recent arrivals, mostly from the German Reich, the Protectorate of Bohemia and Moravia, and Central Europe. They had been among the several thousand allowed to enter Italy on temporary tourist or transit visas between September 1938 and May 1940, on the condition that they return home after their visit or emigrate. Many who wanted to emigrate had not been able to do so.[1] Until June 1940, their primary problems involved searching for places abroad, avoiding repatriation when their temporary visas expired, and securing food and shelter. The Italian declaration of war on the side of the Germans on June 10, however, brought immense new hardships. Within just a few weeks nearly all Jewish men from the German Reich and its occupied countries, along with at least a third of their women and children, were arrested and either interned or placed in supervised residence. By March 1941, those interned numbered at least 1,891.[2] Another several thousand in supervised residence, especially women and children, lived on a government pittance in designated housing in some four hundred small towns and villages, where they were obliged to report to local authorities twice a day, could not go outside between dusk and dawn, and could leave town only with official permission.

Foreign Jews were not the only civilians interned in Italy in June and July 1940. Non-Jewish citizens of enemy countries—French and British, especially, along with some Chinese and others—were also subject to arrest. Only about 1,921 of these, however, representing just a small percentage of those present, were in fact interned. According to one government account, at least 676 Italian citizens suspected of political disloyalty were also arrested in 1940 and interned, in most cases separately from foreigners. The proportion of Italian Jews arrested on suspicion of dissidence far exceeded that of their non-Jewish countrymen. Although they represented just one-tenth of 1 percent of the overall Italian population, Italian Jews constituted about 12 percent of the citizens arrested in 1940.[3]

During the first weeks of the Italian war effort, then, several thousand Jewish men and women were held for weeks in filthy city prisons before being marched in handcuffs to the trains that carried them to such wretched camps as Ferramonti Tarsia in the province of Cosenza, and Campagna in the province of Salerno. There they lived in flimsy huts without electricity, heat, or running water until they could construct better facilities for themselves. Food was scarce, medicine almost nonexistent, and malaria and typhus endemic. And the population of internees continued to swell. At the end of September 1940, Ferramonti, by far the largest camp and almost entirely for Jews, held 718 prisoners from Germany, Poland, the former Czechoslovakia, and Romania. Of these, 143 were women.[4] By March 1941, the camp held 958 Jews and 33 non-Jews, all foreigners.[5] By September 1942, the number had increased to about 1,500, still predominantly Jewish.[6]

The Vatican became involved with Jewish and non-Jewish civilian internees in Italy in three ways. First, it sent diplomatic envoys and priests to the camps. Second, it offered a communications network by which inmates could hope to correspond with their families. Finally, for the Jews, it addressed the terrifying issue of the possible deportation of foreign Jews from Italy before Mussolini's fall from power in July 1943. While each level of involvement was useful, the third had by far the most momentous implications. The three activities merit separate consideration.

Toward the end of 1940, Pius XII asked his diplomats to petition the major belligerents for permission to visit inmates in civilian internment centers and prisoner-of-war camps. Great Britain, Canada, Australia, and Italy agreed, and visits began immediately.[7] In Italy, Papal Nuncio Francesco Borgongini Duca spent a difficult Christmas in a train, battling snowstorms while trying to visit the Pollenza and Treia camps in the mountains of the province of Macerata. It is not clear whether he ever reached them, but on the morning of December 27 he was at the Montechiarugolo camp in the province of Parma, where 113 foreign non-Jews and one Jewish man were interned. During a three-hour visit, the prefect reported, he "distributed to all, without distinction, tea, chocolate, religious images and prayers written in different languages. In addition he left 1,000 lire to improve the food for the neediest internees."[8] In the afternoon he continued on to Civitella della Chiana in the province of Arezzo, where he spent another three hours distributing cigarettes, tea, and 30 lire apiece to some 34 non-Jews and 30 Jews, all foreign men.[9] He returned to Rome in the evening.

The papal nuncio's subsequent visits occurred around Easter. A whirlwind tour in April 1941 took him to six camps in the province of Teramo on the seventh and eighth; three in Macerata on the ninth; Fabriano in Ancona on the fourteenth; and Bagni a Ripoli near Florence on the fifteenth.[10] In the six camps in Teramo, which held a total of 342 Jews and 156 non-Jews, all foreigners, he distributed cards with the portrait of the Holy Father along with a medal to commemorate his visit. He also left 200 to 300 lire in each camp, to buy candies for the internees for Easter.[11] He made similar gifts in the province of Macerata, whose three camps held 35 Italian Jews, 21 Italian non-Jews, 66 foreign Jews, and 81 foreign non-Jews, and in Fabriano, with 78 Italians and 1 foreigner, all non-Jews.[12] In Fabriano he also donated 100 lire to buy a ball, since the inmates had expressed the wish to play games in the courtyard in order to, in the prefect's words, "better employ the time."[13] After similar visits in Chieti, Foggia, Avellino, and Salerno provinces, Borgongini Duca arrived in Ferramonti on May 22, 1941. He examined the physical plant, addressed the 1,144 internees, and celebrated Mass for the 85 Jews who were Catholics.[14] He donated about 2,000 lire for wine and sweets.[15]

The papal nuncio's tours continued throughout 1942 and the first half of 1943. He last visited Ferramonti at the end of May 1943. Most internees appreciated the visits, as they did those of other foreign diplomats, Red Cross representatives, and occasional journalists. Government reports frequently echo the observations of an official in the province of Teramo, who wrote that the "heartfelt and noble words pronounced by the apostolic nuncio on the occasion [of his camp visits in the region] produced in the spirits of the internees, especially the Catholics, a lively enthusiasm, so that as he left . . . everyone applauded him vigorously, begging him to thank the Holy Father for his kind thoughts." [16] Such contacts reassured internees that they were not forgotten and that some outsiders cared about the treatment they received. Borgongini Duca seems to have treated all internees, non-Jews and Jews, Italians and foreigners, similarly. If his visits did not necessarily indicate awareness of the special problems and sorrows of Jews, they were nonetheless meaningful to them. Several Jewish internees later wrote to express their gratitude.[17]

While the gratitude of forlorn internees is understandable, that of Delasem, the official Italian Jewish agency for assistance to Jewish refugees, is much less so. In the spring of 1941, Delasem directors wrote to Borgongini Duca, thanking him, as the latter put it in a letter to Vatican Secretary of State Cardinal Luigi Maglione, "for the charitable work of the Holy See in favor of so many unhappy people." [18] The Holy See had done nothing more for Jewish internees than for non-Jews, and that was little enough. Delasem leaders may have hoped to persuade Vatican officials to do more by flattering and shaming them. Instead, their words merely helped initiate the myth of a compassionate Church.

With a single exception, there is no evidence that Borgongini Duca criticized the conditions he found in the camps. On the contrary, most government reports of his visits declared that he expressed satisfaction with what he saw—despite flimsy barracks, inadequate food and medical supplies, endemic disease, and pervasive boredom.[19] After a visit to Pollenza in Macerata province the papal nuncio suggested only that three prostitutes interned there be sent elsewhere.[20] About his visits in general, he wrote to officials at the Ministry of the Interior on June 4, 1941, of his "sincere satisfaction with the good treatment of all the internees," and mentioned only that many Italian inmates would like to be able to work in the camps in order to earn money for their families.[21] The single exception involved the papal nuncio's glimpse of Gypsies interned at Tossicia in April 1943. While he found the condition of other internees in the camp to be acceptable, he observed, as a government official described it, that "many [of the Gypsies] were in torn and threadbare rags." In the name of the Holy Father, Borgongini Duca left 20,000 lire for them, far more than usual.[22]

In their introduction to volume VIII of the Vatican wartime diplomatic documents, the editors claimed that "the Holy See was able to obtain rather

broad concessions from the government in Rome," including "better treatment in the internment camps from the point of view of material and
morale." [23] Given the evidence, it is difficult to accept these claims. There can,
of course, be no dispute about the effect on morale. Borgongini Duca's visits
certainly reassured Jews as well as Catholics, as did his promise of a Vatican
channel of communications to families outside the camps and the assignment of a popular new priest at Ferramonti (see below). But the material effect of the visits was minimal. Camp directors learned that the Vatican was
watching them, but they learned also that it was not prepared to be particularly critical.

In early July 1941, not long after Borgongini Duca's visit to Ferramonti,
Vatican officials assigned a feisty sixty-five-year-old former missionary, a
French- and German-speaking Alsatian Capuchin priest named Calliste
Lopinot, to the camp. Lopinot's formal mission was to minister to the 85
Catholics among the 1,144 foreign Jewish internees present at the time. To
that end he built a chapel and held Mass every day. He also tried to improve
the inmates' image of the Church. He wrote to his superiors in Rome, for ex-
ample, asking that they prevent further visits from a military chaplain who
had included provocative anti-Jewish sentiments in an anti-British sermon at
Ferramonti, because, Lopinot wrote, he would "destroy the work of the Holy
Father [and] make the Church look ridiculous." [24]

The hope of winning converts certainly motivated Lopinot, as it did his
superiors. Even before his arrival at least four Jews were converted and baptized at Ferramonti in November 1940, and the diocesan priests involved in
their instruction eagerly sought government permission to continue their visits.[25] After Borgongini Duca's first trip to Ferramonti, a French Catholic publication printed the following statement: "Numerous are the Christians who
have returned to religious practice, *numerous also are the non-Christians whose
unhappiness and personal reflections help them to understand the message of the
Saviour.* . . . We could cite many interesting episodes, for example that of a
great concentration camp [at Ferramonti], a real village, where entire families
of Jews (a thousand people) are interned, who received the nuncio with enthusiasm and whose children ran before him with bouquets of flowers." [26]
While it is difficult to believe that many flowers were available at Ferramonti,
the text clearly demonstrates churchmen's excited conviction that a real opportunity for conversions was at hand. Thanks to the efforts of a Chinese

priest and an Italian missionary at Tossicia in the province of Teramo, Borgongini Duca baptized thirty-eight Chinese inmates on July 31, 1941, and another sixty in May 1942.[27] Could not the same thing occur at Ferramonti?

According to Mirko Haler, an internee at Ferramonti between October 1941 and December 1942, Lopinot baptized about fifty Jews during that period.[28] Lopinot himself claimed to have baptized seventy-nine Jews during his entire stay at the camp, from July 1941 to September 1943.[29] Conversions naturally provoked tensions and resentment among observant Jews. Haler, however, although he was not a convert, nevertheless described Lopinot as *"molto simpatico."* He hastened to add, "It is worth mentioning that Father Lopinot had many [unconverted] Jewish friends in the camp, but I never heard it said that he made propaganda for a change of religion."[30] Not all agreed, but it is a tribute to Lopinot that some did.

Lopinot also made friends in other ways, for he quickly became an advocate of all internees in practical matters. Scarcities and deprivation at Ferramonti were indeed grave, for internees, except for a small daily bread ration, were not fed free of charge. Instead, they were given small subsidies with which to buy food, clothing, and medicine wherever they could. By mid-1942, when a cooked meal prepared in a camp kitchen cost 6 or 7 lire, men at Ferramonti received 8 lire a day, women 4, and children 3.[31] A family with two children thus received about 540 lire a month, at a time when Lopinot was writing that he alone could not live on his monthly salary of 700 lire.[32] Most families were obliged to buy their own food from local peasants and prepare their scanty meals themselves. Often there was nothing to buy. Father Lopinot observed with some desperation in June 1942, "*Everyone* is suffering from hunger."[33] Pants and shirts worn since 1940 were in tatters, but there was little money for new clothing. In December 1941, Father Lopinot had noted indignantly in his diary, "If the state is going to put people of the Jewish race in prison, it must also take care of their clothing."[34] But the state did not respond.

Let us return to the Vatican claim, mentioned above, that "the Holy See was able to obtain rather broad concessions from the government in Rome," including "better treatment in the internment camps from the point of view of material and morale." That claim has been shown to be greatly exaggerated. But if Borgongini Duca, representing the Holy See and dealing with the Italian government, achieved little, Lopinot, acting on his own, achieved more. The elderly Capuchin missionary was not diplomatic, discreet, and polite like Borgongini Duca. Nor was he a bureaucrat, prepared to make a proper request through the appropriate channels merely to be able to say that he had done his best. Lopinot was, instead, loud, pushy, and persistent. Also unlike Borgongini Duca, who never seemed to notice the suffering that he confronted on his camp visits, Lopinot lived and shared it every day for three years. Imaginative where Borgongini Duca was dull, he saw what needed to be done and he did it.

Father Lopinot was not unconnected in Rome, for he had served as a consultant at the Vatican's Congregazione di Propaganda Fide since 1937.[35] Through his contacts he obtained a donation from the Vatican of 3,000 lire to help the 494 Jewish survivors of the shipwrecked *Pentcho,* transferred from Rhodes to Ferramonti in February and March 1942.[36] The contribution was small, but Lopinot estimated in another context that in the late winter of 1942–43 that amount could provide a nourishing soup for thirty people once a day for a month.[37] Thus, the money made some difference.

More important, during his trips to Rome, Lopinot was able to interest several private Catholic benefactors in the plight of the internees at Ferramonti. He reported that an anonymous Yugoslavian monsignor gave a total of 312,100 lire for the Yugoslavians there. In 1942 a Czech monsignor provided 281,700 lire for his countrymen and for the survivors of the *Pentcho.* The Swiss Legation and others, including the papal nuncio, made additional donations.[38] Lopinot supervised the use and distribution of funds and saw to it that Jews and non-Jews benefited equally.

Father Lopinot was not the only outsider to funnel aid into Ferramonti, of course. Jewish organizations, especially, did much more.[39] But the Capuchin priest was the only Catholic clergyman, in a Catholic country, to demonstrate compassion and concern for the material welfare of foreign Jews at Ferramonti who had not converted. He had been sent to the camp to minister to Catholics and, if possible, bring others into the fold. While he never lost sight of that mission, he far exceeded it. He was a precursor of the many gallant priests in Italy who became involved in rescuing Jews after the Germans occupied the country in September 1943. He was an honor to his Church, but the Vatican cannot claim credit for his dedication, vision, and personal initiative.

On November 23, 1940, several months before Lopinot was sent to Ferramonti, Monsignor Mario Besson, the bishop of Lausanne, Geneva, and Fribourg in Switzerland, sent a lengthy appeal to Pius XII. The bishop was concerned about the "appalling misery that is ravaging a great number of countries." He continued:

> All the great organizations that are concerned with the victims of the war and whose headquarters are in Geneva are Protestants or neutrals. With very rare exceptions the agents who visit the prisoner-of-war camps and the concentration camps are strangers to Catholicism. The non-Catholics are ahead of us everywhere. They alone, better welcomed than we, it is true, by the authorities of certain belligerent countries, have truly undertaken meaningful actions. Our Swiss Catholic Mission in favor of victims of war is a very small thing at the side of so many other institutions. . . . At the present moment, countless unfortunates will go to those who give them aid, and among those who give them aid the Catholics are only a small number.[40]

The bishop went on to suggest some ways in which aid could be provided to prisoners in the camps.

Monsignor Filippo Bernardini, the papal nuncio to Switzerland, forwarded the bishop's message to the pope. In his covering letter, Bernardini wrote, "What Monsignor Besson writes . . . is so evident that all documentation can be dispensed with. It is a fact that almost everywhere, non-Catholic philanthropic and humanitarian associations abundantly provided with means and animated by unquestionable zeal have preceded us and are arriving there where we have not or cannot arrive."[41] Coming as it did from a papal nuncio, this is like a breath of fresh air. A week later, Monsignor Giovanni Battista Montini, secretary of the Section for Ordinary Ecclesiastical Affairs within the Vatican Secretariat of State, wrote instructions for a reply. "Seen by the Holy Father," he declared. "Answer: we are aware of this and we are already thinking about it, thank you. Be encouraged."[42]

The precise issues raised by Bishop Besson are beyond the scope of this book. However, the portrait of the Church's social services drawn by the Swiss prelate reinforces impressions that have emerged here. We see again that the Roman Catholic Church in the 1930s and 1940s remained a narrow institution, unimaginative, inflexible, and inward-looking. Accustomed to and adept at protecting its own institutional interests, it was far less committed to humanitarian goals. It remained the Fortress Church in a world perceived as hostile and threatening.

In addition, the Vatican bureaucracy itself was rigid, conservative, and much too small to respond creatively to the complex problems it faced. Montini's Section for Ordinary Ecclesiastical Affairs, after all, had only thirty-four employees in 1944. Monsignor Domenico Tardini's Section for Extraordinary Affairs, the only other department within the Vatican Secretariat of State, had just sixteen.[43] All of these bureaucrats had forged their careers within an institution that did not encourage or reward innovation. Infighting and maneuvering were intense, and a single mistake or personal enemy could mean demotion. Over and over again, as a result, we find bureaucrats responding to requests and appeals in a purely perfunctory way, as if they wanted only to shuffle one more piece of paper off the desk. These conditions made a proper response to the sufferings of Jews during the war virtually impossible.

Lopinot was able to boost the morale of internees at Ferramonti in many ways. While most of the Jews remained unimpressed by the new chapel and regular Catholic Masses in the camp, they responded enthusiastically to the Capuchin priest's offer to forward mail to their relatives abroad. Lopinot was in effect introducing the Vatican Information Service, established in the early days of the war to allow civilian and military prisoners-of-war in all countries to communicate with their families. Letters were to be collected in the camps by Catholic priests there, distributed via the Vatican to its papal nuncios in foreign countries, and then given to local bishops and priests for final delivery. The system functioned with many difficulties—the British objected for a time on the grounds that the same service could be provided by the Red Cross, while the Germans refused to cooperate with no explanation at all. But the Italians were receptive to the Vatican offer, and letters from prisoners there were delivered to families in most belligerent countries except Germany. During Borgongini Duca's visits to Italian internment camps he invariably informed internees about the service. As that service's representative at Ferramonti, Lopinot encouraged and helped inmates to send hundreds of letters.

The letters that prisoners received, however, whether through the Vatican Information Service or the regular mail, did not always enhance morale, for during the spring of 1942 internees began to learn of deportations and other horrors occurring in Poland. In terror over the fate of their families, they asked Lopinot if anything could be done to bring their loved ones to Ferramonti. Lopinot, probably unaware that the German government had prohibited Jewish emigration in the autumn of 1941, promised to try. On March

25, 1942, he relayed the request to Borgongini Duca, adding that the numbers could be limited to parents, spouses, and children. "It would never involve a mass invasion of Jews," he explained, "and the overload on the government coffers would remain minimal." [44] He nevertheless ran into a brick wall. A note from Borgongini Duca explained, "We have looked into it, but the government cannot accept these people; their demands already exceed 6,000. Also, the German government will not permit them to come to Italy." [45]

Throughout the summer of 1942, Jewish internees at Ferramonti and other Italian camps remained in agony about their families. Letters stopped arriving from Central Europe, and BBC broadcasts warned of deportations from Western Europe as well. Then in August and September, rumors arrived of roundups and deportations of foreign Jews in southern France. Internees in Italy now perceived that they were in danger as well. If officials at Vichy could condone such outrages on unoccupied French soil, what was to prevent Mussolini's Fascists from doing the same? How much longer would Mussolini tolerate and pay for the presence on Italian soil of Jews without legal documents who had been ordered out of the country as long ago as 1938?

Again the Jews of Ferramonti turned to Lopinot, and again, while he had little influence on events, he tried to calm their fears. On September 10, 1942, he wrote a heartfelt letter to Borgongini Duca which read in part:

> For some days morale in the camp has been very bad. News has arrived of the deportations of German Jews from free France to Poland. The general facts seem secure, [but] the details are still unknown.
>
> This news has hit the internees like a thunderbolt. They are terrified that the same standards will be applied to them.
>
> I have tried to calm them by saying that for now there is no indication and that for the moment there is no danger for them.
>
> I have not succeeded in calming them.
>
> Their anxiety is understandable. . . .
>
> I feel myself obligated in good conscience to advise Your Eminence of this state of affairs and I beg you in the name of all the internees to intervene so that these inhumane measures will not be taken by the Italian government. [46]

There is no evidence that any official of the Holy See intervened with an Italian government counterpart on behalf of Jewish internees at this time. [47]

If inmates at Ferramonti had any lingering illusions in September about the fate of Jewish deportees elsewhere in Europe, they were shattered three months later by the arrival of three young escapees from Poland. Herzl Kawa, Hersch Liverant, and Moschk Nelkenbaum were from Siedlce, forty-two kilometers east of Warsaw. In August 1942 they witnessed the brutal clearing of the two ghettos in their city. Hundreds of Jews were murdered on the spot by German SS and their *Volksdeutsche* and Polish police assistants. Thousands of others were jammed into trains for Treblinka, from which they did not return. The three survivors were among the strong young men selected in Siedlce on the night of the roundup for hard labor rather than immediate death. After being warned by a supervisor that Jewish workers would eventually be shot, they decided that their only hope was to try to escape. While repairing a rail line on October 23, they managed to climb into a nearly empty Italian troop train returning from the Russian front. They traveled safely to the Brenner Pass, on the Italian border with Austria. There they were discovered by Italian customs officials, turned over to local police, interrogated, and jailed for forty days. They were finally admitted to Italy and taken to Ferramonti for internment. They arrived at the camp on December 8. The eyewitness testimony they brought with them dramatically increased the fears and apprehension of inmates.[48]

In January 1943, two spokesmen for the Jews at Ferramonti sent a desperate letter to Myron Taylor, the official diplomatic representative of the United States to the Holy See, for delivery to high-level American government officials. They begged the United States to accept foreign Jews who felt threatened with deportation from Italy. In imperfect English, they added, "A dreadful awe keeps the minds of the Jewish prisoners because almost everybody among them has near relatives who had been deported to Poland some months ago and they know that there is no hope to see them any more because there is no way back from that Hell of despair."[49] But the world was not listening.

CHAPTER SEVEN

What the Pope Knew About the Holocaust

ROLF HOCHHUTH'S play *Der Stellvertreter,* sharply critical of the pope's silence during the Holocaust, set off an international furor when it opened in Berlin on February 20, 1963. As part of the public debate that followed, Father Robert Leiber, Pius XII's personal secretary during and after the war, wrote a long article that appeared in the *Frankfurter Allgemeine Zeitung* on March 27, 1963. Among other things, Leiber wrote, in his usual convoluted style, "We must disregard [the idea] that the pope had certain absolutely reliable material at hand, the reliability of which he personally considered irrefutable; that he did not tell the world-wide public [information] that the Allies had not known already for a long time, and perhaps better than he. The whole extent of the Jewish persecutions, the number of six million victims of the extermination camps, could only be verified after the war."[1]

Other papal defenders soon echoed similar themes. "The enormous dimensions and monstrous cruelty [of the destruction of the Jews] were apparent in their full sinister light only after the war," wrote Father Alberto Giovannetti, an official Vatican historian, in *L'Osservatore Romano* on April 5, 1963. He continued:

> The information about these crimes that reached the Vatican was scarce and vague. For the most part it originated on one side of the struggle (the Allied powers), and was based on revelations and news that even those who conveyed it could not guarantee. . . .

The absence of papal representatives in countries occupied by the
Reich, the isolation and inaction to which the nuncio in Berlin
was condemned, the answers given when he dared hint at certain
rumors, the lack of precision in the scarce information, all advised
against taking a public position that might provide a basis for
Nazi accusations of a violation of neutrality on the part of the Holy
See. . . . Giving Hitler even a vague foundation for an accusation of
this type could be expected to lead to a complete paralysis of every
charitable activity in favor of the victims of the war and even perhaps a break in diplomatic relations between the Reich and the
Holy See.[2]

The following year, Jesuit Father Angelo Martini, another Vatican historian and one of the editors of the *Actes et Documents du Saint Siège relatifs à la
seconde guerre mondiale,* repeated some of these claims. "The complete statistic of six million dead, in the case of the Jews, was calculated and known only
at the end of the war," he declared in an article in *La Civiltà Cattolica.* "The
decision leading to the Final Solution. . . , suspected after the middle of
1942, was known in detail only after the extermination was completed, after
the defeat." Martini admitted that the information gathered by Jewish organizations during the war had proved accurate. Then, differing slightly from
Giovannetti, he continued, "The pope also received news, unfortunately
not frequently nor with the desired accuracy, from the clergy of occupied
countries, from military chaplains passing through, from soldiers and
civilians. Unfortunately all this data lacked proof, the verification that could
confirm the accuracy and provide a case for denouncing the effective
reality."[3]

The official Vatican position on what was known about the Holocaust
during the war appeared in Volume IX of the *Actes et Documents du Saint
Siège,* published in 1975. Vatican officials knew a great deal about massacres
of Jews in the Soviet Union, the editors of the volume admitted, and about deportations as they occurred. They knew that Jewish deportees rarely wrote
home, but they claimed that occasionally a deceptive letter arrived to kindle
hope. The editors continued, "This situation of uncertainty and fear, alternat-
ing with bursts of hope, continued for months, even until 1944. Apparently
the pontifical representatives and the Jewish communities with which they
were in contact did not possess any concrete information."[4] According to the
editors, some details filtered in from Vatican diplomats in several European

capitals. There were rumors of killings by gas. But there was no mention of Auschwitz, and no concrete proof.

In contrast to this position, many historians have argued that the Vatican was, as Walter Laqueur put it, "better informed than anyone else in Europe."[5] In agreement is Gerhart M. Riegner, in 1942 the thirty-year-old representative of the World Jewish Congress in Geneva who received reports from Jewish agents in German-occupied Europe and relayed them to the Allies. Riegner wrote in 1998, "The Vatican was probably better informed than we."[6] An understanding of the distribution of Vatican diplomats tends to confirm this opinion. The Holy See had papal nuncios in, among other cities, Berlin, Rome, Vichy, Budapest, Bucharest, Bern, Madrid, and Lisbon. It also maintained apostolic delegates in Istanbul, Athens, London, and Washington, and other representatives elsewhere, most notably in Zagreb (Croatia) and Bratislava (Slovakia). Papal diplomats received information from officials at all levels in the governments to which they were accredited. Many of them also heard frequently from prelates and priests, who in turn collected information from the faithful, including soldiers, guards, and civilians who witnessed atrocities and were sometimes disturbed by them. Vatican envoys were able to send communications by diplomatic pouch or telegraph, or entrust messages to the many priests permitted to travel to Rome. The Vatican was far from isolated.

The situation within the prewar borders of Poland, where the actual extermination camps were located, was admittedly more difficult. The papal nuncio in Warsaw escaped with the Polish government in September 1939 and was not allowed to return. His duties were assumed unofficially by the nuncio in Berlin, who could not visit Poland and was not allowed to maintain an observer there. Polish bishops were only rarely permitted to communicate directly with the Vatican Secretariat of State, and Polish clergymen could not leave the country. But there were other ways to make the story known. Information acquired by the Polish underground was conveyed to the Polish government in exile in London, and from there to the local apostolic delegate. Data collected by Jewish organizations from their own contacts in Poland was reported especially to agents in Switzerland, who passed it along to the papal nuncio in Bern or to government officials in London and Washington, who in turn relayed it to the apostolic delegates there. From the Vatican's point of view, of course, information from anti-German Poles and Jews eager for a papal commitment to their own side was suspect. As it accumulated, however, it must have made some impression.

More credible to Vatican officials were reports from German and Italian businessmen, bureaucrats, journalists, and military men who traveled in Poland or maintained close contacts there. These individuals, presumably, had less reason to exaggerate tales of German atrocities for propaganda purposes. Still better was information carried by priests. While Polish clergymen could not leave their country, Italian chaplains frequently traveled through central Poland with Italian troop trains on their way to the eastern front, stopping at regular supply depots along their route. Once back in Italy, they moved about freely and had unrestricted access to the Vatican City. To claim that these priests did not inform the pope of what they certainly knew about the destruction of the Jews is the equivalent of saying that they did not care about it. That surely was not the case.

It is not, of course, possible to prove the existence of verbal messages. Nor is it currently possible to examine Vatican documents not selected for publication in the eleven volumes of the *Actes et Documents du Saint Siège*. Cardinal Agostino Casaroli, secretary of the Council for the Public Affairs of the Church, assured Walter Laqueur in 1979 that all documents indicating what Vatican officials knew about the murders of the Jews had been published, but his statement cannot be confirmed as long as the Vatican archives remain closed.[7] But a careful examination of documents that have been published, along with reports to the Holy See from other sources, is instructive.

Soon after the German invasion of Poland on September 1, 1939, Jews began to be moved into ghettos where many died from starvation and disease. Individual Jews were often worked to death or murdered arbitrarily. Vatican attention was initially diverted from these events, however, by similar Nazi persecutions of Catholic Poles. During the war, some 1.8 million to 1.9 million Catholic Polish civilians were killed, including, by one estimate, more than 2,300 men and women of the Church. Another 5,400 clergymen, monks, and nuns, not to mention hundreds of thousands of Catholic laypersons, were imprisoned.[8]

Reports of Catholic suffering prepared by Polish clergymen and smuggled into Rome said little or nothing about the Jews. Examples include two messages carried to the Vatican by Abbot Pirro Scavizzi, an Italian chaplain on a hospital train of the Order of the Knights of Malta who frequently traveled through Poland on trips between Italy and the Russian front. The first message, delivered on November 21, 1941, was from a Dominican priest who described the complaints of Catholic Poles about the failure of the pope to protest their sufferings at the hands of the Nazis.[9] The second was from Archbishop Adam Stefan Sapieha of Cracow, the most important prelate in the country in the enforced absence of Cardinal August Hlond, archbishop of Gniezno and primate of Poland. On February 28, 1942, Sapieha wrote to Pius XII about the dreadful Nazi persecutions of Catholics—the concentration camps from which few returned, the typhus epidemics, the scarcity of provisions. He did not mention the Jews.[10] As will be seen below, Scavizzi, the message bearer, later reported anti-Jewish atrocities. Those later reports, however, originated with him, not with the Polish hierarchy.

Historians have often pointed out that Pius XII remained almost as silent about the sufferings of Catholic Poles as about the Jews.[11] One might perhaps infer from this that both silences were motivated by diplomatic and political considerations rather than by anti-Semitism or indifference—factors which could only have affected the Jews. Other historians have attempted to defend the pope against charges of silence regarding both Catholics and Jews in Poland.[12] While the complex subject of the papal silence will be treated in more detail in the conclusion, one aspect of the question, at least, deserves mention here. Pius XII had good reason to fear that a condemnation of the Nazi persecutions of Catholic Poles would make matters worse for them while changing nothing. The Nazis would probably have intensified their persecutions of Catholics in response to a protest, and the entire population could not have gone into hiding. The pope's decision to remain silent was a difficult judgment call with which some, though certainly not all, Polish Catholics agreed.

With regard to the Jews, the situation was different. As will be discussed, some categories of Jews might have been subjected to deportations and death sooner if the pope had protested. For them, things could also have been worse. But at the same time, a public papal condemnation would have warned other Jews to hide and convinced more Christians to open their doors to them, or at least refrain from turning them in. For the Jews, a papal protest would have made a difference, and should have been issued.

Large massacres of Jewish men, women, and children did not begin until the Germans invaded the Soviet Union in June 1941. The Vatican had no diplomatic representative in that country, and Roman Catholic priests and laymen on the scene were few. Information about the massacres leaked out slowly. In October, however, Monsignor Giuseppe Burzio, the Vatican chargé d'affaires in Bratislava, informed Secretary of State Cardinal Luigi

Maglione that the Germans were systematically shooting Jewish men, women, and children in occupied Soviet territory. Burzio had learned the news from a Slovakian bishop, who had heard it from his military chaplains on the eastern front.[13] Catholic German soldiers disturbed by the atrocities they witnessed were also a source of information. A military officer named Dr. Alfons Hildenbrand, for example, returned from his unit stationed near Minsk to tell Cardinal Michael von Faulhaber, the archbishop of Munich, about the massacres he had seen.[14]

Also in the autumn of 1941, information about the recent murders by Croatian Fascists of thousands of Jews and hundreds of thousands of Serbs in Italian- and German-occupied Croatia began to trickle into Rome. In September, for example, Italian authorities in Dalmatia unearthed appalling evidence of murder at two abandoned camps for Jews on the island of Pago, and sent reports of their inquest to Catholic prelates, among others.[15] Less official reports originated with Italian soldiers who had also seen the evidence. But none of this was yet perceived as systematic Nazi genocide.

Some 6,000 Jews from Vienna, Prague, Moravska Ostrava, and Stettin were deported into the Polish General Government at the end of 1939 and the beginning of 1940.[16] After a pause of several months, deportations from Germany and Austria resumed in early 1941 and became regular and systematic in October. The Vatican was fully informed of these developments. As early as January 20, 1941, for example, Cardinal Archbishop Theodor Innitzer in Vienna wrote directly to Pius XII, describing the dangers threatening Vienna's 60,000 Jews and begging for help at least for the 11,000 of them who were Catholics. He repeated the request on February 4.[17]

Jews deported in 1941 were not yet being systematically murdered. Most were sent to urban ghettos especially in Lodz, Riga, Kaunas, and Minsk, where conditions were grim, especially for the youngest and the oldest among them. The Jesuit Father Pietro Tacchi Venturi, however, had few illusions about their ultimate fate. As seen in Chapter Five, he wrote to Vatican Secretary of State Maglione as early as December 17, 1941, about two elderly Jewish women who were "on the point of being sent from Vienna to die in a concentration camp in Poland."[18] In another report to Maglione on January 20, 1942, Tacchi Venturi referred to "horrible deportation."[19] Five days later an official at the Secretariat of State noted that Jews from the Protectorate of Bohemia and Moravia were also being moved to Poland, adding that shortages of food, lodging, and work made "the transfer rather dangerous for life."[20]

Vatican officials had good reason to be apprehensive. On January 30, 1942, the ninth anniversary of his appointment as chancellor, Hitler delivered a radio harangue against the Jews. According to the British minister to the Holy See, Sir d'Arcy Osborne, the speech was reported the next day in the Roman newspaper *Il Messaggero*. It included Hitler's declaration, "The Jews will be liquidated for at least a thousand years!" Also according to Osborne, who was confined in the Vatican City during the war and met frequently with Vatican officials, Secretary of State Maglione saw it.[21] Few at that time took Hitler literally, of course, but the words were ominous.

The 89,000 Jews in Slovakia were the first to be deported to Poland from outside the German Reich and the Protectorate of Bohemia and Moravia. When that action began in March 1942, the Vatican was immediately informed. Like Croatia, Slovakia was a predominantly Catholic country. Even more embarrassing to the Holy See, Slovakia's president, Josef Tiso, was a Catholic priest, as were many members of the Parliament and of the Hlinka Slovak People's Party. Slovakia was, furthermore, an independent state, allied with but not occupied by Germany. On March 9, Chargé d'Affaires Burzio informed Maglione by telegraph from Bratislava that all Slovakian Jews were about to be deported, regardless of their sex, age, or religious faith. He added, "The deportation of 80,000 people to Poland at the mercy of the Germans is the equivalent of condemning a great part of them to certain death."[22] Like Tacchi Venturi, Burzio had no illusions. The following day, Papal Nuncio Filippo Bernardini in Bern sent Maglione the same information, begging the pope to intervene, "to save, if possible, so many people from atrocious suffering."[23] Bernardini's information came from representatives of international Jewish organizations in Switzerland. Three days later Papal Nuncio Angelo Rotta in Budapest forwarded two similar requests for intervention for the Slovakian Jews. One appeal was from the vicar general of Budapest; the other was from the Jewish Community in Bratislava.[24] On March 20, Rotta added an appeal from the chief rabbi of Budapest, who had told him that most deported women and children were destined to die.[25]

On March 19, the day before Rotta's message from the chief rabbi, Papal Nuncio Bernardini forwarded to Maglione a remarkably accurate report from the World Jewish Congress and the Jewish Agency for Palestine.[26] The report described massacres of Jews that had already occurred: some 18,000 mostly foreign Jews expelled from Hungary and shot by Germans in Galicia; 2,000 Jews and non-Jews murdered by the Iron Guard in Bucharest; 170,000 Jews deported from Bucovina to the Russian frontier, of whom more than a quarter had died; 92,000 Jews shot in Bessarabia; and several thousand Jewish families incarcerated in Croatia, of whom many had died. The report described preparations for the deportation of 90,000 Jews in Slovakia, and expressed fear that they too would be killed.[27] In the eyes of Vatican officials, of course, this report was from a biased source. It could, however, have been used as confirmation of the many other reports that were arriving nearly every day.

Secretary of State Maglione first responded to the appeals on March 14, when he informed Slovakian Minister to the Holy See Charles Sidor that he "greatly hoped that the news [of pending deportations] was not true, not being able to accept that in a country inspired by Catholic principles, measures so grave and laden with such painful consequences for so many families could be adopted."[28] On March 24 or 25, at the request of the pope himself in response especially to Rotta's report about women and children destined for death, Maglione contacted Slovakian Minister Sidor again and asked him to intervene with his government to stop such horrors.[29] But the roundups and deportations of Jews had already begun. Burzio so informed Maglione on March 31, in a long letter consigned to Sidor, who was present in Bratislava and about to leave for Rome. Burzio complained that some members of the Church hierarchy in Slovakia had expressed approval of the events. He went on to describe the brutalities that accompanied the arrests, especially in the cases of Jewish women believed to be destined for prostitution.[30] On April 10, Monsignor Domenico Tardini, secretary of the Section for Extraordinary Ecclesiastical Affairs in the Secretariat of State, noted on the letter, "Seen by the Holy Father."[31]

Burzio informed Maglione again on April 9 that deportations were continuing.[32] At about the same time, Sidor was able to confirm much of Burzio's information during a private meeting with Maglione, although he denied reports that Slovakian Jewish women were being forced into prostitution. Maglione again asked the minister to convey a Vatican protest to his government.[33] About a month later, another credible report of the deportations reached the Holy See. This time, Papal Nuncio Rotta in Budapest forwarded a moving letter from a parish priest in Slovakia to Hungarian Jews, describing the brutal manner in which Jews were being treated in his own country and imploring the Hungarians to inform the world.[34]

At the end of June 1942, the roundups and deportations of Jews from Slovakia ceased. About 52,000 men, women, and children had been deported, while some 30,000 remained. Another 7,000, approximately, had escaped into Hungary.[35] There is little truth to the claims of papal apologists that diplomatic interventions of the Holy See saved Slovakians who were Jewish by religion or culture.[36] Of the 30,000 Jews still in the country at the end of June, most enjoyed official exemptions from deportation because they had converted to Christianity before March 14, 1939, were the family members of converts, had married non-Jews before September 10, 1941, or were engaged in professions declared essential to the national economy.[37] They were spared not because of Maglione's interventions but because the Slovakian government respected their usefulness or their Christian status. Catholic prelates, priests, and laypersons who saved some non-exempt Jewish individuals from deportation in the spring of 1942 acted on their own initiative, with little encouragement from their superiors.[38]

In the months that followed, Nazi agents pressed hard for the rescinding of exemptions, with little success. Until the Germans occupied the country and resumed large-scale deportations in August 1944, just a few thousand additional Jews lost their exemptions and were deported. The resistance of the Slovakian government to German demands is explained in part by well-placed bribes and in part by its increased knowledge of the fate of deportees. When Slovakian authorities sometimes appeared to waver in 1943, however, Maglione was again immediately informed, and he made occasional inquiries.[39] Those mild interventions may in some cases have strengthened Slovakian resolve to resist German demands. The potential victims, of course, were by this time largely converts or their family members, or Jews with special privileges.

The Vatican's record in Slovakia is indeed dismal. It had done nothing to protest anti-Jewish legislation in Slovakia before the onset of deportations, except when it affected converts. The pope did not speak out against the early deportations of 52,000 Jews from a predominantly Catholic and independent country. He did not rebuke President Tiso or other priests like him in positions of power. He did little even to influence individual prelates and priests. Indeed, until the spring of 1943, Slovakian bishops' public letters were appallingly inappropriate. On April 26, 1942, for example, at the height of the deportations, the bishops informed the faithful: "The influence of the Jews has been pernicious. In little time they have seized control of almost the entire economic and social life of the country to the damage of our people. Not only economically, but also in the cultural and moral fields, they have damaged our people." [40] The bishops went on to protest against what they called "those measures that violate honestly acquired private property and violently destroy family ties"—a phrase deleted by the government censors from the Catholic newspaper in which the letter was published.[41] But this, in light of the anti-Jewish remarks that preceded it and in the context of the ongoing deportations, was very little.

The pope failed in Slovakia. Furthermore, the failure to act or to issue a public expression of disapproval when deportations first began from a country outside the German Reich made it much more difficult to intervene later, when similar events began in Croatia, France, Belgium, and the Netherlands in the early summer of 1942. As Father John Morley concluded in his fine study of the subject, "Vatican diplomacy [in Slovakia during the war] . . . was content to limit itself to the narrow confines of strictly Catholic interests, and an opportunity for a great moral and humanitarian gesture was lost."[42]

The diplomats and priests who reported the deportations of Jews before the summer of 1942 suspected that many were dying from starvation, disease, and exposure. They did not know that gassings of Polish Jews had begun at Chelmno in December 1941 and continued against Jews from Poland, Slovakia, and the German Reich at Belzec, Sobibor, and Auschwitz the following spring.[43] That most horrible detail was slow in trickling out, but more general information about mass murder was not. The same Abbot Scavizzi, for example, who frequently traveled through Poland with a hospital train and had delivered messages to the Vatican regarding the sufferings of Polish Catholics in November 1941 and February 1942, prepared his own report about the Jews on May 12, 1942. He wrote directly to Pius XII:

> The struggle against the Jews is implacable and constantly intensifying, with deportations and mass executions.
>   The massacre of the Jews in Ukraine is by now nearly complete. In Poland and Germany they want to complete it also, with a system of mass murders.[44]

Confirmation was not long in coming. On July 17, 1942, Apostolic Visitor Giuseppe Ramiro Marcone reported from Zagreb that the Croatian police chief had told him that 2 million Jews had already been exterminated in Germany.[45] Like Scavizzi's, this was information from a reliable source. Papal Nuncio Orsenigo was less certain when he wrote from Berlin on July 28 that all traces of deportees were intentionally hidden, but that rumors of "disastrous trips and even mass slaughter of Jews" were rampant.[46] Less than a month later the rumors were confirmed by an impeccable source when

Prince Otto von Bismarck, grandson of the Iron Chancellor and minister of state at the German Embassy in Rome, met with Marchese Blasco Lanza d'Ajeta, chief of cabinet of Foreign Minister Count Galeazzo Ciano. During the meeting Bismarck confided that the deportation of Jews from Croatia would result in their "dispersion and elimination." [47] As will be explained in the next chapter, it is difficult to believe that Foreign Ministry officials eager for Vatican help in their own efforts to prevent the delivery to the Germans of Jews in Italian-occupied Croatia did not relay this news to the Holy See.

The summer of 1942 witnessed the deportations to Auschwitz of thousands of Jews from France, Belgium, and the Netherlands, and the onset of systematic selections and gassings at the camp. News of the roundups and deportations could not be hidden, but the precise destination and fate of deportees remained unclear. Suspicion, however, was rife. On August 7, for example, Valerio Valeri, papal nuncio in Vichy, informed Maglione that trains were already leaving the unoccupied southern French zone, carrying foreign Jews north to Paris and on to Germany. He added: "The definitive destination . . . is not yet known, it is thought that they will be sent to Poland, the General Government, or the Ukraine. This disposition and the the fact that the sick and the old are also forced to leave, which excludes the idea of making use of them for labor, has given rise to much discontent among the population." [48] Interestingly enough, Valeri also observed: "On several occasions I have not failed to explain, especially to diplomats from South America, that it is not true that the Holy See has enclosed itself in silence in the face of such an inhuman persecution, since many times the Holy Father has made clear allusions in order to condemn it while on the other hand the danger of new rigor and an extension of the draconian measures in other parts of Europe, as for example in Italy and Hungary, could incline him to a prudent waiting and an enlightened reserve." [49] While ponderous, the language is no less startling. Valeri suspected that people were being deported to their deaths, yet he was willing to fabricate papal responses and point out reasons for "prudent waiting." His mentality, as well as his writing style, was typical of his colleagues in Rome.

Reports from France and other countries continued. On August 31, for example, the vicar general of Fribourg, Switzerland, reported to Papal Nuncio Bernardini in Bern that 20,000 foreign Jews had been delivered from unoccupied southern France to the Germans in the north. While the number was closer to 10,000, the fact of the delivery was correct. The vicar had learned of these events from Swiss charity workers present at the scene. He asked

Bernardini to plead with the pope to intervene with governments in Portugal and North and South America to accept 3,000 to 5,000 children under sixteen who had been left behind, separated from their parents whom, "without a shadow of a doubt, they will never see again."[50] The vicar stressed that the children were still in danger, and that it was crucial to act quickly. Bernardini forwarded the report to the Holy See the next day. Maglione did not even request verification from his nuncio in France until more than two weeks later, and did not acknowledge receipt of Bernardini's message until September 23.[51] He ultimately did little for the children.[52]

During the month of September 1942, the fate of Jews in deportation became even clearer. On September 18, Monsignor Giovanni Battista Montini, secretary of the Section for Ordinary Ecclesiastical Affairs in the Vatican Secretariat of State, wrote that he had met with a Count Malvezzi, a businessman with the Istituto per la Ricostruzione Industriale (IRI), a governmental industrial holding company. Malvezzi had just returned from Poland. Of the meeting, Montini wrote, "In these last weeks there are two grave facts to note: the bombings of Polish cities by the Russians and the systematic massacres of the Jews. . . . The massacres of the Jews have reached fearful and execrable forms and proportions. Incredible slaughter takes place every day; it seems that by the middle of October they want to empty entire ghettos of hundreds of thousands of languishing unfortunates to make room for the Poles, who are being removed from their own homes, where Germans remaining in Germany without roofs because of the war are being transported."[53] Montini expressed no doubt about the veracity of the news.

Nine days later, on September 27, Myron C. Taylor, President Franklin Roosevelt's diplomatic representative to the Holy See, personally delivered an urgent communication to the Vatican. To his brief letter to Maglione, Taylor attached a copy of a memorandum sent to the Geneva Office of the Jewish Agency for Palestine by two individuals described as "reliable eye-witnesses (Aryans), one of whom came [to Geneva] on August 14th from Poland." Among other things, the memorandum stated that the Warsaw ghetto was being "liquidated" and Jews were being killed in special camps, one of which was said to be at Belzec. It declared that "Jews deported from Germany, Belgium, Holland, France, and Slovakia are sent to be butchered, while Aryans deported to the East from Holland and France are genuinely used for work." It added, also, that "during the last few weeks a large part of the Jewish population deported to Lithuania and Lublin has already been executed." In his letter, Taylor asked Maglione if the Vatican had any information to confirm these reports, and any ideas about what should be done.[54]

According to Montini, Pius XII saw Taylor's report the day it arrived. His reaction is not known, but Maglione, who saw it a day or two later, was skeptical. "I don't believe that we have information that confirms . . . this very grave news," he wrote. "Isn't that the case?" But someone in his office noted on September 30, "There is that of Signor Malvezzi." [55] Indeed there was. And there would be more. On October 3, the ambassador to the Holy See from the Polish government in exile reported that Jews were being murdered by the thousands, "by different methods, among others, by asphyxiation in specially adapted centers." One source of his information, he added, was a citizen of an Axis country who had visited that part of the world.[56] Like Malvezzi, this was, in Vatican eyes, a reliable source, but there would be a still better one four days later.

Abbot Pirro Scavizzi, back from another trip through Poland on a hospital train of the Order of the Knights of Malta, delivered a fourth message, his second about the Jews, on October 7, 1942. Scavizzi reported to the Vatican Secretariat of State: "The elimination of the Jews, with mass killings, is almost complete, without regard for children even if they are nursing. . . . Before being deported or killed, they are condemned to forced labor . . . even if they are from the cultivated classes. . . . It is said that over two million Jews have been killed. . . . Poles are allowed to take refuge in the houses of the ghetto, which daily is being depopulated by the systematic killings of the Jews." [57] Scavizzi was a trusted source. His description of Poles being moved into the recently depopulated ghetto was consistent with Malvezzi's report of September 18. His October statistic of 2 million Jews killed echoed the information provided by Apostolic Visitor Marcone in Zagreb on July 17, mentioned above. That statistic, from two distinctly different but reliable sources, seems to have made some impression. In 1963, Father Robert Leiber, the pope's personal secretary, remembered that the figure of 2 million Jewish victims had been spoken of at the Vatican during the war.[58]

Despite the recent reports from Malvezzi, an unnamed citizen of a Nazi country via the Polish government in exile, and Scavizzi, Vatican officials declined Taylor's request for confirmation of reported atrocities. Nine days after the American Chargé d'Affaires Harold Tittmann asked for an answer to Taylor's request, and three days after receiving the Scavizzi report, Maglione replied:

The Secretariat of State has the honor of communicating that news of the severe measures taken against non-Aryans has also arrived at the Holy See from other sources.

It has not yet been possible, however, for the Holy See to check the exactness of such news.

As is known, however, it avails itself of every possibility that is offered to ease the suffering of non-Aryans.[59]

Apparently, help to "non-Aryans" did not include cooperation with efforts to learn what was happening to them.

Still the information flowed in. At the end of October, Helmuth James Graf von Moltke, a driving force of the small anti-Nazi Kreisau Circle in Germany, learned about the gas chambers. He had not seen them but had been told of them by a man recently returned from Poland who provided many details. "Previously I had not believed it but he assured me it was true," Moltke wrote in his diary. "Six thousand people are 'processed' daily in these chambers."[60] Moltke was frequently in contact with Bishop Konrad von Preysing of Berlin, keeping him informed of his resistance activities. It is known that the two men also discussed the persecution of the Jews during at least one meeting.[61] Preysing was in turn a friend of the pope from the latter's days in Germany. It is probable that Moltke shared the secret of the gas chambers with Preysing, and that the bishop passed the information along to Pius XII. In any case, Papal Nuncio Borgongini Duca knew enough by November to ask Italian acting Minister of the Interior Guido Buffarini Guidi a crucial question during a meeting. As the nuncio informed Maglione on November 10, "When I asked him whether, in [Hitler's] allusion to retaliation [against the Jews, in a recent speech in Munich], asphyxiating gas was meant, he twice answered decisively no."[62] The answer was of course wrong, but Buffarini Guidi was clearly suspicious.

By November, talk of the mass murder of Jews was rife among Italian officials, and officials at the Vatican Secretariat of State certainly heard it. On November 4, Foreign Ministry officials sent a report to Mussolini, stating that Carabinieri General Giuseppe Pièche, who had recently traveled throughout the Balkans, had learned that Jews deported from German-occupied parts of Croatia had been " 'eliminated' by means of poison gas in the train in which they were enclosed."[63] Pièche was wrong about the place of death, but right about the means. Two days later industrialist Alberto Pirelli noted that Mussolini had joked about the Jews, declaring that "they are making them emigrate . . . to the other world." [64] About three weeks after that, Count Luca Pietromarchi, head of the Department of Occupied Territories in the Italian Foreign Ministry, noted in his diary that some 6,000 to 7,000 Jews a day had been taken from the Warsaw ghetto and gassed in special trains. He estimated that about a million Jews had been killed. [65]

Pietromarchi's information came partly from Pièche; partly from the Polish government in exile in London, well informed by its agents in Poland; and partly from Italian journalist Curzio Malaparte, who had visited the Warsaw ghetto and spoken about gassings with German military officers. As will be seen in the next chapter, Pietromarchi, a member of the papal nobility, was eager to persuade Vatican officials to intervene to protect Jews in Italian-occupied territories. It is inconceivable that he would not have relayed his information to his friends and contacts at the Holy See.

On November 23, 1942, the American Chargé d'Affaires Harold Tittmann relayed to his superiors in Washington a document identified as a report from Warsaw to the Vatican. The document referred to the immense suffering of Poles and Jews alike. Of the Jews it declared, "Mass execution of Jews continues. At Warsaw, Lwow, Vilno, Lublin, Przemyśl, Przeworsk, Tarnow—the number of Jews killed is numbered by the tens of thousands in the case of each of the towns in question, without mentioning all the others. They are killed by poison gas in chambers especially prepared for that purpose (often in railway cars) and by machine gun fire." [66] The pope and officials at the Secretariat of State had certainly seen this devastating report. The information undoubtedly came from the Polish underground, considered an unreliable source, but again it confirmed the recent reports from Pièche, Pietromarchi, and Malaparte.

British Minister to the Holy See Osborne seems also to have seen the Warsaw document, for an entry in his diary on November 30 referred to reports of Jews gassed in trains. He probably also heard the news from Pietromarchi, for his wording is almost exactly the same as that in Pietromarchi's diary. Osborne's diary entries in December reveal that he spoke to Maglione twice about the extermination of the Jews, and delivered a full report of everything he knew to Tardini. [67] Then in mid-December the ambassador of the Polish government in exile advised the Vatican Secretariat of State of mass murders of Jews in his country, estimating the dead at about 1 million. [68] Some independent confirmation also arrived in December from the eyewitness testimony of the three young Jewish men who had escaped from a work camp near Siedlce, Poland (Chapter 6). They had seen hundreds of brutal casual murders of Jews during the Siedlce roundup in August, and later at work. They had not actually viewed the gas chambers at Treblinka where their families had been sent to die, but they had spoken with a cousin who had escaped from a train waiting outside the camp. The cousin had no doubt about what was going on inside. That the cousin could have grasped the horror is confirmed by the diary entry of an Austrian soldier on a troop train that had also paused at Treblinka. The soldier wrote, "Every day ten or fifteen thousand [Jews] are gassed and burned. Any comment is totally superfluous." [69]

Amid the many reports arriving in the second half of 1942, one unique description should have served as confirmation of all the others. SS Colonel Kurt Gerstein was a religious Protestant who joined the Waffen SS early in the war to investigate rumors of Nazi brutalities, especially the ongoing program of killing the mentally handicapped. In August 1942 he personally witnessed a mass gassing of Jews at Belzec. He first attempted to inform Papal Nuncio Orsenigo in Berlin of the atrocity, but was turned away. He then delivered his report to a Dr. Winter, the coadjutor in Berlin of Bishop von Preysing, the pope's good friend. Gerstein asked that the report be forwarded to the Vatican. Its arrival there has never been denied. [70]

At least two other German Catholic insiders replicated Gerstein's efforts. Both Dr. Hans Globke, an official in the Ministry of the Interior charged with racial matters, and Dr. Josef Müller, an officer in the Abwehr (German Military Intelligence Service), kept German bishops aware of the ongoing murders of the Jews. [71] The bishops presumably relayed the information to Rome. Furthermore, Müller, an anti-Nazi lawyer from Munich who had been involved in a plot to assassinate Hitler in late 1939 and early 1940, traveled frequently to Rome on Abwehr business and met several times with Father Leiber. His last meeting with the German priest and papal secretary was in August or September 1943, when the Abwehr was considering using the Vatican to communicate with the British about Allied responses in the event of Hitler's removal from power. [72] It seems likely that Müller, a fervent Catholic, would also have told Leiber what he knew about the Holocaust at that time.

Reports multiplied throughout 1943. Dino Alfieri, formerly the Italian ambassador to the Holy See and presently the ambassador in Berlin, was a trusted source if there ever was one. On February 3, Alfieri informed Foreign Minister Galeazzo Ciano:

Regarding the fate of [deported German Jews], like that of Polish, Russian, Dutch, and even French Jews, there cannot be much

doubt. . . . Even the SS talk about mass executions. . . . A person
who was there recalled with horror some scenes of executions by
machine guns of nude women and children lined up at the mouth
of a common ditch. Among the tales of torture running the gamut I
will limit myself to one told to my colleague by an SS official, who
confided that he had hurled babies of six months against a wall,
shattering them, to give an example to his men, tired and shaken by
an execution that was particularly horrible because of the number
of victims.[73]

Noted on the document is the fact that Mussolini saw it. Vatican officials certainly learned of it, if not from top bureaucrats at the Foreign Ministry then
from Ciano himself. Just a few days later Ciano was removed as Italian foreign minister and appointed to be Italy's ambassador to the Holy See.

Throughout the next two years the Vatican received many more messages
about the extermination of European Jewry from Italian diplomats, Jewish organizations, and Polish, British, and American representatives to the Holy
See. Many of these will be discussed in the next chapters. It may be more useful here, therefore, to examine only communications from Catholic churchmen, to determine what they believed about the reports they heard and read.
On March 6, 1943, Bishop von Preysing asked the pope to try to save Jews still
in Berlin who were facing imminent deportation that would, he indicated,
lead to certain death.[74] Preysing was certainly believable. On March 7, Vatican
Chargé d'Affaires Burzio in Bratislava forwarded to Maglione a letter from a
parish priest in that city, declaring that Jews who had escaped from Poland
were reporting that Jews were being killed with asphyxiating gas. The parish
priest added that he had been told of the efforts of Slovakian bishops on behalf
of baptized Jews, but he protested, "The non-baptized are also human beings,
and they also want to live."[75] On April 14, Father Pietro Tacchi Venturi, the
Vatican's unofficial liaison with the Italian government, wrote to Maglione
about an intervention he had made to try to save Jews still in Croatia from "deportation, the first step, as is known, toward a not distant, most difficult
death."[76] Then on May 5, an official at the Vatican Secretariat of State prepared
a memo summarizing the situation of Jews in Poland. It said, in part:

In Poland, there were, before the war, about 4,500,000 Jews; it is
calculated now that there remain (including all those who came
there from other countries occupied by the Germans) only
100,000.

In Warsaw a ghetto containing about 650,000 was created: now there are only 20–25,000 Jews there.

Naturally many Jews have gotten away; but *there is no doubt that the majority have been killed.* After months and months of transport of thousands and thousands of people, they have made nothing more known of themselves: something that can only be explained by their deaths. . . .

Special death camps at Lublin (Treblinka) and near Brest Litovsk. It is said that *several hundred at a time are jammed into large rooms, where they die by gassing.*[77]

The author of this report erred about the location of Treblinka, which was northeast of Warsaw. The death camp in Lublin itself was Majdanek, while Belzec and Sobibor were in the Lublin district. The author still knew nothing about Auschwitz. The memorandum itself may have been a summary of a report brought to the Vatican by a third party. What is remarkable about it, however, is that it did not say so. The Vatican official wrote the document as if he believed it, expressing no skepticism or doubt.

Two months later Monsignor Angelo Giuseppe Roncalli, apostolic delegate in Turkey and Greece (and Pope John XXIII from 1958 to 1963), wrote to Montini of a meeting with Franz von Papen, the German ambassador to Turkey from 1939 to 1944. Papen had spoken of the massacre by the Russians in the Katyn Forest near Smolensk early in the war of several thousand Polish officers, whose bodies had recently been found. He had commented that the incident should convince the Poles that cooperation with the Germans was more in their interests than cooperation with the Russians. As Roncalli reported to Montini, "I answered [Papen] with a sad smile that first it would be necessary to make them forget the millions of Jews sent to and executed in Poland."[78] Roncalli, also, seems to have had no doubts about the exterminations.

Vatican officials, then, knew and apparently believed the reports of, as Roncalli said, "millions of Jews . . . executed in Poland." However, they may not have learned the details about a place called Auschwitz until 1944. On April 7 of that year, two young Slovakian Jews, Rudolf Vrba and Alfred Wetzler, escaped from the immense death and labor complex in Upper Silesia. They promptly prepared a thirty-page report on the camp, describing the selection and killing processes in great detail and presenting thorough statistics of those killed. The Auschwitz Protocol, as it is called, reached Switzerland

and the Allied governments in June. There was no longer any doubt about the manner of death. The two escapees gave Chargé d'Affaires Burzio in Bratislava a copy of the Protocol on May 22, begging him to relay it to the Vatican. Burzio did so immediately.[79] It is not clear when it arrived. Editors of the Vatican diplomatic documents claim that it did not reach Rome until October, but it almost certainly arrived much earlier.[80]

When considering what Vatican officials knew about the Holocaust, it is important to remember who is included in the term. A letter written in 1965 by the French Cardinal Eugène Tisserant, the only non-Italian cardinal in the Curia during the war, is instructive in this regard. Tisserant wrote, "It was very difficult during the war to know exactly what was going on. I often regretted that the office of the [Vatican] Secretary of State never thought to keep the cardinals informed by bulletin. I did the best I could by subscribing to two Swiss dailies, the *Basler Nachrichten* and one of two French-language papers, the *Journal de Genève* or the *Gazette de Lausanne*." [81]

The letter points to yet another source of information available to Vatican residents and suggests again that they were not as isolated as commonly supposed. But more important, it indicates that not all cardinals were as informed about the ongoing destruction of European Jews as were the pope, officials at the Secretariat of State, and some papal nuncios. Nor did bishops and priests have a clear picture of events, especially in the provinces. What people knew probably varied from individual to individual, and from place to place. Their information was undoubtedly often hazy, contradictory, based on rumor, and impossible to verify. Our story, however, does not concern the broader spectrum of cardinals, bishops, and priests. Our focus is on the pope, along with his closest advisors and officials at the Secretariat of State who helped him formulate diplomatic policy. Those men knew and believed a great deal about the exterminations, but they did not necessarily share their information.

Even the pope, of course, did not know everything. He and officials at the Secretariat of State did not know and understand in detail the entire chain of events now referred to as the Holocaust or the Shoah. The point here is simply that they had enough information to know that millions of Jewish men, women, and children had been and were continuing to be murdered. Pius XII in fact admitted as much in his traditional address to the Sacred College of Cardinals on his name day, June 2, 1943. As mentioned in the introduction to this book, this was one of only two times during the entire war when the pope publicly referred, however elusively, to the killings of Jews. He spoke of his compassion for "those who have turned an anxiously imploring eye to Us, tormented as they are, for reasons of their nationality or descent [*stirpe*], by major misfortunes and by more acute and grave suffering, and destined sometimes, even without guilt on their part, to exterminatory measures." Pius XII certainly did not act or speak lightly, and he would have been very sure of his facts before speaking in such a way.

It does not matter whether the pope and his highest diplomatic officials understood that the Nazis intended to deport *all* Jews under their control, although by mid-1943 it certainly looked that way. Nor did they need to understand that *all* Jews who arrived at the death camps underwent a selection process, after which the great majority, judged incapable of work, was immediately gassed. It does not matter whether they had heard of Auschwitz, understood the precise manner of death, or had complete and impeccable statistics. Nor is it relevant that they could not personally verify all of the many reports they received. The repetition of the information over an extended period by widely different sources, many of whom were Italian priests or trusted Italian businessmen, constituted adequate confirmation. It does not even matter whether they could imagine, visualize, or emotionally comprehend the full depth of the horror. What matters is that the pope and his diplomatic officials knew enough about the Jewish genocide to believe and understand that it was a disaster of immense, unprecedented proportions. Given what they knew, they should have acted vigorously.

CHAPTER EIGHT

Italian-Occupied Croatia

April 1941–July 1943

ALTHOUGH fears of deportation from Ferramonti in the autumn of 1942, described at the end of Chapter Six, were clearly premature, Jews in Italian-occupied parts of Yugoslavia had good reason to be terrified. In April 1941, the kingdom of Yugoslavia had been defeated and divided among the conquering German, Italian, Hungarian, and Bulgarian armies. The Italians annexed part of Slovenia, including the capital city of Ljubljana, much of the Dalmatian coast between Zara and Split, and additional territory south and east of Fiume (Rijeka). They also occupied Montenegro and Kosovo, while the Germans seized Serbia, with its capital at Belgrade. Croatia, apart from the Dalmatian coast but including much of Bosnia and Herzegovina, remained nominally independent. Its government at Zagreb was headed by the notorious Ante Pavelic, founder of the Fascist Ustasha movement, longtime admirer of Mussolini, and fervent Catholic. While independent, however, Croatia was in fact divided into zones of occupation by the German and Italian armies, which exercised a degree of control that varied somewhat with time and place.[1]

During the terrible summer of 1941, Ustasha assassins roamed freely throughout Croatia, butchering hundreds of thousands of resident Serbs and provoking a brutal civil war. Other victims of the Ustasha's ethnic cleansing were tens of thousands of Jews who were sent to camps in Croatia and either brutally murdered or worked to death during the last five months of 1941. By the end of the first year of occupation, only about 12,000 of Croatia's 35,000

Jews were still alive.[2] The German and Italian occupying forces did little to interfere with the violence.[3] The German army actually added to the horror by executing another several thousand Serbs and Jews in reprisal for partisan attacks. Nor were the Italian forces innocent of the killing of hostages and the harsh repression of Serbian and Slovenian partisans. Jewish civilians, however, were not among their victims.[4]

Even though Croatian authorities in Zagreb were devout Catholics, the Holy See did virtually nothing to diminish the violence and suffering that summer. Pius XII received Pavelic in Rome on May 17. Communications with the new state were formalized in July, as massacres and disorder escalated into chaos. In a step short of establishing full diplomatic relations, the Vatican sent Giuseppe Ramiro Marcone, a Benedictine abbot, to Croatia with the title of apostolic visitor. The new envoy arrived in early August. In his reports to the Secretariat of State, later published in the *Actes et Documents du Saint Siège,* he did not mention Jews until August 23. In that message he made no reference to massacres but focused on policies toward Jews who were requesting conversion in the hope of escaping persecution.[5] Other published reports from Marcone in 1941 and early 1942 reveal a similar concern almost exclusively for Jews who had become Catholics.[6]

Despite Marcone's silence, Vatican officials were informed of the sufferings of Jews in Croatia. On August 21, 1941, Lionello Alatri, a spokesman for the Union of Italian Jewish Communities, sent a desperate appeal to Vatican Secretary of State Cardinal Luigi Maglione. Alatri did not mention the ongoing murders, but he described appalling conditions in the camps where thousands of Croatian Jews had been sent. He described men forced to work in salt mines in Bosnia and 6,000 women, children, and elderly people living in the open, without a roof over their heads and with insufficient food, water, and medicine. He emphasized that many of the Jewish prisoners were Catholics. Since many of the camps were in Italian-occupied zones, Alatri begged Maglione to intervene with both the Croatian and Italian governments to improve conditions.[7] There is no evidence that Maglione did so. His only known response occurred on September 3, when he instructed his new envoy Marcone, "When the occasion arises, you should try to recommend moderation with regard to the treatment of Jews residing in Croatian territory, confidentially and always in a way so that an official character cannot be attributed to your steps."[8]

This response is inadequate and puzzling. Maglione requested only a personal and confidential recommendation for moderation from Marcone.

The recommendation was to entail no publicity and no "official character"—no Vatican backing. What was Maglione afraid of here? Marcone would have intervened with the Croatian authorities, not the Germans. In response to an appeal from the apostolic visitor, those authorities would hardly have taken reprisals on their own Catholic citizenry or argued that the Vatican was violating its neutrality. Also, it is hard to argue that a Vatican intervention in Croatia would have made no difference, or that it would only have made things worse. That argument was made after the war to justify the papal silence with regard to the Germans, but it did not apply to the Croatians. The Ustasha fanatics who were tormenting Jews and Serbs were practicing Catholics. Some of them might have been beyond the reach of moderating influences at the time, but not all. The Church leadership in Rome should at least have tried.

When Maglione made this request on September 3, 1941, he had learned from Alatri about the massive arrests, imprisonment, and suffering of Jewish men, women, and children in Croatia. He may not yet have known about massacres, but he received that gruesome news within the month. Not many outsiders observed the atrocities as they were being committed, but Italian soldiers in the area soon uncovered evidence of them. When the Italian army took over two Croatian camps for Jews on the island of Pago in September 1941, for example, they unearthed the bodies of 407 men, 293 women, and 91 children, many killed by knives and hatchets. Some victims had been buried alive, while many women had been raped. The results of a careful military investigation were sent to Italian bureaucrats, army officers, the king, and prelates of the Church.[9] They surely reached Maglione and the pope. But there is no evidence of another Vatican inquiry or appeal on behalf of Jews in Italian-occupied Croatia until the late summer of 1942.

Nearly all of Croatia's prewar Jewish population originally lived in the area occupied by the Germans in 1941. The largest Jewish Communities were in Zagreb, with roughly 12,000 members, and Sarajevo, with 8,000. Only about 800 or 900 Jews lived in areas annexed or occupied by the Italians.[10] To escape destruction during the first year of the war, however, thousands of Croatian Jewish survivors tried to flee to Italian-annexed areas in Slovenia, the enlarged province of Fiume, or the Dalmatian coast, all firmly in the hands of Italian troops rumored to be well disposed to them. Unfortunately, the rumors were not always true. Because refugees needed visas to enter Italian-annexed territory, at least half of the Jews who reached the border of the province of Fiume were turned back.[11] Some were even delivered to the Croatians, with results that can be easily imagined. Most of the other half entered illegally and remained without papers, subject to instant expulsion. Meanwhile, still other Jews simply moved into areas of Croatia under some Italian influence, where they were even less secure than their brethren in the annexed areas.

In May 1942 the Croatian authorities, apparently losing interest in doing their own killing, agreed to deliver the roughly 12,000 Jewish survivors to the Germans for deportation. An embarrassing dilemma then arose, for several thousand of the potential victims had moved into areas occupied by the Italians, who were growing more reluctant to release them. For several months Croatian and German officials tried to get at the Jews through Italian army officers on the scene. When that failed, Prince Otto von Bismarck, minister of state at the German Embassy in Rome, was sent to the Italian Foreign Ministry. In a meeting on August 18 with Marchese Blasco Lanza d'Ajeta, the chief of cabinet of Foreign Minister Count Galeazzo Ciano, Bismarck asked that the Italian army be ordered to deliver the Jews in its zones of occupation to the Croatians and Germans, "for a transfer in mass . . . to territories in the East." Probably because of his own personal distaste for what he knew was happening in the East, Bismarck then confided that the transfer would result in the "dispersion and elimination" of the Jews in question.[12]

Three days later, Italian Foreign Ministry officials sent a memorandum to Mussolini, describing Bismarck's request as well as his warning about the consequences. They added that their own inquiries had confirmed that the "liquidation of the Jews in Croatia" was already occurring. Mussolini did not blanch. In a bold hand he wrote across the top of the memorandum, "Nulla osta."[13] He had "no objections" to the deliveries of the Jews. That response was duly conveyed to the Supreme Command of the Armed Forces, but the Duce issued no subsequent directives and no timetable for action. Nothing happened.

Mussolini's vagueness gave those Italian military and diplomatic personnel in Croatia who were increasingly uneasy with the prospect of turning over the Jews the leeway they needed. While their Axis partner fumed, they stalled. The matter was highly complicated, they explained, for most of the Jews in their zone were refugees whose citizenship and residence papers required verification. German Embassy officials in Rome approached Mussolini several times that autumn, hoping to prod him into action. Even SS

Chief Heinrich Himmler, at a meeting with the Duce on October 11, attempted to persuade him to enforce his own decision. The only result was an unexpected order approved by the Duce on October 23, 1942, for the roundup and internment along the Dalmatian coast of all Jews in Italian-occupied Croatia. Those in areas that had been annexed were not involved.

The stated purpose of the internment policy was to facilitate a verification of citizenship. Jews recognized as Croatian subjects, it was implied, would be handed over to the Croatian government.[14] The roughly 4,000 people eventually interned had every reason to be frightened. Some of the Italian diplomatic and military officials directing this scheme, however, were determined to keep the Jews safe under their control indefinitely. These men eventually included Lanza D'Ajeta himself; Count Luca Pietromarchi, head of the Department of Occupied Territories in the Foreign Ministry; Roberto Ducci, responsible, under Pietromarchi, for Croatia; Vittorio Castellani, Foreign Ministry liaison officer with the Italian Second Army in Yugoslavia; General Mario Roatta, commander of that army; Giuseppe Bastianini, governor of Dalmatia; and some others. But even their own junior officers and lower level bureaucrats did not understand what they were doing. They continued to fear that some Jews would ultimately be delivered to the Germans, and occasionally even appealed to their chiefs to prevent it.[15] Mussolini, meanwhile, remained undecided, swaying toward whomever he spoke to last.

The Germans naturally perceived internment as a first step toward deportation. After all, Jews interned by local police at Drancy in France, Malines in Belgium, and Westerbork in the Netherlands had been deported throughout the summer of 1942 by the tens of thousands, with no apparent obstruction. Why should the case be any different in Croatia, where the occupying forces were the Germans' partners and where the Jews were not even Italians? Since Mussolini's agreement to internment seemed to promise that Jews who were Croatian subjects would be delivered to the Croatian authorities, why not move them north to Trieste immediately, from where they could easily be transported to Poland? The Germans made that suggestion on December 9.[16]

Mussolini had indeed declared his willingness to deliver the Jews in Italian-occupied Croatia at the end of August 1942, hesitated in September, and ordered their internment at the end of October. But throughout November, he remained reluctant to order his diplomats and army officers to cooperate with his German ally in this grisly matter. The German suggestion for a transfer to Trieste was ignored. When pressed, the Italians simply replied that they lacked the necessary ships. The Jews interned along the Dalmatian coast were safe for a while longer.[17]

Given the gravity of the moment and Mussolini's obvious uncertainty in the autumn of 1942, there is surprisingly little evidence of Vatican intervention with the Italian government officials on behalf of Jews in Croatia. Officials at the Vatican Secretariat of State were certainly aware of the gravity of the moment. Already in July, Apostolic Visitor Marcone in Zagreb had informed Secretary of State Maglione that Jews throughout Croatia were in imminent danger of deportation. As seen in the previous chapter, he added that the Croatian police chief had told him that 2 million Jews had already been exterminated in Germany.[18] At about the same time, the BBC began to broadcast reports of the mass murders of Jews in the German-occupied areas of the Soviet Union and large-scale evacuations of Polish Jews from ghettos to sinister camps. Officials at the Vatican Secretariat of State may not have listened to the BBC, but British Minister to the Holy See Sir d'Arcy Osborne, who resided in the Vatican City, did. He then made certain that Maglione was aware of the broadcasts.[19] Such information, initially regarded as Allied propaganda, was gradually confirmed not only by many Church sources, as seen in the previous chapter, but by Italian officers and soldiers, journalists, and businessmen returning from the Russian front. Not all reports reached the Vatican, but many did.

Deportation, then, meant probable death, a linkage also established by Prince von Bismarck's comments to Foreign Minister Ciano's chief of cabinet on August 18. Bismarck's comments, of course, were made in confidence, but it is difficult to believe that they did not reach the pope. Vatican officials and diplomats met frequently with their counterparts in the Italian Foreign Ministry throughout the war. In addition, many high-ranking officials at the Foreign Ministry bore noble titles and were practicing Catholics, presumably on good personal terms with the Holy See.[20] Count Luca Pietromarchi, for one, was a member of the papal nobility. These men hoped to prevent the delivery of Jews in Italian-occupied Croatia to the Germans, and they were eager to secure Vatican support for their position. For that purpose they would have kept the Secretariat of State informed, not only of what deportation entailed, but of Mussolini's own uncertainty.

Maglione and his deputies had still other sources of information. On August 14, 1942, a week before Mussolini's first expression of "no objections"

to the delivery of Jews to the Croatians and Germans, the Yugoslavian Legation at the Holy See appealed to them for help. The appeal declared that the
Italian occupying forces along the Dalmatian coast seemed anxious to rid
themselves of the Jews in their charge. It then pointed out that a "great number of Jews [in Croatia] have been exterminated in a most inhumane fashion,"
and asked the Vatican to intervene with Italian authorities. On the document
itself Monsignor Domenico Tardini, secretary of the Section for Extraordinary Affairs in the Secretariat of State, wrote that the papal nuncio to Italy and
the apostolic visitor to Zagreb should be notified. That step was not taken
until twelve days later, on August 26, some five days after Mussolini's expression of no objections.[21] Sixteen days after that, on September 11—nearly
a month after the Yugoslavian Delegation's original appeal for help—
Borgongini Duca reported that he had been assured at national police headquarters that the Jews in Dalmatia would not be sent back to Croatia.[22] The
papal nuncio may not have understood that Italian policies toward the Jews in
Dalmatia had not been finalized, and that such assurances, at that time, were
the highly tenuous products of wishful thinking. He had asked for information at a relatively low level of government bureaucracy. Although he had
demonstrated that the Vatican was informed and watching, he had not made
a formal request or a decisive diplomatic intervention.

On September 4, a week before receiving Borgongini Duca's optimistic
report, Monsignor Tardini wrote a vague aide-mémoire about Dalmatia. He
declared categorically that the Holy See had on several occasions recommended moderation to Italian occupying authorities in that area, but he provided no details, and he never mentioned Jews. He continued, "I believe that,
for the prestige of the Holy See, to establish the truth, to show that we assumed some responsibility, it would be good to prepare a nice note or memorandum . . . to the ambassador of Italy [to the Holy See], recording the facts,
suggesting principles and norms of moderation and alluding especially to arguments of a religious character."[23] Tardini wrote this aide-mémoire at the
very moment when Italian policy was being decided. Furthermore, he had
seen the appeal from the Yugoslavian Legation, informing him that many
Jews in Croatia had already been exterminated. He had probably also been informed of Prince von Bismarck's warning to Foreign Ministry officials on
August 18 of the fate of deported Jews. Yet in his aide-mémoire he revealed
himself to be more concerned about the prestige of the Vatican than about the
issues involved, and he recommended giving discreet suggestions rather

than making a firm intervention. In addition, his reference to "arguments of a religious character" sounds suspiciously as if he were considering a special appeal for converted Jews.

It took a full two months for Tardini's idea to come to fruition. Finally, on November 5, Italian ambassador to the Holy See Raffaele Guariglia contacted Foreign Minister Ciano. Guariglia informed his superior that "the office of the [Vatican] secretary of state has asked me to intervene with Your Excellency for the purposes of avoiding if possible the consignment [to the Germans and Croatians] of [the Jews in Croatia]."[24] This was, at last, a clear and unambiguous diplomatic request, prompted probably by the recent decision to intern Jews along the Dalmatian coast. It was, however, again rather mild and discreet. It conveyed no sense of urgency or emotion. Guariglia delivered his appeal only in writing, not in person, and mentioned no Vatican diplomat by name. The Holy See seemed to have decided to distance itself somewhat from the issue, thus reducing the risk of rejection and loss of face.

As seen, the order for the internment and census of the Jews in Italian-occupied Croatia was issued on October 23, during the interval between Tardini's idea and Guariglia's response. Reports of more possible trouble along the Dalmatian coast soon reached the Vatican from several sources. On November 6, for example, Carlo Morpurgo, secretary of the Jewish Community of Trieste, described to Monsignor Giovanni Battista Montini the internment of at least 1,700 Jewish men, women, and children in a camp at Porto Re (Kraljevica), south of Fiume. Internees were, Morpurgo declared, living in terror of expulsion from the Italian-occupied zone.[25] On November 13, again after a rather long delay, given the circumstances, Vatican Secretary of State Maglione forwarded a copy of Morpurgo's report to Borgongini Duca, asking if he "could possibly do something in favor of these unhappy people."[26] Nearly a month later, on December 7, Borgongini Duca replied that his approach to the police chief had achieved nothing.[27] This was certainly a paltry and desultory effort at the very time when the fate of the internees was being decided.

As it turned out, papal intervention was not necessary to save the Jews in Dalmatia in 1942, although Pius XII and Maglione could hardly have known that at the time. Italian military and diplomatic officials in both Italy and occupied Croatia had been maneuvering since August to see that Mussolini's expression of no objections to the delivery of Jews to the Germans did not become policy.[28] As Nazi pressure intensified, so did their numbers and their efforts. Carabinieri General Giuseppe Pièche, for example, advised Mussolini on November 14 that "the decision to consign the Jews would be the equivalent of condemning them to death and has provoked very unfavorable comments . . . among the troops . . . and among the rest of the [Serbian] Orthodox and Moslem populations who fear that they too will be exposed in future to some similar provision whereas today they stand confident under the shadow of our flag. . . . At this particular moment, perhaps, an act of clemency would, in the opinion of most people, be very opportune." [29] Pièche had not initially opposed the consignment of the Jews. He had, however, recently learned that some 5,500 Jews deported from Zagreb in six trains in August had been killed by poison gas. He apparently thought that they had been asphyxiated in the trains rather than in fixed gas chambers in a death camp, but he clearly believed that they had died. He changed his mind about delivering Jews in the Italian zone to the Germans.[30]

Giuseppe Bastianini, a committed Fascist of long standing and governor of Dalmatia since May 1941, traveled to Rome in mid-November 1942 to express similar objections to the Duce. General Mario Roatta, commander of the Italian Second Army in Yugoslavia, arrived a few days later to explain to Mussolini that a deportation of Jews from Croatia would irritate the local population, agitate the Serb minority, and make Italian control more difficult. Their arguments were ultimately persuasive.

In addition to the purely practical considerations of Pièche, Bastianini, and Roatta, there were several other reasons why many Italian diplomatic and military officials opposed the delivery of Jews to the Croatians and Germans. As Hitler's junior partners they had always been touchy about encroachments on their autonomy, especially when the encroachments sounded like orders and those who delivered them appeared to be overbearing and condescending. As the Italian war effort ground to a halt after massive defeats in North Africa and the Soviet Union in the autumn and early winter of 1942–43, the sensitivity was compounded. Furthermore, by November even the German partner was looking vulnerable. Allied landings in Morocco and Algeria on November 8, 1942, and German defeats at El Alamein in November and Stalingrad in December created growing apprehension about who would win the war. Ever larger numbers of Italians began to question the wisdom of a relationship with the Nazis and to think in terms of their own future accountability.

Finally and perhaps most decisively, many Italian military and diplomatic personnel opposed the delivery of Jews to the Croatians and Germans on sheer humanitarian grounds. They had not always been so magnanimous. Italian officials had, as seen, looked the other way as the Ustasha rounded up Jews and Serbs in the fearful summer of 1941. At the same time, they denied sanctuary in Italian-annexed portions of the former Yugoslavia to terrified Jewish refugees. But then, slowly, information about atrocities began to spread. News of the Ustasha's massacres of Jews and Serbs circulated in the autumn of 1941. BBC broadcasts about the fate of Jews in deportation began in July 1942. The same stories from Italians returning from the Russian front that filtered into the Vatican also reached Italian military officers and diplomats. At the highest levels, Bismarck's confidential warning on August 18, 1942, about the "dispersion and elimination" of deported Jews also made the rounds. Attitudes began to change. General Pièche's change of mind in November, described above, was typical, but later than that of many others.

It is useful to recall that when Italian military and diplomatic personnel first began to obstruct Mussolini's approval of the delivery of Jews in Italian-occupied Croatia to the Nazis in August 1942, the German army was still victorious in North Africa and the Soviet Union. There was not yet talk of defeat and future alibis, but there was much talk of what was compatible with the honor of the Italian army and a civilized nation. Other factors came into play by the late autumn. Injured pride, concern for order in their own territories, and apprehension about a lost war and a future settling of accounts were concepts with which Mussolini could be reached and manipulated. But over it all hovered moral revulsion, as Italian diplomatic and military personnel backed away from complicity in the Holocaust.

The problems involving Jews in Croatia, however, were far from settled at the end of 1942. German military reverses that winter did not discourage Nazi efforts at genocide. On the contrary, those charged with deportations seemed to intensify their activities, perhaps recognizing that time and opportunity were running out. After many less formal appeals by others, German Foreign Minister Joachim von Ribbentrop discussed the "Jewish question" with Mussolini in Rome on February 25, 1943. Although there is no evidence that the German minister made any reference to Jews in Italy itself, he certainly mentioned those in Italian-occupied Croatia and France. The situation in France will be examined in the next chapter, but with regard to Croatia, Mussolini was apparently evasive.[31] Again a period of terrible uncertainty ensued. Again the Duce met a flurry of protest against deportations from his military and diplomatic officers. These included Bastianini, acting secretary at the Ministry of Foreign Affairs since Ciano was removed and Mussolini assumed the portfolio on February 6; General Vittorio Ambrosio, recently promoted to be chief of the General Staff of the Armed Forces; General Roatta, who replaced Ambrosio as chief of the Army General Staff; General Mario Robotti, Roatta's successor as commander of the Second Army in Yugoslavia; and many others. In the face of their objections, Mussolini finally decided against delivering the Jews in Croatia to the Germans.[32]

By this time, rumors of deportations of foreign Jews not only from Croatia but from Italy itself were circulating freely. The arrival of Ribbentrop in the capital further intensified the alarm. But in contrast to its reaction at the end of 1942, the Holy See now chose to become involved. On February 17, a week before Ribbentrop's visit, Vatican Secretary of State Maglione advised Borgongini Duca that he had heard that Polish Jews at Ferramonti were to be delivered to the Germans. Could the papal nuncio investigate the truth of the rumor, and try to avert such a development if it was true?[33] As Jewish refugees in Italy were not being threatened with deportation, that assignment was easy. Borgongini Duca answered promptly and correctly on February 27, after Ribbentrop's visit, that there had been no request for the Ferramonti Jews, "at least for now."[34]

A request from Maglione involving Jews in Italian-occupied Yugoslavia, however, created a more difficult problem for his papal nuncio. Maglione asked Borgongini Duca on February 13 to intervene on behalf of 1,700 Jews believed to be assembled in Split and threatened with expulsion and the "gravest dangers."[35] The latter did not feel secure enough to reply for over a month. On March 21, however, he was finally able to report that he had learned from a top police official that the threat of expulsion was nonexistent.[36]

As the uncertainty continued in March, rumors and requests for intervention continued to reach the Vatican from frantic churchmen and diplomats abroad. The English Catholic cardinal archbishop of Westminster was asked to seek Vatican intervention on behalf of four hundred Czechs in Italy, almost certainly Jews, who were believed to be in danger of deportation. He did so, through the apostolic delegate to Britain, in early March.[37] Rabbi Stephen Wise and the Yugoslavian ambassador to the United States asked Myron C. Taylor, President Franklin D. Roosevelt's diplomatic representative to the Holy See, to request papal intervention for 15,000 Yugoslavian Jews believed to be in Italy and its occupied territories in the Balkans. Taylor obliged, telling the Apostolic Delegate Amleto Giovanni Cicognani in Washington, D.C., that deportation to Poland would mean condemnation to death.

Cicognani passed the request along to his superiors on March 6.[38] Then on March 20 the British Legation at the Holy See asked for help for Polish and Yugoslavian Jews at Ferramonti, believed to be in danger of deportation.[39]

Each appeal to the Vatican eventually received some sort of bureaucratic response. Since no deportations from Italy itself had been planned at that point, answers to the first and third appeals were simple. Regarding the 400 Czechs in Italy, Borgongini Duca was easily able to tell the British inquirers that he had learned from "competent sources" that rumors of their deportation were totally unfounded.[40] Regarding the Polish and Yugoslavian Jews at Ferramonti, the same British inquirers were informed the day after their initial appeal that the Holy See "had already concerned itself fruitfully" with the Jews in question.[41] Monsignor Montini seems to have remained uneasy on the matter, for on April 10 he asked Borgongini Duca to investigate again and to intervene with the appropriate Italian authorities if deportations from Ferramonti seemed imminent.[42] The nuncio repeated on April 13 what he had said several times before—there was no truth in the rumors.[43]

Given the recent uncertainty about the Jews in Italian-occupied Croatia following Mussolini's meeting with Ribbentrop on February 25, the inquiry from the United States on March 7 about the 15,000 Jews in Italy and Yugoslavia proved much more difficult. Maglione noted on March 13 that while he had recorded on January 22 that "Mussolini had suspended measures to send Jews out of Croatia, I now know that the Germans have again insisted upon obtaining from Italy a more resolute attitude toward the Jews." Thus, he continued, he would ask Borgongini Duca or Tacchi Venturi "to intercede yet again."[44]

Secretary of State Maglione contacted the Jesuit Father Pietro Tacchi Venturi, the Vatican's unofficial liaison with Mussolini, four days later. He asked him to "intercede, in the manner that you believe to be most opportune, with the relevant Italian authorities, so that so many [Jews in Croatia] will be spared such a harsh fate [delivery to the Germans]."[45] This was a request for a real face-to-face intervention, not just an inquiry or a polite suggestion. Maglione's choice of the experienced and well-connected Tacchi Venturi was also a reflection of real concern, for the Jesuit had an uncanny ability to gain access where more official papal diplomats could not. Meanwhile, on the same day that he contacted Tacchi Venturi, Maglione sent a typically noncommittal response to Washington. The apostolic delegate there was merely told that "the Holy See, as it has already recently done, continues to concern itself strongly in favor of the Jews mentioned."[46]

Even Tacchi Venturi was not able to secure an answer for Maglione for nearly a month. Finally, on April 14, he had something impressive to report. Maglione had originally asked him, as he put it, to try to save Croatian Jews from "deportation, the first step, as is known, toward a not distant, most difficult death." He had, consequently, met for forty-five minutes on April 13 with acting Minister of Foreign Affairs Giuseppe Bastianini, to discuss what he called the "Jewish question."[47] Tacchi Venturi had justified Maglione's confidence by going straight to the top.

As it turned out, however, Tacchi Venturi's inquiry on April 13, like Borgongini Duca's before him, was not decisive. The decision to protect the Jews interned in Italian-occupied Croatia by moving them all to a single camp close to Italy was approved by Mussolini on March 31.[48] "After all," Bastianini told Tacchi Venturi at their meeting, "we do not want to be butchers." Mussolini had always endorsed separation but not persecution of the Jews, the minister informed his Jesuit interlocutor, adding with a little dig that the Duce's policy was not unlike that of the Church itself. Thus, Bastianini continued, the 4,000 refugee Jews in Dalmatia would be held on an island off the coast that was "extremely civilized, with superb climate, where there is no scarcity of inns of first, second, and third class."[49] That island, just a few miles from the Italian mainland and annexed to the province of Fiume in April 1941, was called Arbe, or Rab. Although its facilities did not meet Bastianini's glowing description, between 2,600 and 3,600 Jews were in fact transferred there between May 20 and July 10.[50] They remained safe until the Italian armistice with the Allies in September.

Careful examination of Vatican interventions with the Italian government on behalf of Jews in Italian-occupied Croatia reveals a gradual increase of involvement and concern. During the summer and autumn of 1941, as Ustasha militia were murdering some 26,000 Jews in nominally independent Croatia, there was no intervention. During the late summer and autumn of 1942, when the issue involved German and Croatian demands for the delivery of Jewish survivors in the Italian-occupied zone, little changed. Until virtually the end of the year, urgent appeals to the Vatican from overseas regarding rumors of possible deliveries received perfunctory bureaucratic attention at best. Vatican documents give no indication of genuine worry. They reveal, rather, a sense that there was plenty of time. Officials at the Vatican Secretariat of State usually asked their diplomats to make inquiries or suggestions. They took no independent initiatives but limited themselves to responding to appeals. Such complacency was clearly inappropriate, for a real danger of deportations existed as early as August 1942, when Mussolini recorded no objections to German requests for deliveries of Jews.

In 1943, however, the tone changed. In at least three cases—Maglione's on March 17, Montini's on March 18, and Tacchi Venturi's on April 14—Vatican diplomats showed real concern. The resulting interventions were never confrontational. There were never any threats of a broad public condemnation of Italian policies toward the Jews. Such threats turned out to be quite unnecessary, for Italian diplomatic and military officials blocked the delivery of Jews to the Germans without Vatican pressure. It is impossible to know what the Secretariat of State might have done had it been otherwise. But the fact that even moderate interventions turned out to be unnecessary does not diminish the fact that the efforts were made. And the efforts themselves, as they finally became more than merely perfunctory, may have helped strengthen the determination and effectiveness of those who were already acting to protect the Jews. The efforts were commendable, but their impact must not be exaggerated or portrayed as decisive.

CHAPTER NINE

Italy and Italian-Occupied France

November 1942–July 1943

W H I L E Italian military and diplomatic personnel were struggling to protect Jews in their Croatian territories at the end of 1942 and the beginning of 1943, their problems were also multiplying elsewhere. Following the Allied landings in North Africa in November 1942 the German army had seized all of unoccupied southern France except for seven departments and two parts of departments in the southeast, east of the Rhône River, plus Corsica. Those areas fell to the Italians. Some 20,000 Jews lived in southeastern France in November, but at least 5,000 others arrived as refugees fled into the Italian zone to escape the Germans to the north and west.[1] Most of those newcomers were foreign Jews, eagerly sought by Vichy French officials to satisfy German demands for deportees while sparing French-born Jewish adults. In part for humanitarian reasons and in part from a desire to assert their own authority, Italian military commanders refused to allow Vichy police to arrest Jews in their zone of occupation. They informed French officials of the proscription in early December, and subsequently repeated it several times. The French necessarily backed down. The Germans were understandably furious.[2]

As in Croatia, German diplomats intervened with Mussolini in Rome. During his meeting with the Duce on February 25, Foreign Minister Joachim von Ribbentrop complained about numerous cases in which the Italian army had protected Jews from arrest by Vichy French police.[3] Mussolini replied that these were incidents staged by the French to divide the Italians from their German partner. Obeying Ribbentrop's instructions after that interview, German Ambassador Hans-Georg von Mackensen met with Mussolini on the evening of March 17 to demand the immediate release of Jews in Italian-occupied France to Vichy and German police. According to Mackensen, the ever-compliant Duce told him everything he wanted to hear. In a telegram to Berlin on March 18, 1943, the delighted ambassador confidently reported that Mussolini had said, "This is a question with which the [Italian] Generals must not meddle. Their attitude is the result not only of lack of understanding, but also of sentimental humanitarianism, which is not in accord with our harsh epoch. The necessary instructions will therefore be issued this very day to General Ambrosio, giving a completely free hand to the French police in this matter." [4]

But if Mussolini really meant what he said to Mackensen, he changed his mind two days later. At 11:30 on the morning of March 19 the Duce attended a regularly scheduled meeting with acting Foreign Minister Bastianini and Chief of the General Staff of the Armed Forces (since February) General Vittorio Ambrosio. According to Bastianini and Foreign Ministry official Luca Pietromarchi, he informed them at that time of his latest decision. Both men were dismayed, and Bastianini tried to dissuade him. Pietromarchi later noted that Bastianini informed Mussolini that deported Jews, including old women and babies, were being indiscriminately gassed. Did Mussolini really want to associate himself with that? Visibly shaken, the Duce reversed himself. It was agreed that the French police would not be given a free hand in the matter, as Mussolini had promised Mackensen. Instead, to create the impression of a change, authority over the Jews in Italian-occupied France would be transferred from the Italian army to the Italian police. [5]

As Bastianini intended when he informed Mackensen of the new policy after his meeting with Mussolini, the Germans were not entirely displeased. The short-term implications seemed clear enough to them. Since Italian Foreign Ministry and military officials had been too lenient toward the Jews in Italian-occupied France, just as they were in Croatia, the police and the notoriously more anti-Jewish Ministry of the Interior would simply bypass them. Bastianini also assured Mackensen that foreign Jews in the Italian zone would be immediately interned. [6] But his long-term intentions remained murky.

On the evening of March 19, Mussolini summoned Guido Lospinoso, a fifty-eight-year-old police inspector from Bari, to his office. According to Lospinoso's later account, the Duce ordered him to go immediately to Nice to arrange the transfer of thousands of Jewish refugees in Italian-occupied

France from the coast to internment areas at least one hundred kilometers inland. He was to complete the assignment by the end of the month—an obvious impossibility. The following day, Lospinoso arrived in Nice and began his work with the Italian police, independent of the occupying army.[7] But the transfer of authority over the Jews from the army to the police changed nothing. Some 4,000 to 5,000 foreign Jews were eventually consigned to supervised residences in the interior—a condition far more benign than internment—but an equal number remained free to live as they liked or could manage along the Côte d'Azur.[8] Lospinoso, meanwhile, managed to evade most meetings with the Germans that could lead to direct demands. Mussolini's fall and his replacement as head of government by Marshal Pietro Badoglio on July 25, 1943, simply provided Lospinoso with another excuse to stall. On August 18 he carefully explained to the Germans that he had to return to Rome for new instructions. Until the Italian army withdrew from France after the armistice, not a single Jew was deported from its zone of occupation.

It seems to have been a close call, but Mussolini was ultimately not prepared to permit in France in mid-March the same kind of deportations that he had decided against in Croatia earlier that same month. If the Germans were deceived about the Duce's intentions, however, so too were other concerned observers. Thus, on March 18, Monsignor Giovanni Battista Montini instructed Monsignor Francesco Borgongini Duca to act that very evening to seek an audience at the Italian Foreign Ministry for the following morning. The papal nuncio was to ask Bastianini to intervene for the Jews in Italian-occupied France, to save them from delivery to the French and Germans.[9] Somehow, Montini had learned of Mussolini's concession to Mackensen on the 17th. Borgongini Duca did as he was told. According to Bastianini, the two men met early on the morning of March 19, just be-fore Bastianini's previously scheduled meeting with Mussolini at 11:30. Borgongini Duca informed Bastianini of Mussolini's meeting with Mackensen on the evening of March 17, and of Mussolini's agreement to give the Vichy police in Italian-occupied France a free hand against the Jews there. Bastianini knew nothing of the matter, and was astounded that Vatican officials had heard the news before he did. He assured Borgongini Duca that he would oppose such a measure.

The two men met again later that day, soon after Bastianini's meetings with Mussolini and then with Mackensen. At their second encounter Bastianini informed the papal nuncio that the Duce had changed his mind again, and that Italian police would merely transfer Jewish refugees in Italian-occupied France to supervised residence away from the coast.[10] The vastly relieved Borgongini Duca immediately passed the news along to Montini.[11]

Montini and Borgongini Duca's activity on March 18 and 19 constituted a real Vatican intervention—high-level, personal, timely, and more urgent than anything exhibited so far. It had the purpose not of questioning or suggesting but of pressing firmly for a particular policy. It represented, also, a direct initiative, not a perfunctory bureaucratic response to an appeal from abroad. It is, however, difficult to assess the impact of the intervention. Italian diplomatic and military officials certainly had their own reasons to oppose the delivery of Jews in Italian-occupied territories to the Germans for deportation, and did not need a nudge from the pope. Furthermore, some historians suggest that Mussolini himself never intended the delivery, but lied to Mackensen from the beginning.[12] According to this view, Bastianini and Pietromarchi exaggerated their own input in his ultimate decision to save the Jews, at least for a time.

The Vatican intervention is nevertheless laudable. If Mussolini had indeed intended to give the Vichy police a free hand concerning Jews in Italian-occupied France, as he told Mackensen, the knowledge that Vatican officials were watching and concerned might have been an element in his change of mind. If he had been lying to Mackensen all along, the intervention could only have strengthened his resolve. It also served to fortify the determination of Italian Foreign Ministry officials, both that day and in the future, when Mussolini threatened to change his mind yet again. Montini's action in mid-March, then, was probably not decisive, but it was useful. More frequent and more public reminders of papal concern for all Jews, not just for converts, and in all involved countries, not just in Italy, would have been more useful still.

The fate of the Jews in France was discussed again during Father Pietro Tacchi Venturi's interview with Bastianini. It will be recalled that on March 17 Secretary of State Cardinal Luigi Maglione had asked the Jesuit intermediary to intercede for Jews in Italian-occupied Croatia, and that on April 14 Bastianini had assured the latter that they would be interned on an island off the Dalmatian coast. During that same meeting, Bastianini added that foreign Jews in Italian-occupied France would be concentrated in Savoy, the mountainous area along the Swiss and Italian frontiers. Unfortunately, Italy could do nothing for Jews in German-occupied areas. Tacchi Venturi therefore closed his report to Maglione with the statement that he was "grieved that he had not been able to obtain anything for [those] unhappy sons of Abraham."[13] Here at last, in the spring of 1943, were indications not just of bureaucratic punctiliousness but of genuine concern and emotional involvement in the tragedy engulfing the Jewish people.

It is clear that Jews in Italian-occupied areas of Croatia and France came close to deportation in the spring of 1943. Mussolini seems to have acquiesced in their removal only to yield to pressures from his own diplomatic and military personnel. Appeals on behalf of those Jews from the Holy See were not lacking, but neither did they prove decisive under the circumstances. In the third Italian-occupied territory, southern Greece, the Germans were too busy deporting Jews from their own northern zone to demand from the Duce the far fewer Jews elsewhere in the country. Italian diplomatic and military officers nevertheless distinguished themselves in Greece by protecting Jews in the German zone who had some Italian connection and escorting them to temporary safety in the south.[14] Published documents indicate no Vatican intervention with officials in Italian-occupied Greece. It was not necessary.

One area of possible danger remained, however, and that was Italy itself. As was also the case in unoccupied Vichy France until the Germans arrived in November 1942, native Jews were safe from deportation from Italy as long as the country was free from German control. The threat developing for foreign Jews in unoccupied Italy, however, is less clear. Those in internment or supervised residence were under the jurisdiction of the Ministry of the Interior, whose officials were usually far less sympathetic toward Jews than were their counterparts in the Foreign Ministry. Furthermore, foreign Jews in Italy still remained subject to the expulsion decree of September 1938, which had been suspended but never revoked. It could be reactivated at any time. Finally, there was the awful precedent of Vichy France, which delivered some 11,000 foreign Jews from the unoccupied zone to the Germans in northern France between August and November 1942. Some of those sent north had been in internment camps or supervised residences since the summer of 1940. Others had been living freely throughout the southern zone and were arrested precisely in order to be delivered to the Germans. Nearly all the Jews sent north were deported to Auschwitz, most within days of their arrival at Drancy, an internment center outside Paris.

Fears for the foreign Jews in Italy began to circulate as early as September 1942. As seen in an earlier chapter, Father Calliste Lopinot wrote to his superiors in Rome that month, begging for an intervention for the Jews of Ferramonti. There is no evidence of a response, but Vatican intervention was not necessary in 1942. The previous chapter described several later appeals to the Vatican from outsiders on behalf of foreign Jews in Italy in February, March, and April 1943. All elicited polite Vatican inquiries and reassurances. There was, again, no real danger. But gradually, almost imperceptibly, the situation began to change.

In July 1942, at the same time that they were initiating pressure for the release of Jews in Croatia, German officials began to petition the Italian Ministry of the Interior for the extradition of individual German subjects, including Jews, with scarce reference to the offenses allegedly committed. By May 1943 some bureaucrats at the ministry were proposing the extradition, always on an individual basis, of former subjects of all countries controlled by Germany, again including Jews, political offenders, those threatening to military security, and common criminals.[15] Then on June 14 an official Fascist Party resolution in nine parts recommended, in point eight, that "all foreigners who cannot justify their presence in Italy should be repatriated, and, if that is not possible, they should be isolated in spots not used for vacations."[16] News of the resolution was publicized in Italy, and it appeared in *The Times* of London within a few days.[17]

Mussolini's public response was limited to calling for greater vigilance with respect to foreigners in a speech reported in *Popolo d'Italia* on July 5. Privately, however, he seems to have been shifting again to a hard line regarding foreign Jews under Italian control. On July 15, Lospinoso's police superiors in Rome ordered him to comply with a German request for some 1,000 to 1,200 German Jews in Italian-occupied France, in exchange for a handful of Italian Jews recently repatriated from France. Such a direct and unequivocal order could not have been issued without Mussolini's approval, and Lospinoso would not have been able to evade it. The Jews concerned were saved only by Mussolini's fall a few days later.[18]

On July 25, the day Mussolini fell, a secret directive from the cabinet office of the Ministry of the Interior to the Office of Police revealed a new danger for foreign Jews in Italy itself. It declared, "There is an opportunity to transfer 2,000 elements (including forty Communists) now interned in the concentration camp of Ferramonti, possibly to the province of Bolzano, for the purpose of removing them from the possible zone of military operations."[19] The report did not specifically mention Jews, nor did it speak of actual extradition, as opposed to internment at Bolzano on the northern Italian frontier. It made, also, no reference to a specific German demand. But the tenor of the report was ominous. Everyone knew that nearly all the internees at Ferramonti were Jewish. The report included no suggestion of also moving internees from other camps northward and away from future military zones, although Communists were far more numerous elsewhere than at Ferramonti. The report was chilling and the possible consequences terrifying.

Vatican officials seem to have been unaware of the escalating menace to foreign Jews. When Maglione wrote again to Borgongini Duca on the subject of Italy and the Jews on June 13, 1943, the day before the Fascist Party resolution to repatriate foreigners, he demonstrated much less urgency than a few months before. He explained that he had received a notice from the Yugoslavian Legation at the Holy See a full two weeks previously, warning that the Germans had requested delivery of all Yugoslavian Jews in Italy as well as in the Italian-occupied territories and asking if the Vatican would use all its influence with the Italian government to prevent such a development. Almost apologetically, Maglione informed his papal nuncio, "Although Your Excellency has already communicated to this Secretariat of State that the Italian government is opposed to the deportations of the Jews, in order to be able to respond with great security to the Legation, I beg you to inform yourself of the present dispositions of the government relative to the Yugoslavian Jews in general, interned in Italy or in the occupied territories." [20] Maglione had his answer the very next day. The director of political affairs at the Ministry of Foreign Affairs informed Borgongini Duca that nothing had changed—that no Jews would be delivered to the Germans. [21] Yet that same day, the Fascists issued their resolution.

Vatican officials apparently never questioned the contradiction between the reassurances of the Ministry of Foreign Affairs and the Fascist Party resolution. In late June, however, they received three more appeals for Jews in Ferramonti, all prompted by the resolution itself. Those appeals evoked only mild responses. The first two were from British sources. On June 29, the British chargé d'affaires at Cairo relayed to Maglione a message from Grand Rabbi Israel Herzog in Egypt. In typical abbreviated telegram style, it declared, "Have learned with anxiety measures contemplated for deporting refugee Jews at present interned Ferramonti and beg Holy See intervene in order these may remain in Italy under vigilant protection Holy See whom Jews of world consider their historic protector in oppression." [22] Then on July 1, Sir d'Arcy Osborne, the British minister to the Holy See, personally delivered a memorandum. It acknowledged the Vatican's verbal reassurances in March that deportations from Italy were not under consideration, but it expressed fear that Italian authorities might change their minds and begged the Vatican to become involved. [23] Both the British petitioners and their Vatican recipients would have known of the Fascist Party resolution of June 14. Yet the telegram from Cairo received only a perfunctory response on July 1, reading, "Please assure the Grand Rabbi that the Holy See has already involved itself with the relevant authorities so that the Jews interned in Italy will not be deported, and it will continue to do so with every care in the future." [24] Osborne reported to his superiors in London that he was told that the Vatican could not intervene again. To do so, he said he had been told, "would risk doing more harm than good." [25]

The third appeal originated with a letter on June 25 from Rabbi Stephen Wise to Myron C. Taylor, the American diplomatic representative to the Vatican, informing him of the report in *The Times* of London that the Fascist Party had resolved that foreigners in Italy should be repatriated. Wise asked Taylor to inform the Holy See. Four days later Taylor duly wrote to Monsignor Amleto Giovanni Cicognani, the Vatican's apostolic delegate in Washington, D.C. [26] Cicognani obviously knew nothing about the resolution that had been so well publicized in Italy, for he told Taylor on July 3 that "I trust that the report from London is false." [27] He promised to relay Taylor's question to Maglione, but he was slow in doing so. Only on July 23 did he contact the Vatican secretary of state, informing him of Wise and Taylor's information and adding that Wise asked the Holy See to intervene. [28] Notes by both Maglione and Monsignor Domenico Tardini, secretary of the Section for Extraordinary Ecclesiastical Affairs, written just after Mussolini's fall on July 25, also claimed ignorance of any Fascist Party resolution and of any recent threats affecting foreign Jews. Maglione added that nothing was likely to happen because of the change of regime. [29] Nevertheless, Cicognani received a telegram on July 26, requesting him to tell Taylor that "the Holy See, whenever it may be necessary, will do everything possible to avoid the enactment of the feared measure." [30]

Vatican officials clearly remained unaware of Mussolini's hardening attitude toward Jews during the last weeks of his regime. If the Duce had remained in power, it is unlikely that they or anyone else would have been able to countermand the orders to Lospinoso to deliver 1,000 to 1,200 German Jews in Italian-occupied France to the Nazis. The Jews in Ferramonti were probably a little safer because the government had not yet actually decided to move them north but was merely considering it. But the situation was becoming increasingly dangerous for foreign Jews under Italian control, and Vatican officials seemed not to realize it.

Pius XII, Maglione, Montini, and Tardini acquired more knowledge of the destruction of European Jewry with each month that passed. Atrocities that may have seemed spontaneous in 1941 appeared as part of a master plan by 1943. Even with that knowledge the pope never made a public protest, but, as seen, he did send Tacchi Venturi, Borgongini Duca, and other Vatican envoys to speak privately with Italian diplomats, military officials, and police authorities. It is interesting that Vatican representatives never intervened with the Germans in quite the same way as with the Italians. They made mild private protests to the Germans, polite inquiries through bureaucratic channels, and pleas for individuals, especially for Catholics or for Jews who were Catholics or spouses in mixed marriages. But there was nothing remotely similar to the lecture delivered by Borgongini Duca to Foreign Minister Ciano during a meeting on June 22, 1942. The nuncio literally scolded the Fascist statesman for the Italian army's execution of seven civilian hostages in Slovenia in reprisal for the assassination of an Italian citizen by local Communists. He dared to remind Ciano of his duties and responsibilities, saying, as he reported to Maglione, that "the Italian army claims to be a bearer of civilization, and is accompanied by a large number of chaplains; thus these reprisals can be attributed to the Catholic religion by those who wish us ill, with evident benefit to the propaganda of the Communists and those not in agreement with the Church." [31]

The lecture is the most dramatic incident among many that reveal Vatican perceptions of a special relationship with Italy. Priests, bureaucrats, and other employees at the Vatican, after all, were almost all Italians at that time, and clearly retained special affection for the country of their birth. Most of them passed frequently through the gates of the Vatican City, visiting friends, colleagues, families, and residences in Fascist Italy. What Mussolini did affected them personally in ways that the actions even of other Catholic rulers like Philippe Pétain of France, Monsignor Josef Tiso of Slovakia, or Ante Pavelic of Croatia never could. That special relationship was tacitly acknowledged by those who appealed to the pope for the Jews. Desperate appeals for Jews throughout occupied Europe were arriving regularly by 1943. But appeals on behalf of Jews connected with Italy have a different tone—a subtle assumption that here, at least, the pope had special influence and responsibilities. Here, at least, the Vatican could and should achieve results.

The deportation of Jews from an independent Italy and its occupied territories would have constituted a significant blow to papal prestige. Secretary of State Maglione and Pius XII himself seem to have been slow to grasp that basic fact in 1942, and they did little to involve themselves in Italian policies toward the Jews. As seen, there was little risk of deportations from the peninsula itself or from Italian-occupied France in 1942, but Jews in Italian-occupied Croatia were in great danger by the end of that year. They were spared, but not because of anything the Vatican did for them. By 1943, however, Maglione was fully aware of the danger not only in Croatia but in France. Vatican involvement and concern escalated accordingly, reaching levels not attained elsewhere. Interventions remained private and polite, but they let Mussolini know that the pope was watching. They may also have strengthened the resolve of Italians to continue to oppose deportations. Ultimately, however, they were not decisive. Jews were not deported from Italy or its territories before the German occupation of the country in September 1943, but the credit goes to Italian diplomatic and military personnel who had made their decisions to protect even foreign Jews well before the papal interventions occurred.

CHAPTER TEN

The Forty-Five Days

The Vatican, Badoglio, and the Jews

ON MAY 13, 1943, the German and Italian armies in Tunisia surrendered to the Allies. The war in North Africa was over. The war in Western Europe was about to begin. The Allies landed on the Italian island of Pantelleria on June 11. Lampedusa fell two days later. Then on July 10, British and American forces landed on the southern beaches of Sicily, and the race for Palermo ensued. Combat and devastation would clearly proceed up the Italian peninsula. Equally clearly, Italy had lost the war. In desperation, King Vittorio Emanuele III, with the more or less enthusiastic backing of his army and the Fascist Grand Council, demanded Mussolini's resignation and had him arrested. In a radio broadcast at 10:45 on Sunday evening, July 25, Marshal Pietro Badoglio announced that the king had asked him to head the new government. A regime in place since 1922 crumbled without resistance. Huge crowds cheered in the streets as young men toppled statues of the Duce and stripped buildings of their Fascist trappings. Few noticed, that first night, that Badoglio had added that the war would continue. They would remember in the morning.

For the community of about 33,657 Italian and 6,500 foreign Jews in the country, as well as for several thousand Jews on the island of Arbe off the Dalmatian coast and at least 25,000 in Italian-occupied France, the change of government raised several new questions.[1] Would the Fascist anti-Jewish laws, imposed by Mussolini five years earlier, now be rescinded? What would happen to the several thousand foreign Jews interned or held in supervised residence in Italy itself, deprived of documents and the right to work and barely supported by a small daily government allowance? Would their confinement and maintenance continue? What should be done, especially, about some 2,000 Jews interned in Ferramonti, in a region declared a zone of military operations in June and rapidly being overrun with German combat troops? And most troublesome of all, what was to become of the thousands of Jews in the occupied territories, now that the Italian army seemed to be losing control there? How could they be protected from the French police and Croatian Ustasha who were determined to deliver them to the Germans?

Since Italy remained a fully autonomous partner of the Germans, the problem was not yet one of direct Nazi control over the Jews. Although many must have suspected that Badoglio would negotiate with the Allies for a separate peace, few could foresee that he would obtain it within only forty-five days. Certainly no one dreamed that the armistice would prompt an immediate German seizure of most of the Italian peninsula, driving the king and Badoglio into exile at Brindisi, in Apulia, adjacent to the growing Allied zone. In late July 1943 such complications were still in the future. There seemed to be time to solve problems concerning Jews within Italy itself. In the occupied territories, however, the situation was quite different. The Italian Second Army in Yugoslavia and the Fourth Army in southeastern France were needed to defend the homeland against the Allied invaders. Protection for Jews in the occupied territories required immediate special attention.

For officials at the Vatican Secretariat of State, Jewish issues did not have high priority. An overwhelming question for them was how to prevent Italian Socialists and Communists from profiting from the escalating political disorder. How, more specifically, could the Badoglio government and the war effort be sustained until the Allies could enter Rome and ensure an orderly transition? Equally urgent, how could the Eternal City be protected from destruction by Germans and Allies alike? All other issues were secondary to these two problems. For that and other reasons, including, with regard to occupied France, a colossal lack of imagination and attention, Vatican officials rarely attempted to influence Italian policies toward Jews during the forty-five days of the Badoglio regime.

Italian Jews naturally expected that the fall of Fascism would prompt the immediate revocation of anti-Jewish laws. To their great surprise, that was not to be. Throughout the forty-five days Jewish students and teachers remained barred from public schools, Jewish adults could not resume careers

in the professions or the public sector, property could not be reclaimed, intermarriage continued to be prohibited, and foreign Jews did not regain the
right to work. The disappointment and humiliation were hard to bear. Only
later did Italians understand that the continuation of the laws entailed one
well-disguised benefit. While Badoglio was secretly negotiating for an
armistice with the Allies, he desperately needed to deceive the Germans. The
anti-Jewish measures contributed to the image of Italy as a firmly committed
Axis partner.

Unaware of Badoglio's negotiations with the Allies and expecting the war
to continue for some time, Italian Jews and their supporters attempted to secure a total revocation of the laws. They apparently sought some help from
the Vatican, but their requests were rejected.[2] The refusal should come as no
surprise, for it has been shown that the enforced legal separation of Christians and Jews was a policy not displeasing to the pope and his associates. Jesuit Father Pietro Tacchi Venturi's admission to that effect bears repeating in
this context. In a letter to Vatican Secretary of State Cardinal Luigi Maglione
on August 29, 1943, he explained that he had proposed three precise changes
in the laws to the new Italian minister of the interior. His proposals would
benefit only Jews who converted to Catholicism. He had not, he stressed, "alluded in any way to the total abrogation of laws which, according to the principles and tradition of the Catholic Church, have some dispositions that
should be abrogated but contain others worthy of confirmation."[3]

The problems of converts, however, were of intense concern to the
Church during this period. In his capacity as unofficial liaison between the
Holy See and the Italian authorities, Tacchi Venturi immediately initiated efforts on their behalf. On August 10 he asked Maglione for permission to seek
from the new government virtually the same changes that he had been suggesting to Mussolini since 1939. His three proposals included the designa-
tion of all members of mixed families as "Aryans," and thus their exemption
from all anti-Jewish provisions; the granting of Christian status to all offspring of mixed marriages who had taken preparatory catechism classes before the date specified for conversion in the anti-Jewish laws, but who had not
had time for actual baptism; and the civil registration of all mixed marriages
in which the Jewish partners had in fact converted and which had consequently been sanctioned by the Church since the prohibition in 1938. In his
request to Maglione, Tacchi Venturi added that "couples whose children are
considered illegitimate by the state, and themselves, the parents, are regarded
as living in concubinage, are not few in number."[4] Clearly, the Church had

been ignoring the anti-Jewish laws and conducting mixed marriages despite the state's refusal to recognize them.

Maglione gave Tacchi Venturi permission to present his three proposals to the Ministry of the Interior on August 18, and the latter did so in writing on the 24th.[5] The announcement of the armistice on September 8 and the subsequent German occupation precluded any decision.

For foreign Jews in Italy, also, little changed during the forty-five days. Delasem continued to offer moral and material aid to Jews in need, although it usually excluded converts because of lack of resources. The Church in Italy still offered little organized help specifically to refugees. The only alternatives for converts were parish aid to the indigent in general or government subsidies to foreigners in internment. Subsidies were increased slightly, but recipients still found them inadequate to sustain life.[6]

Bureaucrats at the Ministry of the Interior began discussions in early August regarding the evacuation of internees in the zone of military operations in the south to greater safety in central Italy. Plans were made to enlarge the camp of Farfa Sabina in the province of Rieti and to construct two new internment centers near Siena and Arezzo. In the context of Italy's overwhelming difficulties at the time, such ambitious projects were patently absurd. Consequently, on August 29 the minister of the interior ordered Ferramonti closed and the Jews liberated, "with the exception of special cases."[7] Freed Jews were to be allowed to reside wherever they wished. As communications with Ferramonti had already been disrupted, however, the order was slow in arriving. Acting on his own initiative, the commander of Ferramonti finally opened the gates of the camp on September 5. More than half of the internees chose to leave, to deal on their own with a rapidly changing set of problems. Two days after the announcement of the armistice, most other foreigners interned in Italy were released. With the German army pouring into the country, many had already fled.

In Croatia, as seen, Italian occupying forces had initiated new measures to protect Jews even before Mussolini's fall from power. Between May and July 1943, 2,600 to 3,600 Jews interned along the Dalmatian coast had been transferred to a single camp on the island of Arbe. After Mussolini's dismissal, Foreign Ministry officials repeatedly instructed the Army General Staff that the Jews on Arbe should not be released unless the internees themselves requested it. They also began desperate negotiations with other agencies at home to arrange for the transfer of the Jews to Italy itself. They quickly ran out of time.

At 6:30 P.M. on September 8, 1943, General Dwight David Eisenhower announced the armistice. Badoglio repeated the announcement at 7:45 but left the Italian army without precise instructions. In the resulting confusion, most of the Jews on Arbe were able to go into hiding or join Tito's partisans before the Germans occupied the island. About 200 others secured a boat and escaped to southern Italy, where they hid until the Germans left that region. Another 200, roughly, mostly sick or elderly, chose to remain where they were. When the Germans reached them in March 1944 they were deported to die at Auschwitz. Roughly 275 of those who joined or were protected by the partisans also died before liberation.[8] The rest—between 2,125 and 3,125 men, women, and children—survived. They did so because Italian officials in Dalmatia had moved them to an island close to the Italian mainland, and because, when the army withdrew, Yugoslavian partisans reached them before the Germans did. They were lucky. Given information available at the time, the proper course for ensuring their protection would have been to move them into Italy proper. Many Italian Foreign Ministry officials, with the best of intentions, were trying to do exactly that. Even though Italy was no longer a Fascist state, they were opposed by counterparts at the Ministry of the Interior who wanted no more foreign Jews in the country. There is no evidence that Vatican officials intervened to support the transfer of Jews from Arbe to Italy.

On July 20, 1943, five days before Mussolini's fall, Vatican Secretary of State Maglione received a note from his apostolic delegate in London, forwarding an appeal from A. L. Easterman of the World Jewish Congress.[9] Easterman wished to draw the attention of the Holy See to some 20,000 Italian and refugee Jews "concentrated either in internment camps or otherwise in Northern Italy and notably in the regions of Fiume and Trieste, Milan, Como, Bologna, Modena and Parma." He continued, "Should the Allied invasion of Italy progress, there is every danger that these Jews may either be subject to persecution, like Jews in other Axis-occupied countries, or deported to Eastern Europe, where they may suffer the same fate of extermination as the many hundreds of thousands who have already perished there at the hands of the Nazis."[10] Easterman asked Pius XII to intervene with the appropriate Italian authorities so that Jews could be moved from the north of the country to the south, "where, in the event of an Allied invasion, they may come under the protection of the Allied Forces."

Easterman's appeal differed from those sent to the Vatican a month earlier, for he was pleading for, as he put it, "Nationals as well as Refugees." Mussolini had not yet fallen, and Easterman was rightly afraid that Fascist policy toward all Jews would be radicalized by the approaching conflict. But Mussolini did fall before Vatican officials began to consider the appeal, and the issues changed. Ironically, as seen, Italian bureaucrats not hostile to Jews and indeed eager to protect them then began to consider moving them into central Italy, out of the war zone, rather than south into it. In any case, Easterman must have known that the idea of moving 20,000 people, most of whom were Italian citizens still living securely in their homes, south into the zone of military operations, was impracticable at best. Yet he repeated the request on August 2, in a telegram sent directly to Pius XII.[11]

Easterman was on decidedly firmer ground with the second part of his original appeal, in which he asked that the Vatican intervene for "2,500 Jews who are now concentrated in the Yugoslavian coast areas." He pointed out that in the event of an Italian capitulation to the Allies, the Jews would be "left to the mercy of the Axis-controlled 'Croatian' authorities who are notoriously anti-Semitic," and he suggested that they too might be moved to southern Italy.[12]

Vatican officials did not respond to Easterman's appeals until August 6, nearly three weeks after receiving the first one. They may have thought that the situation of Jews in Italy had improved somewhat under the more favorably disposed Badoglio regime. In addition, they seemed unable to visualize the danger threatening the Jews on Arbe. When their answer finally came, it consisted of a bland message to the apostolic delegate in London, telling him "to communicate . . . to Mr. Easterman . . . that the Holy See will continue to do everything possible in favor of the Jews."[13]

Despite the slow response to Easterman, however, the Vatican Secretariat of State had indeed made an inquiry, for on August 12 Maglione received a special report from an Italian diplomat. The latter assured the secretary of state that there were no camps for Jews in northern Italy, as Easterman had believed, and that Jews in the area had no cause for alarm.[14] This was a simplistic response at best. It totally ducked the issue of Jews still interned on Arbe and ignored any possibility of future complications for those in Italy.

Sixteen days after the announcement of the armistice and the onset of the German occupation of Italy, Easterman again wrote to the apostolic delegate to say that he had learned that the Jews in Dalmatia had been moved to Arbe and recently freed by Yugoslavian partisans. He added, "I feel sure that the efforts of your Grace and of the Holy See have brought about this fortunate result, and I should like to express to the Holy See and yourself the warmest thanks of the World Jewish Congress."[15] Easterman must have known better. The Jews had been moved to Arbe well before his appeal. The appearance of Yugoslavian partisans was fortuitous. He had asked that the same Jews be moved to southern Italy—a step which, as it turned out, would have exposed them to more danger, but which was the logical rescue policy at the time. There is no evidence that the Vatican had done anything at all.

While the Jews in Italy, at least, seemed relatively secure during the forty-five days of the Badoglio regime, their far more numerous coreligionists in southeastern France were increasingly exposed. As it became apparent by the end of July that the Italian occupation forces would have to be withdrawn to fight the Allies in southern Italy, panic began to set in. A few hundred Italian or Italian-connected Jews were admitted to Italy itself, but many more Jewish noncitizens who attempted to flee across the border were rejected. The possibility of being abandoned to the mercies of the Vichy French and the Germans became a certainty on August 15, when Italian and German negotiators agreed that the Italian Fourth Army would withdraw from all of its zone of occupation except for a tiny enclave around Nice. The move was scheduled for completion by September 9, a date naturally unrelated to the still unforeseen armistice. Confronting the frightful consequences for the 25,000 to 30,000 Jews in the zone, some Italian diplomats and military officers began searching for new solutions.[16] As a beginning, they agreed at the end of August that the 4,000 or 5,000 Jewish refugees sent a few months earlier to supervised residences in the mountainous interior should be summoned back to Nice. A Jewish relief agency operating out of Nice hired some sixty trucks to fetch them. The refugees arrived on the morning of September 8. The armistice was announced at 6:30 that evening, and the Germans began to move in. Meanwhile, Jews still living independently along the coast also drifted into what they thought would be a remaining Italian enclave. Few of these thousands of refugees had false papers. The Germans came looking for them within a few hours of their arrival.

Months before these last-ditch efforts to help Jews in Italian-occupied France, however, an Italian Jewish banker and refugee relief organizer from

Modena named Angelo Donati had foreseen trouble and embarked on more ambitious rescue plans. Donati, a liaison officer between the French and Italian armies during the First World War and a founder and director of a Franco-Italian bank afterward, had become involved with German Jewish refugees in Paris in 1933. When the Germans occupied northern France in 1940, he moved to Nice and continued his refugee work there. After the Italians occupied much of southeastern France in November 1942, Donati naturally became involved with them. In December he was the first to inform Italian military officers of attempts by Vichy police to arrest foreign Jews in the Italian zone and deliver them to the Germans. The following March he met and befriended Guido Lospinoso, Mussolini's recently appointed commissioner for Jewish affairs in Italian-occupied France. Lospinoso's orders were vague and his knowledge of Jewish issues in the area, limited. Donati's objective was to ensure that the new commissioner for Jewish affairs would be sympathetic to the Jews.

Whatever the attitudes of Lospinoso and his government, Donati already understood that thousands of Jews could not remain in Italian-occupied France indefinitely, partially surrounded by hostile German forces and totally dependent on Italian protection. In the late spring of 1943, therefore, with Mussolini still in power, he attempted to persuade officials at the Italian Foreign Ministry to accept into their country at least the foreign Jews in the Italian-occupied zone. He received a sympathetic hearing but made little headway.[17] At that point he enlisted the services of his friend Pierre Petuel, otherwise known as Father Marie Benoît, a remarkable Capuchin priest from Bourg-d'Iré (Maine-et-Loire) in France. On his own initiative and responsibility, Father Benoît had become involved in Jewish assistance and rescue in Marseilles at the beginning of the war.

Father Benoît later related that he had known nothing about the problems of Jews in France until June 1940, when a stranger knocked on the door of his monastery in Marseilles to seek help for a young relative. The lad was a Jewish refugee trying to avoid internment by the Vichy authorities. "I was a refugee myself," Benoît explained. As a forty-five-year-old French national he had been obliged to leave a monastery in Rome when France and Italy went to war. "I had no assigned role at Marseilles. I could carve out my own niche."[18] For the next three years he did exactly that. Hundreds of refugees, nearly all of them observant Jews rather than converts, called at the monastery to receive false documents, some food and money, and a guide to Switzerland, to Spain, or to a French family or institution willing to hide them for the duration of the war. Father Benoît met Donati while providing false papers to help move Jews into the Italian zone.

Father Benoît's order called him back to Rome in late June 1943.[19] At Donati's request he immediately sought an audience with Pius XII, which he obtained on July 16. At that audience Father Benoît presented several documents describing the situation of Jews in France, prepared for that purpose with help from leaders of the French Jewish Community.[20] Among other matters, the pope was asked to intervene with Italian authorities to secure the admission into Italy of what Benoît described as 8,000 to 10,000 foreign Jews in supervised residence in Italian-occupied France, whose situation would become "immediately catastrophic" if the Germans were to invade. Two days later, Monsignor Tardini wrote in the margin of the request, "We can say a good word to Italy."[21] But Mussolini fell about a week later, and nothing more was done.

In mid-August, Donati learned that the Italian army would turn over most of its occupation zone in France to the Germans on September 9. With officials at the Ministry of the Interior still blocking his requests to move foreign Jews into Italy, he developed a more ambitious plan. This time he proposed that an estimated 30,000 to 40,000 people be moved temporarily to Italy and then transported in Italian ships funded by the American Jewish Joint Distribution Committee to camps in American- and British-occupied North Africa. A complex series of negotiations ensued. Italian government officials agreed in principle. In an Italy at war with the Allies, however, American and British diplomats who could commit their own governments were not readily available.

Again Father Benoît was helpful. Through his friend Monsignor Hérissé, who had a private apartment at Santa Marta in the Vatican City, the Capuchin priest was able to contact Harold Tittmann and Sir d'Arcy Osborne, respectively the American chargé d'affaires and the British minister to the Holy See.[22] Also through Hérissé, he was able to smuggle Donati into the Vatican City for a meeting with the two diplomats, who also lived at Santa Marta. By the end of August both diplomats had expressed some interest and agreed to the plan.[23] But thorny details remained.

It is not clear whether Father Benoît or Monsignor Hérissé initially informed anyone else at the Vatican about what they were doing. Nor is there evidence that they ever received formal Vatican encouragement or approval of the negotiations. In late August, however, Benoît drafted another memorandum for the Holy See, briefly describing Donati's plan for transferring to

North Africa what he described this time as 50,000 Jews. He did not mention that the negotiations had taken place within the Vatican City and with the co-operation of the British and American diplomatic representatives to the Holy See. He did refer, however, to the "agreement in principle" of the British government. He asked for two types of assistance from the Vatican itself. "Could the Holy See ask its representatives in London and Washington to support and activate this enterprise?" he inquired. And, "Would it be acceptable for me to introduce Mr. Angelo Donati to the Secretariat of State in order to expose and treat the matter in a more direct and concrete manner?"[24] The editors of the Vatican wartime diplomatic documents reported that they found no other references to these requests in the archives.[25] There is no evidence that officials at the Vatican Secretariat of State ever considered Benoît's proposals.

Some days later Father Benoît prepared still another memorandum, probably dictated by Donati. The document, intended for representatives of the American Jewish Joint Distribution Committee in Lisbon, was delivered on September 8 by a colleague of the French Capuchin.[26] Benoît apparently also delivered a copy to Vatican officials, for it appears in the published Vatican documents.[27] Such a step is entirely credible, for it is not likely that a devoted priest like Father Benoît would have wanted to deceive his superiors. This time he and Donati provided even more details about the rescue project. They explained that some 40,000 to 50,000 Jews in southeastern France would fall into German hands in the event of an armistice. They wrote that the British government was considering the matter and advising the American government of it, but that "almost unsurmountable obstacles on a practical order" were foreseen. Funding from the Joint, they added, seemed virtually assured. They named and described, finally, the four Italian ships that were prepared to move refugees, in three shifts of 10,000 at a time, to North Africa.

Officials at the Vatican Secretariat of State, then, were informed of the Donati plan before the armistice rendered it impossible. There is, however, no evidence that they ever took steps to help. Time was, admittedly, very short, and the proposal was innovative and daring—exactly the kind of project that causes conservative bureaucrats to hesitate. But the danger, also, was obvious and overwhelming. Rumors of an armistice were rife by early September, and Vatican officials were, as always, at least as well informed as other Italians. And while the implications of an armistice for Jews in Italy proper may have been uncertain, they were crystal clear for the Jews in Nice. At the very least, Maglione could have instructed his diplomats in Britain and the

United States to speak favorably of the project, as Benoît asked at the end of August.

Interestingly enough, the American Jesuit Father Robert A. Graham, one of the editors of the Vatican wartime diplomatic documents, later wrote that the "project of the four ships was . . . not presented to the Vatican before the armistice—too late for any Vatican intervention." [28] He cited the two reports by Benoît, mentioned above, without explaining the contradiction. Only the second report, however, written on about September 7, actually mentioned and named the four ships, and it is possible that it was not delivered or read before the armistice. Father Graham may have been technically correct—the Vatican may not have been informed specifically about the four ships. But it is impossible to believe that Father Benoît's earlier report, with its more general information about the project and its specific requests for help from the Holy See, was not delivered. Reports of that nature were not misplaced. Father Graham, then, was being misleading. The Secretariat of State was informed of the project and asked for help well before it became "too late for any Vatican intervention."

In something of an overkill, Graham also described Donati's plan as "easily seen as unrealizable in time of war." [29] Are we, then, to believe that it received no Vatican support because it was so preposterous? Yet the four ships offered for the project by the Italian government had been used earlier to transport Italian civilians from East Africa back to Italy, by way of the Cape of Good Hope and the Straits of Gibraltar, with British approval and protection. They were already painted with Red Cross colors, and their crews had received British security clearance. [30] The plan was not unrealizable because of the war, but because of the lack of time and, perhaps, good will. Vatican officials seem to have been, again, highly conservative, unwilling to risk the loss of prestige that failure might have entailed, and much too ready to decide that a difficult project was an impossible one.

Alternatively, Maglione could have urged Italian bureaucrats at the Ministry of the Interior to reverse their policy and allow Jewish refugees from France to enter Italy, as Benoît asked on July 16. Nor was Benoît the only one to ask. On August 20, Apostolic Delegate Amleto Giovanni Cicognani in Washington relayed a similar request from leaders of the World Jewish Congress, begging the pope to intervene "to save Jews residing in countries from which the Italian government is withdrawing its troops." [31] The Jewish leaders specifically suggested that Jews in France and northern Italy be given refuge in central or southern Italy. The idea of moving Jews already in Italy was not practicable, but, given the knowledge of imminent Italian with-drawals from France and with the illusion that Italy would remain unoccu-pied, a transfer of refugees from France to Italy made sense. On August 26, Cicognani was informed, "Please tell [the Jewish leaders] . . . that the Holy See has already involved itself in favor of the Jews mentioned." [32] But there is no evidence that it ever did so.

The Jews assembled in Nice on the eve of the armistice, without false documents and expecting to be transported to North Africa, were caught in one of the most brutal and terrifying roundups of the war in France. SS Cap-tain Alois Brunner entered the city on September 10 with his own team of about fifteen highly trained SS police. Without lists of Jewish names and ad-dresses, they could only identify victims through informers, indiscriminate arrests and body searches, torture, intimidation, and sheer terror. In the days and weeks that followed, some 1,100 Jews were seized in Nice and at least 300 others were caught elsewhere along the Côte d'Azur. [33] Unlike previous roundups conducted by Vichy police with some German help, the Nazis now made no distinction between French and foreign Jews. The victims were sent to Drancy in Paris, from where they were deported to die at Auschwitz. Their numbers might well have been higher, but Brunner's forces were small and unprepared, and French non-Jews, observing the ferocious methods of a German SS unit unassisted by French police, helped hide French and for-eign Jews alike. [34] But the raid's essential failure was small consolation to its victims.

Those lucky enough to escape Brunner's roundup in Nice struggled to find hiding places with French families and institutions. Those still in the countryside did the same, or made their way into Italy. The stories are varied, and hair raising. Some 200 to 250 mostly Polish Jews in supervised resi-dence in Saint-Gervais and Megève in Haute Savoie were too young, old, sick, or weak to make the journey by truck back to Nice as the Italians retreated there. They embarked by train from Chambéry, therefore, on September 7. Their train was diverted to Turin, in Italy, where they learned of the armistice, disembarked, and, for a short time, at least, counted their blessings. [35] Their subsequent travails will be recounted in Chapter Twelve. A few other Jews caught rides to Italy in Italian army trucks. A much larger group, some 800 foreign Jewish men, women, and children in supervised residence in Saint-Martin-Vésubie in Alpes Maritimes, hiked with the retreating army through high mountain passes into Italy. [36] They experienced not only the most arduous escape but the most devastating consequences. As the exhausted refugees staggered into the villages of Valdieri and Entraque, in the province of Cuneo, they learned that the Germans had occupied Italy. On September 18, German posters appeared, ordering all foreigners to report to the occupying authorities, on pain of death for themselves and their protectors. Some 349 people, frightened and without resources, obeyed. They were arrested and imprisoned in an old army barracks at nearby Borgo San Dalmazzo. On November 21, 1943, 328 of them were deported in sealed box cars, first back to Nice, then to Drancy, and finally to Auschwitz. Only ten are known to have survived.[37]

Luckier new arrivals in Italy—probably numbering 1,200 to 1,300—scattered quickly throughout the country. Some found refuge with Italian non-Jews in remote towns and villages in the mountains near the French frontier. Others tried to hide without assistance, in the open or in makeshift cabins useful only until the snow began to fall. Still more tried to make their way south, without money or documents, to Genoa, Turin, Florence, and ultimately Rome. In the chaos following the armistice, with Italian soldiers trying to escape the German occupiers and hundreds of thousands of citizens on the move, they had some success. The 200 who had arrived in Turin by train, for example, managed to get to Rome within five days, where they found Father Benoît and assistance. Many others were able to contact the Jewish assistance organization Delasem or sympathetic non-Jews. Most eventually found shelter, and survived. The dramatic story of those admitted to Catholic convents, monasteries, and schools will be told in the remaining chapters of this book.

CHAPTER ELEVEN

Under the Pope's Very Windows

The Rome Roundup, October 16, 1943

THE ITALIAN armistice with the Allies did not catch the Germans unprepared. With several divisions already in Italy and others massed and ready on the northern frontier, the army swept through the peninsula to occupy most of the country in just a few days. The Allies who landed in Reggio Calabria on September 3 and Taranto and Salerno on the 9th would not reach Rome until June of the following year. On September 12 an SS parachute unit rescued Mussolini from the mountaintop ski resort in the Apennines where he had been confined soon after his removal as head of government on July 25.[1] He was taken to Berlin, from where he announced the reconstitution of the Fascist Party on September 15 and the formation of the collaborationist Italian Social Republic (RSI), headed by himself, a week later. The new puppet regime became known as the Republic of Salò, from a town on Lake Garda around which many government offices clustered.

Accompanying the German army into Italy were SS military units. Some of these promptly conducted the first anti-Jewish atrocities of the occupation. On September 15 in the idyllic resort towns of Meina, Baveno, and Arona around Lago Maggiore, soldiers from the Second Regiment of the SS Panzer Division Leibstandarte Adolf Hitler arrested scores of Jews from some twenty different families. Most of the victims, both citizens and foreigners, had fled to the tranquil lake country to escape Allied bombing raids on northern Italian cities. Fifty-four men, women, children, and elderly people were shot or drowned, some that same day and others on September 22 and 23, after a week's confinement at the Hotel Meina. The bodies of many victims were thrown into the lake. Similar murders occurred in nearby Stresa, Mergozzo, Intra, Pian Nava, and Orta San Giulio.[2] Townspeople may not have witnessed the actual killings, but they certainly knew that Jews in German custody were disappearing.

On September 16, the day after the earliest murders around Lago Maggiore and just eight days after the announcement of the armistice itself, the first deportation train carried twenty-two Jews from Italy to an "unknown destination." The victims were from Merano and Bolzano, near the Brenner Pass leading into Austria. They and thirteen others had been arrested a day or two earlier by German SS police aided by local pro-Nazi volunteers. Just one of them returned from Auschwitz after the war.[3]

Two days later, on September 18, other SS soldiers in northern Italy began to arrest the exhausted foreign Jews who had plodded painfully across the French Alps into the province of Cuneo. As seen, they ultimately seized 349 men, women, and children, of whom at least 328 were deported. Ten of the 328 survived.[4] Ten days after that, in the city of Cuneo, about twenty-four Italian Jews were arrested in their homes. They were eventually released on November 9, thus confusing perceptions of who was actually in danger of deportation and death.[5]

Although few Italians further south knew about the atrocities on the northern frontier in mid-September, it is inconceivable that the pope and officials of the Vatican Secretariat of State were not informed within a day or two of their occurrence. German troops now occupied Rome and surrounded the Vatican City, but they did not seriously disrupt lines of communication between the neutral Holy See and the outside world. As the Italians had done before them, the Germans often interrupted and monitored official Vatican correspondence, conveyed by telegram or diplomatic pouch to and from its representatives abroad, but they did not prohibit it. Nor did they prevent the use of the Vatican pouch by those diplomats from Allied countries accredited to the Holy See who were obliged to remain within the Vatican City. Allied diplomats had left their offices in Rome and moved behind the Vatican walls when their individual countries declared war on Italy, but until the German occupation, they and, more frequently, their families could come and go occasionally with permission from the Italian authorities. During the German occupation they were confined but could still communicate with their governments. Information circulated.[6]

Still more information, especially of a local nature, was conveyed by word of mouth, for contact between individuals on either side of the wall did not end in September 1943. German soldiers guarded the opening between the two wings of Bernini's colonnade and scrutinized the crowds entering the Piazza San Pietro to attend Mass in the Basilica. They searched suspicious-looking characters, but it was not difficult to look innocuous. Once inside the Basilica, outsiders could go no further, but they could easily exchange information with those who lived in the Vatican City. They were inhibited only by the presence of German and Italian spies. Meanwhile, those with business in the Vatican City, such as priests, day-to-day employees, and tradesmen, were questioned by Vatican, not German, guards at the several entrances, and admitted. Members of the Curia and other priests whose offices were in properties of the Holy See outside the walls came and went freely, as did the Vatican policemen themselves. All of these people brought information and occasional fugitives with them. Vatican officials were not isolated.

Italian priests were a constant source of information. As soon as arrests of Jews from France began in the province of Cuneo on September 18, a handful of local clergymen began hiding them. Along with their colleagues from around Lago Maggiore and Bolzano, they reported what they saw and heard to their immediate superiors. Those prelates informed their own superiors in Rome. The war was inching toward the very walls of the Vatican. Jews were clearly to be among its principal victims, and Vatican officials knew it.

After the initial atrocities on the northern frontier, anti-Jewish incidents declined in number for a week or two. On October 5, German police arrested several dozen Jews in the province of Ascoli Piceno, near the Adriatic coast north of Pescara. On the 9th, they attempted a similar roundup in Ancona but failed completely because the local Jews had been warned and had gone into hiding.[7] Also on the 9th, a major roundup of Jews occurred in Trieste.[8] That same day and on the 11th, the prominent Ovazza family—Ettore, his wife Nella, son Riccardo, and daughter Elena—were murdered in Intra and Gressoney, both near the border, as they tried to escape into Switzerland.[9] But apart from Italian government officials and the clergy, who had their own networks of information, the general public knew little of these incidents. About 5,500 Jews fled to safety in Switzerland, and 500 were able to reach the small Allied-occupied zone in the south, but most of the roughly 33,350 Jews who remained stayed uneasily in their homes, awaiting events until early October.[10]

The most terrifying event of the Holocaust in Italy, as it happened, developed in the Eternal City itself. The actual decision to extend the Final Solution into Italy, with all that it entailed regarding a possible German confrontation with the pope, had probably been reached a week or two after the armistice, if not sooner. It was communicated to those responsible for Jewish roundups throughout occupied Europe on September 23.[11] SS Lieutenant Colonel Herbert Kappler, chief of the German security police in Rome, had undoubtedly been informed of the decision even earlier, but he received specific orders from his Berlin office on the 25th. He was to prepare a coordinated surprise action to arrest and deport all Jews in Rome regardless of their nationality, age, and sex. Until the action could take place, Kappler was to avoid incidents that would arouse popular suspicions.[12] Deception was the order of the day.

Kappler acted quickly. On the evening of Sunday, September 26, he summoned to his office in the Villa Wolkonsky two of Italy's most prominent Jewish leaders. Dante Almansi, a former prefect, was president of the nationwide Union of Italian Jewish Communities. Ugo Foà, a retired magistrate, headed the Jewish Community of Rome. Kappler bluntly informed the two men that the Germans considered Jews among their worst enemies and would treat them as such. But, he added, according to Foà, "it is not your lives nor those of your children we will take, if you fulfill our demand. It is your gold we want to provide new arms for our nation. Within thirty-six hours you must bring me fifty kilograms of gold. If you do so, nothing bad will happen to you. If you do not, two hundred of you will be taken and deported to Germany."[13] The extortion of the gold of the Jews of Rome had begun.[14]

Fifty kilograms of gold is the equivalent of about 110 pounds. For a small community, the German demand was daunting. Foà immediately began collecting donations at his office adjacent to the central synagogue, along the Tiber and on the edge of the former Roman ghetto. Word spread slowly, but by the afternoon of the first day a long line of contributors had formed. Some of the most prosperous Jews had already left the city for security and anonymity elsewhere. Remaining to make donations were middle-class Jews and the poor from the former ghetto or Trastevere, along with some sympathetic non-Jewish neighbors. Gifts tended to be small—a ring or two here, a bracelet there. After all, many of these same people had loyally contributed their gold eight years previously, when Mussolini had called for donations to finance the invasion of Ethiopia that began on October 3, 1935. Kappler twice extended his deadline, to forty hours and then to forty-four. By 4:00 P.M. on Tuesday, September 28, fifty kilograms of gold had been conveyed to Gestapo headquarters in the Via Tasso, carefully weighed, and accepted. Believing their security to be bought and paid for, Jews breathed a collective sigh of relief. The great deception continued.

Pius XII's response to the extortion of Jewish gold is subject to some debate. Papal defenders sometimes maintain that the pope was so outraged when he learned of the German demand that he spontaneously offered a gift to the Jewish Community.[15] Some even contend that the contribution was actually made.[16] Ugo Foà, who was nothing if not respectful of the pope, remembered the matter differently: "The Holy See, learning immediately of the fact [of the extortion], spontaneously made it known to the president of the Community [Foà himself] through official channels that if it was not possible to collect all the fifty kilograms of gold within the specified thirty-six hours it would place at his disposition the balance, which could be paid back later without hurry when the Community was in a condition to do so."[17] Foà hastened to add that this "noble gesture of the Vatican" had not been needed. A Vatican official at the time informed Maglione also that a contribution from the Holy See was not necessary.[18]

Pius offered, then, not a gift but a loan, and even that was contingent on the failure of the Jewish Community to collect the gold itself. But there is more, for some reliable first-hand witnesses contend that Foà was being generous when he wrote that the pope's offer was spontaneous. Renzo Levi, a local businessman and Delasem activist, later declared that he and a colleague had actually requested a Vatican loan in the frightening first hours of the gold collection, when contributions were coming in slowly.[19] Whether spontaneous or solicited, the Vatican's willingness to make a loan is commendable, especially because it made Roman Jews feel less abandoned in a time of need. But it should be seen honestly for what it was, and not exaggerated.

Unfortunately, the pope's agreement to make a loan had one disastrous consequence, for it inadvertently contributed to Roman Jews' sense of security in the shadow of the Vatican. The Holy Father seemed to care about them, and he would never permit their arrest and deportation. Although such an implication could hardly have been foreseen, it contributed to the success of the Nazis' deception. The extortion itself had done the same, for the Jews believed Kappler's promises of safety. In reality, the Nazis were interested less in the gold than in deceiving the Jews until they themselves were ready to conduct a roundup. After the war, the entire fifty kilograms were found in the office of Ernst Kaltenbrunner, chief of the Reich Security Main Office (RSHA). The box had never even been opened.[20]

The deception was so successful that it survived the contradictory evidence of the next few days. Early Friday morning, September 29, little more than twelve hours after the delivery of the gold, SS police surrounded the administrative offices of the Jewish Community of Rome. They seized 2 million lire plus archival documents, including lists of the names and addresses of Community contributors. On Thursday, October 14, they returned, this time carting away precious manuscripts, prints, rare books, and medieval documents.[21] The evidence was difficult to decipher. Did the Nazis want cash, precious manuscripts, or the lists? Many Roman Jews still did not read the handwriting on the wall, and they remained in their homes.

Disaster struck early in the morning of the Sabbath, October 16, 1943. In the cold rain of a dreary dawn, German SS security police and military police surrounded the former ghetto of Rome and began knocking on every door. Other agents raced toward apartment buildings throughout the city where Jews were known to reside. They carried lists of names and addresses compiled from the special government census of Jews conducted at the time of the racial laws, updated regularly since then, and possibly supplemented by documents seized at the Jewish Community's offices. Hundreds of terrified men, women, and children, many still in their nightclothes, were soon shivering in the central square of the old ghetto, waiting to be hustled into trucks and driven away. By the time the roundup ended, about 2:00 P.M., 1,259 people had been transported to a temporary detention center in the Italian Military College, in the Palazzo Salviati in the via Lungara, less than half a mile from the Vatican City. Among the prisoners were 896 women and children.[22] Believing the raid to be for labor, they had helped their men and older boys flee to safety over the rooftops. A proper warning would have saved them, too.

At the Military College that same afternoon, the prisoners were screened. About 236 were released, including non-Jews arrested by mistake, Jewish spouses and children from mixed marriages, and Jewish citizens of countries where deportations were not occurring. For the most part, these categories of persons were not being deported from the German Reich. The Nazis initially applied the same standard in Rome. There is no evidence of Vatican intervention in this screening process, but officials of the Secretariat of State tried to get a number of converts released when it was over. They apparently had no success.[23]

About 1,023 people remained after the screening.[24] In the early morning hours of October 18, these unfortunates were driven to the city's Tiburtina Station. There they were crammed into freight cars and transported to Auschwitz. Within a week, all but 149 men and 47 women had been gassed and burned in the camp's crematoria. Of the 196 admitted to the camp, seventeen returned after the war. They included sixteen men and one woman.[25]

During the fearful hours between the roundup on October 16 and the departure of the train for Auschwitz two days later, Italians and Germans alike awaited the pope's response. After all, officials from the Vatican Secretariat of State had, as seen, shown some concern about the threat of deportations of Jews from Italian-occupied Croatia and France. How much more care might they demonstrate about arrests and expulsions from Italy itself? Deportations from the Eternal City would attract criticism from around the world, focus attention on the pope's silence and lack of influence, and constitute a devastating blow to papal prestige.

And yet, through it all, the pope remained silent. Shockingly enough, his advisors, if not he himself, had almost certainly heard rumors that Roman Jews were to be deported several days before the actual roundup. Eitel Friedrich Möllhausen was the representative in Rome of the new German ambassador to Italy, Rudolf Rahn, whose embassy was transferred to the north with the government of the Italian Republic of Salò. Möllhausen learned almost immediately of the orders to Kappler on September 25 to prepare for the arrest of the Jews of Rome."[26] Deeply concerned, both for humanitarian reasons and for fear of a papal condemnation and damage to Germany's public image, Möllhausen tried to convince Kappler and Field Marshal Albert Konrad Kesselring, commander of the German forces in Italy, to prevent deportations. When he failed with them, he sent telegrams to the Foreign Ministry in Berlin on October 6 and 7, describing the orders, expressing his conviction that the Jews were to be "liquidated," and urging that they be engaged in building fortifications instead.[27] On October 9 he received a peculiar answer from his ministry. The Jews of Rome were to be sent to Mauthausen as hostages. He was to leave matters to the SS, and not get involved.[28]

Möllhausen found it difficult to remain uninvolved. He later claimed that within a day or two he passed on the answer he had received from Berlin on October 9 to the office of Baron Ernst von Weizsäcker, German ambassador to the Holy See since July 1943. Like Möllhausen, Weizsäcker feared that Jewish deportations from Rome would damage Germany's image and fuel enemy propaganda. A papal protest would make matters still worse, embarrassing the Germans, further diminishing the possibility of a compromise peace negotiated by the Holy See, and perhaps unleashing the Italian Resistance, public disorder, and even a German invasion of the Vatican City. The ambassador was eager to see that the Jews were privately warned and dispersed before they could be arrested.[29] According to Möllhausen, Weizsäcker's office therefore informed officials at the Vatican Secretariat of State of German plans for a roundup.[30] Those officials certainly notified the pope.

Möllhausen's testimony constitutes a terrible indictment of the Vatican. Neither he nor Weizsäcker nor the Vatican officials whom Weizsäcker informed knew the exact day of the planned roundup, but specific knowledge of Nazi intentions should have been enough. The 1,259 Jews arrested on October 16 were caught in their homes. Many had considered hiding but ruled it out as too dangerous and expensive. They could not believe that the Germans would act against them under the pope's very windows. A quiet private warning from the pope to Jewish Community leaders would have been passed along and believed, and hundreds of lives would have been spared.

In addition to Möllhausen, many other Germans and Italians opposed to the deportation of the Roman Jews knew of plans for a roundup. It is hard to believe that some of them did not inform their priests, who in turn advised Vatican officials. The published Vatican documents reveal that tips on other matters were received. An Italian military intelligence agent, for example, informed his friend in the Vatican Secretariat of State on October 11 that the Germans were planning a large roundup in Rome for the 18th of the month. He did not mention Jews.[31] An Italian priest informed another official at the Vatican Secretariat of State on October 25 of his conversation with a German chaplain, who told the priest of unease in German military circles after the deportation of the Jews from Rome. Some Germans were apparently unhappy with what the Vatican official described as the "absenteeism of the ecclesiastical authorities in that sad affair."[32] The German chaplain promised to keep the Italian priest informed of future SS projects. Both of these documents are symptomatic of the kind of information that Vatican officials must have frequently received.

Vatican officials are not the only individuals to be blamed for not telling the Jews what they knew. Others equally informed could have warned Jewish leaders directly. Möllhausen himself, or one of his assistants, could have done so. After all, the warning that helped save Jews in Denmark came originally from a German, Georg Ferdinand Duckwitz, a shipping expert at the German legation in Copenhagen. Around the end of September 1943, Duckwitz learned of plans for a Jewish roundup scheduled for October 1 and 2. He informed prominent Danish acquaintances, who promptly passed along the information to Jewish leaders and potential rescuers. Danes rallied in defense of Jewish citizens so clearly in danger. All but 474 of Denmark's 8,000 Jews had time to hide or escape to Sweden, and they survived.[33]

Rome's Jewish Community leaders are themselves sometimes criticized for keeping the synagogue open and not advising their people to hide. Even though their knowledge of the danger in Italy was much vaguer than that of German diplomats and police and some Vatican officials, they knew more about deportations from other countries than average Jews. Deceived by Kappler's promises after the gold incident, however, they were reluctant to recommend changing residences, which could cause panic and, because it was illegal, provoke the German police.[34] In addition to the leaders, Jews already in hiding, like Rome's Chief Rabbi Israele Zolli and hundreds of average people, might have made a greater effort to convince their coreligionists of what they suspected.[35] But it may be argued that Pius XII was the most guilty in this respect. His knowledge of the danger was more solid than almost anyone else's, with the exception of the Germans. A warning would not have put his institution at risk, for it could have remained secret. He, above all others except perhaps Möllhausen, would have been believed and would have made the most difference. And he, unlike Möllhausen, was a spiritual leader, dedicated to service toward other human beings.

Why did the pope issue no warning? Did he disbelieve Möllhausen and others? Did he, as he told Princess Pignatelli on October 16, really believe Kappler's promise to the Jews that they would not be harmed if they delivered the fifty kilograms of gold? Ignorant of the exact date of the roundup, did he think that he had plenty of time? As a conservative diplomat anxious to avoid confrontation, was he holding out for still further verification, or discussing an appropriate response while hoping that the problem would go away? Did he think that the Germans would never dare, despite information to the contrary? Or did he simply believe that the deportation of the Jews of Rome was not a matter in which he should become involved?

According to Princess Enza Pignatelli Aragona Cortes, the pope first learned that the roundup was in progress from her. Early on the morning of October 16 she was wakened by a telephone call from a friend who lived near the former Jewish ghetto. The caller told her that the Germans were arresting Jews and driving them away in trucks. The princess, who had been received several times by Pius XII in connection with her charitable work, decided to inform him of the terrible news. Unable to secure other transportation, she called the one acquaintance whose automobile she knew had not been requisitioned. Karl Gustav Wollenweber, a bureaucrat in Weizsäcker's embassy to the Holy See, agreed to drive her to the Vatican. She had no appointment, but she managed to meet with the pope and tell him what she knew. Pius XII expressed surprise, she later claimed, saying that the Germans had promised after the gold incident that they would not touch the Jews of Rome. In her presence, however, he made a telephone call. As Father Robert Graham, the Jesuit historian and archivist who recorded the princess's story, expressed it, "Maglione's protest was now in preparation." [36]

There is no authoritative account of whom the pope called in the princess's presence, nor of what he said. Vatican Secretary of State Cardinal Luigi Maglione, however, recorded that he summoned Ambassador Ernst von Weizsäcker to a meeting that same day. According to Maglione,

I asked him to intervene in favor of those poor people. I spoke to him as best I could in the name of humanity, of Christian charity.

. . . I told him simply: Your Excellency, you who have a tender and good heart, try to save these many innocent people. It is painful for the Holy Father, painful beyond words that here in Rome, under the eyes of the Common Father so many people are made to suffer simply because of their particular descent [stirpe] . . .

The ambassador, after some moments of reflection, asked me: "What would the Holy See do if these things continued?"

I answered: The Holy See would not want to be obliged [essere messa nella necessità] to express its disapproval.

The ambassador observed: For more than four years I have admired the attitude of the Holy See. It has succeeded in guiding the boat between shoals of all types and sizes without collisions and, while it may have had greater faith in the Allies, it has maintained a perfect equilibrium. I ask myself if, now that the boat is about to reach the port, it is appropriate to put everything at risk. I am thinking of the consequences that a step by the Holy See would provoke. . . . The directives come from the highest level . . . "Will Your Eminence leave me free not to report this official conversation?"

I replied that I had begged him to intervene appealing to his sentiments of humanity. I was leaving it to his judgment whether or not to mention our conversation, that had been so friendly. [37]

Maglione's meeting with the German ambassador to the Holy See should be described not as an official diplomatic protest of the roundup but as a desperate plea for Weizsäcker's intervention to save the victims. Only when specifically asked what he would do "if these things continued" did the Vatican secretary of state mention the possibility of a public expression of disapproval. The effect of that imprecise threat was further weakened by Maglione's willingness to leave matters in Weizsäcker's hands—to allow him to refrain from reporting the Vatican's request and the mention of a possible protest.

Why did Maglione act as he did? He seems, in part, to have lost his nerve, frightened by Weizsäcker's allusion to the "consequences that a step by the Holy See would provoke." Pius XII and his officials at the Vatican Secretariat of State did not want a break with Germany, especially at that particularly sensitive time. In addition to their long-standing fear that a papal protest of the Holocaust would endanger or alienate German Catholics, weaken the Reich in its stand against the Soviet Union, and destroy the possibility that the pope might be called upon as a neutral party to negotiate a peace, they had new and more immediate concerns in the autumn of 1943. The Lateran Accords guaranteeing the sovereignty and integrity of the Holy See constituted a bilateral agreement between that state and Italy. It was not clear whether the Germans would respect it. But with or without a treaty the German occupiers of Italy who surrounded the Vatican City could invade it at any time. The Holy See was completely vulnerable and without effective defenses. Rumors were rife that Hitler planned to seize the Vatican City and perhaps even kidnap the pope and take him to Germany. The truth of these rumors is less relevant here than the fact that Vatican officials feared them.[38] So too did the Allied diplomats confined within the Vatican, who had begun to burn their confidential documents even before the Germans entered Rome.[39]

By the time of the October roundup, however, the situation had clarified and the pope's advisors had reason to feel more secure than they had in September. On October 7, German Foreign Minister Ribbentrop officially informed Maglione, by means of Ambassador Weizsäcker, that "the sovereignty and territorial integrity of the Vatican will be respected and . . . the German troops in Rome will behave accordingly."[40] In return, to silence Allied propaganda about Nazi threats against the Vatican, Ribbentrop sought a public Vatican statement that the German occupying forces had behaved correctly with regard to the integrity of the Holy See and had promised to continue to do so. After some internal discussion, a statement to that effect was printed in L'Osservatore Romano on October 30, acknowledging that "German troops have respected the Roman Curia and the Vatican City" and provided assurances about the future.[41] But if Vatican officials felt better after Ribbentrop's promises they could never be completely confident that the Germans would not change their minds. As long as the Germans remained in Rome, disturbing rumors circulated and the men inside the Vatican felt vulnerable.[42] As will be seen in Chapter Fifteen, their fears increased still more when Fascist fanatics accompanied by some Germans invaded Vatican extraterritorial properties in Rome in December 1943 and February 1944.

A second recent cause of Maglione's reluctance to confront the Germans in the autumn of 1943 involved the issue of public order. Like Weizsäcker, but for different reasons, Pius XII worried that a possible papal protest against German policies might play into the hands of the Italian Resistance and spark a popular uprising in Rome. Weizsäcker and those of his colleagues who were sensible hoped to avoid domestic disorder because it would necessitate a diversion of German fighting forces and an unwelcome intensification of violent repression. The pope, on the other hand, feared a popular uprising because it might create a power vacuum in which Communists and Socialists could seize control. He and his advisors preferred that the Germans remain firmly in control until they could ensure an orderly transition of power to the Allies.

Maglione may also have agreed to allow Weizsäcker to refrain from reporting their meeting and the mention of a papal protest to his superiors in Berlin because he feared that the threat of a protest would ensure the very deportations it was designed to prevent. Weizsäcker had indeed said as much at the time, telling his friend Gerhart Gumpert at the German Embassy to Italy that "any protest on the part of the pope would have as a consequence that the deportations would be carried out in a truly complete fashion. I know how our people act in these cases."[43] The Vatican secretary of state was certainly eager to stop the deportations, both for humanitarian reasons and because they would highlight the pope's failure to protest and his weakness even in his own diocese. But equally eager to avoid a protest, he in effect turned the matter over to the German ambassador.

It is not clear exactly what either Weizsäcker or Maglione thought that the former could achieve. The German ambassador was, however, almost certainly involved in the next episode in the diplomatic response to the Rome roundup. In the early evening of October 16, a letter from Bishop Alois Hudal, rector of the German ecclesiastical college at the Church of Santa Maria dell'Anima, near the Piazza Navona, was delivered to General Rainer

Stahel, the German army commander in Rome. The letter, which was immediately forwarded to the Foreign Ministry in Berlin by Weizsäcker's friend and Stahel's new aide, Gumpert, said in part, "A high Vatican source in the immediate entourage of the Holy Father has just reported to me that the arrests of Jews of Italian nationality began this morning. In the interests of the good understanding existing hitherto between the Vatican and the High Command of the German Forces . . . I earnestly request you to order the immediate cessation of these arrests in Rome and its environs. I fear that if this is not done the pope will make a public stand against it, which could not fail to serve anti-German propaganda as a weapon against us." [44]

This was not the full report that Weizsäcker could have made if he had so desired. It did not mention an actual meeting between himself and the Vatican secretary of state. Nor did it declare that Maglione had actually mentioned the possibility of a public protest. It softened the facts and relayed them gently. Furthermore, it did not ask that the arrested Jews be released, but simply that further arrests cease.

Historians speculate that Bishop Hudal may have been prompted to write by Weizsäcker, or by Weizsäcker's aide Albrecht von Kessel with input from Gumpert.[45] Weizsäcker never claimed to have initiated the letter, but Gumpert later declared that he wrote it, and that Kessel then gave it to Hudal to sign.[46] Hudal, known to be sympathetic to National Socialism, which he saw as a last bulwark against Bolshevism, always insisted that he wrote it himself. His claim was not inconsistent with an initiative from Weizsäcker, Kessel, or Gumpert. It is, in any case, highly unlikely that the pope or Maglione initiated the letter, although they may have known about it. Hudal was apparently not a confidante of the pope and had little influence in the Vatican.[47] More to the point, Maglione had agreed to let Weizsäcker act as he thought best. He would not have wanted to disrupt Weizsäcker's plans by acting independently, without his knowledge.[48]

In a move that was part of the original plan, Weizsäcker sent a telegram to the German Foreign Ministry the following day, elaborating on Hudal's letter. He wrote in part:

> I can confirm the reaction of the Vatican to the removal of Jews
> from Rome, as given by Bishop Hudal. . . . The Curia is
> dumbfounded, particularly as the action took place under the very
> windows of the pope, as it were. The reaction could perhaps be
> muffled if the Jews were employed on work in Italy itself.

Circles hostile to us in Rome are turning the action to their own advantage to force the Vatican to drop its reserve. It is being said that in French cities, where similar things happened, the bishops took up a clear position. The pope, as supreme head of the Church and bishop of Rome, could not lag behind them. Comparisons are also being made between Pius XI, a much more impulsive person, and the present pope.[49]

Weizsäcker did not tell his superiors about his own meeting with Maglione. Indeed, he made it look as if his information about the Vatican reaction came from Hudal rather than from the secretary of state. Nor did he mention the actual Vatican reference to a public protest. He did, however, report the pope's concern about roundups in the Eternal City, altering Maglione's phrase "under the eyes of the Common Father" to "under the very windows of the pope." He certainly conveyed the possibility of a protest, with all that it would mean for the German Reich. Several French bishops and archbishops had indeed protested loudly when foreign Jews were delivered from the unoccupied zone to the Germans in Paris for deportation in August 1942. By reminding his superiors of that fact, Weizsäcker strengthened his claim that the pope might speak, beyond even what he may himself have believed. Finally, he suggested a face-saving alternative, as a good bureaucrat should. The Jews need not be released. They could be put to work in Italy.

Weizsäcker's warning was not heeded. The Jews of Rome were deported the following morning. Nor did the pope ever utter a real protest. On October 25–26, after most of the deportees were already dead, an article on the front page of *L'Osservatore Romano* lamented in broad and general terms the sufferings of all innocents in the war.[50] A second article, printed beside the first, spoke of the pope's reaction to that suffering. Its tone, however, was more one of self-justification than indignation. It read in part:

> As is well known, the August Pontiff, after having tried in vain to prevent the outbreak of the war . . . has not for one moment ceased employing all the means in His power to alleviate the sufferings that are, in whatever form, the consequence of this cruel conflagration.
>
> With the growth of so much evil, the universally paternal charity of the Supreme Pontiff has become, one could say, even more active; it does not pause before boundaries of nationality, religion, or descent [stirpe].

> This manifold and incessant activity of Pius XII has been
> greatly intensified recently by the increased sufferings of so many
> unfortunate people.[51]

Neither article used the ugly word "race" (*razza*) or mentioned the recent roundup, Jews, or Germans. The second article did not imply that "increased suffering" meant death. While it declared that the pope had employed "all the means in His power to alleviate the sufferings," it provided no evidence. Nor did it offer proof of any "manifold and incessant activity of Pius XII" on behalf of "so many unfortunate people." Readers were apparently expected to take these claims on faith. Some sensitive readers, however, might have detected a veiled recommendation to succor those in need, without consideration of "boundaries of nationality, religion, or descent." In view of the fact that more than a thousand Roman citizens had just been hauled away, one might wish for more. There was no more.

In an assessment of the second article for his superiors two days later, Ambassador Weizsäcker wrote:

> By all accounts, the pope, although harassed from various quarters,
> has not allowed himself to be stampeded into making any
> demonstrative pronouncement against the removal of the Jews
> from Rome. Although he must count on the likelihood that this
> attitude will be held against him by our opponents and will be
> exploited by Protestant quarters in the Anglo-Saxon countries for
> purposes of anti-Catholic propaganda, he has done everything he
> could, even in this delicate matter, not to injure the relationship
> between the Vatican and the German Government or the German
> authorities in Rome. As there will presumably be no further
> German action to be taken in regard to the Jews here in Rome, this
> question, with its unpleasant possibilities for German-Vatican
> relations, may be considered as liquidated.[52]

Weizsäcker went on to describe the same second article from *L'Osservatore Romano*, which he enclosed. He commented about it, "No objection can be raised to this public statement, the less so as its text . . . will be understood by only very few people as having special reference to the Jewish question."[53] That last sentence was probably wrong, for most Romans reading ten days after the roundup would have understood the word stirpe, meaning descent, lineage, or bloodlines, to be a reference to the Jews. But Weizsäcker was right in declaring that the pope's reaction to the October roundup was indeed mild.

Years later, Vatican historian Father Robert Graham bitterly accused Weizsäcker of deliberately minimizing the extent of the pope's displeasure in his reports to Berlin.[54] Weizsäcker never informed anyone that Maglione had called him to a meeting on the morning of October 16 to plead for his, Weizsäcker's, intervention to save the Jews and to threaten a papal protest "if these things continued." That action of Maglione, in Graham's view, had fully demonstrated the pope's overwhelming concern for the Jews. "Perhaps no other incident has contributed more than this one to the legend of the 'silence' of Pope Pius XII," Graham complained, referring to what he called Weizsäcker's "falsification of the Vatican reaction to the tragic arrest of a thousand Roman Jews on October 16, 1943." He continued, "For years it has been believed, on the word of the ambassador of the Reich, that the pope did not bat an eyelash or make any protest on that occasion."[55]

The charges are unfair to Weizsäcker. As seen, Maglione agreed that the ambassador need not report to Berlin about their meeting and the mention of a possible protest "if these things continued." Weizsäcker was to use the information as he thought best, and he did so. He certainly advised his superiors of the possibility of a Vatican protest in his report on October 17. With his reference to the French bishops, he seems even to have exaggerated that danger beyond what Maglione had actually implied. If Pius XII had wanted to issue a public protest, he was free to do so at any time. If Vatican officials later wanted the world to know of the meeting between Maglione and Weizsäcker on October 16, they could have published Maglione's description of it at any time. They did so only in 1975.

Were Maglione and Weizsäcker correct in fearing that a papal protest on October 16 or 17 would simply have made matters worse? For the victims, matters could hardly have been worse. The deportation of more than a thousand Roman Jews was scheduled for October 18. But neither diplomat knew that at the time. It was probably reasonable for them to fear that a public condemnation would ensure continued arrests and immediate deportation, while a private threat of a protest might persuade the Nazis to end the roundup and divert the arrested Jews to forced labor. It was a difficult judgment call.

It is at least arguable, then, that Pius XII cannot be faulted for delivering no public condemnation of the October roundup during the short period of less than forty-eight hours when the arrested Jews were still detained at the Military College. But there are other steps he should have taken before, during, and after the disaster. He should have informed the Germans privately, long before October 16, that he would take a public stand against any Jewish deportations from Rome, or, better yet, from Italy. Many Germans agreed with Weizsäcker, Möllhausen, and Stahel that a confrontation with the Church was undesirable, for it would provoke disorder in Italy and international criticism of the Reich. Faced with the certainty of a papal condemnation, the Germans might possibly have postponed anti-Jewish actions in Italy. But the pope gave the Germans no reason to believe that he would respond any differently to deportations from Italy than he had from any other occupied country.

During the forty-eight-hour crisis period, Maglione and the pope should have been clearer in their threat of a public protest. As it happened, Maglione mentioned a protest only vaguely on October 16, answering Weizsäcker's question about what the Vatican would do "if things continued" by saying that it "would not want to be obliged to express its disapproval." Instead, the German ambassador should have been officially informed from the outset that the Holy See *would* protest if the Jews of Rome were deported.

Once the deportation train left Tiburtina Station, Pius XII also had an option. He should have issued an immediate loud and vehement protest. Jews still free in Italy and elsewhere would have been alerted and persuaded to hide. If Jews were being deported from the city of the pope, there was no hope anywhere. Furthermore, with the world's attention focusing on it, the actual deportation train might have been diverted from Auschwitz to another camp. As seen, Möllhausen had been told by his superiors at the German Foreign Ministry on October 9 that the Jews of Rome were to be sent to Mauthausen, the Nazi concentration camp closest to Italy, as hostages. It is just possible, then, that Nazi intentions for those victims were not absolutely fixed. Had the pope objected publicly, the instant that the train's actual departure ended the option of forced labor in Italy, the Jews might have been diverted to Mauthausen or even Theresienstadt. Neither of these were death camps where Jews were selected for the gas chambers upon arrival. In them, more of the deportees from Rome might have survived.

The example of the Jews of Denmark, different in many respects, may nevertheless offer a relevant comparison. From the moment that Danish officials heard rumors about a roundup, only a few weeks before the same event occurred in Rome, they bombarded the German occupying forces with questions and objections. The roundup went forwarded as planned, and, because of the help of Danish civilians, most Jews escaped. But in part because of the incessant interest shown by Danish officials both before and after the roundup, the 474 Jews who were caught were not sent to Auschwitz but to Theresienstadt. Representatives of the Danish and the International Red Cross were allowed to visit them there, and 422 survived.[56] Might not an equal expression of Vatican interest in the Jews of Rome have achieved a similar outcome?

In the days and weeks following October 16, 1943, Vatican officials made polite inquiries about the whereabouts of the deportees. By their own admission, however, most inquiries concerned specific individuals, primarily what they called "baptized non-Aryans."[57] But even these attempts were half-hearted. On October 25, for example, two days after most of the deportees had already died in the gas chambers of Auschwitz, the Jesuit Father Pietro Tacchi Venturi informed Secretary of State Maglione that many relatives and friends of the victims had begged him to urge the pope to make inquiries. The priest added pointedly, "A step like this by the Holy See, even if it does not obtain the desired effect, will without doubt help increase the veneration and gratitude toward the August Person of the Holy Father." Two days later, Vatican official Monsignor Dell'Acqua wrote, "We can try . . . but I do not believe that we will succeed in getting any news of the deportees: the experience in other countries is rather eloquent in this regard."[58] Five days after that, Montini learned that General Stahel himself had sent an envoy to a prominent Italian senator and government official. The envoy told the senator, in Montini's words, that "these Jews will never again return to their homes."[59]

Some of the reasons for the pope's silence just before, during, and after the Rome roundup resemble those for his failure to protest the Holocaust generally. As mentioned above, he did not want to anger or endanger German Catholics; he feared making matters worse; he did not want to weaken the German Reich in the face of the Bolshevik peril; and he wanted to preserve Vatican neutrality in order to help achieve a negotiated peace. Other reasons were more unique to the time and place. As also seen, Pius XII was worried, in the autumn of 1943, about a German invasion of the Vatican City and about popular disorder in Rome. But in the autumn of 1943, Pius XII was in an awkward position for yet another reason. He had said nothing when hundreds of thousands of Jews were massacred on the eastern front and in Croatia in 1941. He had remained silent when hundreds of thousands more were seized in Catholic Slovakia, Poland, France, and Belgium, as well as in Protestant countries, in 1942 and 1943. A protest in October 1943 would draw attention to those earlier silences. He was supposed to be a moral spokesman for all people. Could he intervene for one small group of local Jews only?

The final explanation of Pius XII's silence at the time of the Rome roundup is the one most often cited by papal defenders. Soon after October 16 it became apparent that hundreds if not thousands of Jews were seeking shelter in convents and other Catholic institutions throughout Italy. The extent of Vatican involvement in that process will be examined in the remaining chapters of this book. Here it will suffice to say that after the Roman roundup, the pope may have feared that a condemnation from him would provoke German searches of church institutions and seriously endanger those in hiding. At least four Vatican properties in Rome were in fact invaded by German SS and Italian Fascists during the occupation, along with several convents elsewhere in Italy.[60] A papal protest against deportations from Italy might have made that situation even worse without, according to some, helping anyone.

There are several problems with this last explanation. For the most part, as will be seen, the movement of Jews into Church institutions throughout Italy occurred gradually during the weeks *following* the Rome roundup and the departure of the deportation convoy. The pope would not have foreseen the extent of that development before or immediately after October 16, when his own moves should have been made. Second, it is highly questionable that a papal protest before or immediately after October 16 would have made matters worse without helping anyone. Some Jews who eventually hid in Church properties might have been rendered less secure, but they were insecure in any case. But if some became less secure, more of those arrested on October 16 might have survived. A prompt papal response might have led the Germans to divert the train to Mauthausen or Theresienstadt. A vigorous response might even have prompted Italian Resistants to attack the train and free the prisoners.

A papal protest in October 1943 would have helped in still other ways. Jews continued to be arrested in their homes in Florence in November, in Venice in December, and throughout Italy, France, and most other occupied countries until the end of the war. A papal warning would have helped them to believe and understand their danger, and to flee. Finally, while many non-Jews, including men and women of the Church, did hide Jews throughout Italy during the German occupation, many more remained indifferent or even hostile. A papal protest of the Rome roundup, or of any other anti-Jewish activity during the war, would have prompted many more Catholics in Italy and elsewhere to rethink prevailing propaganda and help Jews in trouble.

In June 1963, just before his election to become Pope Paul VI, then Cardinal Giovanni Battista Montini addressed this issue. Montini had been second only to Maglione in the Vatican Secretariat of State during the war. "An attitude of protest and condemnation [of the persecutions of the Jews] . . . would have been not only futile but harmful," he wrote, adding, "that is the long and the short of the matter." [61] As Montini himself knew perfectly well, nothing is ever that simple. And in this case, Montini was wrong.

Papal defenders occasionally maintain that Maglione's mention of a possible protest and Weizsäcker's communications with Berlin had two positive consequences. First, Bishop Hudal later wrote that General Stahel told him on October 17 that SS Chief Heinrich Himmler, informed of the possibility of a Vatican protest, had personally ordered the roundup to cease.[62] There is no evidence for this position. On the contrary, the chronology refutes it. Himmler could not have learned of the possibility of a papal protest until Gumpert forwarded Hudal's letter to Stahel on the evening of October 16, as seen. Sometime that same evening, Kappler, the chief of the security police in Rome who had organized and conducted the roundup on Himmler's orders, informed SS Lieutenant General Karl Wolff, commander of the SS in Italy, that arrests had ceased that afternoon. He added that the roundup had lasted from 5:30 A.M. to 2:00 P.M. He carefully explained that 1,259 persons had been arrested, that those not eligible for deportation had been released, and that deportation was set for Monday, October 18.[63] Clearly there were no plans for continuing the action.

As a second positive consequence of Maglione's reference to a possible papal protest on October 16, it is sometimes alleged that, as Father Robert Graham put it, "Rome was excluded from the mass deportations of Jews." [64] Nothing can be further from the truth. Although most Roman Jews went into hiding after October 16, at least an additional 657 men, women, and children were arrested and deported before liberation less than eight months later.[65] No other deportation trains left for Auschwitz directly from Rome. Most from this group of 657 were held in filthy conditions at the Regina Coeli Prison, on the banks of the Tiber, again virtually in the shadow of the Vatican and again without a flicker of a papal protest. Toward the end of February 1944 many were sent to an internment camp called Fossoli, five kilometers from Carpi in the province of Modena. Others, arrested later, followed them. They were included among the 2,445 Jews from Italy who were deported from Fossoli, mostly to Auschwitz, in six different convoys.[66] Other Roman Jews may have been aboard the seven deportation trains that originated in Milan, Mantua, Verona, Bologna, or Florence. They may even have been on the three from Bolzano and the many others from Trieste.[67] From October 1943 to June 1944, Rome was a city of terror.

And so the incident of the Roman roundup came to a tragic close. When the deportation train made an unscheduled stop at Padua on October 19, Jews allowed to descend briefly for water begged observers to ask the local bishop to inform the pope, who might help them. Six days later, the bishop did so.[68] By then, most of the deportees were dead. Jews and Catholics alike waited for words from the pope. Those words never came.

Pope Pius XI (Achille Ratti), pope from February 1922 to February 1939. The Lateran Accords with Italy (1929) and a concordat with Germany (1933) were signed during his pontificate. Major encyclicals included *Non abbiamo bisogno* (1931), *Mit brennender Sorge* (1937), and *Divini Redemptoris* (1937). (Courtesy of CNS, Washington D.C.)

Pope Pius XI. (Courtesy of CNS, Washington, D.C.)

Pope Pius XII (Eugenio Pacelli), pope from March 1939 to October 1958. He was the papal nuncio in Germany from 1917 to 1929, and Vatican secretary of state from 1930 to 1939. (Courtesy of CNS, Washington, D.C.)

Pope Pius XII blessing his audience after a radio broadcast in 1943. Second from right is Monsignor Giovanni Battista Montini, secretary of the Section of Ordinary Ecclesiastical Affairs of the Vatican Secretariat of State. Montini became Pope Paul VI in 1963. (Courtesy of CNS, Washington, D.C.)

The internment camp of Ferramonti Tarsia, in the province of Cosenza in southern Italy, where thousands of foreign Jews were interned from the time of Italy's entry into the war in June 1940 until the armistice with the Allies in September 1943. (Courtesy of CDEC, Milan)

Father Calliste Lopinot, a Capuchin priest who lived at Ferramonti and worked on behalf of all the prisoners there. Here he is talking with an archimandrite of the Eastern Orthodox Church. (Courtesy of CDEC, Milan)

Jewish forced laborers working on the Tiber embankment in Rome in 1942. In the background is the Castel Sant'Angelo, just a few hundred yards from the Vatican. (Courtesy of Publifoto, Rome)

Jewish refugees after the Italian armistice with the Allies on September 8, 1943, fleeing across the mountains into northern Italy from the former Italian-occupied zone of south-eastern France. They knew that the Germans were about to seize the former Italian zone in France, but they did not expect them to occupy Italy also. (Courtesy of Charles Roman)

Jewish refugees in one of the mountain huts where they were obliged to live in hiding after fleeing into northern Italy. (Courtesy of Charles Roman)

German paratroopers in front of St. Peter's Basilica during the German occupation of Rome, September 1943 to June 1944. They were required to remain outside the piazza, which was the territory of the Holy See, but they checked those wishing to enter. They allowed most worshippers to enter the basilica for religious services, but they tried to obstruct fugitives seeking refuge in the Vatican City. Vatican guards stationed at several gates did the same, often—but not always—with less zeal. (Courtesy of Publifoto, Rome)

Father Maria Benedetto (known in France as Marie Benoît), a Capuchin priest who helped hide thousands of Jews, working first in Marseilles until June 1943 and then in Rome until the city was liberated in June 1944. (Courtesy of CDJC, Paris)

Settimio Sorani, a director of the Jewish refugee assistance organization Delasem in Rome. In September 1943, Sorani asked Father Benedetto to help Jewish refugees, entrusted Delasem funds and lists to him, and worked closely with him until liberation to hide several thousand Jews. (Courtesy of CDEC, Milan)

Don Francesco Repetto, secretary to Cardinal Pietro Boetto, the archbishop of Genoa.
When Lelio Vittorio Valobra, a national director of Delasem, asked Boetto in September
1943 to help distribute Delasem funds to Jewish refugees, the cardinal agreed and
assigned Repetto to the task. A large regional rescue network evolved, and thousands of
Jews were hidden and saved. Don Repetto is standing amid the ruins of the Archbishop's
Palace in Genoa, after an Allied bombing raid on May 19, 1944. (Courtesy of his sisters
Teresa, Vittoria, and Anna Repetto)

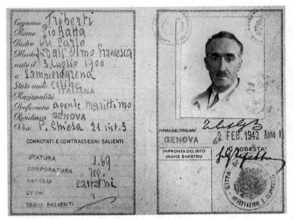

The false identity card of Massimo Teglio, the Jewish businessman who worked with Don Repetto throughout the German occupation to save Jews in and around Genoa. (Courtesy of CDEC, Milan)

At left, Cardinal Elia Dalla Costa, the archbishop of Florence, in front of the Baptistery of San Giovanni in the early 1950s. At right is his secretary, Monsignor Giacomo Meneghello, whom he asked to help with the rescue of Jews. (Courtesy of the Archdiocese of Florence)

Father Cipriano Ricotti, a Dominican priest, in the cloister of the Convento di San Marco in Florence in 1985. (Courtesy of the Archdiocese of Florence)

Don Leto Casini, during the war a parish priest in Varlungo, near Florence, in 1990. Father Ricotti and Don Casini worked closely with Cardinal Dalla Costa and Monsignor Meneghello to hide Jews.

Bishop Giuseppe Placido Nicolini of Assisi. The bishop established a committee in July 1943, to assist refugees from Allied bombing raids in more industrial cities who saw Assisi as a legal safe haven. When Jews sought to hide in the city during the German occupation, Nicolini allowed the committee to engage in clandestine rescue, and he helped it in every possible way. (Courtesy of Don Aldo Brunacci)

Don Aldo Brunacci, years after the war, with Graziella Viterbi, whose family he helped save. (Courtesy of Don Aldo Brunacci)

CHAPTER TWELVE

Hiding Before the Roundup

September 8–October 16, 1943

ON SEPTEMBER 8, 1943, as the Italian armistice with the Allies was being announced, about 200 mostly Polish Jewish refugees were on a train in Italian-occupied France, traveling from Chambéry to Nice.[1] As seen, most of them had spent several years in France, had been assigned to supervised residence in the mountains by the Italians, and were now hoping to be evacuated from Nice to North Africa. When the armistice prompted an Italian retreat from France and a German move to replace them, the refugee train was rerouted to Turin. The refugees' joy at evading Germans entering Nice, however, turned to fear when they learned that the Germans were also occupying Italy. There would be no safety in Turin.

With the help of two remarkable advisors, Aron Kastersztein from a Jewish assistance committee in Nice and Stefan Schwamm, a young lawyer from Vienna, the refugees decided that their best chance lay in moving south. The Allies, they believed, would soon move up the Italian peninsula to liberate Rome, and perhaps Florence as well. They climbed aboard yet another train, this one bound for Rome. They arrived to find chaos. Everyone, it seemed, was on the move—Italian soldiers evading service, draft dodgers, supporters of the previous Badoglio regime, Communists, civilians bombed out or fleeing the war zone. The chaos helped the refugees to escape notice, but only for a time.

The refugees from Chambéry were among the first, but not the only, foreign Jews to reach Rome that September. Others poured in every day. Some had drifted out of internment camps or supervised residences, often with the connivance of their Italian guards, when the German army approached. Others were among the more than one thousand foreign Jews from Italian-occupied France who had followed the retreating Italian army over the Alps on foot after the armistice. Not all of these headed for Rome. Some stayed in mountain huts or barns in the Alps until winter drove them out, or until non-Jews took them in. Others wandered into various northern cities—Turin, Genoa, Milan, Florence—and looked for help there. All were frightened. With no money, documents or friends, no ability to speak Italian, and no legal right to be in Italy at all, much less to work there, they were extremely vulnerable. With the exception of the province of Cuneo, where some 349 Jewish refugees from France were arrested after September 18, the Germans were not yet paying much attention to them. But there was no way to know when that would change. Foreign Jews throughout Italy felt helpless and alone.

But not entirely. Until September 1943, the Delegazione per l'assistenza agli emigranti (Delasem) continued to function with financial donations from prosperous Italian Jews. Established in December 1939 primarily to help Jewish refugees with emigration problems, the organization was also able to distribute funds to impoverished foreign Jewish families in cities, internment camps, and supervised residences. After the German occupation, dedicated Delasem activists perceived a new, far greater problem in the form of Jewish illegal aliens in danger of arrest and possible expulsion. They promptly set out to locate the refugees, itself not an easy task, escort them to suitable living quarters, and provide them with the financial support necessary to live. As will be seen in subsequent chapters, the story of the survival of foreign Jews throughout German-occupied Italy, but especially in Rome, Turin, Genoa, Milan, and Florence, is to a large extent the story of Delasem.

On behalf of the Jewish refugees newly arrived in Rome, an unnamed Italian Jewish lawyer met on September 17 with Monsignor Giuseppe Di Meglio from the Vatican Secretariat of State. The lawyer was probably Ugo Foà, president of the Jewish Community of Rome, to which the local Delasem organization reported. According to Di Meglio, the lawyer asked if the refugees could be accommodated in small groups in various religious institutions throughout the Eternal City. Di Meglio's answer was politely negative. In a report of the meeting to his superiors the following day, he wrote:

> I told him [the lawyer, probably Foà] that, by so doing [hiding in religious institutions in Rome], they [the foreign Jewish

newcomers] would not escape eventual searches by the German
police! Since he insisted, I found it opportune to refer him to
Monsignor Riberi, who also conveyed to him the absolute
inadvisability [*inopportunità*] of having those Jews remain in Rome,
if they wanted them to escape from the feared danger of being
taken. There was no other alternative than to make them leave,
possibly for the Abruzzi or the Marches, sending with each group a
Jew who was an Italian or spoke the language.

    The above-indicated gentleman [probably Foà] did not seem to
be satisfied with this answer![2]

It is important to point out that on September 17, when Di Meglio met
with Foà and declined his request, officials at the Vatican Secretariat of State
probably did not yet understand the full extent of the danger that threatened
native and foreign Jews alike throughout Italy. As seen, the massacre of 54
Jews around Lago Maggiore began on September 15, the first deportation
train departed with 22 Jews from Merano and Bolzano the following day, and
the arrests of 349 Jewish refugees in the province of Cuneo began on the 18th.
But that was all, or almost all, at first, and the news took time to trickle in. On
September 18, Di Meglio described his meeting with Foà of the previous day,
but already on the 17th he had sent another report to his superiors at the Secretariat of State. "Measures against the Jews in Italy are feared," he declared.
But he continued, "While we have news of German authorities detaining Italians trained to bear arms . . . we do not have . . . news of similar measures
directed specifically against the Jews." He added that the Jews themselves
were nevertheless terrified, for rumors were rife. He suggested that his superiors make a general recommendation to the German ambassador to the
Holy See "in favor of the civilian population regardless of race [*razza*], especially the weakest."[3] There is no evidence that such a step was taken.[4]

    Although Di Meglio had probably not yet learned of events on Italy's
northern frontier, he certainly suspected trouble. His report of his meeting
with Foà, with its references to "eventual searches by the German police" and
the "feared dangers of being taken" made his suspicion clear. He also knew
that foreigners caught without papers by the police would be arrested and
possibly expelled. With his access to the Vatican Secretariat of State's information about the destruction of European Jewry elsewhere, he certainly understood that expulsion for Jews could mean death. He was, nevertheless,
completely unwilling to help. Di Meglio's report makes it obvious that any ac-

ceptances of Jews in convents in Rome before his meeting with Foà on September 17 were individual acts of charity in which the pope and the Secretariat of State were not involved.

On September 17 the German occupation and the accompanying danger period for Jews were still very recent. Few Jews, including the newly arrived refugees, had decided to hide themselves completely, but their numbers would increase during the next few weeks. The question then arises: how many Jews in Rome found shelter in Catholic institutions before the October 16 roundup, as well as after, and what was the extent of papal involvement in that sheltering? Was there any papal directive to Catholic institutions in Rome to accept Jews? The issue is further complicated by the special problems of refugees with distinct needs. This chapter will examine Vatican involvement with both Italian and foreign Jews in Rome before the roundup. The issue of involvement in Rome after the roundup will be discussed in the next three chapters.

For the Jews of Italy, the autumn of 1943 was the most critical period of the war. The decisions they made between September 8 and the end of December largely determined whether they would survive the conflagration or die in a concentration camp like Auschwitz, where most Jewish deportees from Italy were sent. But in Rome until the roundup of October 16, decisions had to be made with little information. According to a deliberately articulated policy, German occupying forces were usually pleasant and courteous, buying watches, cameras, and souvenirs from ghetto shopkeepers and paying the full price without quibbling. At the same time, most Jews were only vaguely aware of Nazi atrocities throughout occupied Europe in general and on Italy's northern frontier in particular. In Rome, many let themselves be persuaded by Kappler's promises on September 26 to spare them if the Jewish Community contributed fifty kilograms of gold. Pius XII's willingness to lend gold, as seen, inadvertently helped lull them into immobility by reassuring them of Vatican concern. In addition, Italian non-Jews had, on the whole, observed the racial laws with little overt hostility, and violent anti-Semitic incidents had remained rare. Italian Jews consoled themselves that "it could not happen here."

To avoid the possibility of arrest for "racial" reasons, individuals had to discard identification documents marking them as Jews and abandon homes recorded as Jewish residences in census data since 1938. Valid documents had to be replaced by false ones, while new living places had to be secured

under the new names or, if that was impossible, without the required registration. All of this was illegal, punishable by instant arrest. It was also expensive. New rental space or hotel rooms had to be paid for, while abandoned
homes with all their contents were subject to confiscation.

Reliable new identification documents were equally costly, as well as
difficult to obtain. They had to be carefully prepared by expert counterfeiters,
for they were constantly scrutinized. They were necessary not only to rent
new homes, but also to move about the streets, maintain some form of employment in order to live, and obtain essential ration books for food. Foreign
Jews hoping to live openly also needed them to obtain residence permits. The
best documents were created from authentic but illegally acquired government forms with fabricated seals or stamps. The new false names and addresses had to be carefully chosen, ideally identifying bearers as residents of
municipalities behind Allied lines or with town halls destroyed by bombing
raids, so that their authenticity could not be confirmed.

Good false documents were rare and precious commodities, but they did
not guarantee survival. False identities could be betrayed deliberately by an
informer or inadvertently by a former acquaintance, by a child or elderly person unable to maintain the pretense, or even by an accent inconsistent with
the alleged region of residence. Italian and German authorities were always
on the lookout for dissidents. Jews in hiding were simply added to a long list
of Italians living outside the law and being hunted relentlessly.

In the face of such difficulties, many Roman Jews declined to hide during the first five weeks of the occupation. Surprisingly enough, they included
many middle-class individuals who had limited access to inside information
about the Nazi menace and for whom hiding would not have been an unsur-
passable financial burden. Dante Almansi and Ugo Foà, for example, respectively presidents of the nationwide Union of Italian Jewish Communities and
the Jewish Community of Rome, remained at home and refused to order the
closing of the central synagogue adjacent to the former ghetto of Rome. The
Jews were law-abiding, they argued, and should do nothing to provoke the
wrath of the authorities. They set what they believed to be the correct example
by refusing to hide. They barely escaped arrest on October 16. They both went
into hiding after that date but continued to work actively and courageously for
their people throughout the occupation.[5]

Other well-connected and affluent Roman Jews who stayed home too
long were not so fortunate. Sixty-one-year-old Alina Cavalieri, described by
local Delasem director Settimio Sorani as a "cultivated and distinguished

benefactor" of the Jewish Community, had won a silver medal in World War I for nursing services at the front. After the armistice in 1943 she refused Sorani's urgent plea to obtain false papers and change her residence, declaring that she had "nothing to hide." She was arrested on October 16 and gassed upon arrival at Auschwitz.[6] Others like her who were caught in their homes during the roundup and murdered at Auschwitz include Admiral Augusto Capon, the seventy-one-year-old, half paralyzed father-in-law of Enrico Fermi; Amelia Treves Segre, the seventy-four-year-old wife of Commendator Giuseppe Segre, seized from her sickbed; and Lionello Alatri, owner of one of Rome's largest department stores and a prominent member of the Jewish Community, arrested with his wife and her ninety-year-old mother.

At the opposite extreme was a small minority of Roman Jews who arranged a complete clandestine existence before October 16. They usually rented apartments or hotel rooms, preferably in other cities and always with false documents. Settimio Sorani, for example, who had urged his friend Alina Cavalieri to hide, posed as a non-Jewish refugee and rented a house in the country as early as August. He moved his family there the day after the announcement of the armistice. He himself moved to a new apartment in Rome, under a false name, on September 12, but he courageously continued his work for Jewish refugees throughout the occupation.[7]

The controversial chief rabbi of Rome, Israele Zolli, also went into hiding in mid-September, but unlike Sorani, he did not continue to help his people. Born in Eastern Europe in 1881 and a rabbi in Trieste for nearly thirty years before coming to Rome in 1940, Zolli had talked with hundreds of Jewish refugees in northern Italy and was much more suspicious of the Nazis than most Italian Jews. He turned over his rabbinical duties to his assistant, but his absence from services at the central synagogue was vaguely attributed to illness. It was not allowed to constitute a warning. Zolli spent the nine months of the German occupation of Rome in the home of a young working-class Catholic couple. Claims that he was sheltered in the Vatican are untrue.[8]

Many Roman Jews with foresight and some means fell somewhere between the two extremes of refusing to move and hiding completely. This group simply moved, unofficially and without changing documents, into the homes of relatives or friends. Such partial measures only slightly lessened the danger, for the fugitives usually remained in households linked with Jews. Enough people moved, however, that a joke began to circulate in the city by the end of September. Tourists ask their guide where Michelangelo's statue of Moses is. The guide replies, "For some days now, he has been in the home of friends."⁹

Other Roman Jews made plans but postponed moving. In mid-September, for example, author and publisher Luciano Morpurgo quietly began to stockpile food and blankets in a room in a distant neighborhood in Rome where he would not be recognized. He decided to move there after hearing that the Germans had seized the Community's lists on September 29.¹⁰ Piero Modigliani planned but delayed even longer. He located a room for his wife and himself in a simple pensione on October 3 but did not move there until after the roundup.¹¹ Enzo Finzi obtained false papers for himself and moved into the house of a friend in order to avoid the obligatory labor service, but he left his wife and young daughter at home.¹² The family of a survivor identified only as David moved into the home of an uncle on the outskirts of Rome soon after September 8, but returned to their own apartment near the former ghetto early in October, when the danger seemed to have receded.¹³ The Germans came for the Modiglianis and the Finzis and for David's family on the morning of October 16, but all three groups narrowly escaped capture.

Twenty-nine-year-old Arminio Wachsberger, his wife, Regina, and his five-year-old daughter were not so lucky. On September 29 they watched from their apartment window as the Germans looted the office of the Jewish Community. They pondered the implications and debated moving. But the little girl was ill, and moving would have been difficult for her. They were arrested at home on October 16 and deported to Auschwitz. Of the three, only Arminio survived.¹⁴

As the above cases suggest, most of those who hid before October 16 turned to relatives or friends, or rented new living quarters outside religious institutions rather than within them. After all, life in a convent or religious school was an unappealing prospect for anyone not dedicated to the contemplative life. Even the best-intentioned nuns or monks could offer only sparse and crowded accommodations along with a strict Spartan daily routine. Men were invariably separated from their women and children. Youngsters in Catholic schools, furthermore, were obliged to participate in the religious life of the institution in order to maintain their fictitious identities. Even in cases where nuns promised not to proselytize, parents feared conversions among lonely children eager to please their teachers and conform among their peers.

There were, of course, exceptions to the reluctance to turn to Catholic institutions before October 16. The young university graduate Lea Di Nola was one. Unusually well informed about anti-Jewish atrocities because of her work among refugees for Delasem, Lea asked for lodging for herself and her mother at several convents around September 15. She was always refused. She moved into a pensione that did not demand identification papers, but she was uneasy there because of the presence of Italian soldiers also hiding from the Germans. By October 9 she knew about the gold extortion on September 26 and the looting of the Jewish Community offices on the 29th, and had heard rumors of more terrible incidents to the north. She decided to try again.

This time Lea and her mother were accepted at the convent of Santa Maria Ausiliatrice, near Monte Mario. Some thirty people, all women, eventually hid there. Not all were Jews. Some were the female relatives of partisans or escaped Italian soldiers. Like most Jews and non-Jews sheltered in convents, Lea Di Nola paid room and board for herself and her mother. Also like most other laypersons in convents, the two women never wore habits or disguised themselves as nuns. Like many other convents, Santa Maria Ausiliatrice had always maintained rooms for guests, religious pilgrims, or Catholics on retreat. It was easy to explain the presence of female outsiders in these facilities at a time when thousands of non-Jewish refugees escaping military operations in the south and Allied bombardments in the north were pouring into Rome and seeking shelter. The Di Nola women lived there, slightly apart from the nuns, who paid little attention to them and probably never suspected that they were Jewish. Only the Mother Superior and her assistant officially knew their real identity.

At 4:00 A.M. on October 16, an hour before the main roundup, German police went looking for the Di Nola family at their former apartment. Of course they were not there. Lea's foresight had saved their lives. After that she obtained false documents. She chose a new name that preserved her initials, in case some of her jewelry, luggage, or linens bore monograms. She continued her work as an accountant, indispensable if she was to pay her room and board. She also became acquainted with Father Marie Benoît, the French Capuchin priest who, as seen, had worked among endangered Jews in southeastern France and had even appealed to the pope on their behalf. Now in Rome and known as Father Maria Benedetto, by which name he will subsequently be called, the dynamic priest was working closely with Settimio Sorani and other Delasem activists to help Jewish refugees. Through him, Lea Di Nola became involved in clandestine rescue work.[15]

There were other exceptions to the general pattern of Roman Jews either not hiding or turning to non-Church sources before October 16. Soon after the gold incident and the looting of the Community's offices, the mother of eleven-year-old Lia Levi placed her and her sister in a Catholic boarding school called the Istituto San Giuseppe, at Casaletto near Monteverde. The children lived as normal students at the school for the duration of the occupation. They were not required to convert in order to be admitted, although friendly nuns responded eagerly to any expressions of interest in the Catholic faith.[16]

Similarly, Silvana Ascarelli Castelnuovo began petitioning convents for a place soon after September 8. Like Lea Di Nola, she was refused many times. On September 30, she finally found places for four children, her mother, and herself at the Convento del Sacro Cuore del Bambino Gesù. She paid a modest rent for three rooms, one for her mother and her six-year-old son, another for herself and her nine-year-old daughter, and the third for her two older daughters. She told the Mother Superior that her family was Jewish, but that nun told the others that they were refugees from Sicily.[17]

Did the Vatican have any role in the sheltering of Jews before October 16? Although a few observers believe that the pope asked convents and monasteries to open their doors to Jews in this early period, there is no evidence to support the allegation and much reason to doubt it.[18] Most convents, monasteries, and Catholic schools needed no formal papal authorization to accept guests as boarders outside their cloistered areas, so long as adult newcomers were of the same sex as the religious residents. On the contrary, these institutions were often eager to have extra guests or students, who represented welcome revenue sources at a time when their regular guests or boarders—most often pilgrims or Catholic pupils—were not forthcoming because of the penury and the dangers of the war. By mid-September they were already accepting many non-Jewish refugees and illegal fugitives, as well as a few Jews, for residence outside cloistered areas. Jews were not yet in desperate straits, and not yet pounding frantically on closed doors. Nor were the dangers of harboring illegal fugitives as apparent as they would become later. Under these conditions it is not reasonable to suggest that Pius XII would have risked compromising his relationship with the Germans, not to mention with Vatican officials opposed to helping Jews, by intervening when it was not necessary.

Might the pope, at the very least, have suggested to a few convents that they accept Jews during the few days just before October 16 when, as seen in the previous chapter, he almost certainly knew about the pending roundup?

Again, it seems unlikely. If Pius XII failed to warn Jewish leaders of what he knew, it is not reasonable to think that he facilitated Jewish hiding. There was no surge of Jews into convents just before October 16. On the contrary, some Jews continued to be turned away, not only just before the roundup but afterward as well. No Jewish survivor or Catholic director of a Church institution has testified to the existence of a papal directive before October 16. The published documents of the Holy See from the period of the German occupation of Italy provide no evidence either of an actual directive or of an internal suggestion or debate about such a step.

Quite apart from a general directive, published Vatican documents provide only one reference even to an individual request for shelter directed to the Holy See and actually considered before October 16. On October 1, Monsignor Giovanni Battista Montini, secretary of the Section for Ordinary Ecclesiastical Affairs in the Secretariat of State, noted that an eighty-four-year-old man "of the Jewish religion, and manifesting very good sentiments" had asked the Vatican to authorize his lodging in a Roman convent of nuns. The Suore Oblate Agostiniane di Santa Maria dei Sette Dolori were willing to accept his seventy-six-year-old wife, an elderly domestic servant, and a niece. The wife was ill, however, and needed her husband's help. To accept a man, even outside cloistered areas, the nuns needed authorization. In his note, Montini added that the supplicant had indicated an interest in bequesting his assets to a Catholic charity. The following day he recorded that he had spoken of the matter of lodging in the convent with Monsignor Luigi Traglia, assistant to the vicar of Rome, who "seemed to be favorable." [19] The published Vatican documents provide no information about the outcome.

Montini's note confirms that the Vatican was generally not directly involved in the admission of Jews to Church institutions in Rome before October 16. In this case, the elderly Jewish couple had gone first to the convent, as other Jews did, and only afterward, because of a problem, to the Vatican. The convent itself needed no special permission to accept women into its non-cloistered areas, but it did need authorization to accept a man. There is currently no way to know how many other special requests reached the Holy See, how many were considered, or even how aware Vatican officials were of the few Italian Jews actually being sheltered in church institutions before the roundup. Certainly, Montini was aware of this case.

If few Roman Jews moved into convents, monasteries, and Catholic schools before October 16, however, the situation was different for the Jewish refugees who were pouring into the Eternal City without money, documents, or friends. As their numbers swelled, Settimio Sorani, Aron Kastersztein, Stefan Schwamm, and other Delasem activists tried desperately to feed and house them in Jewish schools, orphanages, and other institutions. It was becoming increasingly evident, however, that such places would soon become untenable, and that Delasem itself would have to disguise its operations. The Jewish activists needed help. They found it in the French Capuchin priest Maria Benedetto.

Father Benedetto's already extraordinary Jewish rescue work in France, under his French name of Marie Benoît, was described in Chapter Ten. After his order called him to Rome in late June 1943, he continued his efforts to help by asking Pius XII on several occasions to intervene on behalf of Jews trying to escape from Italian-occupied France to safer parts. As also seen, he had no success. After the German occupation of Italy in September, however, Father Benedetto found himself again involved in assisting Jews directly. On July 20, 1944, more than a month after the liberation of Rome, he recorded how he first became involved with Delasem.

Of the Jewish refugees newly arrived from France in mid-September, Father Benedetto wrote, "I was advised of their presence by my friend Lionello Alatri (who was unfortunately deported after October 16) [Benedetto's parenthesis]." After conferring with Alatri, an important figure in the Jewish Community of Rome, Benedetto made a fateful decision. As he wrote:

> I went to find [the foreign Jews] at the Jewish orphanage where they had been temporarily lodged and I recognized a good number of those I had known in Marseilles and Nice. Unable to extricate myself from an obligation to resume helping, I became acquainted with "Delasem," with which I collaborated for nine months [until liberation], taking part in all its activities. . . . Very soon the offices of "Delasem," Lungo Tevere Sanzio 2, had to be closed and little by little the monastery at Via Sicilia 159, with its internal and external visiting rooms and its second entrance at Via Boncompagni 71, became the central seat of the committee.[20]

Through Alatri, then, Father Benedetto met Settimio Sorani, the local director of Delasem, whom, the priest later wrote, "I did not yet know." [21] Father Benedetto did not give the precise date of the onset of his involvement, but Alatri, arrested on October 16, could naturally only have contacted him before that date. Sorani, with whom Benedetto cooperated during the entire nine months of the occupation, also made it clear that the priest's involvement began well before the roundup. Sorani wrote after the war, "At the end of September 1943, after the ransom of the fifty kilograms of gold . . . and the requisition or, rather, the theft at the two [Jewish] libraries . . . we left our offices at Lungotevere Sanzio 2 and transferred all our work to the monastery at Via Sicilia 159."[22]

What exactly went on at that monastery? Delasem's initial, more or less legal efforts to find housing for Jewish refugees and maintain them financially were gradually transformed into something quite different. The story extends well beyond October 16, the cut-off date for this chapter. Father Benedetto described it succinctly:

> [The monastery was] the central headquarters and processing center, because it was necessary to create other centers where those being helped, divided by category, could be received. The categories were: foreign Jews coming from France, foreign Jews who had lived in Italy for several years, Yugoslavian Jews, Jews who were Italian but not Roman, and Roman Jews. . . . In addition to distributing subsidies, foodstuffs, clothing and medicine, [the assistance committee's] functions consisted of obtaining identification documents . . . [and] ration booklets. . . . The work was really immense and required the greatest courage, because the risk . . . was enormous and constant, and there was no lack of threatening letters, denunciations, and spies against us and our centers.[23]

The Capuchin monastery in the Via Sicilia became, in effect, the center of a large clandestine Jewish rescue network. The Delasem committee used the building for meetings and for hiding its funds and records. False documents were made there, on an old hand-operated printing press discovered on the premises.[24] Refugees were taken there before being referred elsewhere. Some stayed at the monastery for a time, waiting for the false documents and subsidies that would allow them to take rooms in apartment buildings, hotels, or pensioni. Priests, nuns, Jewish social workers, and Catholic laypersons all went there to receive their assignments—to escort a group of refugees arriving from the north into Rome; to guide another group, already in Rome, to a hiding place; to distribute a supply of food or money to those in hiding; to fabricate and give out false documents. About 4,000 Jews were directed to hiding places and supplied by Delasem representatives and Catholics working together at the Capuchin monastery. About 1,500 beneficiaries were foreigners, but by the spring of 1944, an additional 2,500 were Italian Jews.[25] None of the refugees in Delasem's care in Rome were caught on October 16, for the roundup was directed against Italian Jews with registered addresses.[26] About sixty-two Delasem beneficiaries were caught during the entire nine-month occupation, most after May 1, 1944.[27]

For his heroic rescue work in Rome and, earlier, in southeastern France, Father Maria Benedetto was awarded the Medal of the Righteous Among the Nations by Yad Vashem in Israeli.

Father Benedetto always made it clear that the initiative for his own rescue work came from the Jewish Community, in the persons of Alatri and Sorani. He did not receive a directive from the Vatican to become involved. By September 1943 he had already been working to help Jewish refugees in France for more than three years. He resumed that activity in Italy in response to the appeals of Jewish leaders. Benedetto also declared unambiguously that "Signor Sorani, except for the two-week interruption when he was arrested, remained at the head of the committee, helped by a certain number of representatives of the group of foreigners who maintained contact with the others and carried out the multiple functions of assistance."[28]

The money for the Sorani-Benedetto operation also came from Delasem, which in turn was funded by the American Jewish Joint Distribution Committee and by private Italian Jewish contributors. At first, funds arrived from Delasem headquarters in Genoa.[29] By January 1944, however, that money was exhausted. Raffaele Cantoni, the Delasem courier from Genoa, had been arrested, escaped, and was forced into hiding. It was impossible to get more money from the north. Since it was also impossible to transfer dollars directly from the United States to Rome because of the war, the desperate Benedetto and Sorani devised an ingenious system. In the spring and early summer of 1944, individual Italian non-Jews advanced lire on credit, with the guarantee of being repaid in dollars when peace was restored. The amount thus secured eventually totaled $120,000.[30] The American and British diplomatic representatives to the Holy See verified the Joint's deposits of funds in a bank in London from which the postwar reimbursements would and did come.[31] Those two diplomats thus gave invaluable help to Delasem at a critical time, but they acted independently of the Vatican. In fact, the Secretariat of State had been asked in March to provide a similar service, receiving dollar deposits and converting them to lire through a Vatican institution. Maglione categorically refused, writing, "I do not intend to give orders or assume responsibility [for converting the available dollars]. I do not even want to give suggestions." [32]

The money for the rescue project, then, came from Delasem and the Joint. After the war, Father Benedetto could not have been clearer on this subject. "I with the real heads of Delasem did not receive any money from the Vatican," he wrote in July 1961. He added that toward the end of September 1943, he had visited Monsignor Antonio Riberi, who would become head of the Pontifical Commission for Refugee Assistance after its founding in April 1944. Accompanied by Sorani, Dante Almansi, and Raffaele Cantoni, Benedetto requested a Vatican loan. Riberi replied, "The Vatican does not make loans; if it has it, it gives it." The supplicants left with nothing. [33] There is no reason why Benedetto would have lied about this matter. He maintained friendships with some prelates close to the Vatican and was in no way disrespectful of the pope. He was committed to his religious order and his Church. Such a man would have been glad, even proud, to give credit where credit was due. He could not do so.

Nor, apparently, did the rescue group receive much in the way of supplies from the Vatican. Again Benedetto was clear, writing in 1961 that on only one occasion did he receive food from the Vatican, in the form of a delivery of 300 kilograms of flour. [34] He never referred to other items, but Sorani wrote vaguely in 1983 that Delasem's representatives *tried* to get contributions of clothing from Riberi. Sorani did not mention food or money, nor did he say whether clothing was actually received. [35] Much earlier, however, during the final month of the occupation of Rome, he had been more forthright, writing on May 16, 1944, that Monsignor Riberi had again been asked for clothing and foodstuffs. He added, without elaboration, "Despite the promises, nothing has been granted as of today." [36]

Benedetto and Sorani's reports should be read in connection with a claim by an official at the Vatican Secretariat of State on January 9, 1944, that the Holy See had been giving the Capuchin priest money and foodstuffs for Jewish refugees since the onset of the German occupation. Monsignor Riberi, the official wrote, was charged with the matter. [37] This claim is difficult to interpret, but in light of Benedetto and Sorani's comments, any Vatican contributions must be regarded as exceedingly sparse. In the immediate postwar period, when Jews and Catholics alike were eager to foster Jewish-Christian reconciliation, Benedetto and Sorani had every reason to record such assistance, if it was true. They did not do so.

Also in 1983, Sorani referred tantalizingly to Delasem's requests at the Vicariate of Rome for "more secure hospitality in convents for refugees and Italians."[38] The Vicariate was the agency responsible for the day-to-day administration of the diocese of Rome, of which the pope was, by virtue of his office, bishop. Throughout the German occupation, most of Delasem's protégés were lodged precariously in hotels and pensioni, somewhat protected by their false documents and supplied by the Benedetto-Sorani committee. Clearly, more secure refuges were desirable. But Sorani provided no details to indicate that the requests at the Vicariate for "more secure hospitality in convents" were ever granted. It seems reasonable to suppose that if the requests for shelter had been granted, he would have said so.

Far from claiming receipt of material aid from Vatican officials, Benedetto never even wrote that they encouraged him. Nor did he ever mention that they discouraged him, but that seems to have been the case. On November 19, 1943, for example, a priest at the Vatican Secretariat of State reported that he had learned that Father Benedetto was already in trouble with the Italian authorities for forging documents for Jewish refugees. The following day an exasperated higher official in the same department, Monsignor Angelo Dell'Acqua, wrote, "I have repeatedly (and the last time very clearly) told Father Benoît [Benedetto], Capuchin, to use the maximum prudence in dealing with the Jews . . . : it can be seen, unfortunately, that he has not wished to listen to the humble advice given to him."[39] About a month later, after reading a Secretariat of State note about rumors of a joint Jewish and Catholic rescue group with links to the Vatican, Dell'Acqua denied its existence and commented petulantly, "Several times . . . I have observed that persons employed at the Vatican or close to it interest themselves too much (in a manner that I dare to call almost exaggerated) with the Jews, favoring them. . . . I have always believed . . . in using the maximum prudence in speaking with Jews, to whom it would be better to speak less."[40] In this second note, Dell'Acqua was undoubtedly thinking not only of Benedetto but of other priests who, as will be seen in the next chapters, were sheltering Jews in Vatican properties. But rather than encouraging Father Benedetto and others like him, some Vatican officials were actually trying to subdue them.

There is, of course, no doubt that bureaucrats at the Secretariat of State knew something about what the Capuchin priest was doing. Dell'Acqua mentioned it in November and December; the official who claimed that the Holy See had been contributing money and foodstuffs wrote of it in January; and Maglione was asked for help in financial transactions in March.

Benedetto himself seems to have kept Vatican officials informed, at least initially. On November 5, for example, the irrepressible priest appealed personally to Montini for a letter of recommendation, which would help him with a complicated scheme to provide false documents for some 500 Jewish refugees. Benedetto did not receive the recommendation, apparently because, at Vatican urging, he changed his mind about the details of the plan.[41] Soon after that, however, he spoke with Dell'Acqua about other ways to help the refugees.[42] He received little but a reprimand, as seen. But some of his activities were known. And while Dell'Acqua and others tried to restrain him, they did not stop him.

In their wartime and postwar reports, Benedetto and Sorani were always quick to acknowledge the outside help they had received. This tendency provides another indication that if material aid from the Vatican had been forthcoming, they would have mentioned it. Among those who were mentioned, however, were two individuals close to the Vatican. Benedetto referred to Monsignor Hérissé, for example, as "our very precious friend."[43] Hérissé was the elderly French priest with the private apartment in the Vatican City who had, in July 1943, helped the Capuchin secure a private audience with the pope and establish contact with American and British diplomats Harold Tittmann and Sir d'Arcy Osborne. The monsignor later served as the liaison between Delasem, Tittmann, and Osborne (whose apartments were in the same building as Hérissé's), and the Italians who were selling lire and buying future dollars from the Joint. Sorani and Schwamm both mentioned him. Sorani wrote of that eventful spring of 1944, "I used to go to see Monsignor Herissèe [sic], who kept the receipts [of the transactions] along with the promises [to pay dollars after the war] signed by me. And I left St. Peter's with my packet of thousand lire bills wrapped up in newspaper, passing under the eyes of the German guards at the boundary between the Vatican City and Italy."[44] Hérissé provided an essential service, but his activities were inconsistent with Maglione's expressed refusal in March, mentioned above, to become involved in financial transactions benefiting Benedetto's rescue operations. The French monsignor acted on his own authority.

Help also came in December 1943 from a priest at the Vicariate, whom Father Benedetto and Stefan Schwamm later identified as Monsignor Umberto Dionisi. Father Benedetto and the Delasem rescue group were preparing 500 special identification certificates, essential if refugees were to obtain residence permits and ration books from the municipality. The refugees, of course, were not identified on the certificates as Jews. Benedetto, posing as the head of an assistance committee for general refugees, signed the certificates, but he needed verification from the Vicariate that his signature was authentic. Dionisi provided that verification. It is not clear how much the latter understood about the refugees in question, but if he knew anything about Father Benedetto he must have suspected that they were Jews. Nor is it clear if high-level officials at the Vatican knew what Dionisi had done. In any case, the signature verification was only that. For Italian government authorities it did not imply knowledge or approval of the recipients of the special certificates. It was a purely bureaucratic maneuver, but it made the certificates convincing for a time.[45]

Other helpful members of the secular and regular clergy were further removed from the Vatican. Father Benedetto made it clear that his superiors at the Capuchin monastery in the via Sicilia strongly supported and protected him.[46] Individual priests and monks, some whose names are recorded and some who remain nameless, along with several nuns, participated in the rescue activities. At least one convent and three parish churches served as additional meeting and distribution centers for refugee assistance.[47] Finally, and most intriguingly, the Salvatorian Fathers whose monastery was just north of the entrance to St. Peter's Square were sometimes able to send warnings of raids being prepared by German police. The Salvatorian Fathers' superior general, Father Pancrazio Pfeiffer, a German, was Pius XII's personal liaison to the German military command in Rome. Father Benedetto and Stefan Schwamm, who recorded the help, unfortunately do not tell us whether Father Pancrazio intentionally shared tips acquired at German headquarters with his monks, or whether the monks somehow obtained their information without his cooperation and passed it along without his knowledge.[48]

The story of Father Benedetto's work with Jewish refugees in Rome extends well beyond the date of the October 16 roundup. It demonstrates in microcosm, however, the complexity and subtlety of the Vatican's involvement in Jewish rescue. Vatican officials took no initiatives to help Jews. Some individuals connected with the Vatican, however, like Monsignor Hérissé, participated independently in acts of assistance that were formally illegal, with full knowledge that the beneficiaries were Jewish. They almost certainly did not inform their superiors of the details. Their superiors did not wish to know. Other individuals connected with the Vatican, like Monsignor Dionisi at the Vicariate who verified Benedetto's signature on certificates for "general refugees," did not ask too many questions about those being helped.

Finally, some high officials at the Vatican Secretariat of State knew what Benedetto, who was not connected with the Vatican, was doing, and positively disapproved. They did so not necessarily because the refugees were Jewish but because the illegal rescue network, if discovered, would compromise the pope and increase the danger of a German invasion of the Vatican City. Those officials certainly informed Maglione of what they knew, as demonstrated by the fact that they wrote memoranda of the events. And Maglione certainly told the pope, who expected to be informed about everything. The best that can be said for Pius XII's role in all of this is that he allowed Benedetto's activities to continue.

CHAPTER THIRTEEN

Hiding After the Roundup

Roman Convents, Monasteries, Catholic Hospitals and
Schools, October 16–December 1943

THE ROUNDUP on October 16 changed everything. The trickle of Roman Jews appealing to the Church for help was transformed into a flood. The former ghetto adjacent to the central synagogue was in the heart of Rome, with many convents and monasteries nearby. On the morning of the Nazi operation, terror-stricken Jews lucky enough to have escaped arrest turned instinctively to those institutions for temporary shelter. Just as instinctively, sympathetic nuns and monks in the vicinity of the ghetto and aware of the raid let them in. A dozen or more Jews, for example, fled along the Ponte Fabricio to the Isola Tiberina, facing the synagogue across the Tiber. There they knocked on the doors of the Ospedale San Giovanni Calibita, known as Fatebenefratelli, They were immediately admitted. At one time or another during the occupation at least sixty-seven Jews were hidden there, often disguised as patients among the genuinely ill.[1] They were not the only simulators. Political and military fugitives had been hiding in the hospital since September 8.

The Convent of the Sisters of Our Lady of Sion, also across the Tiber from the former ghetto but up the Janiculum hill, had been a Catholic boarding school for girls before the war. The pupils, fearing the Allied bombing raids that had begun in Rome in the summer of 1943, did not return for classes in the autumn. The mansion was serving primarily as a study center for about twenty-four novices. Two men, an air force general and a naval captain, found hiding places there soon after the armistice. Fleeing Jews arrived on October 16—about forty, by one estimate; perhaps one hundred by another.[2] There was plenty of space in the big house, and the Jews—men as well as women and children—were all accepted. The men lived separately from the women, with prepared hiding places in the event of a search. Their presence in a female convent-school could never have been explained, but the women and children could be disguised as non-Jewish refugees. The female guests were not disguised as nuns.

The numbers of Jews at the convent-school grew with time, although the total is difficult to determine. Some individuals stayed for only a few days. Others came, left, and returned, while still others remained until liberation. One estimate places the total number at an impressive 187.[3] A nun who was present as a novice at the time believes that number to be somewhat high, explaining that so many were certainly never present at one time.[4]

There are countless other examples of convents that received fleeing Jews on October 16. Enzo Finzi's wife and young daughter, warned by telephone that the roundup was in progress, fled to the Monastery of the Carissimi in the Via dei Serpenti, where they knew someone. The monastery was already crammed with others in hiding: supporters of Badoglio's former regime, Italian soldiers and carabinieri who did not want to serve the Germans, draft dodgers, Communists, and other dissenters. But the monks admitted Finzi's family as well.[5]

Eleven-year-old David, who did not give his last name in later testimony, also narrowly escaped the Germans who came to his door in the former ghetto that same morning. David fled with his family and uncle to the nearby Convent of Santa Rufina, in the Via della Lungaretta in Trastevere. The nuns there had been customers of his uncle's haberdashery business. The uncle remembered them as he fled across the Tiber, wondering where to go. The nuns were already sheltering some female students. They would accept only David's mother and her younger children, including David and a brother. To accept older men would attract too much suspicion. David remained there until the liberation.[6]

It seems clear that there was little Vatican involvement in the hiding of Jews in convents, monasteries, and Catholic schools on or shortly after October 16, for several reasons. First, the hospitality was requested and granted so spontaneously that there was no time for a papal directive prompted by the roundup. Second, those involved in accepting Jews in convents and monasteries rarely claimed after the war that they had received a directive, even though such a claim would have redounded greatly to the credit of the pope whom they honored and respected.[7] Most never mentioned a directive at all, while some actually denied it. Brother Maurizio, for example, the steward at the Fatebenefratelli Hospital, declared that the monks there never received a papal order to admit Jews. After they had accepted the fugitives fleeing across the Ponte Fabricio on October 16, they duly notified Vatican officials. They received no response, and they took the silence for approval.[8]

Monsignor Elio Venier agrees. During the war Venier was a young priest at the parish church of Santa Maria della Divina Provvidenza, in the Monteverde section of Rome. About seventy Jews were sheltered in a number of large rooms on an upper floor of the parish house from October 1943 until the liberation of Rome. For the most part, they took care of themselves. Two or three women went out every day to shop. The others helped with the cooking and cleaning. They sometimes exercised in an attached courtyard. Monsignor Venier explained that the pope did not get involved in such matters. Officials at the Vicariate would have been informed, he said, because parish churches were under their jurisdiction. But, he added, "We did not go around broadcasting it. No one expected applause. Even after the war, we did not talk about it as anything special. It was all so natural. You help those in need."[9]

In his study of rescue and charitable activities at the Istituto Pio XI during the occupation, Francesco Motto essentially agreed with Brother Maurizio and Monsignor Venier.[10] Before the war, the Istituto, run by the Salesian Order, was a boarding school for 200 to 250 boys. After the second Allied bombing attack on Rome on August 13, 1943, most of the regular boarders chose not to return. Soon after that, the school began taking in nonpaying orphaned, poor, or homeless boys, offering them shelter, food, and education. At first the Salesians needed authorization from their superiors in Turin to accept boarders who did not pay fees. They not only received the authorization, but they were urged to help those in need and reminded that the mission of the Salesians was to minister to the young, especially the poorest.[11] Many more youngsters arrived, including at least thirty from the war-torn Naples area in early October. Not all of them were present legally. None of these early arrivals were Jews, but some of the older boys were in danger of being drafted for military or labor service.

The first Jewish boys and young men entered the school in mid-October, mostly after the roundup. Of a total of eight that month, three arrived on October 19 and one on the 27th. For the other four there is no precise day of entry recorded. Of the seventy Jews who spent some time at the school, most arrived in November and December, although a few appeared as late as

April.[12] The seventy were never all present at same time. Non-Jews totaled 100 to 150 but were also not all in residence simultaneously.

In his account of the Istituto Pio XI, Motto examined the situations of the Jewish pupils carefully. He explained that most paid fees of about 40 lire a month—low compared with charges of 1,600 to 2,200 lire a year before the war.[13] Some received stipends from Delasem or other Roman Jewish charitable institutions. They disguised themselves as non-Jews, to the extent of going to religious classes, services, and prayers like everyone else. Their parents and relatives could visit them. Most boys, Jews and non-Jews alike, came to the Istituto with a personal recommendation from a Catholic priest or layman, or because they were already acquainted with the Salesians. Some were related to students already there. Such information suggests that many of the Jewish boys may have come from mixed families, or had a relative who was a convert.

Despite all this detail, Motto never declared that the Istituto had received a papal order to admit Jews. On the contrary, he implied that the Istituto's hospitality was impressive, considering that the Vatican secretary of state had urged it on October 25 to observe a "discreet and prudent correctness."[14] That admonition, delivered to the heads of many religious institutions in Rome that day, will be further discussed below. On assistance by Catholics to Jews in Rome generally, Motto concluded, "*Without any written directive* during that terrible period, the Catholics of Rome were very aware that they were responding to the will of the pontiff by contributing in every possible way to saving the largest possible number of human lives, and above all, the most tried, the Jews."[15] Motto did not allege that the "will of the pontiff" was conveyed orally. It was just generally understood.

Nuns present as novices in the Convent of Our Lady of Sion at the time are less certain about a papal directive. One declared that an order to shelter Jews arrived before October 16. Her colleague responded, more plausibly, "That is ridiculous! The issue never even occurred to anyone until that date." Both nuns explained that special permission to accept outsiders into the convent-school was not required; the Sisters of Our Lady of Sion had never been so strict. Besides, the building in Rome was primarily a school.[16] In any case, no written directive to help Jews or any other fugitives exists at the convent today. Surviving nuns, novices at the time, would probably have been too young and unimportant in 1943 to have had first-hand knowledge of a papal order, whether written or oral. They might have been falsely informed of one, however, to inspire their care for fugitives. On the other hand, a directive might have been hidden from them to protect the pope. But given the timing of the arrival of their fugitives and the absence of any subsequent claims to the contrary, it is most likely that there was no papal directive at all.

The Sisters of Our Lady of Sion are, however, clearly eager that Pius XII receive credit for the work of their order to help Jews. They insist, probably correctly, that the pope ultimately knew that they were sheltering many Jews. They also point out that the Vatican Secretariat of State provided their convent with a special protective placard to be displayed at the entrance, reading, "This building serves religious objectives, and is a dependency of the Vatican City. All searches and requisitions are prohibited." [17] That placard, however, printed in Italian and German and signed by General Rainer Stahel, the German military commander of Rome, was distributed on October 25 to many religious institutions throughout the Eternal City, regardless of whether they were harboring illegal fugitives. Its intent was to affirm and protect the special prerogatives of the Church rather than to protect fugitives.

Vatican properties declared extraterritorial in the Lateran Accords between Italy and the Holy See in 1929, such as the Seminario Romano Maggiore and the Basilica of San Paolo fuori le Mura, were indeed exempt from searches and requisitions as a matter of law. More humble parish churches, convents, monasteries, and schools, however, enjoyed no such privileges. German General Stahel, eager to minimize anti-Catholic incidents and avoid confrontation with the Vatican, issued the placard to remind Fascist fanatics of the status of certain Vatican properties and to extend a degree of protection to some lesser institutions as well. The Convent of the Sisters of Our Lady of Sion on the Janiculum hill, along with the Istituto Pio XI mentioned above and the Seminario Lombardo to be described in the next chapter, were three of many beneficiaries of the policy. As will be seen, the placard failed to protect the Seminario Lombardo from a brutal invasion in December by a Nazi-Fascist paramilitary group contemptuous of instructions from the German army.

Nuns at the Convent of Our Lady of Sion may also not recall that the protective placard of October 25 was accompanied by a letter, mentioned above in connection with the Istituto Pio XI, urging recipients to exercise prudent and moderate conduct. It declared, "The secretary of state of His Holiness expresses the confidence that [your] conduct . . . will be inspired by diligent observation of the dispositions and instructions provided by the Holy See and by that discreet and prudent correctness that is always, but now more than ever, necessary." [18] Since there is, as seen, no evidence that the "dispositions and instructions provided by the Holy See" included directives to hide Jews, the urging of "discreet and prudent correctness . . . now more than ever, necessary" appears to be an admonition not to take advantage of the placard to bring excessive numbers of illegal fugitives into Church institutions.

As a final indication of Pius XII's involvement with their rescue of Jews, nuns at Our Lady of Sion maintain that a special delivery truck regularly brought them foodstuffs from the nearby Vatican.[19] The claim is probably correct in part, but there is no way to know how much food was delivered. There is also no reason to believe that any supplies were intended specifically for Jews. They may have been normal deliveries for the nuns. Also, many convents and monasteries were sheltering non-Jewish civilian victims of air raids and military operations, and Vatican officials were understandably less reluctant to assist in those entirely legal efforts. The knowledge that Jews, former Italian soldiers, draft dodgers, partisans, and political dissidents were illegally present among other legitimate refugees did not necessarily deter Vatican contributions of food, but neither did it increase them.

In addition to the timing and the absence of credible evidence or claims from contemporaries, there are other reasons for questioning papal involvement in the sheltering of Roman Jews in Church institutions. It is apparent that on or immediately after October 16, many individuals escaping the roundup were refused admission to convents and monasteries. Emma Alatri Fiorentino, for example, remembers receiving a telephone warning that the roundup was in progress. She went with her family to two nuns they knew. They were refused admission. They then walked from one convent to another along the Via Nomentana and were rejected everywhere.[20] Piero Terracina was also turned away twice. He does not recall the reason for the first rejection. In the second case, the price for room and board was too high.[21] Another group of Jewish fugitives walked around the city for hours with Don Libero Raganella, a priest at the Church of San Lorenzo, trying to find a shelter. They had no luck. Finally, just at curfew, the group found itself in front of Santa Susanna, a church with an adjoining cloister. The nuns, who apparently did not run a school or guest house, said that it was forbidden to accept outsiders, especially men, in their strictly cloistered area. Only after much discussion, during which Don Raganella promised to assume all responsibility for the violation of the rules of cloister, did the nuns relent.[22]

Many others share these memories of rejection or difficulties in obtaining shelter in Church institutions. Anna Ascarelli and her siblings were taken by their parents to a particular convent, as arranged before October 16. When they arrived, the nuns said that they could not enter unless they converted. They left.[23] The mother and grandmother of Bice Migliau had a similar experience. Nuns at a convent near the Piazza Farnese accepted them for three days after October 16. After that, they were told that they must convert or leave. Such a demand is hardly consistent with a papal directive. Bice maintains that the directors of many Catholic institutions in Rome became more sympathetic toward Jews very slowly after October 16, rather than all at once.[24]

There were many reasons for turning Jews away from convents and monasteries besides anti-Semitism and a fanatic commitment to obtain conversions. Some institutions were already overflowing with refugees of all types. With women and children sleeping on the floor or in crowded, unhealthy quarters, some nuns could not imagine a danger great enough to justify aggravating that situation. Furthermore, how were so many to be fed? Eventually, most guests had to pay room and board and acquire false documents in order to obtain their own ration books. With documents, women and children, if not men, often left their hiding places to shop. But such arrangements were not foreseeable on October 16, and many Jews may have been rejected for fear that they would cause serious shortages for everyone in a particular convent. A papal communication explaining the special dangers that threatened the Jews and promising to share the burden of feeding extra guests could have eased such worries. That, however, would have required a basic agreement among Vatican officials to help, as well as levels of foresight that simply did not exist.

Another reason for refusing to admit Jews to Church institutions involved the understandable fear that throngs of illegal fugitives in a single place would endanger those already there. Simple monks and nuns may not initially have grasped the special dangers threatening Jews, especially women and children, but they knew that anti-Fascist activists were in mortal peril. And the anti-Fascists usually arrived first, soon after September 8. Again, a papal directive could have explained that all Jews were in as much danger as any partisan, escaped prisoner of war, or draft evader. But again, such an explanation did not come.

Still another reason for believing that there was no papal directive to convents, monasteries, and Church schools and hospitals to hide Jews is that it was not technically necessary. As seen, Catholic institutions, with the exception of those convents and monasteries with strict rules of cloister that maintained no guest houses for outsiders, did not need special papal authorization to accept individuals of the same sex as their religious residents. Parish priests often advised the Vicariate of guests already accepted, while nuns and monks notified the superiors of their orders or requested permission to keep outsiders of dubious legality or the opposite sex. There was no need to involve Vatican officials. A papal directive or message of encouragement would have facilitated the hiding process by explaining the special dangers that Jews faced, easing worries about food and space, and warning against efforts to convert guests. But for the actual decision to grant hospitality, it was not essential. It is, therefore, difficult to believe that the cautious, conservative Pope Pius XII would have chosen to become involved, endangering his neutral status and risking his delicate relationships with the Germans who now surrounded the Vatican City, when the hiding process was functioning quite well without him.

One may well wonder why, in the absence of a papal directive and with only a vague understanding of the nature of the dangers threatening Jews, nuns and monks accepted them at all. There are several reasons. The first involved the Catholic Church's longstanding tradition of sheltering those in need. Nor was hospitality necessarily limited to those in the good graces of the secular state. The right of political dissidents and even common criminals to find asylum in churches and monasteries ended during the nineteenth century, with the assertion of the supremacy of the state in matters secular rather than religious. Men and women of the Church, in other words, were bound by the laws of their nation. But the mentality of those prepared to grant asylum did not always change, so that some priests, monks, and nuns who helped fugitives viewed themselves as exempt from secular law and superior in questions of morality. During the German occupation of Italy and other European countries, Jews and political dissidents were the beneficiaries of that mentality. After the war, former Fascists and Nazis benefited as well.[25]

With time and the opportunity to reflect after October 16, still other motives emerged. It should not detract from the magnanimity of men and women of the Church to suggest that some institutions were able to accept newcomers because they were virtually empty during the war. As seen in the cases of the Convent of Our Lady of Sion and the Istituto Pio XI, boarding schools and seminaries were barely functioning. In another example, the Religious Teachers Filippini sent their boarding students home during the last years of the war, for their own safety. They were able to shelter sixty Jews comfortably in the vacant space in their school in the Via Botteghe Oscure.[26] In some cases, paying guests offered welcome relief to institutions deprived of a major source of income. There is no evidence, not the merest suggestion, of an unscrupulous increasing of fees. There is frequent evidence, however, that reasonable fees were required.

How fugitives were able to continue paying fees for room and board for themselves and their elderly parents and young children remains a puzzle. Some Roman Jews, like Lea Di Nola, seen above, held jobs outside the convent and lived precariously with their false documents. Many foreign Jews, like those placed and supported by Sorani and Father Benedetto, received regular subsidies from Delasem and the Joint. But between these two extremes were many with no revenue at all. It is unclear how they managed.

The nuns at Our Lady of Sion solved the problem in their own way, which may not have been atypical. Some of the guests at the convent were able to earn a little money by working for the Vatican Information Service. The nuns received large bundles of letters written to the service by petitioners seeking information about their loved ones. Guests sorted the requests and recorded the data on standardized forms. The nuns then returned the letters and completed forms to the office of the Information Service, which paid them for the work.[27]

It should also not diminish the courage and compassion involved in rescue to point out that many of the Jews sheltered in Catholic institutions were in fact converts, relatives of converts, or the spouses and children of mixed marriages. It is neither possible nor desirable to determine their proportions among the full and observant Jews in hiding, but accounts of rescuers and survivors alike testify to their frequent presence. There are other hints as well, as, for example, Francesco Motto's remark cited above that most of the Jewish pupils accepted at the Istituto Pio XI arrived with recommendations from Catholic priests. Such a circumstance is only to be expected. Converts and others linked by family ties to Catholicism would have turned most quickly to the Church for help, and would have felt most comfortable doing so. Jews less acquainted with the Church may have been more hesitant, and they looked for help elsewhere.

Far less palatable than charging reasonable fees or focusing especially on Jews who were Catholics is the suspicion that men and women of the Church occasionally took advantage of their guests, especially the children, by pressing for conversions. Such a charge is difficult to measure. At least as many survivors testify that they experienced no pressure to convert as the contrary. But pressure could be discreet and subtle. Lonely children separated from their parents for long periods and eager to please their teachers and conform to their peer groups were vulnerable to the merest suggestion. Some nuns who came to care about them then responded to their expressions of interest with excessive zeal. Jewish leaders after the war were understandably reluctant to complain about the conduct of those who had done so much to help them. In a report of July 19, 1966, however, Delasem leader Settimio Sorani, after paying tribute to the courageous nuns and monks who had sheltered Jews, added, "I remember . . . that, after the liberation of Rome. . . , I went from convent to convent to bring out the Jewish children sheltered there and, more than once, I heard the answer that they had no 'Jewish children.' They had evidently been baptized, without much difficulty. All those whom it was possible to recover (about three hundred) were returned to family members or were sheltered in three children's homes." [28]

Yet another reason why men and women of the Church accepted Jews in their institutions is that, very infrequently, important figures within the Church asked them to do so. These rare personal requests in exceptional individual cases are in no way inconsistent with the absence of a general papal directive. Intervention at high levels tended to be for important figures who were usually, but not always, political or military fugitives. When the beneficiaries were Jewish, they tended often to be converts. Evidence of such intervention is scarce, however, and details about the beneficiaries are even scarcer. Prince Carlo Pacelli, for example, the nephew of Pius XII, intervened on October 1, 1943, for an Ettore Jannelli, but the available documents do not indicate whether he was a political, military, or racial fugitive.[29] In another case, Monsignor Giovanni Battista Montini wrote a rather vague letter on October 29, thanking the prior of a monastery for promptly accepting a group recommended by Montini's office. The monsignor did not say that the individuals were Jewish, but the editors of the Vatican's *Actes et Documents du Saint Siège* stated that they were.[30] There is no way to know whether they were also converts.

A better-documented example occurred on November 20, when a fervently Catholic woman, Jewish in origin but converted during childhood and subsequently the wife and mother of practicing Catholics, appealed personally to Pius XII. The woman asked for refuge in the Vatican itself or in a convent. Monsignor Montini wrote on the 21st that the woman was "non-Aryan," and noted that Monsignor Dell'Acqua might be able to help. Someone in his office, probably Dell'Acqua, then wrote on the 23rd, "I told Monsignor Brugnola [who had recommended the woman] that it is not possible in the Vatican." The writer added that he had suggested that Brugnola ask nuns at two convents if they could help in this particular case.[31] Presumably, he did so.

None of this should detract from the basic fact that men and women of the Church in Italy took in Jews above all because they saw them as human beings in desperate need of protection and assistance. They may not have known about Auschwitz, other death camps, or gas chambers, but they knew that women, children, and elderly people should not be arrested without cause and shoved into the backs of trucks, as they were on October 16, 1943. They should not be driven away to internment camps, train stations, and unknown destinations. The monks at Fatebenefratelli witnessed the great roundup and accepted those escaping it. The nuns at the nearby Convent of Our Lady of Sion heard the stories and did the same. The hiding of Jews in Catholic institutions was above all a spontaneous, uncoordinated gesture of compassion and sympathy. It involved little thought of the future, and little understanding of how long the new guests would have to stay.

It is not the purpose of this book to tell the comprehensive story of the rescue of Jews in Rome by men and women of the Church. Examples of rescue in convents, monasteries, schools, and hospitals have been mentioned in order to examine their dates of origin and any possible linkage with the Vatican. But while the full story cannot be told here, a word about the commonly accepted statistics of Jewish rescue in Church institutions in Rome is appropriate. In 1961, the well-known Italian historian Renzo De Felice published an impressive list of 100 female convents and 55 male-operated monasteries, schools, hospitals, parish churches, and Vatican-owned properties that sheltered Jews. Beside the name of each institution he provided the number of Jews sheltered. He concluded that the women's institutions protected 2,775 Jews, while those of the religious and secular male clergy, including eleven parish churches, sheltered 992. About 680 Jews were housed in Church buildings for just a few days, bringing the total of Jews rescued to 4,447.[32]

Although these statistics sound conclusive, they must be regarded with suspicion, for De Felice did not clearly reveal their source. He wrote only that the information had been requested from and provided by the heads of individual Catholic institutions. In fact, the material closely coincided with that published in *La Civiltà Cattolica* the same year by the German Jesuit Father Robert Leiber, Pius XII's closest advisor and friend during and after the war.[33]

If De Felice's statistics originated with Father Leiber, they might be suspect, for Pius XII's advisor and friend is hardly an unbiased source for such sensitive information.

Father Leiber's article was written to defend both the policy of the pope toward the Jews of Rome from 1943 to 1944 and his general silence regarding the persecution of the Jews. As the source of his statistics of rescue, Leiber cited another Jesuit priest, Father Beato Ambord, who directed the German transmissions of the Vatican Radio during the war and also helped distribute a fund from a private Swiss donor to needy Jews. Leiber did not say when the statistics were originally compiled, but he declared that they were "verified in 1954 with research on the individual cases." [34]

Apart from their origin, there are other reasons to question the Leiber–De Felice statistics. First is the problem of duplication. Both men admitted that some Jewish fugitives may have been included in the statistics of more than one institution. Such a situation is to be expected, for Jews frequently moved from one shelter to another. But without some estimate of the size of the overlap, the statistics become almost meaningless. It is, for example, virtually impossible that the Franciscans at the Monastery of San Bartolomeo all'Isola could have housed 400 extra guests all at the same time. The monastery was directly across the Tiber from the former Jewish ghetto. Many Jews, and quite possibly 400, may have passed through it during the terrifying days immediately following the October roundup. They would have been referred to other places, while other newcomers arrived to take their place. But those referred were then counted again elsewhere. Four hundred is a large number, especially if counted twice.

In partial compensation for exaggerated estimates resulting from duplication is the fact that many Church institutions that harbored Jews seem not to have been included on the list. De Felice does not mention, for example, the Convent of Santa Rufina, where the witness named David, mentioned above, found shelter with his mother and young brother. Nor does he list the Convent of Santa Susanna, where Don Libero Raganella found places for a family for at least one night. The list included some Vatican properties, to be discussed in the next chapter, but it omitted San Paolo fuori le Mura, which sheltered at least five Jews, and the Pontificio Collegio dei Sacerdoti per l'Emigrazione Italiana, which had several. It also omitted at least forty Jews hidden in the Vatican City itself, as will be seen. These omissions may have occurred because the original investigators did not contact every institution, or because not all institutions, intentionally or otherwise, responded.

Some may not even have known how many of their wartime guests were Jews rather than non-Jews. Thus, for example, the Fatebenefratelli appear on De Felice's list to have sheltered 46 Jews, while a subsequent investigator counted at least 67.[35]

There were in Rome in 1943 and 1944 hundreds of parish churches, 1,120 religious institutions for women, and 152 for men.[36] Given that surprisingly large number, the statistics of 100 female convents and 55 male institutions (including eleven parish churches) that sheltered Jews become less impressive. Most Catholic institutions, after all, took pride in their reputation as dispensers of hospitality and succor. It should have been the norm rather than the exception for them to shelter Jews and others in distress. Perhaps more did, but perhaps not. What is certain is that we will never really know.

CHAPTER FOURTEEN

Hiding After the Roundup

Vatican Properties, October 16–December 1943

IN AN attempt to escape frequent German roundups of young men for labor service, twenty-two-year-old Michael Tagliacozzo had been living away from home since the end of September 1943. When German police knocked on the door of his relatives' home in the early morning of October 16, he, still in his sleeping clothes, slipped out a window and into the apartment of a Catholic family whom he did not even know. Unable to return home and desperate for refuge, he remembered Maria Amendola, a former teacher, who sheltered him for a few days. Amendola put him in touch with a young assistant parish priest, Don Vincenzo Fagiolo. "It was he," wrote Tagliacozzo, "who warmly defended my cause with the rector of the seminary, Monsignor Roberto Ronca." [1] The seminary was the prestigious Pontificio Seminario Romano Maggiore on the Piazza di Porta San Giovanni, in the vast complex of buildings that also included the Basilica di San Giovanni in Laterano and the Lateran Palace, which today houses the offices of the Vicariate of Rome. Undeterred and fortified with recommendations from Professor Amendola and Don Fagiolo, a former student at the seminary, Tagliacozzo ventured to the Lateran complex, passed through gates patrolled by papal guards, and received asylum on October 22. [2]

Tagliacozzo's place of refuge was not an ordinary Church institution. The Pontificio Seminario Romano Maggiore was a Vatican property, a remnant of the centuries of glory when the Papal States comprised not only all of Rome but a good portion of central Italy. Furthermore, the Seminario

Romano, as it will be called here, was specifically mentioned in the Lateran Accords of 1929 as enjoying the "immunities recognized by International Law to the seats of diplomatic agents of foreign States."[3] Along with the Vatican City itself, it was declared to be "neutral and inviolable territory," with extraterritorial rights and privileges.[4] Of the several Vatican properties that sheltered Jews and will be discussed in this chapter and the next, one other, the Basilica di San Paolo fuori le Mura, enjoyed similar status and protections. Several other Vatican properties that offered refuge were acknowledged by the treaty as belonging to the Holy See, but they were not granted extraterritorial status. Those mentioned in this chapter and the next will include the Seminario Lombardo, the Pontificio Istituto Orientale, the Collegio Russo, and the Pontificio Collegio dei Sacerdoti per l'Emigrazione Italiana. But with or without extraterritorial status, all Vatican properties were more directly linked to the papal authorities than were parish churches, monasteries, and convents. With regard to their role in sheltering Jews during the German occupation, they require separate scrutiny.

At the Seminario Romano, the young Tagliacozzo eventually found himself among an impressive cross-section of Italy's political, economic, and social elites in hiding. Foremost among them was Ivanoe Bonomi, former prime minister and president of the Comitato di Liberazione Nazionale (CLN) during much of the German occupation. The CLN was coordinating the Resistance and planning for a postwar Italy. Bonomi noted in his diary on December 5, 1943, that "the authorized representatives of four of the six movements [or parties] of the Comitato di Liberazione are here, including the Liberal [Alessandro] Casati, the Democrat [Meuccio] Ruini, the Christian Democrat [Alcide] De Gasperi, and the Socialist [Pietro] Nenni."[5] Other prestigious political figures sheltered at the Seminario Romano included Giuseppe Saragat, a Socialist and later the fourth president of the Italian Republic, who arrived at the end of March 1944; Marcello Solari, a Liberal Party minister in prewar cabinets who would serve again after liberation; and four ministers from Marshal Badoglio's government in the summer of 1943. There were also at least three well-known former diplomats, two prefects, several senators, six generals, an admiral, four princes, two counts, and a marquis, as well as engineers, medical doctors, university professors, lawyers, and businessmen.[6] At least two of the senators were former Fascists.[7] There were probably several others.

Perhaps the most surprising guest at the Seminario was the daughter of Marshal Rodolfo Graziani, the current minister of war in Mussolini's Republic of Salò. She was accompanied by her husband and children.[8] Also within the complex, but presumably in another building, were members of Badoglio's family.[9] But surely the most compromising guest in German eyes was General Roberto Bencivenga, Badoglio's commander of military Resistance operations in Rome, and a late arrival at the seminary. The general was present because he had slipped on the marble floor of the seminary and broken his leg during a meeting with Bonomi in May 1944. With such an injury he could not safely leave.[10]

The presence of so many politically involved and often openly anti-Nazi individuals in a Vatican institution renders somewhat hollow the claim that assistance to Jews would compromise the Holy See and antagonize the Germans. The reasons for their acceptance, however, seem clear. The political, economic and social elites protected at the Seminario Romano included many of Italy's most prestigious anti-Fascist but non-Communist leaders. They were the very men who would soon be rebuilding the country and redefining postwar Italy's relations with a Church that had not heretofore distinguished itself by opposition to Fascism. They were also, in the eyes of most Vatican officials, the only men capable of maintaining order and thwarting a Communist takeover in the power vacuum that would follow the defeat and withdrawal of the Nazis and their Fascist allies. The war, by December 1943, was clearly drawing to a close. The Allies were temporarily stalled south of Rome, but their ultimate victory could only be a matter of time.

Among the total of about 200 guests at the Seminario Romano, there were also at least fifty-five Jews.[11] They included Giorgio Del Vecchio, rector of the University of Rome from 1925 to 1927, and his wife; Roberto Almagià, former university professor of geography in Rome, and his son; Federigo Enriques, a former university professor of mathematics in Rome; Gino Cohen, an ex-administrator of the Società Pantanella; and many other professors, businessmen, industrialists, lawyers, doctors, and students. There were also some small nuclear families—men with their wives and children.[12] Some of the Jews had converted to Catholicism years earlier, but according to Michael Tagliacozzo, who knew them all, they were a minority.[13]

With the exception of two or three early arrivals, to be mentioned below, most fugitives entered the seminary in late October, November, and December 1943.[14] The Jews conformed to the same pattern. Of those whose dates of arrival at the seminary are recorded, six entered in October just after the Rome roundup, two in November, and eight in December, after the Republic of Salò ordered that Italian police arrest all Jews on sight.[15] According to Tagliacozzo, however, a few Jews came to the seminary as late as April 1944.[16]

Jews and non-Jews alike entered the seminary with personal recommendations. Tagliacozzo explains that "personal identification of persecuted individuals was essential to prevent the infiltration of Fascist agents like that which occurred [elsewhere]. The recommendations generally came from monks, parish priests, members of Catholic Action, and simple people who appealed to their priests or other Catholic institutions on behalf of the persecuted."[17]

Tagliacozzo has nothing but good memories about the way Jews were treated at the seminary. He remembers:

> There was absolutely no pressure for conversion to Christianity. The respect shown to those being helped was exemplary. I remember fondly that Don Palazzini turned to me, knowing that among the refugees I was the closest to the Jewish traditions. He begged me to instruct him in the Jewish dietary laws, so that the sentiments of the refugees would not be offended. He gave me a Bible in Hebrew that inspired me with faith and hope in the future. . . .
>
> The Jews were treated exactly the same as the political refugees. In fact, if there was any preference it was for us (food, laundry, medical assistance). Here I add a personal memory. In January 1944 I had bronchitis. Don Palazzini immediately provided a doctor and the necessary medicine. After the convalescence he provided a food supplement that continued until the day of liberation.[18]

Like Father Benedetto, Pietro Palazzini, assistant to the rector of the Seminario Romano, and Vincenzo Fagiolo, who helped Tagliacozzo to enter, both eventually cardinals, received the Medal of the Righteous Among the Nations from Yad Vashem in Israel. So too did Maria Amendola, the teacher who first sheltered Tagliacozzo and then sent him to Fagiolo.

Despite Tagliacozzo's reference to adequate food and medicine, the technical problems of feeding so many extra people were enormous. To address them, workers at the seminary kept a large garden, raised thirty dairy cows, traveled long distances to acquire wheat at the lowest possible prices, and ground wheat and made pasta on the premises. On the other hand, funding was apparently less difficult. Although the Seminario Romano neither charged fees nor accepted payments, it received financial contributions from both the Holy See and Badoglio's government in southern Italy.[19] Nor was space an issue, for Ronca had had a new wing for seminary students built just before the war. Many of those students were young priests from Britain, France, and the United States who had returned home at the outbreak of hostilities. Of a total of 130 seminarians before the war, only forty remained in 1943.[20] The outside guests in 1943 filled their vacant rooms and occasionally spilled over into other buildings within the complex. Political and Jewish fugitives were housed in separate wings or on different floors.

The directors of the Seminario Romano also struggled with problems of security and discipline. According to Palazzini, the guests did not disguise themselves in clerical garb. "With regard to false documents," he added, "the seminary never provided them. Some [guests] obtained them from the outside."[21] After the police raid on the Seminario Lombardo on December 21, to be described in the next chapter, CLN members were assigned hiding places to use in the event of a search. Those same individuals, however, occasionally left the seminary to attend CLN meetings elsewhere in the city, or hosted similar meetings in the seminary itself.[22] Those activities, a clear violation of international law and the privileges and obligations of neutral powers, largely ceased after the Italian police raid on the Basilica di San Paolo fuori le Mura on the night of February 3–4, as will be seen.

The relationship between Pius XII and the wartime rescue activities at the Seminario Romano is complex and elusive. It is clear that some of the first individuals to find shelter in the seminary were sponsored by high-level prelates and Church officials. One of these, Ettore Jannelli, was recommended by Prince Carlo Pacelli, the pope's nephew, on October 1.[23] Prince Pacelli's letter of recommendation was addressed to Monsignor Luigi Traglia, the assistant to the vicar. Traglia then passed Jannelli along to Monsignor Ronca at the seminary. While Ronca was more than willing to make his institution a place of refuge, the importance of Jannelli's sponsors also assured him that he had the approval of the vicar and probably of the pope himself. Two weeks after Jannelli's arrival, the equally well-connected Prince Giovanni Torlonia and his young son Alessandro also received asylum at the seminary.[24]

As the number of outsiders at the seminary grew, however, Ronca found himself in an increasingly delicate position. Despite the recommendations from high places for some of his earliest guests, he was increasingly aware of opposition from conservative prelates in the pope's entourage to any steps that might jeopardize Vatican neutrality and incur the wrath of the occupying forces. That opposition had been well expressed in a Secretariat of State memorandum on October 23 that Ronca probably did not see but with whose arguments he was undoubtedly familiar. Just a week after the roundup of the Roman Jews the unidentified author of the note recorded that he had spoken with Father Aquilin Reichert, a German confessor at St. Peter's Basilica. Reichert had asked the author to inform his superiors that, in Reichert's opinion but in the author's words:

> General Stahel [the German military commander of Rome] will probably respect extraterritorial buildings, convents, etc., but the SS, which, as is known, act under the orders of their own commanders, certainly will not.
>
> The attitude of the Vicariate which, according to [Reichert], facilitates the access to convents of Jews, deserters, etc., seems imprudent to him. . . . In the face of the SS, it is necessary to exercise prudence in order not to compromise the interests of the Holy Church and the refugees themselves with an act of poorly understood charity. According to [Reichert], the SS will begin to raid convents and buildings of the Holy See.[25]

Aware of opposition of this type and eager to protect themselves, Ronca and his assistants wrote a memorandum sometime in late 1943 or early 1944. It stated, in part:

> We have tried, as much as possible, to limit the number of requests [accepted] and to remove ourselves from pressure; above all the directors of the seminary are in continuous contact with their superiors, sending information of everything that happens either to the cardinal vicar in one or even two audiences a day or to the secretary of state, particularly by means of the secretary of Monsignor Montini, to whom the seminary for a long period of time sent a priest from the Istituto daily. . . .
>
> The secretary of Monsignor Montini did not fail to make frequent visits to the wing of the Istituto where the guests are, to interest himself in their condition, needs, and desires. . . .
>
> Monsignor Montini similarly sent other persons belonging to the Secretariat of State.[26]

In this memorandum, the rector was answering or anticipating charges that he had shown too much initiative and independence by admitting so many fugitives, and especially, so many with political credentials. His policy, he wanted to remind his critics, had always had backers in high places, including the vicar of Rome and Monsignor Giovanni Battista Montini, the secretary of the Section for Ordinary Ecclesiastical Affairs within the Vatican Secretariat of State.

On December 11, 1943, the rector wrote an even more revealing letter to the pope himself:

> It is with the greatest sorrow that I have learned that I also have added a displeasure to that mass of pain that today weighs upon the paternal heart of Your Holiness. . . .
>
> For all my failings, I humbly beg your pardon. . . .
>
> I believed that it was in the heart of Your Holiness to welcome in your seminary, with the greatest possible reserve, caution and secrecy, some poor unhappy persons caught up in the current storm.
>
> I was confirmed in this through meetings with prelates of the Secretariat of State and with the same persons of authority who presented and recommended refugees to be welcomed at the seminary. The first nucleus of refugees that Your Holiness benevolently deigned to send me served as a guideline. These grew in number: but I thought that it was not necessary to involve the highest responsibility of Your Holiness in individual cases.[27]

Ronca had apparently been criticized for excessive zeal, and the pope was backing away from him. His confusion was understandable, since his first guest had been recommended by the pope's nephew and passed along to him by the assistant vicar of Rome.

Ronca's writings indicate that his rescue activities were well known to his own superiors, as well as to some of those Vatican officials closest to the pope. The significance of that fact, however, should not be exaggerated or extended to apply more broadly to all other Church institutions in Rome. Because it was an extraterritorial property of the Holy See, the Seminario Romano had an exceptionally close relationship with the Vatican. The supervision under which it operated did not extend to convents, monasteries, or schools, whose directors reported above all to the heads of their religious orders. Parish churches in Rome fell somewhere in between, for the priests who headed them were responsible to the vicar of Rome. They enjoyed, however, more independence than did the directors of Vatican properties.

In addition, the fact that Montini was involved in sheltering fugitives at the Seminario Romano does not prove that a general directive came from the pope. Pius XII was certainly informed, but Ronca's letter to him on December 11, 1943, suggests that he was not always supportive. At least one important churchman, Monsignor Emanuele Clarizio, Montini's secretary during the occupation, believed that Montini acted at some personal risk in this and in other cases, and went beyond the expressed will of the pope.[28]

It is interesting to note that in his book about the Seminary Romano during the occupation, Palazzini, by then a cardinal, never claimed that Pius XII directed Ronca to shelter Jews. He recorded that "one day in September 1943 Monsignor Ronca called me and said, 'In the times in which we live we are obliged to open the doors of the seminary not only to clerics, whose number is much reduced, but also to outsiders who need asylum to save their lives."[29] Ronca apparently said nothing of a papal directive. Elsewhere, Palazzini pointed out that since the vicar certainly told the pope about the fugitives at the seminary during his frequent audiences, "Thus, in the last analysis, it was Pius XII himself who allowed this great work of charity."[30] Allowed, perhaps, but not ordered or even supported.

When explaining how it was possible that the seminary accepted the daughters of both the pro-Fascist Graziani and the anti-Fascist Badoglio, Palazzini declared that "the guidelines provided by Pope Pius XII were to save human lives, on whatever side they may be."[31] In keeping with that theme, Palazzini freely admitted that after the war the seminary also sheltered some former persecutors of Jews and anti-Fascists when they were threatened with purge trials.[32] Finally, in the strongest defense of the pope that this honest man could truthfully manage, Palazzini declared: "Under the pressure of events, although so very tragic, men rediscovered the Christian message, that is, the sense of reciprocal charity, according to which it is a duty to charge oneself with the salvation of others. To rediscover it, one voice was often raised among the din of arms: it was the voice of Pius XII. The refuge offered to so many people would not have been possible without his moral support, which was much more than a tacit consent."[33] As evidence of the "voice of Pius XII," Palazzini cited his radio message of August 24, 1939; his Christmas messages of 1939, 1941, 1942, and 1943; and speeches on the pope's name day, June 2, in 1940, 1943, and 1944. As seen in the introduction to this book, only in the addresses of Christmas 1942 and June 2, 1943, did the pope make a brief reference to those persecuted because of their descent [stirpe]. He did, however, often mention the need for compassion for all those who were suffering because of the war.

After hiding for months in temporary shelters after the Rome roundup, Enzo Finzi was admitted to the Seminario Lombardo, across the piazza from Santa Maria Maggiore, on April 9, 1944. The seminary was a Vatican property, but it did not enjoy extraterritorial privileges. Finzi was sent there by a friend, who arranged a meeting with the rector. As the young fugitive later wrote, "When I was accepted there, the seminary had already experienced the most intense and desperate hours of its history."[34] He did not exaggerate. A Fascist paramilitary group with a few German SS agents had raided the institution on the night of December 21–22 and taken away several fugitives.

The first fugitive arrived at the Seminario Lombardo on September 9, as the Germans were occupying Rome. He and most of several others who followed in early October were young non-Jewish men evading conscription for labor or military service.[35] The first two Jews, a middle-aged couple, arrived on September 29 or 30, unusually early.[36] All but two of the twelve other Jews who found refuge at the Seminario Lombardo before October 16 were also young men who feared being apprehended for labor service. Twenty-two additional Jews arrived in October after the roundup, and 27 in November or December. By mid-December they numbered about 63, among a total of 110 fugitives.[37]

Unlike those in the Seminario Romano, most of the Jews at the Seminario Lombardo were average but not prominent citizens. A seminary list described most of them as businessmen, shopkeepers, clerks, housewives, students, and elementary school pupils. There were also two surgeons, one lawyer, one pharmacist, and one bank director.[38] Although it is not possible in all cases to determine their personal connections with the seminary, existing documents provide some hints. At least six of the Jews present were converts to Catholicism.[39] A detailed but informal report written by a seminarian after the liberation of Rome identified four of them. Three had converted before arrival, and one did so soon after. One of the first three was the uncle of a rather important non-Jewish professor of economics who was also hiding at the Lombardo.[40] Many of the other Jews at the seminary were present in large family groups. There were, for example, thirteen Anticolis, probably the families of three adult brothers; six Di Coris; six Mielis; five Di Gioacchinos; five Spizzichinos; and four Astrologos; not to mention the married women who shared one of these names as a maiden name. Furthermore, the Anticolis and the Di Coris had previously lived in the same building. Two other guests had lived in the same building as the four Astrologos.[41] The point is that one person who was either a Catholic himself or had some family connection to a Catholic probably brought a number of others with him when he appealed to the seminary for help.

In contrast to the Jews, the non-Jews at the Seminario Lombardo were all men. Very few of them were accompanied by even one other family member. Before the German occupation, most had been either middle-level government bureaucrats or military officers. Two were recorded as members of the nobility. On the other hand, one, Giovanni Roveda, was an important figure in the Italian Communist Party. Nevertheless, as the same seminarian wrote after liberation, perhaps thinking of the prominent politicians hidden at the Seminario Romano, "There weren't any honest to goodness big cheeses [*pezzi grossi*] at the seminary. The rector, faithful to his convictions and wanting to perform acts of charity, had accepted the poor." [42]

At least fifteen of the non-Jews, but apparently none of the Jews, were inscribed as students at the Università Gregoriana in the scholastic year 1943–44.[43] They carried special identification cards with their photographs and the signature and seal of the assistant vicar of Rome, Monsignor Luigi Traglia, testifying that they were seminarians and students of philosophy.[44] They also wore clerical garb. Jews with families obviously could not be similarly disguised. Instead, they were referred to as "refugees."

The disguise and enrollment of false students at the Università Gregoriana indicates that officials at the Vicariate knew of their presence at the Seminario Lombardo. Whether they also knew about the Jews is uncertain but probable. It is not clear how much officials at the Vatican Secretariat of State knew.

It could not have been easy for priests accustomed to routine and perfect order to maintain 110 men, women, and children in wartime. Their space and resources were more limited than those of the Seminario Romano, and their guests more often young and unruly. When they originally accepted them, they did not expect that they would stay long. As a priest noted on November 1, "A new month is beginning. None of the guests who entered at the beginning of last month, or in September, would ever have thought that they would still be here in November." [45] For their own comfort and protection the guests were required to observe a strict set of rules governing their daily schedule, maintenance of their rooms, and procedures in case of alarms. To ease the boredom, there were lectures, study circles, and concerts. Throughout November and early December a priest described the activities. He always noted Jewish participation. One Jewish physician lectured on diseases, and another spoke about modern surgery. A Jewish organist contributed to a religious ceremony. Many Jews demonstrated their enthusiasm for Bible studies. The priest seemed to have great interest in his Jewish guests, but he did not mention the sensitive issue of conversion.[46]

The priests at the Seminario Lombardo were aware that the Jews in their midst faced special problems and dangers. A seminarian wrote in early November, for example, that while all guests had suffered, it was worse for the Jews because of the "searches, vexations, and thefts in their houses and businesses."[47] He seemed not to have known yet about still worse causes for their terror and concern. On November 27, however, he wrote that many more Jews were arriving and that "we are learning that many have been seized in order to be sent to concentration camps: their property, both furniture and real estate, requisitioned."[48] Tension was mounting in Rome and throughout Italy. December would bring a new Italian government policy toward Jews, and terrifying new problems.

While many Jewish and non-Jewish fugitives from the Nazis and Fascists were being sheltered in properties of the Holy See scattered throughout Rome, a few were even more fortunate. On rare occasions throughout the period of the German occupation, individual priests, prelates, or laymen who worked and resided in the Vatican City were able to bring fugitives in distress within the walls of the Vatican itself. The beneficiaries were usually important Italian political dissenters or military officers, but they occasionally included escaped Allied prisoners of war or Jews, many of whom were converts. Outsiders often simply walked through a gate in the walls in the company of their benefactors, who assured the Swiss Guards or other Vatican sentinels that they were entering on legitimate business. Other fugitives passed through the gates in diplomatic vehicles, again with help from their benefactors, or entered through doorways from the interior of the basilica, which remained open to the public. Once inside they usually resided in their benefactor's private apartments. They were expected to remain indoors and refrain from communicating with the outside world. Above all, they were to avoid attracting the attention of Vatican employees who might be spies and report their presence to the Nazis and their Fascist collaborators.

The number of fugitives residing in the Vatican City at the end of 1943 is unknown. There may have been very few, or none at all. On October 25, 1943, just after the Rome roundup, Monsignor Montini noted that German Ambassador to the Holy See Ernst von Weizsäcker had asked whether it was true that political fugitives, Jews, military officers, or other outsiders were being sheltered there. Weizsäcker was informed that it was not true. It is not clear whether there really were no fugitives present at this date, whether Montini did not know the whole truth, or whether he simply lied. The editors of the *Actes et Documents du Saint Siège* suggest that Weizsäcker received a "diplomatic" response, because no fugitives were *officially* present.[49]

By February 1944 there were about fifty fugitives living in private apartments in the Canonica di San Pietro, just left of the basilica. On the pope's request, Monsignor Guido Anichini, head of the Canonica, made inquiries and provided the statistic, along with some sketchy information about each individual. Nearly all were men. Women were present only in their capacity as wives or sisters of the men. Roughly twenty-four of the guests were non-Jews, often important former government officials or military officers. Another seventeen were Catholics described as "non-Aryans," while seven were Jews whose religion was not mentioned. Three others were described as Catholics, with no hint of their status as Jews or non-Jews.[50]

Monsignor Anichini's statistics were limited to the Canonica di San Pietro. There is no way to know how many other fugitives were housed elsewhere behind the Vatican walls at that time. Certainly there were some, for Anichini did not mention the British and American escaped prisoners of war known to have found at least a temporary refuge at the Vatican in 1944 if not earlier.[51] On June 2, 1944, however, an official at the Secretariat of State investigated the number of fugitives sheltered throughout the entire Vatican City. His resulting calculation came to about 160, of whom about forty were Jews. At least fifteen of the forty had been baptized, some during their stay in the Vatican City. About 120 of the total of 160 were housed in the Canonica di San Pietro.[52]

The official from the Secretariat of State described the outsiders present in June as "all respectable people and some highly distinguished." Obviously impressed, he went on to list nine names, including four counts, two marquis, one *commendatore*, one with the title Sua Eccellenza, and another called *onorevole*. These prestigious figures were the personal guests of monsignors, also listed by name. The other outsiders were described as high-ranking military officers, former government officials, and rich businessmen. The latter, especially, were guests of lower-level Vatican employees.

Pius XII knew that some outsiders were being sheltered within the Vatican City. He may not always have known the extent of the rescue work, but he certainly learned about the reports of Anichini in February and the Secretariat of State official in June. The former report, after all, was addressed to him. The second would have ended up on his desk. It is clear, however, that the initiative for rescue came from individuals. Pius XII did not prohibit these activities, but neither did he encourage or even necessarily approve of them. On the contrary, as will be seen in the next chapter, some officials at the Vatican Secretariat of State strongly disapproved of the presence of outsiders and demanded their departure. They almost succeeded. Their demands continued until the liberation of Rome on June 4, 1944.

CHAPTER FIFTEEN

Raids and Reconsideration

December 1943–June 1944

THROUGHOUT the period of the terrifying Rome roundup and the rush of Jews into hiding, Mussolini's puppet government remained strangely silent and uninvolved. At a special convention at Verona on November 14, however, diehard Fascist delegates overwhelmingly approved, article by article, a political manifesto defining their party's new program. Article Seven of the so-called Carta di Verona declared, "Those belonging to the Jewish race are foreigners. During this war they belong to an enemy nationality."[1] Despite this ominous declaration, official Italian policy remained unclear for another two weeks. Then, on the evening of November 30, the infamous police order number five was broadcast over the Italian radio. At 9:00 A.M. on December 1, Minister of the Interior Guido Buffarini Guidi delivered the order to his prefects, who in turn relayed it to their police chiefs.

The order declared that all Jews in Italy, even if granted exemptions under earlier anti-Jewish laws, were to be arrested by Italian police and carabinieri and interned in camps within the country. It thus made the arresting of Jews, hitherto entirely a German affair, an official Italian policy. Deportation was not specified, but nearly all Jews subsequently arrested were delivered to the Germans and transported, mostly to Auschwitz. According to the same police order, Jewish property and possessions were to be confiscated. Individuals born of mixed marriages but baptized and officially defined as "Aryan" under the anti-Jewish laws were to be placed under police surveillance.[2] Ten days later the order was amended slightly. Italian Jews who were gravely ill, over the age of seventy, or spouses in mixed marriages were not to be arrested.[3]

Police order number five did not greatly alter the situation of Jews in Rome, where Jews fortunate enough to have escaped the great roundup had already left their homes for hiding places. In other cities where many Jews had been arrested, such as Milan, Turin, Genoa, and Florence, the situation was similar. The police order dramatically affected other Jews, however—individuals and families in smaller cities, towns, and villages who now realized that the local Italian police and carabinieri were under orders to arrest them wherever and whenever they could be found. The testimonies of most Jews from cities that had not yet experienced raids indicate that they went into hiding at this time.

Two days after the police order became effective, *L'Osservatore Romano* described the measures and clearly expressed its objections. There was no motive for such a policy, the author complained; no reason to punish innocent women, children, the elderly, the sick, those hitherto exempt from many anti-Jewish measures, or "so many sincere converts and practising Catholics." If the baptized children of mixed marriages were simply to be placed under surveillance, he suggested, why could not a similar policy be applied to all Jews, "given that [personal behavior or responsibility] does not depend upon birth, but upon the will and emerges from facts." In these anguishing times, it was indispensable "to remain worthy of the goodness and help of God by showing charity toward all his creatures."[4]

The author resumed the theme the following day. Article Seven of the Carta di Verona, he declared, was a preposterous justification for the arrests and internment of all Jews. A mere declaration of a political program could not be regarded as the law of the land. Jews born in Italy and enjoying Italian citizenship could not, because of a mere political program, be reclassified as enemy nationals. It was not appropriate "to send [Jews] to concentration camps, especially, we repeat, children, women, old people, the sick; and those with previous exemptions, precisely because it is recognized that their activity has never been directed against the interests of Italy; and [it was not appropriate to send away] Catholics who have never belonged, or no longer belong, to the Jewish Community." The author concluded, "We are confident, we continue to be confident of wisdom and good will, justice and mercy."[5]

Behind these eloquent words there lay, perhaps, an agreement that some Jews, presumably young adult males, might be a risk to the nation and should be interned on an individual basis. But this is nit-picking. The two articles deserve commendation. Readers at the time may have wondered why only *Italian* policies toward Jews were criticized; why roundups of Jews elsewhere in Europe, not to mention the German-conducted raids in Rome, Milan, Genoa, Turin, Bologna, and Florence in October and November 1943, were not equally condemned. After the second article, readers may also have wondered why the Vatican lapsed again into silence while Italian police obeyed the order and arrested thousands of Jews, most notably in Venice. Finally, they may have asked why *L'Osservatore Romano* expressed no objections when Italian authorities allowed the Germans to seize and deport several thousand Jews arrested after the police order and interned for a time at Fossoli and elsewhere. The "justice and mercy" for which the newspaper had pleaded continued to be ignored. But on December 3 and 4, at least, the Vatican took the high ground and sent a message to the faithful. Clearly it felt free to criticize some Italian government policies while it hesitated to speak when Germans acted similarly.

A few days after the articles, the police order, as seen, was modified slightly to exempt Jews who were gravely ill, over seventy, and spouses in mixed marriages. It is possible that the objections of *L'Osservatore Romano* contributed to the modification. As time went on, however, the special exemptions were respected less and less, but *L'Osservatore Romano* did not protest again. Furthermore, the exemption of Jewish spouses in mixed marriages did not represent a major government concession, for the original police order including them resulted from an excess of zeal that not even most Nazis practiced. In the German Reich itself, Jews in mixed marriages and their children were not usually deported. Nevertheless, even the slightest and most temporary government concession saved lives and was welcome. If Vatican protests could help secure any results at all, that was all the more reason why they should be made—and more often.

About two weeks after the articles in *L'Osservatore Romano,* a curious exchange of reports within the Vatican Secretariat of State occurred. An official from the Secretariat reported on December 17 that the archbishop of Ferrara had appealed for an intervention from the Holy See on behalf of "non-Aryans," especially those in mixed families. The writer continued:

> It is clear, however, that a direct and official intervention of the
> Holy See [with the government of the Republic of Salò] is not opportune under the present circumstances.
> We could send a little note to Padre Tacchi [Venturi] begging

him to do whatever possible: Father Tacchi is not the nuncio: thus his intervention cannot be taken as a direct intervention of the Holy See.

We could also ask the nuncio [Borgongini Duca] to say or arrange to be said a little word, confidentially, to Marshal Graziani or Buffarini Guidi, that mercy be applied especially toward the mixed families.

To the archbishop we can respond saying that the Holy See as it has done in the past, also in the present circumstances, is trying to come to the aid, as much as it can, of the "non-Aryans," especially those in mixed families.

Certainly it will be difficult to obtain what is asked because probably the government of the Republic is acting under the influence of the German authorities: but, if nothing else, it will always be possible to say that the Holy See has done everything possible to help these unhappy people.[6]

The cynicism here is undisguised. The Secretariat official had no intention of intervening on behalf of the Jews but was concerned only with preserving appearances. He wanted to be able tell the archbishop of Ferrara, as well as critics in the future, that the Holy See had done everything possible while cleverly arranging a token response that he knew would fail. In addition to those objections, the emphasis on Jews in mixed marriages, as opposed to all Jews, is unsettling. Equally shocking was Secretary of State Cardinal Maglione's response. On December 18 the cardinal wrote to tell Tacchi Venturi that the archbishop of Ferrara had asked for a papal intervention in favor of "non-Aryans" who were Catholics. He thus narrowed the archbishop's request still further, from an emphasis on Jews in mixed marriage to an absolute and deliberate focus only on them. Maglione asked Tacchi Venturi to try to call the attention of the Italian authorities to the issue, "noting the necessity that mitigated treatment be used above all toward mixed families."[7]

As instructed, Tacchi Venturi prepared a formal note of protest that began by stating that Italian non-Jews were essentially not hostile to the Jews in their midst and disapproved of the recent government measures against them.[8] On December 20, however, Maglione wrote that neither Tacchi Venturi's note, which he had seen, nor a "more delicate note from us" needed to be sent. He had just learned that mixed families would not be disturbed. He added that Tacchi Venturi's note would in any case have had to be revised.

As far as Jews not in mixed marriages were concerned, he stated that "the authorities here in Rome and in the province are looking carefully for a convenient place [for their internment]." [9]

The constant emphasis of Vatican officials on converts and Jews in mixed marriages is difficult to interpret. Did they limit their requests for strategic reasons, in order not to antagonize Fascists and achieve nothing at all? Did they intend, after securing mitigation for Jews with Catholic connections, to issue additional appeals for the others? Or did they, even as late as December 1943, define their responsibilities purely in terms of Jews who were Catholics, or married to Catholics? The latter conclusion seems harsh, but official Vatican language often renders it inescapable.

At the same time that Italian police and carabinieri were being charged with arresting nearly all Jews, a local ordinance in Rome made hiding more difficult for Jews and non-Jews alike. The ordinance of December 6 required that the names of all persons present in every building in the city be posted daily at the entrances. Doormen, concierges, innkeepers, and other service personnel were to be held personally responsible for errors and omissions, and all unlisted individuals found in buildings were liable to arrest. It became more imperative than ever that those in hiding have valid identification documents and residence permits. Levels of tension rose.

Despite the articles in L'Osservatore Romano, Vatican officials seem to have backed further away from sheltering Jews and other fugitives at this time. One indication of increased caution is revealed by the letter on December 11, described in the previous chapter, from Monsignor Roberto Ronca, rector of the Seminario Romano, to the pope, apologizing for accepting too many refugees. Another sign of change is suggested by the Foligno case. On December 2, a day after the issuance of police order number five but before the subsequent notice that Jewish spouses in mixed marriages would be exempt, a lawyer named Foligno wrote to Cardinal Maglione to beg for help. Foligno had been arrested during the roundup of October 16, but released because he was a member of a mixed family. He was not only a Catholic since birth who had a non-Jewish, practicing Catholic wife and children, but he was also a high-ranking lawyer at the Vatican. In light of the threat posed by the new police order, Foligno asked if he and his family could be sheltered in the Vatican City or in some extraterritorial Vatican building. Monsignor Giovanni Battista Montini, as seen, had been willing on November 21 to refer a similar case to an assistant, Monsignor Angelo Dell'Acqua, who suggested some nuns who might help. To Foligno's request of December 2, however, Montini answered with terrifying finality. He noted succinctly on Foligno's letter, "Unfortunately what he asks is not in our power. Respond accordingly."[10]

Toward the end of the third week of December, an unidentified Italian colonel provided the Vatican with some disturbing information. The German SS were about to increase their contingent in Rome from the current total of 400 men to 2,000. Once that level of strength was achieved, they planned to search every building in Rome, including many convents and monasteries. All male guests capable of bearing arms would be ordered to leave the buildings. Those who obeyed would be "loaded into freight cars." Those who refused would be shot. Vatican properties with the placard indicating special protection would receive "pro-forma visits." However, SS Lieutenant Colonel Herbert Kappler, chief of the German security police in Rome, had not ruled out the possibility that the Vatican City itself would be attacked.[11]

Little more than twenty-four hours after the colonel's report, his dire warning became a reality at one cluster of Vatican properties. At about 10:30 on the night of December 21, 1943, in a torrential rainstorm, a group of what appeared to be Italian police officers accompanied by a few Germans burst into the Seminario Lombardo. In reality, the Italians were members of a semi-autonomous paramilitary force headed by Pietro Koch, an Italian Fascist fanatic, and the accompanying Germans belonged to the SS.[12] After dragging the rector, Monsignor Francesco Bertoglio, out of the chapel where he was saying his evening prayers, the invaders began a ruthless search of the premises. As planned for such an event, many of the Jewish men whose rooms were on the fourth floor were able to escape to an adjoining building through an entrance at that level. They and some non-Jews—about thirty in all—descended to the cellar, where a secret room had been prepared for just such an emergency. They hid there until the "police" and SS left the next morning.[13]

Many of the guests remaining in the seminary had false documents. The invaders, checking everyone carefully, were probably not fooled by the terrified Jewish women and children who insisted that they were Catholics and prayed loudly to the Madonna. Nor were they deceived by a group of real and false seminarians who marched out of the seminary in the early morning to go to classes. Seeing them leave, Koch remarked to the rector, "All priests, eh? Sure, priests since the eighth of September."[14] But he let them go. He was searching for bigger game. The Koch band had come looking for military officers and Communists, not draft evaders and Jews, and certainly not women and children. As sometimes happened in such cases, they took only men.

At 7:00 A.M., after stealing everything of value, the invaders left with twelve to fifteen prisoners—several Jewish men, the Communist Giovanni Roveda, non-Jewish men suspected of being military officers, and a number of other non-Jews who did not have documents from the Vicariate indicating that they were seminarians.[15] The Fascists were sloppy and disorganized, however, for as they marched out of the seminary one of their most important prisoners, a professor of economics who was also an army officer and had been caught with Resistance newspapers and letters in his room, managed to duck under a table. Another officer, a colonel, slipped into a reception room and then into a chapel where a group of nuns was attending a morning Mass.[16] Among those less fortunate, however, was a fifty-four-year-old Jewish businessman and convert to Catholicism named Enrico Ravenna, who had been asleep in his room when the invaders arrived and had not been able to flee with the others.[17] He was sent to the internment camp called Fossoli, where most Jews arrested after December 1 were held pending deportation. He was sent to Auschwitz on August 2, 1944, after Rome had already been liberated. He did not survive.[18]

As soon as the Koch band left, the Jewish men hidden in the cellar gathered up their women and children and left the seminary. As the seminarian wrote in his account several months later: "Began the exodus of all those poor victims, toward a more secure exile. Women, men, children. Where to go? To whom? There were terrible moments. But everyone left. The Jews, especially, were stupefied from shock. We learned that for several days they slept in places found by chance. Then they took lodgings as best they could."[19] For several days priests and nuns connected with the Seminario Lombardo moved to and from the new hiding places, taking possessions to the fugitives and carrying messages from them to their loved ones elsewhere. After a few days some of the Jews asked to return to the seminary, but it was considered too dangerous.[20] The Koch band and its SS assistants had seen them there, had suspected their identities, and might return. Only the false seminarians remained, for another two months. Then, as will be seen, they too were obliged to leave. The seminary remained without guests for a short time, until a few newcomers, like Enzo Finzi, seen in the previous chapter, were admitted in the spring of 1944.

The Seminario Lombardo was not the only Vatican property attacked on the terrible rainy night of December 21. At about 11:00 P.M. three or four men from the same Koch band and German SS, declaring that they had an urgent telegram, knocked on the door of the nearby Pontificio Istituto Orientale. About twenty political dissenters and Jews were hiding there. As the invaders ran up the stairs, a priest sounded the alarm. The guests scurried for a pre-arranged hiding place in the adjoining Pontificio Collegio Russo, a Jesuit-run school founded in 1928 to prepare priests for the mission of reestablishing Roman Catholicism in the Soviet Union. That institution harbored another twelve illegal guests. The flight was too much for one elderly Jewish man, who suffered a heart attack. The Jesuits persuaded his two brothers and a nephew to leave him, while a young medical student remained to attend to the dying man. That student was arrested, along with two German Jews and two non-Jews. At the Collegio Russo, three other guests were seized.[21] The fate of all those arrested is not clear. At least one of the German Jews at the Istituto Orientale, however, sixty-six-year-old Fritz Warschauer, a convert, was deported from Fossoli on April 5, 1944, and killed on arrival at Auschwitz on April 10.[22]

The three institutions invaded on December 21 did not enjoy extraterritorial status in the strictest sense of the term, since they were not among those Vatican properties specifically granted that privilege by the Lateran Accords. They were, nevertheless, acknowledged by the treaty as Vatican properties. All of them had posted the placards signed by General Rainer Stahel announcing their special status and prohibiting searches. The placards clearly offered no protection at all. Vatican Secretary of State Cardinal Maglione and his assistants, deeply concerned, discussed the invasions with several German and Italian officials. They did not, however, issue a public protest.[23]

The invasion of the Vatican properties greatly strengthened the hand of those Church officials who opposed sheltering fugitives of any kind. Feeling vindicated, they became more vocal. On December 22, for example, an unidentified official of the Secretariat of State wrote:

It does not seem convenient to host those who have military obligations.

We should warn those who find themselves in extraterritorial buildings that they are not at all secure.

Those who find themselves in other ecclesiastical buildings should be urged to change lodgings.[24]

The very next day Cardinal Maglione replied that he had asked Monsignor Luigi Traglia, assistant vicar of Rome, to take those steps.[25]

A month later the focus shifted from men with military obligations to political dissenters. A note of the Secretariat of State on January 31, 1944, declared that:

> The opportunity has arisen . . . to proceed with a change of resi-
> dence for some of the guests presently welcomed at the Seminario
> [Romano] itself, since attention has been called again to the danger
> that could arise if such guests did not abstain from compromising
> activity.
>
> Both His Excellency the lawyer Pacelli [nephew of the pope]
> and Monsignor Ronca [rector of the seminary] have agreed with
> this suggestion.[26]

There is no available evidence that Vatican officials at this time were also
considering urging Jews in their properties to "change lodgings," as the
writer on December 22 so euphemistically put it, but there is no reason why
they would have treated them differently from political activists or men with
military obligations. After all, most Italian churchmen were more likely to be
sympathetic to non-Jews than to Jews. In any case, with the exception of
guests obliged to leave the Seminario Lombardo, the Istituto Orientale, and
the Collegio Russo for security reasons after the raids, there is no evidence
that military service evaders, political activists, or Jews actually left Vatican
properties in December, January, or the first three days of February. But the
situation was about to change again.

The huge Basilica di San Paolo fuori le Mura—St. Paul outside the
Walls—is located on the Via Ostiense south of the Porta di San Paolo and the
center of Rome. According to Catholic tradition, it marks the spot of the mar-
tyrdom and burial of St. Paul. Like the Seminario Romano at the Basilica di
San Giovanni in Laterano but unlike the Seminario Lombardo, the Basilica
di San Paolo and its large Benedictine monastery enjoyed formal extraterritorial status under the Lateran Accords. In February 1944 at least thirty-five
male fugitives were sheltered in the monastery and about fifty more had beds
in a single large dormitory in attached parish buildings. Mostly young men
evading military service, they had been trickling in since September 8.[27]

Toward midnight on the night of February 3–4, 1944, the same Koch
band that had invaded the Seminario Lombardo on December 21, accompanied by about fifteen Germans, surrounded the Basilica di San Paolo fuori le
Mura and its attached buildings.[28] Ignoring papal guards who were not prepared to resist, they blocked all exits, cut telephone lines, and spread through-

out the buildings. With slaps, punches, and worse, they forced monks and their guests into the monastery's entrance hall, leaving the doors to rooms open and lights on. They then proceeded to steal everything of value that they could find, including foodstuffs and linens belonging to the monastery. A puzzled monk commented, "They don't seem like real police agents when they clean out everything of value and steal legitimately owned cash from those who possess it."[29]

When the invaders left at about 11:30 the following morning, they took sixty-four prisoners with them. The others—about thirty, according to the monk who recorded the event—escaped. Among those arrested were General Adriano Monti and four other officers, the principal targets of the raid, who were charged with fomenting acts of resistance.[30] Also seized were at least five Roman Jews, including fifty-five-year-old Carlo Fiorentino, sixty-five-year-old Leonardo Spagnoletto, Leonardo's sons Aurelio and Mario, and Mario's son Leonardo. All five were deported to Auschwitz a few months later. None returned.[31]

Vatican officials were understandably outraged at the flagrant violation of the rights of extraterritoriality guaranteed by the Lateran Accords. They immediately objected to German and Italian authorities, advised other neutral nations—Spain, Portugal, Ireland, Turkey, Sweden, and Switzerland—of the incident, and issued a formal protest in *L'Osservatore Romano* on February 7–8.[32] On February 10 they published another article, conceding that the Church's right to grant asylum might have some legal limits. Although the article did not mention it, the Lateran Accords had, in fact, stipulated that "the Holy See shall hand over to the Italian State persons who shall take refuge in the Vatican City while charged with acts committed in Italian territory which are considered as punishable by the law of both States."[33] But because there had been no formal request for the fugitives or warning of a raid, the article asked, "Who cannot see . . . a clear violation of the rights of extraterritoriality, against all the norms of diplomatic and civil life?"

If their public reaction was strong and defiant, however, the response of Vatican officials behind the scenes was the opposite. The invasion of San Paolo again strengthened those who disapproved of sheltering fugitives, this time with dramatic results. On February 6, Cardinal Maglione wrote that he had "instructed the abbot [of the monastery at San Paolo], in the name of the Holy Father, not to permit disguises in other clothing: no one should wear religious habits if he is not a priest or a monk."[34] To the delight of the Fascist press, General Monti had been caught and photographed wearing a monk's habit at the time of the raid. Vatican officials were determined that that should not happen again.

Within a week or two, if not sooner, official policy regarding fugitives in Vatican properties became still harsher. As a priest from the Seminario Lombardo later recorded:

> Orders from the Vatican to dismiss all non-clerics. Why such a brutal blow? Many were in disastrous conditions: with a death sentence on their heads because they were military officers or deserters from the *repubblichina* [a dismissive reference to Mussolini's regime].
> . . . Where could they go? . . . We didn't know what to say to them. Nor did we understand the reason for such a brutal order. On the other hand there were grave penalties for disobeying: suspension of religious privileges [*sospensione ipso facto a divinis*] for those rectors of colleges, institutions, etc., who kept young people in religious habits.
>
> This happened in the last days of Carnival which were at the end of February.
>
> . . . The rector tried at first to approach the authorities at the Vicariate to put the questions, the gravest cases to them. The Vicariate repeated its categorical order. And then the rector who had risked his life to shelter Jews, Communists, military officers, and had done the impossible, obeyed the order. . . . The young people had to leave.[35]

Little is known about these "orders from the Vatican to dismiss all non-clerics." Exactly who received them, who obeyed them, and how strictly they were enforced remain uncertain. One fact, however, is dramatically clear. Vatican officials ordered the Seminario Lombardo to cease sheltering outsiders—non-clerics, meaning non-seminarians. The orders were not intended merely to impress Nazis and Fascists, for they were not publicized. Nor were they intended to be ignored by priests and monks, for they carried severe penalties. It is difficult to reconcile such orders with the assertions of papal defenders that Pius XII was actively involved in rescue. They are incompatible even with the claim that the pope set a tone for rescue—that he quietly sent messages encouraging hospitality and charity to fugitives from the Nazis and Fascists, including Jews.

No Jews were affected by the orders to the Seminario Lombardo, for, as seen, they had all left after the raid the previous December. The Koch band had discovered then that they were there, and the danger of a second attack was just too great. They and their families could not easily be disguised. But the orders in February forced the many remaining non-Jews to move out, even though they had been well disguised as false seminarians. Because of the December raid the seminary was a focus of Vatican attention, and evasion of the orders was impossible. Their hosts were obviously dismayed.

At the Seminario Romano, the picture is less clear. Don Pietro Palazzini and two of the men he sheltered, Ivanoe Bonomi and Michael Tagliacozzo, all indicated that many fugitives departed within a few days of the raid on San Paolo fuori le Mura. They may have left, then, even before orders for dispersal reached the Seminario Lombardo. All three witnesses from the Seminario Romano imply, however, that guests there were never actually ordered to leave. Instead, according to Palazzini, Rector Roberto Ronca explained to them that the seminary was no longer secure. They were free to choose whether to leave, and most did, only to return later.[36]

Bonomi confirmed that account, writing in his diary on February 5, "There is no longer security in these religious asylums that enjoy extraterritorial rights. . . . The advice of all the prelates who surround us is to abandon this place. We are resigned to the exodus."[37] Bonomi left the Seminario Romano the following day, with Casati, Ruini, and Senator Alberto Bergamini, who had arrived only a few days before. The four men moved to a monastery of Augustinian friars near St. Peter's Basilica. After three days, however, Bonomi wrote that they still were not safe, adding, "The prelates who are responsible for us advise us not to remain in these religious asylums. Better to hide in private homes."[38] All but Bergamini left immediately.[39] Bonomi stayed briefly with different friends and relatives. He and Casati returned to the Seminario Romano on March 24, where they found the Socialist Pietro Nenni.[40]

Tagliacozzo agreed with Palazzini and Bonomi that fugitives were advised to leave but were never ordered to do so. "After the Fascist incursion at San Paolo," he wrote, "Don Palazzini informed us that we at San Giovanni [the Seminario Romano] were also exposed to the danger of an invasion. Each one of us could decide whether to remain in the area or leave."[41] He does not know what the political fugitives in a different wing of the seminary chose to do, but he believes that all the Jews on his floor left. With Palazzini's help, he himself found temporary shelter with the Franciscan Brothers, and also in the home of a Seventh Day Adventist pastor. Palazzini scrupulously kept him supplied with food. He returned to the Lateran complex after twenty days.[42]

Palazzini, Bonomi, and Tagliacozzo have surely written in good faith, but it seems unlikely that Ronca was not under pressure to move guests out of the Seminario Romano in February 1944. There exists, above all, the evidence of the orders imposed on the Seminario Lombardo. Why would the Seminario Romano not have received the same—unless, of course, its guests had already left voluntarily, as most seem to have done. The seminarian at the Lombardo who recorded these events soon after liberation maintained that other institutions received similar instructions. He added, "The other colleges, better protected by nice shadows of red and scarlet [a reference to highly placed clergy, especially cardinals who wore scarlet, who were involved with the prestigious Seminario Romano especially] interpreted the order according to their preferences." [43] There is also the evidence, cited above, that officials of the Vatican Secretariat of State were already exerting pressure for a change of residence for some guests specifically at the Seminario Romano even before the raid.

Finally, there is the evidence of Rector Ronca's appeals at the time. Many guests had left the seminary on February 4 and 5, he wrote on February 6, but some had already asked to return. All those remaining had signed a document promising to harbor no weapons, remain in the seminary at all times, limit contacts outside the seminary to the barest minimum, engage in no political activity, including discussions within the seminary, and accept all other requirements that their hosts regarded as necessary to ensure the neutrality of the Holy See. [44] Such a pledge represented a significant change. As recently as the end of January, as has been seen, CLN members came and went frequently to attend political meetings.

On February 11, Ronca reported that still more former guests were seeking readmission. He added that when they had left, they had been given a "timid promise of being able to return." What answer should he give them now? He suggested that no newcomers or men with military obligations be accepted, that only twenty-five to thirty of "the most illustrious and the most in need of help" of the former guests be readmitted, and that all guests be required to observe the strict rules recently imposed. No one should be allowed to receive visitors or venture out of the seminary for any reason. [45] The rector sounded very much as if he were trying to persuade opponents of sanctuary to change their minds. There is no indication of the response he received, but, as seen, several guests had returned by the end of March.

At the Pontificio Collegio dei Sacerdoti per l'Emigrazione Italiana at 70 via della Scrofa, about fifty-two guests, including many Jews, also left in early February to hide elsewhere. The director of the college, Monsignor Er-

minio Viganò, was deeply distressed by what he called their "forced departure." On March 6 he wrote in glowing terms about his former Jewish guests,
men and women alike. He stressed that many, "having nothing else to do,"
had attended religion classes and Catholic Mass. Two mixed marriages had
occurred. The friendship and gratitude of the Jews, he explained, "had made
a breach in the souls of many." Obviously hoping to persuade Vatican
officials to allow their return because of the opportunity to obtain conversions, he declared that many deeply grateful former Jewish guests were still
in friendly contact with the college.[46] There is no indication of the answer he
received.

Official orders to dismiss all nonclerical guests were also delivered
within the Vatican City itself. As seen in the previous chapter, Monsignor
Guido Anichini informed the pope on February 13, 1944, that about fifty outside guests were being sheltered at the Canonica di San Pietro, which he
headed. Somewhat defensively, Anichini wrote that he did not think that the
presence of the guests violated any rules because they were kept carefully hidden and did not constitute a burden, as he put it, on Vatican provisions. He
proceeded to describe most of the guests, stressing that many were high-
ranking military officers, aristocrats, or converted Jews. A large number were
in danger of losing their lives if expelled. Anichini added that some of the less
endangered guests had voluntarily left the Canonica, but that "those remaining prefer to meet every danger in the Canonica in the shadow of the house of
the father [the pope] to whom they address the anguished invocation: 'save us,
lest we perish!' "[47]

At the bottom of Anichini's report, Monsignor Domenico Tardini wrote:

> This letter was written after Monsignors Anichini, Descuffi and
> Roma were summoned by the Pontifical Commission for the Vati-
> can City State and told by Cardinal Rossi that they must make all
> their guests leave. The matter caused an uproar . . . in the Sacred
> College. At the service for Pius XI on the tenth of February [com-
> memorating his death in 1939], the cardinals begged Cardinal
> Rossi and his colleagues on the commission . . . not to insist. Car-
> dinal Rossi answered that he had spoken on orders from his superi-
> ors. The cardinals then had Cardinal Maglione speak to the Holy
> Father. In reality, those left . . . who wanted to leave [*uscì . . . chi
> volle*].[48]

Like the writer from the Seminario Lombardo, Tardini spoke clearly here of an order for expulsion. Soon after the Facist and Nazi raid on San Paolo fuori le Mura, Anichini and his colleagues had been told "that they must make all their guests leave." They were not merely asked to advise their guests of possible danger, allowing them to decide for themselves. Furthermore, according to Tardini, Cardinal Rossi said that the order came from his superiors. Raffaelo Carlo Rossi was one of three cardinals who directed the Pontifical Commission for the Vatican City State. Chairman of the commission was Cardinal Nicola Canali. The third participant was Cardinal Giuseppe Pizzardo. The commission, responsible for governing and administering the Vatican City State, was independent of the Roman Curia. Its superior was the pope himself. Did Cardinal Rossi mean to imply that the expulsion order came from Pius XII?

The two final sentences of Tardini's note raise another question. The second from the last sentence stated that Maglione eventually appealed to the pope himself. The ambiguous last sentence implied that the order was subsequently not enforced. Did Tardini mean to suggest that there was a connection between the two sentences—that the pope was responsible for the lack of enforcement?

Given the limited evidence available, these two questions about a precise papal role cannot be answered with certainty. It is clear that the pressure for the expulsion of outside guests from the Vatican City in February 1944 was intense. The pressure probably came from the Pontifical Commission for the Vatican City State, charged with the security of the institution in the face of the German threat. Little is known about two of the commission's members, but Cardinal Nicola Canali, the chairman, had a reputation as a conservative and a sympathizer of Fascism and the Italian cause in the war. Determined to avoid conflict with Italy and always deferential to that government's demands, he was in a position to order Vatican guards to deliver British, French, and American fugitives to the Italian police. Apparently he often did so. According to British Minister to the Holy See Sir d'Arcy Osborne, many Vatican prelates and employees disliked Canali. Montini and Canali disapproved of each other, but the pope apparently liked and listened to both.[49]

It is also clear that many prelates within the Vatican City strenuously resisted the expulsion order. "The matter," Tardini recorded, "caused an uproar." Monsignor Anichini wrote directly to the pope, describing the desperation of his fifty respectable guests at the Canonica. The guests were apparently allowed to remain. The incident provides a valuable glimpse at conflicts raging within the Vatican. The pope swayed between the two factions. The worst that can be said about him is that he initiated and ordered the original expulsion decree but then yielded to the objections of certain prelates and did not enforce it. The best that can be said is the reverse: that he knew nothing about the expulsion decree, and that he ordered it rescinded when brought to his attention. The real explanation probably falls somewhere between these extremes. The pope probably allowed the issuing of the expulsion order that Cardinal Canali and others like him wanted, but subsequently permitted prelates to ignore it. After all, Tardini's note concluded that only "those left . . . who wanted to leave." He never said that the pope ordered the decree to be canceled.

Because Vatican and Vicariate archives in Rome are closed to historians, it is not possible to discover how many other Church institutions received similar expulsion orders. The Seminario Lombardo, the Seminario Romano, the Pontificio Collegio dei Sacerdoti per l'Emigrazione Italiana, and several others apparently did. Other institutions may have been permitted to give their guests a choice. In either case, the policy is disturbing. Guests in Church institutions were always in some danger, but almost any other refuge was even more hazardous. Within large institutions, hiding places for use in the event of a raid could have been found. The policy certainly casts doubts upon claims that Vatican officials encouraged men and women of the Church to accept fugitives, including Jews, and set a good example by doing the same. It is difficult to believe, for example, that Vatican officials urged archbishops and bishops in many Italian cities to help Jews—a claim that will be examined in subsequent chapters—while removing them from their own institutions.

The impact of the Vatican policy should nevertheless not be exaggerated. For the most part, the expulsion order seems to have been limited to Vatican properties. Most convents and monasteries were apparently not subjected to it. Furthermore, even many Vatican institutions obeyed only for a short time. As the seminarian at the Lombardo observed, they "interpreted the order according to their preferences." Even inside the Vatican walls at the Canonica, as seen in the previous chapter, there were more than twice as many outsiders in June 1944 as in the previous February. At the well-connected Seminario Romano, at least some of the prestigious guests were allowed to remain or were readmitted, while a few newcomers were actually accepted in April and May. Perhaps alluding to that, the writer at the Lombardo added with some bitterness, "After the arrival of the Allies, ... as life would have it, ... [the institutions that did not expel their guests] received so much credit, so much sympathy, so much support."[50] But even his institution eventually accepted some new fugitives, including Jews, in the months just before liberation. A few newcomers were actually referred there by Assistant Vicar Traglia.[51] But guests were never again disguised in clerical garb.

In addition, fugitives who were dismissed from Vatican properties in early February were not thrown out onto the streets. Michael Tagliacozzo remembered with emotion the aid he continued to receive from Don Pietro Palazzini, assistant to the rector at the Seminario Romano. The seminarian from the Seminario Lombardo also wrote of support provided to fugitives settling elsewhere.[52] Departing guests could be, and were, referred to convents and monasteries that had not received the expulsion order. They were inconvenienced and certainly frightened, but not usually arrested and killed.

If the order to eject non-clerical guests from Vatican properties was not firmly enforced, however, it did put a damper on future acts of hospitality, at least for a time. On March 7, 1944, for example, Monsignor Montini received a request from a third party, explaining that a Jesuit priest, the head of a retreat house in Rome, was seeking permission to accept the sons of several women who were begging him for help. Montini replied coldly, "Let him act on his own responsibility."[53] The priest conveyed his thanks, but this was hardly encouragement.

In April and May, the policy toward harboring fugitives loosened, and some new guests were accepted. Those opposed to offering hospitality, however, were active to the end. On their insistence, the number of fugitives being sheltered within the Vatican was investigated and expulsion was considered again on the very eve of liberation. A somewhat desperate official of the Secretariat of State concluded his investigation on June 2 by writing: "Everyone [priests and laymen within Vatican City] questioned maintained that today it would be rather difficult to dismiss the guests, unless ... the use of force is intended. Some [of the refugees] have in fact been condemned to death, many persecuted by the police, all in serious danger. [One monsignor] ... declared that if the order to leave immediately was given to the refugees by the Vatican, 'some tragic event would occur.' "[54]

Two days later, the Allies entered Rome.

Until the Nazi and Fascist raid on San Paolo fuori le Mura in February 1944, some high-level prelates, especially at the Vicariate of Rome, had permitted the granting of asylum in Vatican properties and sometimes even made referrals. After the raid, officials within the Vatican who had always feared for their institution's safety and neutral status and opposed the sheltering of political and racial fugitives were able to impose their policy for a time. By April or May 1944 fugitives were returning to Vatican properties, but just before liberation the opponents of sanctuary seem to have prevailed again. Pope Pius XII seems to have drifted between these two factions. His wavering, hesitation, and lack of any real commitment to the rescue of fugitives from the Nazis and Fascists were apparent to all who knew of the expulsion order. And many more than those who received the order knew about it. All priests, monks, or nuns who received expelled guests understood that they had been turned out of their former refuges in Vatican properties. After February 1944, men and women of the Church who were honest with themselves could never again delude themselves that by harboring Jews and other fugitives they were following their pope's example.

CHAPTER SIXTEEN

The Vatican and Rescue in the North

Genoa, Turin, and Milan

ALMOST immediately after they learned of Italy's armistice with the Allies on September 8, Renzo Segre and his wife, Nella, both Italian Jews, abandoned their apartment in Biella, about seventy-four kilometers northeast of Turin. Their foreboding was confirmed when, unlike most people farther south, they heard about the murders of Jews around Lago Maggiore and arrests in nearby Vercelli and Novara. At first they took intelligent but not strenuous measures to hide. They secured false identification documents with new names, retaining their own initials in case any possessions had monograms. They chose new places of origin behind Allied lines, impossible to verify. Nella took a different family name, for greater flexibility. But their new hiding place, a sanctuary for religious pilgrims outside Biella, was in a zone permeated with partisans and refugees. It offered only minimum security.

As with so many other Jews throughout the country, police order number five of December 1 requiring Italian police to arrest all native and foreign Jews marked a turning point for the Segres. There could now be no doubt that they were in as much danger of arrest as the foreign Jews who were in the country illegally. With the help of a friend they left their first shelter and moved into a psychiatric hospital. For the next seventeen months they had to feign madness and live in constant fear of being recognized by someone from their former life. But they survived.[1]

Although few Italian Jews in northern and central Italy acted as quickly as the Segres, most, when they decided to hide, could fend for themselves.

They had some resources and contacts, spoke the language, and knew their way around. A friend or neighbor, priest or nun, former teacher, employee, or boss could give them good advice, suggest a refuge, or provide a guide across a frontier. Because Italian Jews looked and spoke like everyone else, they could explain their problems themselves, buy their own train tickets, and secure their own ration books. In this respect, if in no other, they were fortunate. Most foreign Jews, especially those who had just recently been freed from Fascist internment camps or escaped into Italy from southeastern France or Yugoslavia, could do none of those things. Most did not even have the documents necessary to rent a room, buy food, or regularize their status in the country. They were absolutely helpless.

The Italian Jewish assistance organization Delasem had been established before the war to help Jews who wished to emigrate. At first, its activities were entirely legal. After September 8, however, it became clear that those most in need were helpless Jewish immigrants whose very presence was illegal. As already seen in the case of Rome, Delasem workers often began by trying to find them. They combed the mountains of northwestern Italy, where about one thousand Jewish refugees had arrived on foot from France and were sometimes living in huts or with no roof at all over their heads. They searched railroad stations, trying to find foreign Jews without papers before Italian and German authorities arrested them as illegal aliens. Or they just waited until hundreds of desperate refugees staggered into Delasem offices, synagogues, or local Jewish Community headquarters in cities like Turin, Milan, Genoa, or Florence. The refugees were trying to get south, to meet the Allies who were slowly fighting their way north. Those four cities were on or near the route south for Jews coming from France.

At the same time that the demand for its services leapfrogged, Delasem's situation itself became tenuous. In Rome, the German demand for gold on September 26 was followed three days later by a raid on the Jewish Community office in which 2 million lire, along with lists of the names and addresses of members and contributors, minutes of meetings, archival documents—indeed, whole filing cabinets—were seized. Delasem was clearly not going to be allowed to function. Toward the end of the month its leaders were able to transfer assets and documents to Father Benedetto's Capuchin monastery in the Via Sicilia, where they remained for the duration of the occupation. But when would the Germans strike in other cities? It was apparent that other Delasem offices also needed to go underground.

The central office in Genoa was one of the first to move. Don Francesco

Repetto, a twenty-eight-year-old priest in 1943 and the secretary of Cardinal Pietro Boetto, archbishop of Genoa, described the process years later. The occasion was his acceptance in 1982 of Yad Vashem's Medal of the Righteous Among the Nations in recognition of his wartime rescue of Jews. Repetto remembered:

> A few weeks after [September 8, 1943], I met the lawyer [Lelio Vittorio] Valobra who . . . came to test the waters to learn if the cardinal [Boetto] would agree to take over the assistance to the Jews, especially foreigners, in Italy, carried out until then by Delasem of which he [Valobra] was the national president.
>
> I went with this [request] to the cardinal. The situation at the Archdiocese was rather grave: it was already helping those who had lost their homes in bombing raids and was taking on some work collecting news of prisoners of war for a special Vatican office. Standing in front of the cardinal's desk, I asked, with a studied indifference (because my role was only executive, that of a mere secretary) if the Delasem request should be accepted or declined.
>
> The cardinal paused for a moment, but he did not think about it for long; he said: "They are innocent; they are in grave danger; we must help them regardless of all our other problems."[2]

Nothing could make it clearer that the initiative for the Catholic collaboration with Delasem in Genoa was taken by the Jews themselves. The Jews asked for help. The Catholics, no matter how extensive and self-sacrificing their ultimate contribution to the rescue effort, did not offer. They could hardly have been expected to offer, swamped as they were with the problems of parishioners who had lost everything they owned in the air raids. Jews in Genoa were not yet being arrested, and Cardinal Boetto was probably only vaguely aware of the precarious legal and economic status of Jewish refugees. The cardinal was known to be sympathetic to Jews, for he had helped many seeking to emigrate from the port of Genoa several years before.[3] He was a logical person to ask for assistance, and when asked, he agreed immediately.

The fact that Boetto did not volunteer his help does not detract from the impressive contribution to Jewish assistance and rescue made by him and, especially, by Don Repetto, whom he appointed for the task. The fact that Delasem first contacted Boetto is important, however, because several historians have asserted that bishops and archbishops in Italy helped the Jews because Pius XII asked them to do so.[4] Don Repetto's statement makes it clear that

Boetto acted because the Jews, not the pope, petitioned him for help. The cardinal may well have told the pope what he was doing at a later date. If so, Pius XII did not prohibit it. But neither did he initiate or, apparently, even encourage it.

Don Repetto's testimony is sufficient evidence of the origin of his work for Delasem. No one would have been more ready than he to give credit to the pope, had credit been due. But the timing of the events also confirms Repetto's statement. No one at the Vatican at the end of September yet foresaw the roundups of Italian Jews that would begin two weeks later. As for foreign Jews, Monsignor Giuseppe Di Meglio's negative response on September 17 to a request that they be admitted to religious institutions in Rome was seen in Chapter Twelve. It is not reasonable to maintain that Pius XII asked Boetto and other Italian archbishops to help Jews within a week or two after that refusal. Furthermore, Valobra's original request was for help with Delasem's work of distributing subsidies. As Repetto put it, Boetto was asked "to take over the assistance to the Jews . . . carried out until then by Delasem." No one was yet thinking about dangerous clandestine rescue operations. Only gradually did Jews and priests alike make that momentous transition. It is not reasonable to claim that the pope asked Boetto to become involved in distributing subsidies. Nor did Don Repetto ever claim that he did.

After securing Cardinal Boetto's agreement, Valobra delivered to him all Delasem records of contributions received and individuals helped. Boetto in turn asked his secretary Repetto to work with Valobra and Delasem's remaining staff. At the end of November, Valobra was obliged to flee to Switzerland, where he continued to raise money and funnel it into Italy. His position in Genoa was assumed by Massimo Teglio, a courageous local Jewish businessman who directed Delasem's activities until liberation.[5] Just as Father Benedetto in Rome worked side by side with Delasem's local director Settimio Sorani, Repetto worked with Valobra and, after November, with Teglio.

With the help of a small group of Catholics and Jews, Repetto and Valobra began by distributing Delasem funds among needy foreign Jews already on the organization's lists. Don Repetto kept scrupulous records of how the money entrusted to him was spent. He and Teglio also located others in need, including Genovese Jews who went into hiding after the initial German roundup in their city on November 3, 1943. They eventually found themselves providing refugees and citizens alike with shelter, money, food, false documents, ration books and even guides to Switzerland. They had drifted into clandestine rescue.

Lilli Della Pergola, then fourteen, recalls how Don Repetto and Massimo Teglio kept her Italian Jewish family alive with lodgings, money, food, and hope after they had to leave their apartment during the November roundup in Genoa. She records that Don Repetto even arranged work in his own office for her and her sixteen-year-old sister. To ease the boredom of their situation at home, they spent their time stuffing and stamping envelopes. When Lilli's father was arrested on September 15, 1944, Teglio's assurances that the war could not last forever became the most vital ingredient in the family's ability to cope. Lilli's mother and sister survived along with Lilli herself, but her father did not return from Auschwitz.[6]

Don Repetto's special contribution was to recruit bishops and archbishops throughout northern Italy in order to extend Delasem's activities wherever they were needed. He eventually created rescue networks that saved hundreds, if not thousands, of mostly foreign Jews. One of his first recruits was the bishop of Chiavari, whose diocese was a resort town on the coast east of Genoa, between Rapallo and Sestri Levante. Chiavari was on the railroad line leading south from Genoa to La Spezia, Pisa, and ultimately Florence and Rome. It was a critical route for Jews who hoped to find safety behind Allied lines. Men and women of the Church in Chiavari could therefore be especially useful in late September 1943, when Delasem was still focusing more on moving Jews south than on trying to hide them locally or escort them to Switzerland.

Years later, Massimo Teglio remembered Delasem's first contact with the bishop of Chiavari. At the end of September, and thus almost immediately after Repetto had assumed his new responsibilities, Teglio accompanied his friend Valobra to the resort town, ostensibly to have a pleasant lunch near the sea. Teglio was not yet involved with Delasem, but Valobra was there on business. After lunch the two men visited the bishop, delivering a letter of recommendation from the Archdiocese of Genoa, signed by Repetto, asking for help.[7] The bishop agreed, as did others after him.

Don Repetto also mobilized many humbler men and women of the Church within his own diocese of Genoa. Among these, Don Carlo Salvi helped Repetto keep the records of those helped during the first nine months of the rescue work. When Repetto narrowly escaped arrest in July 1944 and was forced to flee to the mountains, Salvi took over his role as chief coordinator with Teglio and Delasem. Like Repetto, he received the Medal of the Righteous Among the Nations after the war. Also active were Monsignors Giuseppe Siri and Giacomo Lercaro, later archbishops of Genoa and

Bologna, respectively. The latter eventually had to go into hiding with false documents, including a false baptismal certificate manufactured for him by Teglio![8] Not so lucky were Monsignors Giacomo Massa and Gian Maria Rotondi. Massa, chaplain at Marassi Prison, was arrested for giving food and money to a Jewish woman detainee. Rotondi was caught with a group of Jewish refugees whom he was trying to escort across the Swiss frontier.[9] Both priests were eventually released, but the Jews in Rotondi's charge were deported to their deaths.[10]

The first major action against Jews in Genoa began on November 2, when the Germans forced Bino Polacco, the janitor at the synagogue, to summon the congregation to a meeting the following day. About twenty Jews responded and were caught, while many others were seized elsewhere in the city and the surrounding area. This is not the place to relate the tragedies that followed, or the rescue efforts conducted by Jews and non-Jews, men and women of the Church and laypersons, private individuals and organizations like Delasem.[11] The purpose here is to examine any possible connection between the rescue of Jews and the Vatican. In this respect also, the testimony of Don Repetto is revealing. In his same speech accepting the Medal of the Righteous Among the Nations, Repetto staunchly defended Pope Pius XII before his mainly Jewish audience and sought its understanding. He discussed the papal silence during the Holocaust. He asserted that, given the fanaticism and irrationality of the Nazis, protest would have changed nothing. He explained that silence had been necessary not only to preserve the Church but to protect both those being hidden and their rescuers.[12] Yet in all that defense, Repetto never implied that the pope ever urged him or Cardinal Boetto to help the Jews. The pope was not only uninvolved at the onset of Repetto's work with Delasem. He remained uninvolved until Genoa was liberated in April 1945, even though the arrival of the Allies in Rome on June 4, 1944, had restored the security of the Vatican City.

Repetto could not have had any illusions about the extent of the pope's involvement in Jewish rescue. The young priest had traveled to Rome in December 1943 in the hope of persuading Vatican officials to intercede for Don Rotondi, who had just been arrested at the Swiss frontier. From December 9 to 13, just a week before it was raided, he stayed at the Seminario Lombardo, where he had lived while a student at the Università Gregoriana.[13] He certainly saw many of the 110 fugitives sheltered there, and he must have realized that more than half of them were Jews. He must have wondered about Pius XII's role in these activities, and whether in Rome rather than Genoa, and in a Vatican property rather than an Archbishop's Palace far to the north, special papal authorization was necessary. He may have learned that the Vicariate had been informed. About the pope, however, he could only have been told that he kept his distance. But he saw firsthand the scope of priestly efforts to help Jews. That in itself must have been encouraging.

Even more than Genoa, the stately Piedmontese capital of Turin was directly in the path of foreign Jews fleeing with the Italian army from southeastern France. As in Genoa but a few days later, Cardinal Maurilio Fossati, the archbishop of Turin, agreed at the end of September or the beginning of October to distribute Delasem funds to indigent foreign Jews in his area. It is not clear whether Cardinal Fossati was initially recruited by Don Repetto or by local Delasem activists who felt obliged, like their colleagues in Genoa, to close their offices, confide their funds and lists of clients to trustworthy Catholics, and operate only in secret. But Fossati's delegate for the work, his secretary Monsignor Vincenzo Barale, was soon working closely with both Repetto and Delasem. At forty, Barale was older than Repetto and already a monsignor, but his position at the Archdiocese of Turin was exactly the same.

On October 5, Monsignor Barale received 50,000 lire from Delasem, probably from its local office. He began distributing it the same day. He gave some of the money directly to needy Jews, mostly foreign, who were already Delasem clients living nearby and able to come to his office. In October, larger subsidies went to eighteen individuals for train tickets to Florence. These relatively large disbursements ceased by November, as it became clear that the Allies were stalled well south of Rome and that foreign Jews speaking no Italian and unable to leave Florence were accumulating there in alarming numbers. Finally, Barale allocated money to individual priests throughout his archdiocese and beyond, for distribution to indigent foreign Jews in their parishes. Despite the risks of leaving incriminating evidence, he carefully recorded all distributions. He took his mandate as an agent for Delasem seriously.[14]

In the days and weeks that followed, Barale received Delasem referrals of other needy families. He preserved some of the written requests, in part to protect himself from any future charges of unauthorized disbursements. He kept, for example, a letter on Delasem stationery received on October 11, 1943, asking him to send aid to a Simona Itzkowitz and a baby just a few months old. Another referral on the same day claimed that Delasem had subsidized a group of thirteen refugees from France until October 10, and begged that

Barale continue the aid. On October 18, Delasem social workers sent four other letters of introduction for individuals or groups in need of financial subsidies. On October 25, as major indiscriminate German actions against Italian and foreign Jews alike intensified in Turin, they sent yet another.[15] Most of the Jews recommended were recent arrivals from France, but some were impoverished foreigners already residing around Turin. A few were poor Italian citizens.

It is impossible to overestimate the importance of Barale's distributions. Delasem's clients were utterly without resources. Many were elderly, sick, handicapped, or parents with small children. All foreign Jews were prohibited from working by the Italian racial laws. Some were hiding in institutions, including religious ones, and needed money to pay their room and board. Without it, they could have been turned out. Others were living independently, often in isolated areas, in rented rooms or houses from which they would certainly have been evicted for lack of payment. Without the services that Barale was able to offer, they would have had to turn themselves in to the police, or starved to death.

Monsignor Barale's connections with Don Repetto in Genoa are as clear as his links with Delasem, for several letters between the two men survive. Repetto's letters, deliberately vague for reasons of security, nevertheless indicate that he, the younger of the two and not a monsignor, was in charge. Repetto, after all, was the Catholic delegate from Delasem's central office, and he controlled the distribution of Delasem funds amounting to some 30 million lire.[16] On October 18 he wrote to thank Barale "for the support given to this work." He reminded his Turinese counterpart that the Delasem money was "solely for the purpose of providing the necessities to enable those being helped to reside where they are," or to pay "for a [train ticket] to Florence and a subsidy for the trip to that city, directing them to the Archbishopric of Florence which is already up to date on the matter and will be able to put them on the right track."[17] By October 18, then, Repetto was also in close touch with the archbishop of Florence, who was doing the same kind of work. Repetto went on to assure Barale that he would try to provide the funds that the latter needed, as soon as possible. But nothing in the letter identified the recipients of Repetto and Barale's efforts as Jews. Any unauthorized readers would have assumed that they were impoverished Catholic refugees.

On October 31, Repetto wrote to Barale again. Without mentioning Jews, he instructed his colleague that "refugees" who did not speak Italian should no longer be sent to Florence. He then remarked that he had originally hoped that the funds for this work could come from the Turinese "committee," obviously the local Delasem office. However, he had received Barale's message that the committee had been dissolved and had no funds available. He assured Barale that he would send someone with 100,000 lire, in order that aid could continue for the "suffering brethren." [18] On November 3 he was obliged to write that he had been able to send only 50,000 lire. [19]

Like Repetto, Barale never claimed that the pope asked him or Archbishop Fossati to help the Jews. The original request clearly came from the Jews themselves, either directly through Delasem in Turin or indirectly through Repetto on behalf of the central Delasem office in Genoa. And as in the case of Genoa, the initial involvement of the office of the archbishop of Turin came too early to be the result of a papal appeal. Repetto and Barale obviously worked hand in hand. The money and the clients definitely came from Delasem. Also like Repetto, Barale did not claim that he later received papal encouragement or support.

Monsignor Barale's records indicate that he worked closely with several other men and women of the Church, whom he most probably recruited personally. Already in October, for example, he sent 3,000 lire to Don Michele Lussu for the Monastery of the Sacramentini in Castelvecchio di Moncalieri. The monastery was sheltering about twelve foreign Jews, some of them baptized. The Church of the Sacramentini in Turin was near the Archbishop's Palace. Barale probably had personal acquaintances there and at the monastery, which facilitated his recruiting. Don Lussu also received several subsequent monthly disbursements. [20]

There are many other examples. The nuns at the Ospizio poveri convalescenti alla Crocetta in Turin regularly submitted a bill to Barale for the room and board of seven elderly foreign Jews who were hiding with them. [21] A parish priest in Aosta seems to have been a more reluctant recruit, for he wrote to Barale that he would comply with the latter's request and deliver a subsidy to a particular woman, although he had heard that she had a dubious reputation. [22] Barale even asked nuns who had access to Jews awaiting deportation in the Carceri Nuove prison in Turin to confirm the presence of particular prisoners or deliver messages to them. The poignant notes assured the prisoners that, for example, a child left behind was being cared for; that relatives were thinking of them; or that a home had not been sealed. [23] Finally, Barale dealt with higher-level prelates. In November, for example, at a time when individual refugees were receiving about 200 lire a month, he sent 25,000 lire to the bishop of Fossano. [24] The bishop must have been supervising an extensive rescue network, for he received additional large amounts later.

If Barale called on bishops throughout Piedmont and Aosta, however, he did not contact or convince them all. Don Giuseppe Peaquin, parish priest of a little village in the Valle d'Aosta, sheltered Italian Jews Davide Nissim and his wife, along with a family of Yugoslavian Jews who spoke no Italian. His was one of those villages where everyone knew what everyone else was doing. Several parishioners complained to their priest about the danger he was bringing to the entire population. Of more relevance here, however, Don Peaquin's bishop also expressed strong disapproval.[25] Barale had not won over that particular prelate. He may not even have tried, for the Nissims had found their protector independently. But the existence of such a bishop—and there were many others—would suggest the absence of any specific papal directive to help the Jews. A papal directive would have gone to all bishops.

The number of Jews whom Barale assisted, directly or indirectly, is not known. Many of an estimated 475 foreign Jews from France remaining in Aosta and Piedmont would have been on his lists.[26] Included also would have been many of the approximately eighty Yugoslavian Jews interned in Aosta between June 1940 and September 1943, but still in the area after the armistice, as well as their counterparts in Piedmont.[27] And there were many others. On July 7, 1944, Barale recorded that he had received 218,000 lire and distributed precisely 183,077. He noted that he had only 34,923 lire left, adding that he would "call for reinforcements."[28] But Barale's rescuing days were nearly over. He was arrested on August 2, after Italian political police raided the Monastery of the Sacramentini at Castelvecchio di Montalieri. In addition to finding several Jews, they discovered letters from Barale indicating his involvement.[29] Barale protested in vain that his financial disbursements came from the archdiocese rather than from Jewish organizations. With three members of the Sacramentini, he was imprisoned in the Carceri Nuove. Cardinal Schuster and his regular liaison with the Germans, Monsignor Giuseppe Bicchierai, intervened with the occupying authorities on behalf of the four men, as they had done for many other priests. They were transferred at the end of August to a religious institution outside Milan, where they lived under strict government surveillance.[30] In Turin, other priests continued Barale's work.

The long and impressive story of Jewish rescue in Piedmont and Aosta by men and women of the Church in Turin extends well beyond the activities of Monsignor Barale and his archbishop.[31] Many priests, nuns, and monks acted independently of him, often without his knowledge. The activities of Don Peaquin have been seen. The Salesians, also, inspired by the presence in Turin of the head of their order, Father Pietro Ricaldone, worked together to shelter scores of Italian and foreign Jews in their boarding schools and other institutions throughout Piedmont.[32] A single individual, thirty-nine-year-old Dominican Father Giuseppe Girotti, hid many Jews in his own monastery, apparently without even informing his superior.[33] Barale and Girotti were friends, but Barale did not know what Girotti was doing. It was safer not to know. Father Girotti was arrested on August 29, 1944, deported to Dachau on October 9, and murdered by lethal injection on the eve of liberation. He was awarded the Medal of the Righteous Among the Nations posthumously.

The story of Jewish rescue in Piedmont also extends far beyond the activities of men and women of the Church, to include hundreds of Christian laypersons as well as Italian Jews who continued to assist their people despite enormous risks to themselves. This book cannot tell the full story. The focus here is on any possible connections between the Vatican and rescuers from within the Church. The conclusion is the same as that for Rome and Genoa— that there was no connection. The courageous men and women of the Church who helped Jews acted on their own initiative, without instructions from the Vatican. They may have been encouraged by Pius XII's occasional public references to the need to succor the victims of war. They may have believed that they were acting according to the pope's will. They may have been influenced by articles in local parish bulletins such as *L'Angelo della famiglia* of San Francesco di Piossasco, which claimed on April 11, 1944, that the pope was offering temporal as well as spiritual assistance to Romans, refugees in the Eternal City, and "those who suffer in every part of the world."[34] But if Archbishop Fossati and Monsignor Barale received no papal directive, it is impossible to believe that the lesser clergy did. Nor have clerical rescuers so claimed. For the most part, assertions to the contrary have been made only by those not directly involved, without evidence.

The city of Milan, in Lombardy, joins Liguria's Genoa and Piedmont's Turin to form Italy's well-known industrial triangle. Distances between the cities are short, and train connections are excellent. While all three cities had flourishing Jewish Communities before the war, that of Milan, with about 10,219 people, was far larger than Turin's, with 4,060, or Genoa's, with 2,263.[35] All three cities, also, were not far from Italy's frontiers, and they were filled with refugees during the war. Because of these circumstances, similarities in the Jewish rescue process are not surprising. Evidence is much scarcer for Milan, largely because the archives of the archdiocese are almost entirely closed. Cardinal Schuster's involvement is clear, however, as is the role of his delegate for the work, the lawyer Giuseppe Sala.

Sala was president of the Society of St. Vincent de Paul, an organization of devout Catholic laymen dedicated to helping the poor. After the war, he testified:

> In November 1943 Cardinal Boetto of Genoa was responsible for
> helping the Jews, I don't know if for all Italy, but certainly for the
> north, and he sent his secretary [Repetto] here to Milan to talk with
> Cardinal Schuster to see about coordinating assistance for the per-
> secuted Jews. I was called on this occasion by the Servant of God
> [Schuster] and he asked me if St. Vincent de Paul could assume re-
> sponsibility for the aid: of course, I accepted. . . . Assistance began,
> developed, and continued until the end of the war: it benefited from
> significant funds that flowed in especially from Switzerland. . . . I
> asked Cardinal Schuster if we should move our headquarters in
> order not to be caught by surprise and cause trouble for him. I re-
> member that he said, "No, no, you must remain here close to me,
> under my protection, because here it will always be easier to defend
> you. Remember that the archbishop is always the last one to be
> touched." [36]

Sala was unaware of the date of Boetto's initial involvement, which was late September, and he may not have known how that involvement began, but he certainly knew when Schuster was contacted. Apparently Boetto and Repetto approached Schuster later than they did Fossati and Barale in Turin. The delay may have resulted from a greater reluctance by Milan's Jewish charities to relinquish their autonomy. Aid in the form of food, financial subsidies, and advice continued to be distributed at the central synagogue, 19 via Guastalla, until the Germans raided it on November 8.[37] About twenty Jewish refugees were seized in that raid, and one was shot while trying to escape. Repetto traveled to Milan not long afterward, to ask for Schuster's coopera-tion. He received it immediately. Despite his speech condemning what he called the "Nordic racial myth" on November 13, 1938, the cardinal arch-bishop of Milan had a reputation as a conservative and as a friend of the Mus-solini regime before the German occupation.[38] Unlike Cardinal Boetto of

Genoa, he was not known for past assistance to Jews who were not converts. But like so many other Italian priests and prelates, his attitudes changed when Jews began to be arrested and deported from his archdiocese in November 1943. In a city that was heavily bombed, full of partisans and refugees, on the route to Switzerland, and of immense strategic importance in the war, he had many other pressing problems, but he was happy to designate a willing layman to cooperate with Don Repetto.

Since Repetto was working for Delasem, the initiative for the archbishop of Milan's involvement in Jewish rescue can be traced to that organization, just as in Genoa and Turin. Sala's reference to "significant funds from Switzerland" provides additional proof of Delasem's involvement. Valobra collected contributions there and sent them into Italy, usually via Genoa, by means of Jewish and Catholic couriers and, eventually, agents of the CLN. As a third indication, Teglio later testified that Valobra instructed him in late November, at the time he assumed Valobra's leadership of Delasem in Genoa, to get in touch with Sala in Milan as well as with Cardinal Fossati and Monsignor Barale in Turin.[39]

In his above-cited testimony after the war, Sala said nothing about a papal directive. Nor did Schuster make any allusion to it when he published documents from the archives of the archdiocese after the war, indicating his activities to help alleviate suffering during the conflict and negotiate peace feelers between the German army and the CLN.[40] That fact must be kept in mind when examining historian Gianfranco Bianchi's statement in 1971 that Sala claimed that Schuster advised him, Sala, toward the end of November 1943 that Pius XII had arranged that the Jews be helped by the Catholic Church in the broadest and most effective manner.[41] Bianchi did not quote Sala or provide a source for his own claim, and other scholars have found no corroborating evidence. Dorina Di Vita, a nun also known as Suor Bernadetta, is one of the few historians who seem to have had full access to the archives of the Archdiocese of Milan. In her excellent and detailed article about Catholic rescuers of the Jews of Milan, she made no mention of a papal directive.[42] It seems highly unlikely that, if there had been such a directive, Sala, Schuster, and Di Vita all would have failed to mention it.

By the time Cardinal Schuster became involved, help to the Jews meant clandestine rescue operations rather than just the distribution of financial subsidies. On Schuster's request, Giuseppe Sala called upon a group of Milanese Catholic men and women, some of whom were already engaged in the rescue of non-Jewish fugitives. In a speech in 1955 accepting a gold medal from the Italian Jewish Community for his wartime rescue efforts, Sala referred to more than a dozen priests, nuns, and laypersons who had worked with him.[43] Especially notable among these were Dr. Adele Cappelli Vegni, president of the Villa San Vincenzo; Carla Uccelli, associated with the St. Vincent de Paul women's section; and Fernanda Wittgens, director of the Brera Museum. Thanks to Sala's collaborators as well as many others not directly connected with him, Milan became the center of a network that escorted to Switzerland hundreds of Jews, along with more than a thousand British prisoners of war, Italian political dissidents and evaders of military service, and non-Jewish foreign refugees. Along the route, fugitives were sheltered in rest homes, hospitals and clinics, schools, parish churches, convents, and private houses. Those who could not make the difficult trip were hidden in surrounding villages. The importance of the Milan rescue networks was revealed in an Italian political police report on February 2, 1945, which declared that "the worst enemies of the Regime are first of all Catholic Action and OSCAR [a Resistance group of priests and laymen, to be described below] . . . and then the masculine and feminine societies of St. Vincent de Paul." [44]

Giuseppe Sala and several of his assistants were arrested in July 1944 and imprisoned in Milan's fearful San Vittore prison. Four months later Monsignor Giuseppe Bicchierai, Schuster's assistant and liaison with the Germans, reported on his own recent activities. In the section of his report entitled "Help for the Jews," he wrote: "After the arrest of the lawyer Sala, I had to take care of the distribution of the sums arriving from Genoa. Altogether 1,200,000 lire—distributed by means of the Conf. S. Vinc.-Opera Cardinal Ferrari; concentration camps of Fossoli and Bozen—and recently sent also to Turin and Cuneo, these zones being by now too difficult to reach from Genoa." [45] The paragraph is cryptic, but it again links Sala with Delasem. The "sums arriving from Genoa" were certainly Delasem funds originally entrusted by Valobra to Don Repetto and later reinforced from Switzerland. Men and women connected to Sala's "Conf. S. Vinc.," a reference to the Brotherhood [Confraternità] of St. Vincent de Paul, had been distributing them, and they continued to do so under Bicchierai's direction after Sala's arrest. The reference to relaying funds to Turin and Cuneo is another indication that the money came from Delasem via Don Repetto, for that is what Repetto had been doing until communications were broken. The brief mention of camps at Fossoli and Bozen (Bolzano) suggested that Jews interned there and awaiting deportation were also receiving Delasem subsidies.

Curiously, Bicchierai later said little or nothing about his efforts for

Delasem. In a letter on September 7, 1984, to Don Giovanni Barbareschi, who was preparing a book on the Resistance activities of priests in Milan during the war, he described his own role. He had saved many priests and Catholic laymen from deportation, obtained permission for an Easter Mass to be said at San Vittore prison in 1944, and worked from Switzerland with representatives of the CLN and the Germans to end the war. He never mentioned Jews. Of the help to Jews described in his own report of November 1944, he said only that he had extended his charitable aid to Genoa, Turin, and the camp at Bolzano. He did not say who received that aid. His reticence is peculiar, to say the least.[46]

As in Genoa and Turin, Milanese clergy and laypersons unconnected with Delasem and Giuseppe Sala were also involved in rescuing Jews and others attempting to escape from the Nazis and Fascists.[47] Many groups straddled the line, predating Sala and working independently of him, but occasionally receiving his referrals. The OSCAR, for example, or Organizzazione Soccorsi Cattolici Antifascisti Ricercati, grew out of the Catholic scouting movement of the 1920s. Firmly anti-Fascist because of Mussolini's efforts to absorb the Catholic scouts into his own Fascist youth groups, the organization included a number of courageous priests along with many laypersons.[48] Long after the war one activist priest estimated that the OSCAR had helped 2,000 people escape from Italy and had provided some 3,000 false documents.[49]

In the late summer of 1943, Don Paolo Liggeri, a young priest from the province of Siracusa in southern Italy, set up a residence in Milan for families whose homes had been destroyed in Allied bombing raids. After the Germans occupied the city Liggeri began to hide Jews among his other guests and help some of them escape to Switzerland. After November he may also have been in touch with Sala, for he later testified that some Jews were sent to him by Fossati and Schuster.[50] On March 24, 1944, his institution, La Casa, was raided, and eleven Jews were caught. They were deported, without return. After imprisonment in San Vittore and Fossoli, Don Liggeri was also deported, to Mauthausen and Dachau rather than Auschwitz. He survived.[51]

On June 13, nearly three months after Liggeri's arrest, the Capuchin Father Giannantonio Agosti was also caught. Born in the province of Trent on the Austrian border, Father Agosti spoke fluent German. As a confessor in foreign languages at the Cathedral of Milan in 1943 and 1944, he naturally met many German and Austrian Jewish refugees, most of them baptized. He hid them in his monastery in the viale Piave, supplied them with false documents, and helped them to Switzerland. After his arrest and detention at San Vittore and Bolzano, he was deported to Flossenburg and Dachau. Like Liggeri, he suffered terrible deprivation but survived.[52]

Father Carlo Varischi, a Capuchin priest like Father Agosti, was also a rescuer. In 1945 he testified that he had helped about fifty Jews, one hundred British prisoners of war, and several hundred former Italian soldiers and officers, political dissidents, and students escape into Switzerland. The students, some of whom, along with university graduates, also served as guides, were from the Università Cattolica, where Varischi worked as an assistant to the rector, Father Agostino Gemelli. Varischi's fugitives needed false documents, safe houses along the route, and money with which to pay guides and smugglers at the frontier. He was able to supply them. He worked also with Father Agosti and was almost captured with him. Warned by Gemelli that German and Fascist police were searching for him, he escaped into the mountains.

Father Varischi is of particular interest here because of his attitude toward the Jews he assisted. The Capuchin later wrote that already in 1940 and 1941 he had been in contact with some "very fine Jewish families" that were trying to cope with the racial laws. He had, he explained, "provided for the instruction and conversion to Christianity of some of them, and for assistance and relocation for others who were already Christians." Conversion of the Jews was, for him, a perfectly natural objective, and one to be proud of. The "very fine Jewish families" he had known were all oriented toward Catholicism.

Toward Jews in general, however, Varischi revealed a certain prejudice. In a letter in 1945 that said nothing of the suffering or bravery of the fugitives, he wrote that many Jews assisted by himself or Liggeri wanted to stay with them rather than flee to Switzerland. Their reluctance, he explained, stemmed from "a lack of courage or also from greed," because it was cheaper to remain than to pay a guide. Varischi made a point of recording that one group cheated their guide at the frontier by telling him falsely that they had already settled with Varischi himself.[53] Describing his Jewish fugitives more broadly, he wrote, "The weakness of character of the Jews in general truly struck me. The great majority of those who came to me had lost their composure and were distrustful and incapable of any initiative, to the point that we had almost to carry them to the rest stops, train station, or frontier."[54]

The best that can be said of these comments is that they reveal Varischi to be a man of limited sensitivity and experience of the world outside his convent door. Certainly he was incapable of understanding the terror and demoralization of his charges, often elderly, sick, or exhausted by years of deprivation, and quite different from the vigorous young anti-Fascist activists whom he also helped. Most Catholic rescuers did not share his attitude. Don Francesco Repetto, for example, virtually dissolved into tears when he recalled, during his acceptance speech for the Medal of the Righteous Among the Nations, the terrified eyes of a Jewish child who arrived at his office with her equally frightened and exhausted parents.[55] Don Paolo Liggeri also remembered, "sometimes we received entire families [of Jews]: father, mother, children. They seemed like helpless animals pursued by hunters. I will never forget the eyes of people who were terrified and had lived with that terror for so many days and nights."[56] Repetto and Liggeri understood suffering. Father Varischi, however courageous, was a less sympathetic man.

Father Varischi is also interesting because of his opinion of the pope's role in Jewish rescue. The impression developed during a trip to Rome at the end of October 1943, his third since September 8. Father Gemelli had sent him twice before to confer with Monsignor Giovanni Battista Montini at the Vatican Secretariat of State about whether the Università Cattolica should remain open during the German occupation. Of his third trip, about a week after the roundup in Rome on October 16, Varischi later wrote, "During my third difficult trip to Rome toward the end of October, I had the opportunity to verify firsthand the effect of the Nazi persecution [of the Jews], and to see what efforts the religious institutions, and first of all the Vatican, were making to save those unhappy people, using every means and defying every danger. A Capuchin Father [later amended by hand to read Benedetto] was famous in Rome . . . for the hundreds of Jews he had already saved in those few weeks, and whom he was planning to maintain in every corner and hiding place while waiting to conduct them to safety."[57]

Like some other priests, monks, and nuns at the time, Varischi seems to have received the impression that the pope was somehow connected with the rescue efforts for Jews that he so clearly witnessed. Yet he could offer no precise examples or proof. The one example he cited, the most impressive in Rome, was that of Father Benedetto, a Capuchin like himself. But Benedetto, as seen, was working with Delasem. Monsignor Angelo Dell'Acqua in the Vatican Secretariat of State had urged Benedetto to use maximum prudence in his dealing with Jews and had complained angrily on November 20 that the Capuchin had not followed his advice. In December, Dell'Acqua had complained again that "several people" close to Vatican circles were too interested in the Jews, "to whom it would be better to speak less." [58] There is no record that Vatican officials ever encouraged Benedetto, while they certainly discouraged him. Varischi knew none of this. And so the myth of papal involvement in the rescue of Jews continued to grow.

CHAPTER SEVENTEEN

The Vatican and Rescue in Central Italy

Florence and Assisi

W I T H I N a few days of the Italian announcement of the armistice and the German occupation of Italy, hundreds of Jewish refugees were passing through Florence in an attempt to reach Rome and, ultimately, the advancing Allies. As in Genoa, Turin, and Milan, many of these refugees were illegal and indigent. To provide them with essential social services, a group of Florentine Jews, including Chief Rabbi Nathan Cassuto, Raffaele Cantoni, Matilde Cassin, Giuliano Treves, and some others quickly set up what they called the Comitato di Assistenza Profughi—the Refugee Assistance Committee.[1] Cassuto was already a leader of Delasem in Florence, while Cantoni was a national coordinator. Cassin was also involved on the local level.[2] The new committee was actually an extension of Delasem itself.

Clients were not difficult to find. Most Jewish refugees arriving in Florence went straight to the central synagogue and the offices of the Jewish Community in the Via Farini. There they were given hot meals and temporary places to sleep, usually in schools owned and operated by the Community itself. Some also received financial subsidies or train tickets for the south. Funds came from the Community, which represented about 1,700 Florentine Jews in 1943, and from private Jewish donors.[3]

As the number of Jewish refugees soared, the committee's work became more difficult. As early as September 13, leaders of the Jewish Community heard rumors from friendly local politicians and police that the Germans had requested lists of all Florentine Jews and of specific individuals who would make useful hostages.[4] As a result, the Community offices were immediately closed, and many of the employees who operated the schools and social services fled. When the synagogue, open on October 1 for Rosh Hashanah, came under German surveillance, services for Yom Kippur on the 9th were held elsewhere.[5] Refugees could no longer be safely housed in Community buildings. The new Refugee Assistance Committee's activities were evolving from the provision of subsidies to the organization of clandestine rescue. It had to make major adjustments.

It is not clear which representative of the Refugee Assistance Committee first asked Cardinal Elia Dalla Costa, archbishop of Florence, for help. Some Italian historians believe that the Refugee Assistance Committee first approached Giorgio La Pira, a well-known Catholic layman and anti-Fascist who had engaged in sympathetic dialogue with Jews before the war and would do so again after it. Matilde Cassin of the committee had known him since 1942. La Pira then relayed the committee's appeal to Dalla Costa.[6] Another author, a young Jewish refugee in Florence at the time, suggests that the idea of petitioning Dalla Costa came from Joseph Ziegler, a Jewish refugee from Belgium in need of shelter but with wealth and ideas to contribute to the cause. According to this interpretation, Ziegler himself first went to Dalla Costa.[7]

Cardinal Dalla Costa readily agreed to help, and he appointed his secretary, Monsignor Giacomo Meneghello, as his liaison with the Refugee Assistance Committee.[8] Meneghello held the same position within the archdiocese as Don Repetto in Genoa and Monsignor Barale in Turin. Dalla Costa also asked for help, probably right away, from Father Cipriano Ricotti, a Dominican priest at the Convento di San Marco, internationally known for its early fifteenth-century frescos by Fra Angelico. Ricotti was a close friend of La Pira.[9] As the number of refugees augmented over the next few weeks, however, many went directly to the archbishop's office to meet Meneghello. That arrangement soon seemed too risky. At that point Dalla Costa also called upon Don Leto Casini, a parish priest from nearby Varlungo. As Casini later remembered, "[Dalla Costa] summoned me to his *palazzo* with a telephone call one evening in October . . . and after describing the tragic situation of the foreign Jews to me . . . asked if I would put myself at the disposition of a committee to search for lodgings, obtain food supplies, provide identity cards—naturally false—in sum, do everything possible to save those persecuted people."[10] Casini agreed, and he met the Refugee Assistance Committee the following morning.

The exact date of Dalla Costa's first involvement with Jewish rescue is uncertain, but it was probably about September 20. Mother Sandra later wrote that he asked her Franciscan convent at the Piazza del Carmine to shelter Jewish women and girls in September.[11] Father Ricotti remembered working with Matilde Cassin of Delasem to find lodgings for Jewish children as early as September 25.[12] Don Repetto informed Monsignor Barale on October 18 that Jews being sent south from Turin should be directed to the Archbishopric of Florence, "which is already up to date on the matter."[13] Casini described the date of Dalla Costa's request to him as "toward the end of October 1943," but he clearly stated that he was recruited late.[14] Whatever the precise date, however, Dalla Costa's involvement began early enough to preclude any kind of papal directive. As seen elsewhere, Vatican officials at the end of September and first two weeks of October were doing nothing to help Jews in Rome. They would not have asked prelates outside Rome to hide foreign Jews when they were not doing the same. Most Jews in Rome did not seek shelter in convents, monasteries, and Vatican properties until after the roundup on October 16—and even then there is no evidence of a papal directive in the Eternal City.

Long after the war Casini wrote that he had acted to help Jews, "feeling myself strong with the full authorization of the cardinal and the example of the pope, a great giver of hospitality to the persecuted."[15] He also told an interviewer, "The example comes to us from the pope who welcomed many Jews in the Vatican."[16] It is noteworthy that Casini wrote of an "example" but did not use the word "order." But there was no papal example in October or, for that matter, later. This book has made it clear that the pope did not welcome Jews in the Vatican. Casini may well have believed otherwise, however, a victim of the myth of a compassionate Pius XII. He may have thought, or been told, that in rescuing Jews he was carrying out the will of the Holy Father in Rome. There is no evidence that Vatican officials acted either to encourage or discourage that conviction.

Cardinal Dalla Costa mobilized the entire structure of his archdiocese for Jewish rescue. He provided Casini and Ricotti with letters of introduction to use in their search for lodgings for Jewish fugitives. The archbishop would have been reluctant actually to order religious houses to accept outsiders, and in some cases he would have lacked the authority, but his request usually received a favorable response. In and around Florence, at least twenty-one monasteries and convents, along with parish churches and trusted parishioners, ultimately accepted more than 110 Italian and 220 foreign Jews.[17] As in Rome, schools run by nuns or monks often accepted Jewish children as boarders and disguised them as Catholics. The school run by the Suore Serve di Maria Addolorato in the Via Faentina, for example, accepted twelve girls. The archbishop's office paid their expenses, primarily from Delasem funds.[18] In addition, the Seminario Minore became a distribution center where foreign Jews assembled before being referred to convents or monasteries. Its large size, with many people coming and going, and its location slightly outside the center of Florence made it an effective gathering point.[19]

In addition to looking for hiding places, Casini distributed false documents and monthly subsidies provided by Delasem.[20] Toward the end of December, when it became too difficult to move around the city, he arranged to be in front of a bust of Cellini on the Ponte Vecchio every morning between 11:30 and 12:30, and at the Chapel of the Madonna in the Duomo every afternoon between 4:00 and 5:00, to meet any refugee who needed him.[21] He miraculously escaped detection, considering that he had already been arrested at a meeting of the Refugee Assistance Committee on November 26 and released only on December 21, after his archbishop intervened. Dalla Costa's secretary Meneghello also distributed funds. Following a request from Eugenio Artom, a leader of the local Jewish Community, his clients after January included needy Florentine Jews as well.[22]

The distributed funds came primarily from Delasem's local and Genovese offices, the Jewish Community of Florence, and private Jewish contributors.[23] Chief among the latter was Joseph Ziegler, who apparently donated 1 million lire to the cause.[24] Casini later testified that he distributed 720,000 lire, given to him on three different occasions by Raffaele Cantoni of Delasem.[25] Meneghello reported after the war that the archbishop's office had helped about 400 Jews and distributed 1.42 million lire. He added that 50,000 lire were returned to the Jewish Community when its offices reopened after the liberation of Florence, and that 15,000 lire were held to reimburse Catholic institutions that had helped Jews.[26]

As in Genoa, Turin, Milan, and Bologna, the first large-scale roundups of Jews occurred in Florence in early November. German SS accompanied by some Italian Fascists caught many mostly foreign Jews near the synagogue, probably at the Community offices, on November 6. None of those arrested are known to have survived.[27] Other arrests occurred that same day throughout the city.[28] Almost from the beginning the SS and Fascist searches for Jews did not spare Catholic institutions. Members of the Refugee Assistance Committee were meeting at the Palazzo Pucci, owned by the archdiocese, when it was raided on November 26. Arrested along with Don Leto Casini were Rabbi

Nathan Cassuto, Luciana and Wanda Lascar, Hans Kahlberg, Joseph Ziegler, and Ziegler's assistant Marco Ischia. Cassuto, the Lascars, and Kahlberg were deported to Auschwitz on January 30, 1944. Only Kahlberg returned.[29]

Joseph Ziegler and his assistant were mysteriously released. Ziegler, who evidently believed that his false documents had deceived his pursuers, returned to the Seminary Minore, where he was hiding with his wife Susanna; his two children, six-year-old Liana and four-year-old Jack; and his mother-in-law. About a week later, on December 8, the Seminary Minore was also raided. The Ziegler family was arrested, along with Monsignor Bartoletti, the rector. Marco Ischia, it seemed, had been a spy and an informer. The Zieglers joined the other Jews on the deportation train on January 30. Joseph Ziegler returned from Auschwitz, but his entire family died there.[30]

Also on the night of November 26–27, German SS troops accompanied by Fascists raided three other Church institutions in Florence. Perhaps the most devastating attack occurred at the Franciscan convent at the Piazza del Carmine, across the Arno from the center of the city. Tourists today visit the famous Brancacci Chapel at the Church of Santa Maria del Carmine to see the Masaccio frescoes. In the autumn of 1943 the Suore Francescane Missionarie di Maria in the quiet convent attached to the church were sheltering about thirty Jewish women and girls, mostly but not all foreign. The guests lived in the convent's public rather than cloistered areas, and did not disguise themselves as nuns. All but two of them were brutally seized in the November raid. The men and boys associated with the women were hidden elsewhere, and escaped.[31]

Wanda Abenaim Pacifici, the mother of twelve-year-old Emanuele and five-year-old Raffaele, was at the convent that fateful night. Wanda's story, full of terror and despair, illustrates the frequent informal contacts between the Archdioceses of Genoa and Florence. Until recently, she had lived in Genoa, where her husband, Riccardo, was the much admired chief rabbi. In September she fled with Raffaele to her parents' house in the province of Pisa. Emanuele joined her there in mid-October. Riccardo, sheltered by Don Repetto, remained valiantly at his post in Genoa.

Around November 18, Wanda was visited at her parents' house by Don Gian Maria Rotondi, who worked with Don Repetto to help Jews in Genoa. Don Rotondi had come to tell her that her husband had been arrested in Genoa on November 3. She and her sons needed to find a better hiding place, in case the Nazis and Fascists should come looking for them too. The Genovese priest gave her a card of introduction for Cardinal Dalla Costa. Accompanied by her brother Carlo Abenaim, Wanda and the two boys arrived in Florence after curfew on November 19. After spending the night in the railroad station, they went straight to the cardinal's office the next morning.

Cardinal Dalla Costa sent the family to the village of Varlungo to see Don Casini. That indefatigable parish priest knew that most convents were already full, but he gave Wanda a list of places to try. With her brother and sons, she trudged from place to place for the entire day on Saturday, November 20. Near dusk, she finally found a place for herself at the Franciscan convent in the Piazza del Carmine. Her youngest son could stay with her in the convent for one night, but Emanuele had to sleep in the reception room. Both boys had to leave the next morning.

Emanuele and Raffaele were sent to the Collegio di Santa Marta, a boarding school and orphanage for boys in Settignano, on the outskirts of Florence. There they and some fifteen other young Jews blended in with about 200 non-Jewish students. Everyone treated them with great kindness, but only two of the nuns knew that they were Jewish. They were often hungry and cold, but they survived. One of Emanuele's most poignant memories of the war, however, was not of his school and the nuns, but of the Sunday after the raid on the convent at the Piazza del Carmine. His mother had been there for only a week. Like other parents, she was planning to visit her sons at the boarding school on Sunday, November 28. Emanuele waited all day for her, until he understood that she was not coming. She had been one of the victims of the raid.[32] She was deported to Auschwitz on December 6, 1943. By chance, she was on the same train as her husband, Riccardo, who had been arrested on November 3. Neither of the two returned.[33]

The other two institutions raided on the night of November 26–27 were the San Giuseppe recreation center in the Via Domenico Cirillo, which was sheltering twenty Jewish men, and the Convento delle Suore di San Giuseppe dell'Apparizione in the Via Gioberti, where the exact number of Jewish women and children present is unknown. All victims of the two raids were deported on December 6, and none returned.[34]

On November 27, the day following the raids on the two convents and the recreation center in Florence, Vatican Secretary of State Maglione wrote to Borgongini Duca, the papal nuncio to Italy. He mentioned the Vatican's concern that so many individuals "of the most disparate social conditions" were being detained throughout the country every day, with so little apparent criteria or reason. The arrests seemed totally arbitrary. He added, amazingly enough, "It is also true, as we have been told, that almost always the agents charged with making these arrests act with tact and courtesy." One wonders whether he thought that the German SS police who arrested Jewish men, women, and children under the pope's very windows had been courteous. It is difficult to imagine what he thought of the massacres of fifty-four Jews around Lago Maggiore. Maglione asked Borgongini Duca to consider conveying the Vatican's concern to the appropriate authorities. He never mentioned Jews.[35]

Borgongini Duca responded to Maglione's request ten days later, on December 7. He had, he explained, met with a high official in the Italian Ministry of the Interior, who wished to remain nameless. The official had confirmed that the German occupying forces were unfortunately making arbitrary arrests, although detainees were often quickly released. He had also stated that the Italian authorities were attempting to restore a more normal situation, in which only the Italian police could arrest citizens. Police order number five declaring that all Jews in the country should be arrested and imprisoned had been issued on December 1. Nevertheless, Borgongini Duca also failed to mention Jews.[36] He apparently believed that he had complied with Maglione's suggestion to convey the Vatican's concern to the appropriate authorities.

With the destruction of the Refugee Assistance Committee in the SS raid on November 26, Cardinal Dalla Costa lost most of the Florentine Jewish leaders who had helped distribute the Delasem funds. Father Benedetto in Rome always worked with Settimio Sorani; Don Repetto in Genoa cooperated with Massimo Teglio; and Monsignor Barale in Turin also had Jewish associates. In Florence, Don Casini and Monsignor Meneghello seem to have continued almost alone. However, one former Delasem activist, Giorgio Nissim, remained to assist the two priests in the area outside Florence, particularly around Lucca, Pisa, and Livorno. Nissim set himself up in the offices of the Sacerdoti Oblati in the Via del Giardino Botanico in Lucca. Working closely with priests whom he identified as Don Paoli, Don Sirio, and Don Guido Staderini, he provided subsidies, false documents, and hiding places for both Jews and partisans. He traveled to Genoa to obtain Delasem funds from Don Repetto and turned them over to Don Paoli, who then distributed them to many of the estimated 800 Jews hiding around Lucca. After the war, both Nissim and the Sacerdoti Oblati testified that they received help and encouragement from the bishop of Lucca.[37]

The priests who helped Nissim, and the nuns and monks who in turn helped those priests, put themselves at great risk. Retreating German forces, particularly the SS, behaved with particular savagery in Tuscany. Some twenty-seven priests were killed in and around Lucca, as well as twelve monks at Certosa di Farneta.[38] Most of these victims were implicated in the military Resistance rather than in Jewish rescue, but many had engaged in both. The monks at Certosa, for example, executed because arms were found in their monastery, had also helped Nissim hide about twenty Jews for a time.[39] And twenty-two-year-old Don Aldo Mei was shot beneath the old walls of Lucca on August 4, 1944, for hiding at least one Jew and some partisans.[40]

In addition to the archbishop of Florence and the bishop of Lucca, several other Catholic prelates in central Italy cooperated with Delasem. In early January 1944, Don Casini traveled to Foligno, about 190 kilometers southeast of Florence, to deliver Delasem funds to the sympathetic bishop there.[41] The bishop of Carpi helped funnel Delasem money and packages into the internment camp at Fossoli, in his diocese, where arrested Jews waited for trains that would take them to Auschwitz.[42] But it cannot be assumed that all bishops were so sympathetic. The bishop of Modena, just eighteen kilometers from Carpi, insisted in October 1943 on the relocation of dozens of orphaned Jewish children from Yugoslavia hiding in a seminary in Nonantola in his diocese.[43] The bishop of Mantua was known as a Fascist sympathizer who refused to have anything to do with the incipient anti-Fascist Christian Democratic Party.[44]

Closer to Florence, Don Casini was surprised to witness a hostile prelate personally. He later recalled that in January 1944 he had been obliged to change trains in Perugia during a trip to deliver Delasem funds to the bishop of Foligno. The connecting train to Foligno was delayed, and the weather was bitterly cold. While waiting, Casini went to see the archbishop of Perugia, hoping, he admitted, that he could leave the money with the archbishop, to be relayed to Foligno by someone else. But, he wrote, "I had barely referred to the 'Jewish' problem . . . he didn't let me finish the sentence, and showing me the door, he asked me to leave." Stranded in Perugia again on his return from Foligno late that cold January night, Don Casini was so intimidated that he did not dare ask for shelter at the archbishop's residence. He preferred to spend the night, as he recorded, "sleeping out in the open, behind a gate."[45] Such a story highlights the courage and strength of character of those clergymen who did help Jews in distress. It also suggests, once again, that they acted independently of a papal directive. A directive to prelates in northern and central Italy would surely have been received by the archbishop of Perugia.

The story of Jewish rescue in the small city of Assisi differs from that in Rome, Genoa, Turin, Milan, and Florence in one crucial respect. In Assisi there was no Delasem to ask Catholic prelates for help. In Assisi the initiative originated from within the Church itself. It clearly came, however, from Bishop Giuseppe Placido Nicolini, who saw what was happening within his diocese and understood what to do about it. The initiative did not come from Pius XII.

Refugees, mostly non-Jews, began to drift into Assisi after November 1942, well before the German occupation. Most of them had left their homes to escape the Allied air raids that were devastating northern Italian cities. Some had actually lost their homes in those raids. The few Jews among them had left their homes for the same reason. These early Jewish refugees were primarily Italians. Most foreign Jews in Italy were still in internment camps or in some form of supervised residence where their mobility was severely restricted. Even those fortunate enough to be free were often impoverished as a result of the law prohibiting foreign Jews from working. They were dependent on the social services offered by Jewish communities or Delasem in the larger cities.

In many respects Assisi was an obvious place of refuge. Set in the hills of central Italy amid fertile farm land, without major industries and far from the principal roads and railroads that connected northern and southern Italy, it was an unlikely target for air raids. In addition, the city of St. Francis and St. Claire had been a place of pilgrimage for centuries. It had a tradition of welcoming visitors. More important, it had scores of inns and guesthouses geared to receive pilgrims and tourists but empty now that tourism was impossible. The same Catholic heritage, however, that made Assisi a visitors' center might have been expected to discourage Jews from coming there. No Jews had lived in Assisi for centuries. It is an indication of Italian Jews' comfort and sense of belonging in their own country that some 100 to 200 ultimately chose to move to such a place.[46] For if they were few in number before September 8, 1943, they increased dramatically after that date, as the Germans occupied Italy and the danger of roundups and deportation gradually became apparent.

As the number of mostly non-Jewish refugees in Assisi began to swell in

July and August 1943, Bishop Nicolini realized that many of them desperately needed food and shelter. He set up a committee, staffed mostly by priests, to help newcomers on a more systematic basis. Government services had virtually broken down in the uncertainty following Mussolini's fall from power on July 25, and Nicolini filled a vital gap. It should be noted, however, that the committee that would play such an important role in Jewish survival in Assisi was originally created to help all refugees, most of whom were non-Jews and present quite legally. The committee had no extralegal purpose at the beginning.

To head his new committee Bishop Nicolini selected a remarkable young priest. Don Aldo Brunacci was a canon at San Rufino Cathedral, a teacher of religion at a local state school, and a dynamic, courageous, and imaginative man. At his bishop's request, he promptly recruited a number of priests to help him. The committee's main purpose at this point was to help newcomers put their papers in order, secure ration cards, and find lodgings at reasonable prices. The committee collected information about available apartments or rooms in farmhouses, hotels, and inns, and passed that information along to the refugees.[47] All of this, again, was quite legal.

Some 4,338 legally registered, mostly non-Jewish refugees ultimately gathered in Assisi to escape the air raids in the north.[48] This was, of course, a huge number for a town of about 5,000 residents, and even in a tourist center it put a strain on the facilities. It was, however, a problem that the committee was able to handle. But after September 8 and the onset of the German occupation of Italy, a different issue developed when scores of Jewish refugees began to arrive. Unlike the Jewish newcomers in the cities previously mentioned, most of the refugees in Assisi were Italian citizens with some financial resources, legal documents, and a perfect command of the language. Consequently, their special needs were not immediately apparent. It gradually became clear, however, that they could not register with the police, as required by law, using their legal documents that identified them as Jews. They had to secure false papers indicating that they were not Jewish, and they had to act quickly. Suddenly, Don Aldo's assistance committee found itself faced with a desperate need for illegal services.

The family of Graziella Viterbi was among those who needed help. Emilio Viterbi, Graziella's father, was a well-known scientist and professor at the University of Padua until he lost his position because of the racial laws. On vacation with his wife and children when the Germans invaded, he did not return to the city where he could easily be recognized. He stayed at a hotel in the mountains until October 9, when he brought his family to Assisi.[49] He had heard that the town was quiet and peaceful, off the beaten track and with a Fascist *podestà* who was a decent man. Other Jewish families were sent to Assisi by priests or bishops whom they knew. Still others came because they heard good things about the town from relatives or friends who were already there. Thus, relatives followed a particular family, or clusters of friends and neighbors arrived from the same city. This created a definite problem, of course, for Jews who had changed their identities and did not want to be recognized by anyone from their former life.

Assisi was a city without an established Jewish Community to offer help. Once in Assisi, therefore, the Viterbis and other families like them could not go to a synagogue or Community office. They turned instead to Don Brunacci's preexisting refugee assistance committee. It was, after all, operating openly and legally, although some of its activities were becoming increasingly clandestine. It was not difficult to discover the committee. Some refugees naturally gravitated to the town square, where they often ran into someone who knew about it. Others went to one of the churches to speak to a priest or monk. The assumption was that although a man of the Church might not necessarily help them and might even be unpleasant, he would not turn them in to the authorities. Many refugees went first to the large Basilica di San Francesco, the church of Giotto's most famous frescos, simply because pilgrims and tourists in Assisi have always gone there first. There they often met a Franciscan from Sardinia named Father Michele Todde, who put them in touch with Don Brunacci.[50]

The committee offered different things to different people. The Viterbis, for example, had some resources but needed false papers in order to register with the police, rent an apartment, and secure ration cards. Don Brunacci found several municipal and provincial civil servants willing to risk their lives to smuggle blank forms out of their offices, to be filled in "unofficially." He located a courageous local printer, Luigi Brizi, to produce other forms, apply photographs, and create false official seals, "proving" that new arrivals came from towns behind Allied lines or destroyed by air raids, where identities could not be verified.[51] Armed with such papers, the Viterbis and other Italian Jews could manage more or less on their own, coping always with a terrible fear.

Jewish refugees without resources and often without an ability to speak Italian faced more daunting problems of room and board. Don Brunacci addressed these issues by calling on nuns throughout Assisi and the surrounding countryside. Religious orders of women had for centuries maintained guest houses attached to their convents, to shelter pilgrims and tourists visiting the holy places of the town. Mostly empty in wartime, those houses were an obvious solution to the need for clandestine residences. They could be searched, it is true, but guests with false documents could be disguised as foreign pilgrims. Most Jews without resources stayed in these guest houses, known as *forestieri*—along with, it might be added, non-Jewish refugees who also could not afford to rent larger quarters.[52] Refugees did not stay with monks, for they did not maintain forestieri.[53]

Despite what is written in some exaggerated accounts of rescue in Assisi, Jews did not stay inside the female convents, in violation of the rules of cloister, except in one exceptional case. Before the German occupation, a couple named Finzi had registered with the regular police, as required by law. At that time, they had declared that the husband was Jewish. After the arrival of the Germans, they naturally became the targets of a police search. From the guest house where they were living, maintained by the Suore Clarisse Francesi di Santa Coletta, or the Colettine, they had to be moved inside the convent. The bishop hesitated until the very last moment, and until the Germans had twice come looking for them, before he granted authorization.[54]

In addition to Don Aldo Brunacci, Father Rufino Nicacci, the father superior of the monastery of San Damiano, was also active in rescuing Jews in Assisi. Father Rufino steered many Jews in need of shelter to the Suore Clarisse di San Quirico. He was also able to help those particular nuns to feed their guests and solve problems that arose concerning them. Graziella Viterbi remembers him as a warm, expansive, and voluble man.[55]

Why did Bishop Nicolini, Don Aldo Brunacci, Father Rufino Nicacci, and others like them act as they did to save Jews? It is apparent that they drifted from legal assistance to illegal rescue rather gradually, almost unconsciously, without making a sudden dramatic decision and without at first understanding the risks involved. They were clearly exceptional people, however, who perceived the needs of newcomers to their diocese and did not cease to help when the going got rough. They had most certainly learned of the Rome roundup of Jews on October 16, 1943. Equally certainly, they knew about the terrifying raids on religious institutions in Florence, only 177 kilometers to the northwest, on November 26. They were also aware that on December 1, the Italian government had ordered that Jews throughout the country were to be arrested and interned. They understood the dangers the Jews faced, and they acted spontaneously to help.

There is an alternative explanation. Don Aldo Brunacci has long claimed that in late September 1943, Bishop Nicolini told him that he had received a letter from the Vatican Secretary of State Cardinal Luigi Maglione asking him to help all refugees, including, the letter specified, political dissenters and Jews. Don Brunacci never said that Nicolini read him the letter, but he maintained that he saw it in Nicolini's hand, and that Nicolini made him aware of its contents. He stressed that he, Don Brunacci, was the only person who knew about the letter, for Nicolini insisted that it remain secret. He also claimed that similar letters went to other bishops in Italy, but it is unclear how he knows this.[56] As seen, no other bishops or their closest assistants have made similar claims.

Nicolini's letter has never been found, nor has any letter like it to any other bishop ever been discovered. Nicolini might have destroyed such a letter, of course, because of its potential to reveal clandestine activities and embarrass the pope in the event of a German search. But this seems unlikely. Single documents are not difficult to hide. Certainly if many letters had gone out, one would have survived. A number of high-ranking archbishops and bishops throughout Europe had long been asking the pope to do more for Jews and others in danger, and Nicolini and other prelates in Italy knew that there was some public disapproval of the papal silence. A letter of the kind that Don Brunacci believes he saw would almost certainly have been preserved by someone clever enough to understand that it might someday help the pope's reputation. Bishop Nicolini of Assisi was clever. Graziella Viterbi later recalled that during the German occupation he saved the real identification cards of her family and other Jews in a hiding place behind a sacred image in his office.[57] If he saved identification cards, risking the detection of himself and those he was hiding, why would he not have saved a papal directive?

Another problem with Don Aldo's claim is the date. Late September 1943 is just too early. As seen, some foreign Jews throughout Italy at that time were worrying about being apprehended as illegal aliens, and Delasem was concerned about protecting its funds and lists, but most Italian Jews had not yet gone into hiding. The incipient danger was not yet strong enough to have caused the pope to jeopardize his relationship with the Germans and the safety of the Vatican City by calling on his Church to help those out of favor with the authorities. As discussed in Chapter Eleven, Vatican fear that the Germans would not respect the integrity of the Holy See was most intense in September 1943, and abated slightly only after German Foreign Minister Ribbentrop sent assurances to Maglione on October 7. There is no evidence that Pius XII called on his prelates to help Jews even after the Rome roundup and the onset of an Italian policy to arrest all Jews. He certainly would not have done so before those events.

Don Brunacci is surely telling the truth as he knows it. He probably did see a letter in his bishop's hand. Nicolini may have considered it useful to make his assistants believe that they were doing the pope's work. Both Bishop Nicolini and Don Brunacci seem later to have implied, more vaguely, to nuns whom they were asking to take in refugees, that it was the pope's will. But it is not likely that the paper in Nicolini's hand said what he, Nicolini, implied that it did. The explanation for rescue in Assisi cannot be traced to the pope but rather rests with the courage and imagination of the individuals directly involved.

CHAPTER EIGHTEEN

The Vatican, the Patriarch, and the Jews in Venice

THE WORD "ghetto" is said to have originated in Venice, where Jews were confined to a carefully circumscribed area in the sixteenth century. "Getto," meaning iron casting in Italian, undoubtedly referred to the iron foundries in the neighborhood where Jews were forced to live. The dark and dirty streets of the ghetto, winding their way toward a few bridges over the canals, were easy to seal off from the rest of the city. Jews there were shut behind heavy gates from dusk to dawn, every night of their lives.

Napoleon Bonaparte had the gates torn down and the ghetto opened in 1797, when French troops occupied Venice. But the tall, rickety buildings remain, and the streets, in the absence of automobiles, look much as they did more than two hundred years ago. The area today is off the beaten track, not far from the railroad station but on the other side of the city from the dazzling Piazza San Marco, the magnificent basilica, and the Palazzo Patriarcale. Many Jews nevertheless still live in the old neighborhood, clustered around its central square, the Campo di Ghetto Nuovo, close to their synagogue, their Community offices, and their memories.

One postwar addition to the central square, however, strikes every visitor. Two large plaques have been erected near the Casa Israelitica di Riposo, as it is now called—a nursing home for elderly Jews. One plaque announces that 246 Jews were deported from Venice during the war, most to die at Auschwitz. The other evokes the Italian police raids of December 5, 1943, and August 17, 1944, when elderly Jews were torn from their beds in that very nursing home and thrown first into local prisons and later into deportation trains and death camps. Today children climb on the walls and play soccer in the square, while mothers keep watch and old people from the same nursing home soak up the sun and gaze at passers-by. The square echoes with voices, as squares in Venice do, but the sounds are of joy rather than terror. It is as if nothing evil ever happened in the Campo di Ghetto Nuovo.

During Mussolini's regime the Jews of Venice lived much like their core-ligionists elsewhere in the country. The racial laws in 1938 hit them hard. Membership in the local Jewish Community, calculated at 1,670 in 1938, dropped to 1,209 by 1942, as some families emigrated and others converted in the desperate but unfulfilled hope that the laws would spare Jews who be-came Catholics.[1] Nor did Venetian Jews receive much sympathy from their Catholic neighbors or solace from the Church hierarchy. A police report in 1938 stated that most Venetians approved of the racial laws, although by 1940 that support had allegedly diminished.[2] And regarding the laws, the cardinal patriarch—the Venetian equivalent of an archbishop—remained silent.

As elsewhere in Italy, hundreds of foreign Jews, mostly from Yugoslavia, were interned in the northeastern provinces before the armistice. Most were freed to fend for themselves as the Germans moved south to occupy the coun-try in September 1943.[3] Without resources, they found a much more fragile support structure than their better organized coreligionists in the northwest. Delasem seems to have been a less dynamic presence here. Nor, apparently, did representatives from Delasem or any other Jewish organization seriously consider asking the local Church hierarchy for help.

Most citizen and foreign Jews in Venice did hide, however, in the tense late autumn of 1943. They were alerted to the danger when Dr. Giuseppe Jona, the president of the Community, committed suicide on September 10, 1943, rather than turn over membership lists to the Germans. They were warned a second time when the train carrying the Roman Jews arrested on October 16 stopped for repairs in nearby Padua. The train was headed for Auschwitz. Some haggard deportees were allowed to descend for water in full view of passers-by, and the news circulated. After these events, about two hundred Venetian Jews fled to Switzerland, where some, including the nearly blind fifty-eight-year-old Chief Rabbi Adolfo Ottolenghi, were refused entry at the border and obliged to return.[4] Hundreds of others hid, sometimes in con-vents, monasteries, and Catholic schools, but usually outside the city. For the most part, those who did not hide were the weakest—the old, the sick, and the poor, including families with many or very young children. Many believed that age or illness would protect them from deportation. They were to be sadly deceived. Others who remained at home were the spouses and children of mixed marriages. They too were often not spared.

Unlike their coreligionists in cities in northwestern and central Italy—in Milan, Turin, Genoa, Florence, and Rome, for example—the Jews in Venice were not arrested in October and November. Change came early in December, immediately following the Ministry of the Interior's issuance of police order number five on December 1. As seen, the original order declared that Italian police were to arrest every Jew in the country. Only those born of mixed marriages but baptized and thus officially defined as "Aryan" under the racial laws were to be spared. Ten days later, the order was amended to exclude also Jewish citizens who were gravely ill, over the age of seventy, or spouses in mixed marriages. In the interval, however, the police in Venice struck fiercely to execute their new orders. They were the first in the country to act on a large scale.

On the night of December 5–6, 1943, Italian police accompanied by some Fascist irregulars but no Germans arrested 163 Venetian Jews, including 114 women and girls and 49 men and boys.[5] Most were arrested in their homes, but police also invaded the Casa di Riposo ebraica, where they pulled sick and elderly men and women from their beds.[6] Probably as a result of the amendments to police order number five on December 10, some of the sick and elderly were temporarily released a few days later. Ninety-three men, women, and children, however, were sent to the internment camp at Fossoli on December 31.[7] Four children between the ages of three and six, too ill to travel earlier, joined them on January 18.[8] From Fossoli, the Venetian Jews were deported to Auschwitz on February 22. None are known to have survived.[9]

The German occupiers of Italy did not initially insist on the arrests of Italian Jews in mixed families. After all, Jewish spouses in mixed marriages in the German Reich, along with their children defined as *Mischling*, were also usually spared from deportation. The Germans did object, however, to exemptions for old and sick Jews. Because of those objections and because no one in the Republic of Salò defended them, the reprieve of the elderly Jews of Venice was brief. On August 17, 1944, Italian police, accompanied this time by Germans, invaded the Casa di Riposo ebraica and seized twenty-one elderly residents.[10] On October 6, the victims were twenty-nine Jewish patients at three city hospitals.[11] Since Fossoli had been closed on August 1, they and other arrested Jews were sent to La Risiera di San Sabba, an old rice factory on a hillside overlooking Trieste that had been converted into a prison, execution grounds, and transit station. The oldest and weakest were murdered on the spot and the rest, the majority, were deported to Auschwitz.[12] Among them was Chief Rabbi Adolfo Ottolenghi, who had been rejected at the Swiss border the previous December. Ottolenghi was deported on September 2, 1944, and killed at Auschwitz.[13]

Nor were the members of mixed families safe for long. Despite their official exemption from arrest by Italian police, many were seized and interned at Fossoli in the spring of 1944. They remained there for a time while others were deported, but they too were moved out when the camp was vacated. Most Jewish spouses in mixed marriages ended their days at Auschwitz. Their baptized children were usually deported to Buchenwald, Ravensbrück, or Bergen Belsen, where their chances of survival were only slightly better.

The family of Paolo Sereni remained intact for a few months longer than many others. He and his Jewish father, Aldo, non-Jewish mother, Giannina Bordignon, brother Ugo, and sister Elena were arrested in Venice on September 21, 1944. All were detained at La Risiera. Aldo was deported to die at Auschwitz in October. The children, between the ages of fourteen and twenty, were sent to Ravensbrück in January.[14] Only Paolo returned. His mother was held at La Risiera for a time and was murdered by an irate guard as she was about to be released. Jews and non-Jews, Italians and foreigners, political dissenters and apolitical civilians—all were victims of brutality and sadism on the hillside above Trieste.

Like most other Italian prelates of his day, Cardinal Adeodato Piazza, patriarch of Venice since 1935, was conservative and fiercely anti-Bolshevik. Although far from being an ideological Fascist, he frequently expressed approval of the Duce, who had signed the Lateran Accords with the Church, waged war in Abyssinia and Spain for the preservation of Catholicism, and opposed the spread of Liberalism and Communism. Regarding the Jews, Piazza shared the attitudes of conservatives within the Vatican and at *L'Osservatore Romano* and *La Civiltà Cattolica,* as described in the first chapters of this book. He viewed Jews as the killers of Christ, doomed by God to perpetual chastisement. He considered them to be, with Liberals, atheists, and Masons, a danger to society and to the Church. All good Catholics were thus obliged to defend themselves against them, even to the extent of separating them from the rest of society by means of special laws.[15] Like Popes Pius XI and XII, however, Piazza approved of discrimination on religious and cultural grounds, but never on racial ones. Nor did they or he remotely sympathize with violence and murder.

The attitudes of the patriarch of Venice toward Mussolini, Fascism, and the Jews did not in fact differ greatly from those of several other prelates mentioned in these pages. Cardinal Schuster, in particular, had often echoed Piazza's sentiments. But with regard to the Jews, Cardinals Schuster in Milan, Boetto in Genoa, Dalla Costa in Florence, and others ultimately supported rescue operations during the German occupation. Because Piazza did not act similarly, he remained a victim of his own unfortunate rhetoric and a target of condemnation by anti-Fascists and partisans who wanted him to have done more. But the patriarch's wartime activities regarding the Jews cannot be inferred from his speeches and writings before the German occupation, from accusations by his enemies, or from often greatly exaggerated and unsubstantiated defenses by his friends. Those activities can be described only after examination of the evidence.

Sometime at the end of November or in early December 1943, Piazza sent a letter to Cardinal Raffaelo Carlo Rossi, head of the Consistorial Congregation at the Vatican. At that time, it will be recalled, the Carta di Verona had declared that all Italian Jews were enemy aliens. Police order number five, which called on December 1 for the arrests of all Jews in Italy, had just been, or was about to be, issued. The police raid against the Venetian Jews on the night of December 5–6 had not yet occurred. Piazza's letter read, in part:

> Permit me to mention to Your Eminence the painful situation of the Jews, who, alarmed by the foreign and enemy declarations [of the Carta di Verona and possibly the police order number five] and by the upcoming Republican law that—they say—will be modeled on the Nuremberg laws, come every day to ask for my help and advice. Having particular apprehension are the baptized, who have already been declared of the Jewish race or who will be so declared, based on the new law. I am certain that the Holy See will do everything possible to save these unhappy people, whose fate cannot not worry [sic—a double negative typical of the writing style of many prelates at the time] the Church. For my part, I have mentioned the painful problem, suggesting moderation, to the German consul [Koester] residing in Venice, who came to see me "privately." He assures me of his interest, but what will he do? I

have been so bold as to write to Your Eminence on the chance that you may wish to point the matter out to the cardinal secretary of state or—even—the Holy Father. It is in truth a matter in which we cannot disinterest ourselves.[16]

Cardinal Rossi forwarded Piazza's remarks to Vatican Secretary of State Cardinal Maglione on December 6, the day following the police raid in Venice.[17] On December 10, Maglione responded. He wrote to Rossi, "I am pleased to assure Your Eminence, so that you may in turn assure Cardinal Piazza, that the Holy See, as it has done in the past, also in today's circumstances will not omit to endeavor, as much as it can, in favor of these unhappy people." [18] Maglione must have known of the brutal Italian-conducted police roundup of Jews in Venice of the previous evening. Yet even with that fresh knowledge, and even with prelates as important as Rossi and Piazza, he employed the usual Vatican style that even Monsignor Domenico Tardini once described, in a different context, as "bureaucratic coldness." [19] There was no passion, no moral outrage, no sense of urgency, no personal touch. The message was stiff and formal, confiding nothing, written, as Vatican communications so often were, as if an overworked and personally uninvolved bureaucrat simply wanted to get yet another piece of paper off his desk. Furthermore, and more seriously, the message offered no guidance for the patriarch of a city whose Jews, men and women, young and old, were now in prison awaiting internment and probable deportation.

Piazza may have been slightly confused about the impact of possible new racial laws on Jews who had converted. Such measures were, in any case, considered but never decreed.[20] More important, however, his letter to Cardinal Rossi basically expressed a concern only for Jews who had become Catholics. There is nothing in the letter to suggest that the "moderation" that he was urging on German Consul Hans Koester was for anyone except converted Jews threatened with arrest by police order number five or about to be affected by new definitions of race.

Despite his narrow vision, Piazza may not have deserved the scathing report that Koester sent to Berlin on December 7, two days after the Italian police raid in Venice. In his report Koester did not mention the meeting that Piazza claimed they had had sometime in early December to discuss "moderation" with respect to Jews who had been baptized. Instead, Koester alleged that a friend, rather than himself, had met with the patriarch. Of that meeting, Koester wrote:

The patriarch pointed out that the Jewish question, as it was now being handled in Venice, was causing him grave concern. Last night [which could only have been December 5–6] many arrests of poor, old and sick Jews were made in their homes by extreme Fascists, while wealthy and carefully screened Jews continued to move about freely in Venice, if they had not already fled from the city. This injustice was disturbing him so much that the only solution he could see would be for the measures against the Jews to be carried out by German authorities, because then justice would at least be guaranteed for all. It is well known that the patriarch's chief wish is to have all Jews and half-Jews shut up in a ghetto.[21]

According to Koester, Piazza went on to praise Germany as a bulwark against Bolshevism, condemn Badoglio as a traitor in league with the Masons and the Jews, and declare his opinion that "an administration in German hands, combined with trustworthy Italian circles, would be the best solution."[22]

Conflicts in the dates and descriptions of the meetings suggest that two separate encounters are involved. The important question, however, is whether Piazza would ever have uttered the words ascribed to him. The patriarch was certainly aware that the Germans had arrested and deported hundreds of Jews in nearby Merano and Trieste, as well as in Rome. It is difficult to believe that he actually wanted all the Jews in Venice arrested, or that he could have said that "the only solution he could see would be for the measures against the Jews to be carried out by German authorities, because then justice would at least be guaranteed for all." Furthermore, other phrases in the report do not ring true. The Jews in December were arrested by regular Italian police, not extreme Fascists, as Piazza must have known. Most wealthy Jews had already fled the city, but if any remained, they certainly did not continue "to move about freely in Venice" after the raid.

It seems prudent to regard Koester's report with suspicion. The German consul may well have been trying, for reasons of his own, to improve the image of the patriarch in the eyes of his superiors in Berlin, or to persuade those same superiors to take a more active administrative role in Venice. He may also have been fed false information by local Nazi sympathizers.[23] Because of his prewar statements revealing religious anti-Judaism, Piazza was an easy target. The patriarch almost certainly preferred, as did most important Vatican officials, that the Germans administer Italy, "combined with trustworthy Italian circles," as the above report said, until the Allies were able to replace them. German and Italian civil servants were vastly preferable to uncontrolled Nazi and Fascist extremists whose violence further polarized the situation. Piazza and those who thought as he did greatly feared civil war and a vacuum of power that would facilitate a Communist takeover and violent partisan retribution against Fascist sympathizers. But Piazza surely did not want the Germans to destroy all the Jews in Venice.

Piazza's record regarding the Jews should not be condemned on the basis of one dubious document. His activities during the German occupation must be examined further. He began, as seen, by urging the German consul to exercise moderation, and by writing to a Vatican official. In both cases his concern was primarily for Jews who had become Catholics. He would continue in the same vein.

After the war the Allied army command in Venice requested a report from the prefect on the activities of the patriarch and the local clergy during the German occupation. The request expressed particular interest in any help given to Jews and Resistants, or, as it described the latter, "Patriots." [24] In response to the request, the patriarch's office prepared a lengthy manuscript describing Piazza's reports to the Holy See about bombing raids and general destruction in his diocese, as well as his protests to the Germans against the brutal seizures and torture of civilians, illegal searches of at least eight churches and monasteries, and arrests of priests. Regarding Jews, a handwritten statement from the patriarch's office dated August 29, 1945, declared, "For the Jews it was possible to obtain that not only the mixed children but also the spouses in mixed marriages were left tranquil in their homes . . . and all the others were helped with all available material and moral means. The patriarch always protested energetically to the German authorities about the inhumane treatment, illegal arrests and iniquitous deportations." [25]

This statement is less than honest. As seen, police order number five had decreed on December 1, 1943, that Italian police should not arrest the baptized children of mixed marriages. Jewish spouses in mixed marriages were originally to be arrested, but the amendment to the police order on December 10 had also exempted them. If those spouses and children were spared for a time, it was because of the policies of the Republic of Salò and not the interventions of the patriarch. Piazza could have done no more than request that an order and an amendment decided elsewhere be respected in Venice—a valid contribution, but not of the sweeping nature described in the post-liberation statement. Furthermore, as seen in the case of Paolo Sereni's mixed family, exemptions proved temporary. Piazza certainly did not "obtain that not only the mixed children but also the spouses in mixed marriages were left tranquil in their homes" on a permanent basis.

Claims of "material and moral" help to arrested Jews also appear to be exaggerated. Documents available at the archives of the Patriarchate provide evidence of only one intervention from Piazza's office. On December 14, more than a week after the raid, Monsignor Giovanni Urbani, the patriarchal chancellor (and a future patriarch), petitioned police headquarters for permission to visit those arrested on December 5–6. He also asked that Father Giovanni Barbaro, parish priest at the Church of San Marcuola near the former ghetto, be allowed to join him. The purpose of the visit, Urbani wrote, was "to offer to the Catholics of the Jewish race . . . the necessary religious assistance."[26] If the patriarch and Urbani did more, either in December or in all the months before liberation, there is no evidence of it.[27]

Finally, the manuscript describing Piazza's wartime activities in support of Jews concluded that he had always protested "inhuman treatment, illegal arrests and iniquitous deportations." Again, the claim is vastly overstated. Documents available for public scrutiny at the patriarchal archives provide no evidence of protests against conditions specifically affecting Jews—and any existing evidence would certainly have been presented. It is, nevertheless, probable that Piazza and his assistants intended that Jews be included in their several petitions to the authorities for better treatment of prisoners in general. They may also have complained privately about the "illegal arrests" of Jews who were Catholics, especially if they were from mixed families technically exempt from arrest. There is, however, no evidence that they did so. Nor did they did ever protest the "iniquitous deportations."

According to available documents, Piazza appealed to the authorities on behalf of only one specific Jewish individual during the German occupation. On December 10, 1943, he wrote to the police chief of Venice asking that a Ukrainian-born convert and nun named Lidia Cressin be allowed to remain in her convent. The request circulated among Italian and German officials for nearly a year. On November 14, 1944, Piazza reinforced his appeal by writing to Lieutenant General Karl Wolff, commander of the SS in Italy, "No person belonging to the Jewish race has ever been hidden in monasteries or convents of this Patriarchate"—a claim that fortunately was untrue. Finally, on November 29, 1944, German Ambassador Rudolf Rahn informed the patriarch that "I have been able to obtain the granting of your request so much more easily because I have been able to demonstrate to the German military and police authorities the good offices of the Curia and the clergy [in the Venice region] for the maintenance of calm and order." Piazza wrote to thank Rahn on December 13 and Wolff on January 10, 1945.[28]

In addition to the above-mentioned report of August 29, 1945, delineating services rendered to Jews by Piazza's office, the patriarchal archives contain a second, much longer manuscript, entitled "In Defense of the Jews." Consisting of three pages handwritten by Monsignor Urbani, probably in connection with the first report, the second manuscript is as tendentious and misleading as the first. For example, after declaring that Piazza and Urbani tried to persuade Fascists and Nazis to spare Jews who had converted, it drew a totally unwarranted conclusion. It stated, "In the beginning [those interventions] permitted the saving of some, but subsequently, when the German SS were charged with the arrests, only with great effort and after the longest discussions was it possible to save the spouses of Jewish race by the merits of their Aryan spouses."[29] It gave no specifics and provided no evidence, nor could it have. Spouses "of the Jewish race" who survived did so because they hid, because they were lucky and overlooked, or because the Republic of Salò exempted them from arrest for a time. Piazza and Urbani could have achieved no more than to have persuaded Italian police to respect those exemptions while they lasted.

Urbani's handwritten re ort also asserted, "after having visited the Jews [arrested on the night of December 5–6] at [the prison of] Santa Maria Maggiore, Mons. Urbani arranged that the sick would be sheltered at the Ospedali Civile e Manicomiale, the children at the Istituto Prinicipessa Giovanna and five young people at the Istituto Canal Marovich and the others concentrated in the Ospizio Israelitico del ghetto."[30] Apart from the vagueness of the wording—did "the others" include all the other Jews arrested?—the report is inaccurate. Monsignor Urbani may well have asked for better treatment for the Jewish prisoners, although there is no evidence that he did so. However, the very first order for the raid issued by the police chief of Venice to his agents had already declared that children were to be held at special preexisting facilities for minors.[31] Urbani's intervention had nothing to do with their transfer. It is not clear what the police originally intended for the internment of the sick and elderly. If Urbani's intervention helped those unfortunates for a time, there is no evidence of it.

For its other claims, the report slipped subtly into the passive voice. It did not maintain that Piazza and Urbani achieved certain results but rather that certain results were achieved. For example, it said, "Suddenly the order for transport to the camp of Fossoli (Carpi) arrived [for the Jews arrested on the night of December 5–6]. In one final attempt it was arranged that the oldest, those over seventy, would be snatched out of the hands of the Germans."[32] It was indeed so arranged, but, again, not because of intervention by the patriarch of Venice. Jews over seventy were spared from transport to Fossoli on December 31 because the amendment to police order number five had said that they should be.

Finally, Urbani's report declared, "However, the struggle was not abandoned. Those [Jews] who were hidden continued to be provided for, those concerned were warned of every new alarm, the snares of *agents provocateurs* were baffled." Urbani went on to name several priests and nuns who had helped to shelter Jews. He concluded that "The most significant episode is that of Sister Lidia Cressin. . . . His Eminence defended the good nun who was ready to die in a concentration camp for the conversion of Russia to Catholicism."[33] Apart from the absurdity of the description of Cressin, this final section of Urbani's report attempted to establish a link between the office of the patriarch and the heroic assistance efforts of some members of the regular and secular clergy. It attempted on a local level exactly what defenders of the pope were trying to do on a national level. The claims were dishonest. Documents in both Catholic and Jewish archives indicate that the archbishops of Genoa, Turin, Milan, and Florence asked their secretaries to work with Jewish rescuers to save Jewish refugees. Those secretaries then recruited a number of other priests, monks, and nuns to help. There is no evidence in the patriarchal archives of Venice of a similar involvement of Cardinal Piazza in Jewish rescue. Nor has any personal testimony unearthed to date suggested such involvement.

Examination of Cardinal Piazza's activity, or lack of activity, regarding Jews during the German occupation of Venice is important in its own right. It is also useful for the light it sheds on the policies of Pius XII. If the pope issued a directive to help Jews, as has occasionally been claimed, to Cardinals Boetto, Fossati, Schuster, and Dalla Costa, and even to the bishop of Assisi, where no Jews officially resided, why would he not have done the same for the patriarch of Venice? According to census figures collected in 1938, 2,189 Jews resided in the entire province of Venice, compared with 2,263 in Genoa and 2,326 in Florence.[34] The differences were certainly not enough to explain papal policies. The answer seems to confirm conclusions already reached elsewhere. Pius XII provided no directive to Cardinal Piazza because he provided no directive to anyone. High-ranking Church prelates in Genoa, Turin, Milan, and Florence worked closely with Jewish rescuers because those rescuers asked for help. The bishop of Assisi drifted into rescue from his initial activities aiding refugees generally. Priests, monks, and nuns often became involved because their archbishops or bishops requested it. Equally frequently, they became involved simply because Jewish fugitives appeared at their doors. In the latter instances, the rescuers were motivated by their own moral standards, reinforced in some cases by the general teachings of their Church and their pope to have mercy on all men and women in distress. But they were not motivated by a papal directive to rescue Jews.

CHAPTER NINETEEN

The Vatican, the Bishop, and the Jews in Trieste

THE PORT city of Trieste, long Austria's lung on the Adriatic, became part of Italy after the First World War. Always a cosmopolitan city, it was a mix of Italians, Germans, Slavs, and Jews, many of whom heartily disliked one another. The Jewish population in the province as a whole, 6,085 in 1938, was the third largest in Italy, following only Rome, with 12,799, and Milan, with 10,219.[1] Trieste also contained the country's largest Jewish community in proportion to the general population. Jews there constituted at least 1.8 percent of the urban population, compared with about one-tenth of a percent in Italy as a whole.[2]

As elsewhere in Italy, most Jews in Trieste were middle class, well educated, and patriotic. While local anti-Semitic elements may have been more outspoken than in other parts of the country, Jews in Trieste expressed a strong sense of belonging to a port city with traditions of tolerance and racial diversity. The anti-Jewish laws, therefore, hit them hard. According to one account, of 419 employees in the insurance company Assicurazioni Generali, about eighty were Jewish. Of these, more than sixty lost their jobs because of the new laws, while only about twelve received exemptions. Among the managers of the company, twenty-one were Jewish and all but three or four lost their positions.[3] These devastating statistics were repeated in other businesses throughout the city.

As Jewish refugees in the 1930s poured into the city from northern Europe and out again in ships provided by Lloyds of Trieste, their local coreligionists gazed upon a vision of the future, and reflected. Then during the first years of the war, hundreds of Jewish refugees from Yugoslavia passed through the city on their way to Mussolini's internment camps and supervised residence. Local Delasem representatives tried to help them, while the unease of the Jewish Community intensified. Meanwhile, Fascist anti-Semites desecrated the synagogue in October 1941 and again on July 18, 1942. In May 1943, Slavic and Jewish businesses in the city were ransacked again during Fascist demonstrations against growing partisan activities in the interior, where Slavs constituted a majority.[4]

All of this was nothing compared with events following the German occupation in September. Along with the provinces of Udine, Gorizia, Pola, and Fiume, all except Udine acquired by Italy after the First World War, the province of Trieste was separated from the rest of the country and attached to a special zone of operations called Adriatisches Küstenland, or Litorale Adriatica in Italian. The zone, which also included most of the province of Lubliana in Slovenia, was administered by an Austrian Gauleiter, High Commissioner Friedrich Rainer, who reported directly to Hitler. His deputy in Trieste was an Austrian baron and Catholic named Dr. Wolsegger, who had served in the city as an official of the Hapsburg Empire before the First World War. In charge of the German SS and police in Trieste was SS General Odilo Lotario Globocnik, a friend of Adolf Eichmann who had, among other things, directed the Jewish roundups in Lublin and supervised killing operations at Belzec, Sobibor, and Treblinka. Other killers working with Globocnik were Franz Stangl, former commander at Sobibor and Treblinka; Arthur Liebehenschel, commander for a time of Auschwitz and Majdanek; Dietrich Allers, director of the German euthanasia campaign in 1940; Christian Wirth, former director of extermination units at Belzec, Sobibor, and Treblinka; and Georg Michalezyk, trained at Belzec, Sobibor, and Majdanek. Globocnik's forces set up the prison called La Risiera di San Sabba, mentioned in the previous chapter, and so began the murders and cremations of what would eventually total at least 2,000 people, mostly Slavic partisans.[5]

Roundups and deportations of Jews also ensued within a month. German police began by raiding the synagogue, where Jews had gathered for Yom Kippur services on October 9. They struck again throughout the city on October 29, and a third time on January 19 and 20.[6] On the latter occasion they not only went from house to house, but they took about seventy elderly or sick Jews from the Casa di Riposo Gentiluomo and the Ospedale Israelitico. Among their victims was fifty-three-year-old Carlo Morpurgo, secretary of

Trieste's Jewish Community, who had been urging the Jews of Trieste to leave since 1938. He himself refused to abandon his people.

Arrests continued in Trieste throughout the terrible spring of 1944. On March 28, police seized at least one hundred patients at local hospitals and mental asylums. Those caught in general roundups and individual arrests were sent to La Risiera, just a few miles from their homes, where they awaited deportation. Between December 7, 1943, and February 24, 1944, 1,173 Jews being held at the rice factory were crowded into twenty-two different trains bound for Auschwitz or, for the children of mixed marriages or after Auschwitz was liberated, Ravensbrück. Their names are known and recorded. Of the 1,173, 1,080 died in deportation; 93 returned. The victims were not only from Trieste but from the surrounding region and from as far away as Venice.[7] From Trieste itself, 710 Jews are known to have been deported. Of these, 687 died in deportation or at La Risiera, and 23 survived.[8]

Forty-three-year-old Antonio Santin, newly consecrated bishop of Trieste and Capodistria, began his duties in early September 1938. From the onset he demonstrated courage, initiative, and an undeniable sympathy for the Jews. The first example occurred on September 18, just two weeks after his arrival in the city, when Mussolini visited Trieste to make a speech about his newly decreed racial policies. During the speech, the Duce, still angry about Pius XI's public charge on July 28 that Italian racism was an imitation of the German variety, declared, "Those who claim that we are adhering to imitations, or, worse, suggestions, are poor defectives whom we don't know whether to disdain or pity."[9] The following day, the fearless new bishop asked him, privately but directly, what he meant and to whom he had been referring. Mussolini, startled by such unaccustomed bluntness, not only felt obliged to deny that he had intended to insult the pope but actually declared as much to a crowd assembled in front of the church.[10] This incident, of course, involved Santin's defense of the pope, not of Jews. In revealing the bishop's indomitable spirit and character, however, it was a forecast of things to come. It also seemed to suggest that Mussolini would not have been, at that point, entirely immune to a direct challenge from the Church.

In December, Santin traveled to Rome to speak with the Duce about problems regarding the local seminary, the Slavs in his diocese, and the Jews. According to his later account of the meeting, the bishop described the Jews as "unfortunate people," referred to the racial laws as "unjust measures [that] had created an infinite number of tragedies," and informed Mussolini that "in Italy, there was no Jewish problem."[11] To a dictator whose closest aides rarely dared make a suggestion, Santin did not mince words. And his words regarded all Jews, not just those who had become Catholics. This, from an important prelate, was highly unusual.

In a long meeting the following day with the Deputy Minister of the Interior Guido Buffarini Guidi, the bishop's objections were more conventional. Like Pope Pius XI, Santin focused mostly on the government's prohibition of mixed marriages and infringement of article 34 of the religious concordat of the 1929 Lateran Accords.[12] Of course he won no concessions in either meeting, but he again proved himself to be outspoken and fearless.

Santin had an opportunity to accomplish more in 1942, after Carlo Morpurgo alerted him that Jews in Italian-occupied areas along the Dalmatian coast were in danger of being turned over to the Croatians or the Germans. On Morpurgo's request, the bishop twice petitioned General Mario Roatta, then commander of the Second Army in Yugoslavia. He asked that the Jews be allowed to remain in the Italian zone or, better still, that they be sent to Italy for internment. Roatta replied that while he could do nothing about getting the Jews into Italy, he would keep them in the Italian zone. As seen in Chapter Eight, the general had many reasons for not wanting the Jews to be deported. Santin's pleas were certainly not decisive. But Santin had again demonstrated his concern and good will. After the war, Jewish Community leaders expressed their gratitude for his intervention.[13]

Santin did more, however, than simply correspond with Roatta about Jewish refugees in the Italian zone. On August 28, 1942, he wrote to the Vatican secretary of state about an even more difficult problem—the Jews in areas of Croatia not under Italian control. He explained:

> [Letters of solicitation] have been repeatedly sent to me asking if some step could be taken to ease the fate of Jews already interned or still being interned in Croatia, a fate that is described as tragic and terrifying.
>
> Here [in Trieste] we have intervened with good effect for those who find themselves in the part of Croatia controlled by the Italian troops. But for those who find themselves [elsewhere] in Croatia an intervention with that government is required.[14]

Santin seems to have received no answer for more than five weeks. Finally, on October 6, Maglione sent him a typical bureaucratic evasion. "I want to assure Your Excellency," he wrote, "that since the Reverend Father Abbot

Marcone, envoy of the Holy See in Croatia, has already intervened in this regard with the competent authorities in Zagreb, I have not failed to ask him again to take the appropriate steps in the desired sense." [15] Maglione had indeed asked Marcone that very day, October 6, to "bring, with the necessary tact, the attention of the [Croatian] authorities" to the sufferings of Croatian Jews. [16] The apostolic visitor was in Zagreb, delivering occasional polite appeals from the Holy See to the Croatian government and police. His requests were not for all the Jews in Croatia, as Santin wanted, but for specific groups, usually young people or spouses in mixed marriages. In his message to Santin, Maglione was essentially telling him that the matter was under control and that he, Santin, should stay out of it. But the matter was not under control, for in the end, little was accomplished. Jewish youngsters were not spared, and the deportations of many mixed families were only postponed until 1943.

Analysis of Vatican diplomacy and the Holocaust in Croatia is beyond the scope of this book, but it is a dismal story indeed. Maglione and Marcone made specific private appeals for Jews there, but they never protested the fact of the deportations themselves. This was true even though Marcone had reported to Maglione on July 17, 1942, "The German government has decreed that within six months all the Jews in Croatia must be transferred to Germany, where, according to what [the chief of the Croatian police] has told me, two million Jews have recently been killed. It appears that the same fate awaits the Croatian Jews, particularly if they are old and incapable of work." [17] Marcone went on to inform Maglione that the chief of the Croatian police "would be pleased if the Holy See could intervene for the withdrawal of this ordinance, or at least propose that all the Croatian Jews be concentrated on an island or in a part of Croatia where they could live in peace." [18] Yet the Holy See never intervened.

As Father John Morley concluded in his fine study of the subject, "Requests for humane or benevolent treatment of the Jews were made [by the Vatican], it is true, but no indictment was given of the whole process that was attempting to remove all Jews from Croatia in ways that were both cruel and unjust. . . . The record of Croatia on the Jews is particularly shameful . . . because it was a state that proudly proclaimed its Catholic tradition and whose leaders depicted themselves as loyal to the Church and to the pope." [19]

After the German occupation of Trieste, Santin's interventions on behalf of Jews intensified. On October 31, after the roundups in his diocese on the

9th and 29th, he wrote to Vice-Gauleiter Wolsegger, asking why the Jews could not be left alone and stating that the entire population of Trieste pitied them. "They are not my faithful," he told the Austrian, "but the charity of Christ and the sense of humanity know no limits. . . . If they are guilty, they should be punished like everyone else. But if they have done nothing as individuals, they should be left in peace." [20]

Three days later, during a service at the Basilica of San Giusto on the occasion of the feast day of the patron saint, Santin delivered an astounding speech in the presence of Nazis and their Fascist collaborators. After speaking of the devastation and suffering caused by the war, he declared, "San Giusto signifies the heroic love of Christ and love of our fellow men and women. Thus, charity, goodness, humanity toward all. . . . In the common misfortune, may every hand offer help, not hide a dagger. As pastor of this diocese, I am asking for this law of humanity in the name of Christ, also for the sons and daughters of that people from whose womb He came as a man and in whose midst He lived and died." [21] Santin's public plea for mercy and assistance to the Jews was far more specific and unambiguous than anything Pope Pius XII ever uttered during the entire war. The bishop spoke, also, as head of a diocese in a region virtually annexed by the Third Reich. Yet nothing happened to him or his flock. He was not arrested. Catholics in Trieste were not mistreated. The speech evoked no intensification of punitive measures against Jews in mixed families. It did not make anything worse. Neither, of course, did the persecution of Jews in Trieste cease. Life went on as before, but Catholics in the diocese knew exactly what their bishop expected from them. His job was to provide moral guidance, and he did so.

About a week later, on November 12, Santin wrote to the pope. His letter said, in part: "For some weeks in Trieste the German authorities have been requisitioning the property of the Jews (baptized and non-baptized), and incarcerating the owners. Terror has spread among these poor people, already so badly treated, and the entire citizenry shares their sorrow. Until now they have not been arrested in mass, but as individuals and families (about 70 people), according to no known criteria, while others have not been touched. Even some Catholic spouses have been imprisoned together with the Jews." [22] Santin proceeded to explain that the district in which Trieste was placed was not under Mussolini's jurisdiction, but neither was it automatically subject to German laws and decrees. The local Gauleiter, he believed, perhaps incorrectly, was empowered to set policies toward the Jews. Then he came to his point:

All this I have said because I humbly beg Your Holiness to intervene with the German ambassador to the Holy See in favor of these
unhappy people.

I ask it for all the Jews, but at least the baptized and the spouses
of the baptized should be left in peace.

Reduced in number and influence and bound in a thousand
ways by the Italian racial laws, they constitute absolutely no danger.

Only victims are being created, which benefits no one. I have
already written to . . . [Wolsegger] and, at [the Basilica of] San
Giusto in front of the provincial authorities, I have publicly asked
for the humane treatment of these poor people.

If Your Holiness could obtain a mitigation of the fate of these
unfortunates, you would have the gratitude of the entire citizenry.
Since the measure [of requisitioning and arrests] is already in effect, I dare to beg Your Holiness benignly to make a prompt intervention.[23]

Santin seemed not to have realized that Jews were being arrested not only in
his own diocese, but throughout Italy. His particular reference to the "baptized," furthermore, was unfortunate. But his concern for all Jews was clear,
as was his determination to do everything in his power to help them.

The letter evoked a curious response from the Vatican secretary of state.
Two weeks later—hardly the "prompt intervention" that Santin had sought—
Cardinal Maglione wrote to German Ambassador Ernst von Weizsäcker, as
the bishop had requested. He informed the ambassador that Santin had
asked for Vatican help "so that the situation of non-Aryans in Venezia Giulia
[at that time, roughly equivalent to the Italian territories in the Adriatische
Küstenland] not be aggravated by the application of new more severe provisions." Maglione added that Santin had also written to Wolsegger, "noting,
among other things, how very provident a merciful treatment of these unhappy creatures would be." He concluded:

The nobility of spirit of Your Excellency and the precious and
effective intervention already experienced on similar occasions
[perhaps a reference to Maglione's conversation with Weizsäcker
regarding the Rome roundup on October 16, which had
accomplished nothing] prompt me to inform you—
confidentially—of the request that the bishop of Trieste, in his
pastoral solicitude, has believed himself duty-bound to advance to

the German authorities, in the security that it will find
understanding in the heart of Your Excellency and your
authoritative support.[24]

As Santin had done to Wolsegger, Maglione was suggesting to Weizsäcker
that it would be "provident," that is, easier, to maintain order in Trieste if the
public were not aggravated by the sight of Jews being arrested and mistreated.
But his wording implied that his primary concern was to do Weizsäcker the
courtesy of informing him of an Italian bishop's letter to a German bureaucrat. Maglione's reference to Santin's "pastoral solicitude" and personal per-
ception of duty served to detach the cardinal himself from the request and
almost to dismiss its seriousness. He also made it clear to Weizsäcker that he
did not intend to do anything more with the information—that his communication with the ambassador would remain "confidential." Nor did
Maglione ask Weizsäcker to do anything. He asked only for the ambassador's
understanding and, very vaguely, his personal support. The Vatican's response to a specific plea from a bishop of the Church, then, was perfunctory,
evasive, and fundamentally dishonest.

About two weeks after Santin's letter to Pius XII and just three days after
Maglione's to Weizsäcker, the bishop traveled to Rome to meet with both the
pope and the Vatican secretary of state. It is not clear why he made the arduous trip. Was it his own wish, or was he summoned by Vatican officials eager
to calm him down and discourage any repetition of his outburst in the Basilica of Trieste? Given the limits on public access to Church archives in both
Trieste and Rome, there is no way to know. Nor is there any available record
of Santin's discussion with the pope. All that is certain is that on December 2,
during his return trip home, Santin wrote a letter to the clergy under his jurisdiction that was published in the diocesan bulletin that same month.

In his letter Santin assured his priests that the pope was greatly concerned about their sufferings, sent money and words of comfort to the people
of Istria, and was doing everything possible to help. He also inserted two curious remarks. "We must love the pope very much and we must have
confidence in him," he declared—a statement so obvious that one would
think it need not have been uttered at all unless confidence was crumbling. In
addition, he wrote, "I found in the house of the pope the solemn silence of the
spiritual holy offices. While the world is in flames, in the Vatican they medi-
tate on the eternal truths and pray ardently." This sounds ironic, bitter, and
startlingly frank, except that it was immediately followed by another com-

ment. "The vast and intense work of the pontiff directed to ease suffering and bring peace does not cease," Santin wrote. "Oh, if the world knew the admirable and wise work that the Church is doing especially in these times." [25]

After his meeting with the pope, Santin never spoke again from the pulpit about the need to show charity to "that people from whom He came as a man and in whose midst He lived and died."

The content of Santin's meeting with Maglione on November 30, during that same trip, is known only from the former's notes. The bishop recorded that discussion focused primarily on the immense problems posed by the partisans, mainly Slavs and Communists, who were terrorizing and alienating the rural population in the diocese. Both men greatly feared a violent Communist takeover in the event of a German withdrawal without an immediate Anglo-American occupation. They also worried that the victorious Allies would not support Italy's retention of Trieste and Istria—a fear that, in the case of Istria, proved justified. But Santin and Maglione also discussed the Jews. As the bishop wrote:

> Jewish question. If normalization in Trieste is desired, as it is by
> the German authorities [there] . . . the police measures [against the
> Jews] that have alarmed the entire population must cease. It is
> necessary to recall that the city shares fully in the pain of these Jews
> (they are the oldest and poorest, because the majority abandoned
> Trieste some time ago). They do not constitute any danger. The
> situation in Trieste is singular, it is a great error to imprison the
> Jews remaining there. [26]

It is difficult to believe that Santin really thought that the arrests of a few hundred Jews would drive the people of Trieste into the arms of the Communists. If public opinion and order in the city had been his only concerns, he would have focused more on the Germans' cruelty toward Italian partisans, Communists and non-Communists alike, as well as on the execution of hostages, forcible recruitment of soldiers and laborers, and other harsh occupation measures against non-Jewish civilians. It seems more likely that Santin deliberately inserted the Jewish issue into a discussion with Maglione in order to attract the latter's attention to a problem that concerned Santin deeply. The bishop had failed to prompt any meaningful action on behalf of the Jews from the secretary of state in his earlier appeal, and he would fail again this time and in the future. But not for want of trying.

The bishop of Trieste seems to have remained silent for more than three months following his return from Rome. If he issued any objections to the roundups of Jews in January in which, among others, his acquaintance Carlo Morpurgo was arrested, there is no record of them. He was back in full form on March 29, however, the day after the brutal seizures of the sick and elderly in city hospitals. In fierce protest, he wrote another fearless letter. This time the recipient was the German-appointed prefect of Trieste, Bruno Coceani, a local Fascist extremist and journalist who had enthusiastically endorsed attacks on Jewish businesses and places of worship before the occupation.[27] Coceani could hardly be expected to be sympathetic. But by now, Santin had few illusions that he could make a difference. To Coceani he declared, "If I thought that my intervention would have even the remotest possibility of obtaining some result, I would not give myself any peace. But I know how much good my recommendations do." Still, he asked the prefect to "intervene energetically in favor of these unhappy people." His anguish for the victims was genuine, as was his rage. "Even barbarians pause before the suffering sick," he fumed. Of the raids by German police, he declared, "The scenes that took place do not even seem possible. In those places [hospitals] of pity and pain, an inhuman and violent whirlwind entered, which left in all the sufferers the most painful and revolting impression. The entire city is nauseated."[28] This was powerful language to use with a Nazi or Fascist official, and Santin was almost unique among the clergy in occupied Europe in using it. He added that he had no objection if the prefect wished to forward his letter to the German authorities. Coceani, fearing the reaction, did not do so. He merely informed them that the bishop had protested the raids.[29]

On April 15, Santin met with Wolsegger and tried to make him realize the dangerous level of unrest in Trieste.[30] When Wolsegger requested facts, he sent him a memorandum on April 23 in which he focused especially on the recent executions of 121 hostages. "The [public] impression," he declared, is terrible." Santin complained angrily that the victims had not been allowed to see priests before their execution. He also protested against both the conscription of civilians for labor in Germany and the terrible reprisals on villagers for partisan activities in their areas. He did not mention Jews.[31] In a report to Maglione on April 24 describing his meeting with the vice-Gauleiter, however, he mentioned the arrests of Jews first among the recent events in Trieste that had upset public opinion: "All the sick and old Jews were brutally taken from the hospitals and transported, it seems, to Auschwitz (Poland). From news that has reached me but that I cannot verify, 62 of the 300 deported Jews died during the five-day voyage. There are also some Catholics among them. . . . If it is in some way possible for clergymen to help them, it would be an act of charity." [32]

Santin went on to describe at greater length the reprisal killings of hostages and the complicated dangers posed by Communist partisans. Again, he had inserted the Jewish issue in a report that was basically about other matters, in the hope of attracting Maglione's attention. And again, he failed.

After April, Santin limited himself to interventions for individual cases, but again he had little success. On July 2, 1944, he wrote to German SS and Police Commander Globocnik, asking for the release of a forty-four-year-old writer from Trieste named Pia Rimini Rivalta. Mrs. Rivalta, he explained, had been arrested on June 17, taken to La Risiera, and sent on June 20 to Udine, Treviso, and "some place in Germany." The bishop was well informed. The prisoner was only half Jewish, he explained to Globocnik, and had been baptized at birth. According to Italian racial law, she was "Aryan." [33] But even in Italy the "Aryan" or baptized children of mixed marriages were being arrested by the summer of 1944, and Trieste was subject to a still harsher regime. Pia Rimini Rivalta did not even enjoy the privilege given to most baptized children of mixed marriages in Italy of being deported to Ravensbrück or Bergen Belsen. Sent to Auschwitz even before Santin wrote his letter, she did not return. [34] Globocnik nevertheless wrote to the bishop on July 5, declaring that he had been looking for her and hoped to be able to make a favorable report soon. [35] On July 26, his office communicated again with Santin, declaring, "Mrs. Pia Rimini [Rivalta] has been for some weeks in an institution in the Reich, where she is being held and kept comfortable. Based on Italian information, she is considered a full Jew." [36] A final notice from Globocnik's office to Santin on September 17 admitted that the victim was the offspring of a mixed marriage, and that she had been deported to Auschwitz on June 21. [37]

In a strange twist of fate, Santin's intervention seems to have saved Pia Rimini Rivalta's parents. Edoardo and Olga Bemporad Rimini were arrested soon after their daughter but subsequently released from La Risiera. [38] The existence of a mixed marriage had not spared the parents of Paolo Sereni of Venice, but that status combined with the sponsorship of the bishop apparently saved those of Pia Rimini Rivalta of Trieste. It also saved the writer Giani Stuparich, arrested on August 25, 1944, with his wife and his eighty-year-old mother, who was Jewish. After Santin's intervention with Wolsegger and the police chief, they were released. [39]

Santin demonstrated his good faith in other ways. On the request of

Carlo Morpurgo he kept many priceless books and historical documents belonging to the Jewish Community safe during the occupation and returned them after the war.[40] Also, he adamantly rejected a German proposal to turn the central synagogue into a church.[41] Santin's assistance, of course, extended far beyond the Jews. He was constantly a thorn in the side of occupation authorities, intervening for arrested priests, local businessmen, genuine and alleged partisans, villagers in partisan-controlled areas, Italian military officials, forced laborers, hostages, and even civilians accused of stealing food.[42]

It is difficult to measure Santin's actual influence, and the difference he made. He himself was, as seen, discouraged because he seemed to be a voice in the wilderness, without listeners. One historian of the Holocaust in Trieste concluded, probably correctly, that "while they contributed to saving some members of well-known families, the actions of the bishop remained vain in the face of general problems."[43] But Santin's influence worked in other, subtler ways. His clergy and parishioners knew where he stood and what he expected from them. They knew it from what he said publicly, from rumors of his private interventions, and, especially, from what was written in the bulletin and the newspaper of the diocese. On February 12, 1944, for example, Santin's message for Lent was printed on the front-page of the newspaper, a weekly entitled *La Vita Nuova*. Among other things, the bishop instructed his flock, "May everyone remember that according to Christian principles, it is not permitted to deprive any person of liberty, property and life simply because he belongs to another nationality, race [*razza*] or political faction, so long as he pursues his ideals by honest and legal means."[44] This moral guidance was clearer, simpler, more straightforward than anything the pope said throughout the entire war.

Unlike his counterparts in Genoa, Turin, Milan, and Florence, Santin did not recruit priests to work in a joint Catholic-Jewish rescue network. But priests, nuns, and monks in his diocese who knew so well what he expected may nonetheless have been influenced by him to give assistance. Sister Alberica Cenci, for example, remembered saving dozens of Jews, including foreigners, during the German raid on the Ospedale Maggiore on March 28. Some were hidden in the operating room and the morgue, while others, younger, were guided to an open window through which they fled. Don Carlo Della Mea, a parish priest, provided those who escaped the raid with the false documents essential to survival.[45] The efforts of nuns and clergymen were replicated by dozens of laypersons who helped Jews in different ways. A few policemen warned families of pending raids. A few bureaucrats issued identification documents they knew to be false. Several individuals hid Jews in their homes, offices, or farms.[46] While the facts of most of these cases have been verified, their links with Santin remain uncertain. But the example was there, for those able to see and follow.

A comparison between Adeonato Piazza, patriarch of Venice, and Antonio Santin, bishop of Trieste and Capodistria, is illuminating. Piazza, just eleven years older than Santin, seemed to be from another generation. Like so many of the prelates at the Vatican, he feared Liberals and Jews as much as Bolsheviks. Santin, with good reason, feared Tito and the Communist threat in Yugoslavia, but he did not harbor the same brooding suspicion of Liberals and Jews. Trieste was a cosmopolitan city and a commercial and business center. He related to it well.

Both men viewed the anti-Jewish laws of 1938 through the lens of their Church. Both resented the infringement of the marriage clause of the religious concordat of the Lateran Accords—the unilateral revocation of the government's agreement to register all marriages sanctioned by the Church. But apart from that, Piazza expressed no opposition to the separation of Catholics and Jews in the schools, the work place, and the public arena. Santin personally informed Mussolini that the anti-Jewish laws were "unjust measures" and that "in Italy there was no Jewish problem."

In the autumn of 1943, as Nazi and Fascist cruelties against Jews intensified, Piazza spoke to the German consul in Venice, asking primarily for moderation with regard to Jews who had been converted. Santin wrote to the German vice-Gauleiter to ask why all Jews could not be left in peace. At the end of November, Piazza wrote to the head of the Consistorial Congregation in Rome, asking for help for converts. He suggested that that prelate might wish to pass his letter along to the secretary of state or the pope. On November 12, Santin wrote directly to the pope himself, asking that he intervene with the German ambassador to the Holy See on behalf of all Jews—with a reference to the baptized. Already on November 3, Santin had called publicly, in his basilica, for "charity, goodness, and humanity" toward the people from whom Christ had come. He would write much the same thing in his Lenten message in 1944. There is no record that Piazza spoke or wrote such words.

It may be argued that neither man did enough—that neither of them specifically and publicly protested the deportations of Jews and called upon clergymen and parishioners to risk their lives to save Jews. Also, both men made specific personal interventions only for Jews who had converted—Piazza for Lidia Cressin and Santin for Pia Rimini Rivalta. Neither man tried to obtain the release of individuals who were Jewish in religion and culture. Finally, both men could have set up rescue networks or, at the very least, tried to hide the sick and the elderly trapped in public institutions. But the arrests and deportations of the sick and elderly were not foreseen until it was too late, and clandestine operations were not the style of prelates of the Church. Santin at least provided moral guidance for those more accustomed to clandestine work. Piazza did not.

The existence of two such different prelates in close geographical proximity demonstrates again the diversity of the Catholic Church in Italy, and indeed throughout the world. Piazza and Santin faced difficult choices and made them according to their different characters and attitudes. Their divergence reveals their isolation from one another. Above all, and most important for the purposes of this book, the divergence also demonstrates their isolation from the Vatican itself. With regard to the Jews, they received little guidance from Rome. Santin, in addition, received little support or encouragement for his efforts to protect Jews from suffering and deportation.

CHAPTER TWENTY

The Vatican and Jews Arrested in Italy

December 1943–May 1945

DURING nearly twenty months of the German occupation of Italy, the focus of most Catholics who would save Jews was on hiding them and supplying the provisions necessary to sustain life. For the pope and officials at the Vatican Secretariat of State, however, the option of diplomatic intervention on behalf of Jews in Italian internment camps constituted another way to be helpful. As seen, the Italian government's police order of December 1, 1943, instructed police and carabinieri to arrest nearly all Jews and intern them within the country. Even then, however, and despite the fact that the Germans had already sent at least 1,469 Jews whom they themselves had arrested to an "unknown destination," the police order did not mention, and probably did not intend, deportation.[1] Germans concerned with Jewish deportations deliberately refrained from demanding control of the interned Jews for a few weeks, to give the Italian police time to complete their work.[2] They did not doubt that those victims would ultimately fall into their hands. Nor could anyone else have failed to understand the danger.

Little is known about how and when Mussolini agreed to the deportation of Jews under his control. A train left Milan and Verona for Auschwitz on December 6, 1943, just days after the Italian police order, but most of its approximately 246 victims had been arrested by the Germans in October and November. Most of the 605 Jews on a second convoy from the same two cities to the same death camp on January 30, 1944, however, had been arrested by Italian police and interned for a time in small camps in the north. The first convoy to Auschwitz from the largest Italian internment camp, Fossoli, in the province of Modena, left about a month later, on February 22. Most of its approximately 489 Jewish victims had also been arrested by Italians. The Germans assumed management of Fossoli on March 15, and three more convoys followed. The last train to leave directly from Fossoli departed on June 26, 1944, almost three weeks after the liberation of Rome. It picked up additional Jews in Verona, and carried some 527 people to the death camp.[3]

On August 1, 1944, as the Allies approached Fossoli, the camp was closed and the remaining internees were moved north to Verona. The following day, most of them were forced into a convoy that carried about 244 Jews to Auschwitz. Including the victims on that train, 2,445 Jews had been sent from Fossoli to Auschwitz.[4] The spouses of non-Jews and children of mixed marriages who had been at Fossoli were sent elsewhere, to Bergen Belsen, Buchenwald, and Ravensbrück, where many more of them survived. The convoys of August 2 proved to be the last Jewish deportation trains to leave from territory that was technically under Mussolini's control, but the terror did not cease. Hundreds of Jews continued to be arrested throughout northern Italy by Italian and German agents, and held mostly in filthy, overcrowded prisons in Turin, Milan, Verona, and elsewhere. They were ultimately transferred to an internment camp in Gries, a suburb of Bolzano, or to La Risiera di San Sabba in Trieste. Both of these prisons were in territories that had been Italian before the German occupation but were now part of two special German operational zones. In both places, conditions were worse than at Fossoli. At least 133 Jews left Gries for Auschwitz, on October 24, 1944. Another train departed on December 14, while a third, in February 1945, could not get through the Brenner Pass because the tracks had been damaged by Allied bombing.[5] Meanwhile, some twenty-two trains left Trieste, mostly for Auschwitz, with at least 1,173 Jews between December 7, 1943, and February 24, 1945. Fifteen of the trains left after Rome was liberated and the Vatican City was freed of the danger of German invasion in the event of a papal protest.[6]

There is no evidence that Vatican officials tried to dissuade Italian police and carabinieri leaders from zealously carrying out the order to arrest Jews. Nor did they attempt to influence Mussolini's policy toward Jews in internment as he faced the inevitable German demands for their deportation in the first months of 1944. There is, furthermore, no evidence of a serious Vatican effort to influence German or Italian authorities later, during the tragic period of deportation and evacuation of Jews from Fossoli between February 22 and August 1, 1944. A belated halfhearted attempt to intervene with the Germans was finally made in August, but it occurred only as a result of an explicit Allied appeal to the pope. Yet there was every reason to intervene sooner, strenuously, and independently of an Allied initiative. Rome was liberated on June 4, 1944, and after that date the pope had no reason to fear that the Vatican City would be invaded and that fugitives hidden in Vatican properties in the Eternal City would be seized if he displeased the Nazis and Fascists. In addition, by the summer of 1944, the pope not only understood that Jews in deportation were being exterminated, as he had realized for at least a year, but he knew all the terrible details. It will be recalled that the so-called Auschwitz Protocol, an unimpeachable detailed description of that death camp from two escapees, reached Switzerland and the Allied governments in June 1944. The Vatican has acknowledged receipt of its copy by October, but it almost certainly arrived much sooner.[7] Finally, there was reason to intervene because there was some chance of achieving results. By mid-1944, as will also be seen, there were numerous individual German and Italian officials with an eye on a future settling of accounts who would have been amenable to pleas for better treatment of the Jews, especially if those pleas came from the pope rather than the Allies. They would not have been in a position to alter Nazi and Fascist policy, but they could have quietly sabotaged it on occasion, and persuaded others to do the same. Some lives would have been saved.

In assessing what the Vatican could or should have done during this period, the intriguing case of Hungary remains to be considered. Some 670,000 Jews in Hungary lived free from deportations until the spring of 1944. On March 19, however, the Germans occupied the territory of their former ally, and two months later deportations of Hungarian Jews to Auschwitz began with terrible intensity. But this time the Allies paid attention. The American and British press spread the news throughout the world. The American War Refugee Board (WRB) warned Hungarian officials that crimes against civilians would be punished after the war.[8] The WRB also called on the neutral nations, the International Red Cross, and the pope to petition the Hungarian regent, Admiral Miklos Horthy, to end the deportations. On June 25, three weeks after the liberation of Rome and the day before a large deportation train departed directly from Fossoli, Pius XII complied with the request and appealed personally to the Hungarian head of state by telegram. The king of Sweden at about the same time, and the International Red Cross somewhat later, acted similarly. On July 6, Horthy announced that the deportations would cease. Some 440,000 Jews had been deported in fewer than eight weeks, but about 230,000 remained alive in Budapest. Of the latter, about 120,000 survived the subsequent slaughter in and around Budapest during the winter of 1944–45, and lived to see the liberation.[9]

A papal diplomatic intervention, then, helped to save some Hungarian Jews. In the country of his birth, however, Pius XII did much less. He seems never to have appealed personally to Mussolini or to any other leader of the Italian Social Republic (RSI) on behalf of Italian Jews, as he did with Horthy in Budapest. His assistants at the time and his defenders later explained that the Holy See never established diplomatic relations with the RSI but recognized instead the Allied-backed government of King Vittorio Emanuele III as the legitimate Italian regime.[10] But lack of formal recognition did not preclude unofficial contact with Italian Fascist leaders. Nor would the Allies, the king, or his government have objected.[11] But Pius XII personally seems to have made no contacts and no appeal to the Italians for the Jews. Likewise, he seems never to have appealed personally to any German officials. At the very least, he might have asked that Italian Jews be allowed to remain in internment on Italian soil. He did not do so. During the second half of 1943 and the first half of 1944, for example, he met several times with the German ambassador to the Holy See, Ernst von Weizsäcker. There is no evidence in the available papers of either the Holy See or Weizsäcker himself that the subject of the Jews ever came up in their discussions.[12]

Vatican officials did not do much more. When Weiszäcker complained to Vatican Secretary of State Cardinal Maglione in January 1944 that "incriminated persons," meaning Jews and anti-Fascists, had been discovered hiding in religious houses, Maglione replied that German measures against women, children, and old people were too severe and were causing terrible suffering.[13] On several occasions Vatican officials received specific requests from the families or friends of Jews who had been arrested, and made inquiries about their whereabouts.[14] But that seems to be all they did.

In midsummer 1944, after their first apparent success in Hungary, representatives of the American War Refugee Board and the multinational Intergovernmental Committee on Refugees (ICR) took active steps to save Jews in Italian internment camps.[15] For most internees, of course, it was too late. Fossoli was rapidly being emptied. But hundreds of Jews would still pass through prisons in the north, the internment camp of Gries, and La Risiera di San Sabba in Trieste. To help them, Myron C. Taylor, President Roosevelt's diplomatic representative to the Holy See, met with Pius XII in July. Taylor asked the pope to intercede with the Germans to stop deportations from Italy and allow Jews and other refugees to move into the Allied-occupied zone. On August 2, Sir Clifford Heathcote-Smith, the ICR delegate in Italy, had a papal audience and made the same plea. He also asked that the approach be made as if it had originated with the pope himself, rather than with the Allies. Pius readily agreed to cooperate, telling Heathcote-Smith, according to one British diplomat, that "neither history nor his conscience would forgive him if he did not make this effort."[16] The pope made that statement, it might be noted, on the very day that the last Jews evacuated from Fossoli were being shipped to Auschwitz. Given his expression of great concern, one might wonder why he had waited so long before intervening. Why, also, had he needed prompting from the Allies? One might also ask why the resulting intervention was so mild.

About a week later, on August 7, the Vatican Secretariat of State sent a formal request in writing to Ambassador Weizsäcker, asking that "all foreign or stateless civilians, especially Jews" in Italy be permitted to move into southern Italy or northern Africa. Contrary to the pope's verbal agreement with Heathcote-Smith, the request stated clearly that the American and British governments had asked for the Vatican intervention.[17] Monsignor Domenico Tardini, secretary of the Section of Extraordinary Ecclesiastical Affairs at the Secretariat of State, personally delivered the note. He recorded that he also told Weizsäcker that the Allies believed that "in the present circumstances, the Nazis might be disposed to an act of clemency: I observed however that I am of a different opinion because the worse things get the worse the Nazis will be."[18] This was hardly the way to persuade Weizsäcker to help. The German ambassador promptly agreed with Tardini and suggested that the papal nuncio in Berlin, rather than himself, should become involved in the matter.

The timid, unimaginative nuncio in Berlin, Monsignor Cesare Orsenigo, was advised of the situation on August 11 and asked to convey the Allied request to the German Foreign Ministry. Orsenigo had delivered requests to the German government cautiously and apologetically on many occasions, always without effect, and had sent numerous messages back to Rome about the utter uselessness of any futher efforts. If he ever conceived of a creative idea about how to assist Jews in distress in the Third Reich or Poland, where he also had jurisdiction, it is not recorded in the published Vatican documents. Predictably enough in this latest case, his approach to the German authorities was formalistic, correct, and ineffective. Eighteen days after he was asked to intervene, he informed his superiors in Rome that "the Foreign Ministry here has replied that in this regard [concerning Jews and

other refugees in Italy] the competent authority is the Italian [Social] Republic." [19] Given the fact that the Germans had taken over Fossoli in March and
controlled the sections of other Italian prisons where most Jews were held,
this was a misrepresentation of the true state of affairs. Vatican officials nevertheless advised the Allies of Orsenigo's intervention and its result on September 8, adding that they did not maintain relations with the Italian Social
Republic. [20] Until that report, they had apparently considered it unnecessary
to keep the Allies informed about how they had responded to their request. [21]

With the conveying of Orsenigo's report to the Allies, the story of Vatican
attempts to intervene with the Germans specifically on behalf of Jewish internees in Italy came to an end. [22] The claim that the Holy See had no relations
with Mussolini's government, however, was not entirely true. It was intended
merely to divert Allied pressure. Behind the scenes, Vatican officials, if they
were so inclined, could approach the Fascist authorities on their own as long
as the Germans occupied Rome. After the liberation of that city, they could do
the same with the help especially of the papal nuncio in Bern, Monsignor Filippo Bernardini. Messages from Allied-occupied Rome to neutral Switzerland moved easily by telegram, diplomatic pouch, or even individuals
traveling by plane. From Switzerland, Bernardini could communicate with
Cardinal Ildefonso Schuster in Milan by means of the Swiss consul general in
Milan, who allowed him to use his diplomatic pouch but expected that the
messages would be limited to Church matters. [23] With much more difficulty,
Bernardini could also engage priests and others involved in guiding fugitives
across the frontier, as well as partisans, Fascist double agents, and even black-
market profiteers, to smuggle letters and reports into still-occupied Italy.
Thus, the papal nuncio could communicate with both priests and Fascist activists in German-occupied Italy.

After Myron Taylor's appeal to the pope for help for interned Jews but before that of Heathcote-Smith, Secretary of State Maglione asked Bernardini to
inform him about the number and condition of Jews at Fossoli. [24] The camp
was in fact being evacuated that very day. According to the editors of the Vatican documents, the papal nuncio in Bern was asked again on September 16,
September 29, and October 2 to "take steps with the representatives of the
RSI" on behalf of "other Jews interned at Fossoli or deported." The editors provided document numbers but did not reveal the content of the requests. [25]
They seem, also, not to have realized that by September 16 there were no
more Jews at Fossoli. It is possible that Bernardini was in fact instructed to
petition the Fascist authorities to allow Jews to remain in Italy, but it is equally

likely that he was merely asked again to inquire about conditions, or to take those steps he thought best. If the Vatican Secretariat of State asked Bernardini to intervene strenuously to save Jews, why would the editors of the *Actes et Documents du Saint Siège* not have published the documents?[26]

Whatever his precise instructions, however, Bernardini in early October 1944 did indeed involve himself in a major effort to help the Jews in Italy. During a meeting in Bern on October 7 with Heathcote-Smith of the ICR, the nuncio agreed to send a letter to Cardinal Schuster by means of his (but presumably the Swiss consul general's) weekly Wednesday courier to Milan. The letter would ask Schuster, according to Heathcote-Smith, "by every possible means to get into direct touch with Sig[nore Guido] Buffarini [Guidi], the Fascist Minister of the Interior, and urge the latter, in his own self-interest, to find means of releasing all internees whose lives are threatened by deportation and/or massacre by the Axis." At the meeting, Bernardini also advised using the services of a Dr. Bruno Kiniger, whom Heathcote-Smith described vaguely as "formerly the Fascist unofficial representative in Switzerland, but who, since May or June, had been thrown out." The ICR delegate continued, "With [Bernardini's] letter [to Schuster] was to go an extremely strongly worded letter from Bruno Kinniger [*sic*] to Buffarini of which letter I have seen the text. It said, among other things, that a certain Signor Koch and his band of criminals, were known to be in the employ of 'you [Buffarini Guidi]: you are down on the list of those who will be treated as war criminals; if you wish to try to save your skin, now is the opportunity.' "[27]

Little is known of this curious last-ditch effort to save Jews arrested and still imprisoned in Italy. The two letters apparently did not go out by Bernardini's courier but were carried to Milan by Kiniger himself. The enigmatic Italian did not succeed in crossing the frontier until December 1, and he returned to Switzerland on January 1. He personally delivered Bernardini's letter to Schuster, who was sympathetic and offered to be helpful, but who told him that the situation in Italian "concentration camps" differed from Allied perceptions. If Schuster was implying that there were very few Jewish prisoners left in Italy, he was wrong and he must have known it from the several priests and nuns who were visiting them. Kiniger also met with Buffarini Guidi, who professed to be sympathetic, promised favorable treatment of internees, and claimed to have passed information about the request on to Mussolini.[28] But Buffarini Guidi, too, left Kiniger with the incorrect impression that the Germans had by then deported most prisoners.

Although information provided in the *Actes et Documents du Saint Siège* does not prove it, there is some reason to believe that Bernardini was acting on Vatican instructions, if not on its initiative. Bernardini himself implied as much to the Allied rescue workers with whom he was cooperating, and they were convinced. Heathcote-Smith, for example, reported on October 27 that Bernardini "had received very direct instructions from the Vatican when I saw him on the 7th of October." [29] In another report that same day, Heathcote-Smith expressed the opinion that "Bernardini might, by a judicious telegram to the Vatican elicit there stronger instructions, recommendations or persuasive arguments" to be used to persuade others to help the Jews. This was not necessarily proof that Bernardini did so, but it did indicate the ICR delegate's appraisal of his position. In the same report, however, Heathcote-Smith added that Bernardini "might himself (for he is a very wise, worldly and cunning prelate), be able to devise still further means of bringing pressure to bear on Buffarini, or it may be that Mgr. Schuster may suggest some other approach." [30] But the British delegate remained convinced of the Vatican's involvement, reporting from Rome on January 19, 1945, that "last week Monsignor Tardini of the Vatican sent a further message to Monsignor Bernardini urging him to further efforts" on behalf of Jewish internees in Italy. [31]

Many other individuals involved with the Buffarini Affair, as the British and Americans called it, shared Heathcote-Smith's belief that Bernardini was acting on Vatican instructions. Roswell McClelland of the WRB telegrammed Heathcote-Smith on November 22: "Feel you overrestimate role Schuster might be willing to play this affair. He enjoys poor reputation for having compromised for many years with Fascists. Any positive instructions Schuster might receive, therefore, from Vatican via Bernardini would help." [32] A Fascist bureaucrat referred, in a brief letter to Kiniger on December 15, to "the Note of the Holy See sent by means of the Nunciature in Bern to the Government of the Italian Social Republic (Ministry of the Interior)." [33] The bureaucrat had not himself seen the note, but it was clearly being represented as coming from the Holy See. Kiniger himself spoke of the "dispatch from the Vatican" that he carried to Buffarini Guidi. [34]

There are several reasons why Bernardini might have exaggerated the extent of his instructions from the Vatican. His superiors in Rome had undoubtedly advised him to act as he thought best, and he was not reluctant to award the credit to the pope. His claim of papal instructions, also, lent moral authority to the requests he was making of Schuster, Buffarini Guidi, and others. Convincing evidence that the initiative for Bernardini's effort came from Rome would redound to the pope's credit, but in the last analysis, it makes little difference. Pius XII and his advisors undoubtedly knew what Bernardini was doing, and approved.

The real questions lie elsewhere. Why did Bernardini act only in October 1944, and not a year earlier? Why was an Allied request necessary before the Vatican took any action? Why weren't prelates throughout Italy mobilized to bombard Italian political authorities and police agents with requests to do their jobs less well, to decline to arrest Jews, to allow arrested Jews to escape, and to keep interned Jews in Italy? Buffarini Guidi was not the best target for an appeal, for he was a committed Fascist whom even Mussolini considered to be too pro-German.[35] But why weren't multiple approaches made, to Italian authorities at all levels?

Would it have made much difference? Official Fascist policy would probably have remained the same. But to answer the question, let us look at a description of a Fascist bureaucrat written by an Italian Jewish rescue worker in March 1945: "It is important to point out that in service at the central police headquarters (office on race) in Turin, there is a certain Conti (a career civil servant) who has given serious proof of his humanitarian sensibility by trying to ease as much as possible the suffering of Jews arrested or detained in the prisons. It seems that Conti has already succeeded in obtaining the release of some arrested Jews."[36] Conti was not the only Italian civil servant to have acted with courage and compassion. But if the pope had asked priests and prelates to urge bureaucrats and politicians at all levels to act similarly, would there not have been a significant response? The effort on the part of the pope and his churchmen would not have been difficult, there was little to lose, and precious lives could have been saved.

Conclusion

IMMEDIATELY following the liberation of Rome on June 4, 1944, Jews from all over the world began to acknowledge the compassion and help provided in Italy by Pope Pius XII during the Holocaust. A Jewish chaplain with the French Expeditionary Forces in Italy, for example, wrote on June 22, 1944, to thank the pope "for the immense good and the incomparable charity that your Holiness extended generously to the Jews of Italy and especially the children, women and elderly of the community of Rome."[1] A month later, on July 21, two spokesmen for the National Jewish Welfare Board wrote gratefully, "Word comes to us from our army chaplains in Italy of the aid and protection given to so many Italian Jews by the Vatican and by priests and institutions of the church during the Nazi occupation of the land."[2] On August 5, an unnamed resident of Rome, explaining that he and his family had suffered greatly since the onset of the anti-Jewish laws, wrote to thank the pope "for everything that has been done to help us Jews."[3] Then on October 29, Father Calliste Lopinot led a group of former internees from Ferramonti to an audience with Pius XII, again to thank him.[4]

After the war ended, Jewish expressions of gratitude multiplied. On September 21, 1945, for example, Dr. Leon Kubowitzki (later, Aryeh Kubovy), an official with the World Jewish Congress, met privately with Pius XII. During the audience he thanked the pope on behalf of the Union of Italian Jewish Communities for all that the Church had done for Jews during the war. After the meeting he delivered to Monsignor Giovanni Battista Montini a check for

2 million lire, or about $20,000, for papal charities, in token of the gratitude of his people.[5]

The German Jesuit Father Robert Leiber, the pope's private secretary and closest advisor throughout his papacy, proudly remembered other expressions of thanks in an article in 1961: "On November 29, 1945, a group of more than 70 Jews, survivors of German concentration camps, thanked the pope with all their hearts for his great help. On May 26, 1955, a Jewish symphony orchestra, directed by Paul Kletzki, with 95 Jews from 14 nations, played the second part of Beethoven's Seventh Symphony, 'in recognition and gratitude for the great work of humane assistance given by His Holiness to save a large number of Jews during the Second World War.' "

When Pius XII died in 1958, Mrs. Golda Meir, then foreign minister of Israel, paid tribute to him for having "raised his voice in favor of the Jews." Although she used the word voice, she must have been referring to allegations of papal intervention on behalf of the Jews. She certainly knew that there had been no meaningful public protest. About the same time, the chief rabbi of Rome, Elio Toaff, declared: "More than all others, we [Jews in Italy] had the opportunity of experiencing the great compassionate goodness and magnanimity of the pope during the unhappy years of the persecution and terror, when it seemed that for us there was no longer an escape."[6]

Defenders of Pius XII invariably evoke these and many other expressions of gratitude by Jews after the war, as if the phenomenon itself were proof of the veracity of the claims. Even the official statement of the Holy See's Commission for Religious Relations with the Jews, issued in March 1998 and entitled "We Remember: A Reflection on the *Shoah*," included the phrase, "During and after the war, Jewish communities and Jewish leaders expressed their thanks for all that had been done for them, including what Pope Pius XII did personally or through his representatives to save hundreds of thousands of Jewish lives."[7] This book has shown the gratitude to be misplaced. Men and women of the Church in Italy certainly deserved to be recognized and thanked, but the pope had very little to do with their activities. Why, then, were so many observers mistaken?

The error was often rooted in benevolent ignorance. Fugitives sheltered in Church institutions had no way of knowing why they had been allowed to enter. Many must have been surprised to find themselves where they were. Many, also, had an exaggerated notion of centralization within the Catholic Church, and they assumed that no individual convent, monastery, hospital, or school would act without prior papal approval. Nuns, monks, and priests—

some, perhaps, embarrassed by the pope's silence on one of the most important moral issues of the century—were quite willing, even eager, to share
credit for their own dedication and heroism with the Holy Father. Indeed, to
their own subordinates who sometimes questioned why they were crowding
their institutions, endangering themselves, and sharing scant rations with
men, women, and children who did not even share their faith, the heads of religious houses occasionally referred vaguely to papal benevolence. As seen,
archbishops and bishops sometimes did the same. They did not, however,
mention a papal directive.

Father Lopinot, from the period before the German occupation, is
nonetheless a good example. This dedicated Capuchin priest knew that the
pope had never spoken out against Italy's anti-Jewish laws. He knew that the
Vatican had done little to provide extra food, clothing, or medicine to ease the
situation of the refugees at Ferramonti. He, Lopinot, had to scramble and pull
strings to secure private donations. He probably knew, also, that the danger
that Mussolini would deport Jewish internees from Italy was remote, at least
until the last few weeks of his regime. Certainly he had no evidence that the
pope acted on their behalf. Yet he led his internees to believe otherwise. They
knew little more than what he told them, and he did not tell them the full
truth. The truth was not that Pius XII had intervened on their behalf or sent
many supplies, but that Father Lopinot had defended them with all his immense energy and dedication.

As Jewish chaplains, soldiers, officers, and journalists with the Allied
troops moved north through Italy, they met Father Lopinot and his internees,
along with others who had heard their story. They also witnessed the often
friendly relations between Jews and non-Jews in so-recently Fascist Italy—
a condition they had not expected to encounter. They received similar explanations and impressions of a papal role. Thus it is not by chance that several
of the earliest expressions of gratitude to Pius XII originated with foreigners,
who in fact had only a minimal understanding of what had occurred in the
country they had liberated.

There are, of course, other reasons for the postwar flurry of recognition
of papal assistance that never occurred. Jewish chaplains with the Allied army
in Italy, Chief Rabbi Toaff, and others like them were anxious to protect and
preserve the fragile good will between Jews and non-Jews that seemed to be
emerging from the rubble of the war in Italy. The last thing they wanted was
recrimination for past offenses. Why had the pope not condemned the Italian
anti-Jewish laws? Why had he remained silent about the atrocities perpe-

trated against Jews throughout Europe? Why had he not protested, at the very least, the deportations from the Eternal City? At the time, many Jews believed that such embarrassing questions were better left unasked—that it was more important to promote healing and to build bridges for the future. Men and women of the Church had helped Jews, after all, in great numbers. The pope was, if not the initiator of their actions, at least the symbol of their faith. In thanking the pope, Jews were thanking the Church and the people associated with it. Distinctions may have seemed petty. The important fact was that human lives had been saved.

A few of those who expressed their gratitude to Pius XII, finally, acted for more concrete reasons. They had specific goals and objectives that seemed more important than a critical evaluation of past omissions. Kubovy, for example, frankly admitted that he sought his meeting with the pope in September 1945 because he wanted something from him. The Union of Italian Jewish Communities, which sponsored him and arranged the audience, asked that he also use the occasion to convey their gratitude. Of that request, Kubovy later wrote, "After some hesitation I agreed, not only because I realized that these people were truly grateful to the Church, but also because I could not miss the chance of bringing my requests before the pope." [8]

What were Kubovy's objectives? He desired, first, the cooperation of the Vatican and the religious and secular clergy in recovering Jewish children who had been placed in Church institutions throughout Europe during the war. Second, he urged the pope to issue an official statement, emphasizing the spiritual linkage between Christians and Jews and refuting the age-old concept of the responsibility of Jews for the death of Jesus. Kubovy believed, as he later explained in his account of the audience, that "unless the Church were to abandon its teaching that the Jews were cursed to all eternity for having crucified Christ, hostility towards the Jews was bound to recur through all subsequent generations in all the lands of Christianity." [9] In 1945, preventing a recrudescence of anti-Semitism was more important than historical truth. Living as he was in the immediate aftermath of the Holocaust, Kubovy's priority is understandable.

Within a short time, Jews dedicated to the creation of the state of Israel also realized that Vatican recognition of their dream was a desirable objective. Memories of past commissions and omissions were readily sacrificed to the goal of constructing a better future. Some of those who praised Pius XII for his generosity shared that outlook. Certainly, the two Jewish authors who have most ardently defended the pope's historic record did so as well. Pinchas

E. Lapide, whose book *The Last Three Popes and the Jews,* published in 1967, is often refuted in this work as being replete with egregious mistakes and distortions, was an Israeli diplomat in Italy in the 1960s, during the meetings of the Second Vatican Council. Dr. Joseph L. Lichten—whose equally erroneous article "A Question of Judgment: Pius XII and the Jews" of 1963 was so popular among Catholic defenders of the pope that it was reprinted by the Catholic League for Religious and Civil Rights in 1988—was a director of the Intercultural Affairs Department of the Anti-Defamation League of B'nai B'rith.[10]

There is no need to decide here whether these writers' errors were intentional or inadvertent. Certainly, however, they were conducive to the cause of better Catholic-Jewish relations. And certainly, also, they were damaging to the task of establishing historical truth. Since the work of Lapide and Lichten, Christian defenders of the papal role during the Holocaust have cited them with frequency and vigor. For if Jews, they imply, usually without actually saying so, can write such words of praise, they surely must be true.

About the time that Lapide and Lichten were writing, Settimio Sorani was preparing an assessment of his own experiences during the war. Sorani, it will be remembered, a director of Delasem in Rome, had worked closely with Father Maria Benedetto during the entire period of the German occupation to save both foreign and Italian Jewish fugitives in the Eternal City. If anyone knew the extent of wartime help and support from the pope, it was Sorani. On that issue, he wrote:

> Regarding the subject of the work of the Vatican, it must be
> specified precisely that much more was requested by many, and
> also much more was hoped for by the Jews: a more decisive atti-
> tude, more constructive, because if a certain number of human
> lives were saved, other results could have been achieved if the
> Church had acted differently from the beginning of the racial cam-
> paign in Germany, in Italy, and in the occupied countries, with an
> open condemnation of racism and the persecutions. In principle,
> no danger threatened the Pontifical State, and the Vatican was
> aware of the creation of the camps and of their real destructive pur-
> pose. Yet, in the Church, even in Italy, paintings were still shown
> that portrayed "ritual homicide" [a reference to the popular belief,
> not officially endorsed by the Church, that Jews murdered Chris-
> tians to obtain their blood for ceremonial purposes].[11]

Sorani was addressing the issue of the papal silence here, more than the facts of physical assistance to Jews in need. He did not tell us that help was requested and refused. But neither did he temper his words by a reference to acts of generosity. "A certain number of lives were saved," he said, in the passive voice, omitting the agent. Sorani did not want to appear rude, confrontational, or ungrateful, but neither was he among those who were abundant in their praise.

What, then, did Popes Pius XI and XII and the highest ranking officials in the Vatican Secretariat of State actually do to help Jews in Italy during the years of Fascist and Nazi persecution? Concerning the Italian anti-Jewish laws of 1938, it has been demonstrated that intervention was limited almost entirely to Jews who had become Catholics. Vatican spokesmen objected only to laws affecting the Church's authority to determine who could marry and who could convert and thus be considered "Aryan." Indeed, as late as August 1943, the Jesuit Father Pietro Tacchi Venturi, knowing full well that millions of Jews had been murdered throughout Europe, nevertheless referred to the Italian anti-Jewish decrees as "laws which, according the the principles and tradition of the Catholic Church, have some dispositions that should be abrogated but contain others worthy of confirmation." [12] Regarding Jewish emigration, the same limitation applied. With the exception of only a few special individuals, help was restricted to converts.

When Italy entered the war on the side of the Germans in June 1940, thousands of foreigners and political dissenters were interned throughout the country. Archbishop Francesco Borgongini Duca, the papal nuncio to Italy, visited most of the camps more than once, bringing small gifts and words of comfort. He did not criticize substandard living conditions observed in the camps, but the visits themselves may have encouraged the government to make improvements. Prisoners were, above all, consoled by the knowledge that the world had not forgotten them. They were also grateful for the Vatican Information Service, which enabled them to correspond with their families in other countries. The nuncio and the Vatican Information Service treated Jewish internees no differently from non-Jews. At the primarily Jewish camp of Ferramonti, however, Father Lopinot, initially sent to minister to internees who were Catholics, worked with exceptional dedication and tact, easing anxieties and advocating better treatment for all.

Vatican diplomatic interventions on behalf of Jews in the Italian-occupied territories of Croatia and southeastern France have been analyzed in these pages and shown to be, with two or three exceptions, perfunctory, polite, and dilatory. Generally consisting of questions rather than requests directed at the Italian authorities, and certainly never rising to the level of threats or ultimatums, these interventions served primarily as an indication that the Vatican was following events. The pope clearly did not want the Jews to be deported from territories controlled by Italy, the country where his own influence was strongest. He let Mussolini know it, to a degree never demonstrated elsewhere. The mild interventions may have caused the Duce to reflect, and may have strengthened the resolve of Italian diplomatic and military personnel who already opposed deportations. The interventions were not decisive, but they were commendable. There is no way to know how Vatican officials would have reacted if Italian authorities had actually begun to deliver the Jews in their occupied territories to the Germans, Croatians, or Vichy French. Given their silence when deportations began in Italy, however, as well as their weak responses to deportations from Catholic countries like Slovakia, Vichy France, and German-occupied Croatia, it is not easy to believe that they would have publicly protested.

The issue of the papal response to the deportations of Jews from German-occupied Italy after September 1943 can be divided into two questions: What did the pope do to prot ct Jews in his own diocese of Rome, where he was in fact the bishop, and what did he do elsewhere? It is clear that he ultimately decided not to protest publicly when 1,259 Jews were arrested in the Eternal City on October 16. Vatican Secretary of State Maglione summoned German Ambassador to the Holy See Ernst von Weizsäcker that same morning, informing him that "the Holy See would not want to be obliged to express its disapproval" if "these things continued." [13] But things did continue. More than a thousand Jews were deported on October 18, and the Vatican remained silent. On October 25, a full week later, an article in L'Osservatore Romano mentioned the Supreme Pontiff's charity, which "does not pause before boundaries of nationality, religion, or descent." [14] That was all.

In a broader context, L'Osservatore Romano did object unequivocally and strenuously to the infamous Italian police order number five of December 1, 1943, which declared that all Jews in Italy were to be arrested by Italian police and carabinieri and interned in camps within the country. The objections were commendable. They may have caused some readers to pause and consider, and even to criticize or ignore the police order. They may even have influenced the government's decision a few days later to exempt sick and elderly Jews, and Jewish spouses in mixed marriages. Unfortunately, the objections were never repeated publicly, while the police order continued to be enforced, exemptions were ignored, and thousands of arrested Jews were not merely interned in Italy but were delivered to the Germans and deported.[15]

If the pope remained silent, however, he allowed nuns, monks, priests, and prelates in his diocese, including several at the Vicariate, to involve themselves in Jewish rescue. Many Church institutions, including Vatican properties, sheltered Jews along with other types of fugitives for long periods. Vatican authorities may have provided extra food to institutions it knew to be harboring fugitives, as well as some clothing and money—although the latter two types of aid were minimal in comparison with the need. There were other indications of good will. A high-level prelate at the Vicariate told Father Raganella that he had done well to persuade an order of cloistered nuns to accept a group of Jews for a time.[16] The same or a similar prelate at the Vicariate verified Father Benedetto's signature on official documents, certainly suspecting that his purpose was to disguise the identities of illegal Jewish immigrants.[17] Some prelates who resided within the Vatican City itself even invited individual fugitives, including Jews, many of them converts, to live in their private apartments. Pius XII undoubtedly knew about these activities, although he seems not to have known of their extent. Nor did he particularly approve. Nuns, monks, and priests were urged to use prudence and moderation—not unreasonable, but not encouraging either. The rector of the Pontificio Seminario Romano Maggiore apparently received a reprimand for excessive zeal.[18] Then in the early spring of 1944, directors of Vatican properties were informed that their guests must hide elsewhere. When certain prelates strenuously objected, however, the pope apparently allowed those orders to be enforced only temporarily, or not at all.[19]

There is no evidence of a papal role in the efforts of men and women of the Church to save Jews in dioceses outside Rome. In Genoa, Turin, and Florence the local archbishops became involved in Jewish assistance in late September or early October, well before the roundup in Rome made everyone aware of the danger that Jews would be deported. They acted at the request of Delasem, which, fearing the confiscation of its lists and funds, was forced to go underground. In Rome toward the end of September, Father Benedetto did the same, for similar reasons. A few other prelates in this early period, like the bishop of Assisi, acted entirely on their own initiative, without prompting from Delasem. Others, like the patriarch of Venice, did nothing at all. There is no reason to suspect that the pope sent rescue directives at this early date, before significant numbers of Jews began the flight into Church institutions in Rome itself. Nor did men and women of the Church present on the scene, in Rome or in other cities, claim that he did.

There is also no reason to believe that Pius XII sent a rescue directive after October 16, or even a message of encouragement to continue a process already begun. Surely at least one copy of a written message would have been hidden and preserved by churchmen all too conscious that the pope would be criticized after the war for his silence and lack of assistance to Jews in distress. Other compromising documents have survived. Archives in the archdiocese of Turin, especially, contain Monsignor Barale's notes of funds distributed to Jews in hiding. The bishop of Assisi, as seen, hid the original identification papers of a Jewish family he had helped.[20] But there is no letter from the Vatican instructing or urging men and women of the Church to help fugitives, including Jews. Nor is there a letter authorizing the lifting of rules of cloister, in order that fugitives might be admitted to areas forbidden to outsiders.

Might such an order have been conveyed orally? Again, there is no evidence. Although they invariably believed that they were acting according to the pope's will, men and women of the Church present on the scene almost never claimed after the war to have received precise oral instructions from the Vatican. Their rescue activities began spontaneously, when someone in need knocked on their doors, or, in some cities, on the request, but not the order, of a bishop working with Delasem.

Rather than specifically order or suggest that Catholics help Jews in Italy, it may be argued, Pius XII made his wishes known indirectly through his general public speeches and writings published at the time. The argument is shaky indeed. As seen, in his public pronouncements during the war the pope mentioned only twice that people were dying because of their "descent [stirpe]." He never used the word "Jews," or mentioned the agent responsible for the deaths. He spoke more often in general terms of his compassion for suffering humanity, but on only two other occasions did he add that the compassion exceeded distinctions of nationality or descent. One of these occasions was the publication, a week after the Rome roundup, of the article in L'Osservatore Romano mentioned above, not necessarily written by him but perceived as coming from him. The other was a speech to the assembled cardinals on June 2, 1944.[21] There was, finally, the article of admonishment of the Italian government printed in L'Osservatore Romano in response to police order number five. Such limited allusions may have provided spiritual guidance and encouragement to those already inclined to assist Jews. Fortunately enough, many men and women of the Church in Italy were so inclined. Unfortunately, however, many others were not. For them, the pope provided little leadership or inspiration.

Nor, apparently, did the pope provide much private guidance when specifically asked or given the opportunity. As seen in this book, for example, the patriarch of Venice informed the Vatican in December 1943 about his concern for the Jews in his diocese, especially those who had been baptized. He was assured blandly that the Holy See was doing everything it could. No one encouraged him to continue to be concerned, or to offer assistance.

A better example of this lack of guidance takes us further afield, to an exchange between Vatican Secretary of State Maglione and Monsignor Andrea Cassulo, the papal nuncio in Romania, in the summer of 1943. Cassulo wrote on July 21 that the bishop of Timisoara had reported that laypersons in his diocese, predominantly ethnic Germans, were complaining that the Vatican Information Service was favoring Jews over non-Jews.[22] On August 20, Maglione replied:

> In its charitable work of relieving suffering produced by the war, the Holy See makes no distinction of religion or nationality. If a great number of the requests addressed to the Information Office regarding Romania involve Jews, it is certainly not from any "preference" of the Office for non-Aryans, but from the simple fact that the non-Aryans who reside or used to reside in the Romanian territory are very numerous and their relatives who find themselves in diverse parts of the world desire to have news of them.
>
> To give any other explanation for the prevalence of requests for non-Aryans . . . would destroy the work of the Holy See.
>
> I beg Your Excellency to convey this with your usual prudence to the bishop of Timisoara, whose diocese may perhaps be in a more unfavorable condition than others if the percentage of the non-Aryan population is higher there than elsewhere, and at the same time I propose [that] some channel of transmission to non-Aryans of the forms from this Information Office [be established] that will not implicate the direct participation of the local curia.[23]

At first glance, Maglione's response seems praiseworthy. He assured his papal nuncio that "the Holy See makes no distinction of religion or nationality." But one would wish for much more. There was no moral guidance for the bishop of Timisoara. He was not told that the Jews had suffered extraordinary hardship, disruption, and destruction during the war. He was not reminded that Jews are part of the great human family, as deserving of help and compassion as all others. He was not asked to provide that help, or to instruct his flock to do so. Instead, he was encouraged to disguise the Church's role in helping Jews communicate with the outside world. He was to avoid injuring the sensibilities of his virulently anti-Semitic parishioners.

It is clear, then, that Popes Pius XI and XII did little to help Jews in Italy just before and during the war. What options, however, did they have? What more could they have done, and why did they not do it? The most radical, obvious, and frequently cited answer, of course, involves the option of a loud, vehement public protest by Pope Pius XII against the deportations and murders of Jews by the Nazis throughout Europe between 1941 and 1945. Such a protest could have been accompanied by the threat of excommunication of all who participated in the killings. It could have included information that the pope knew to be true—that hundreds of thousands of Jews had been murdered in the Soviet Union, Lithuania, Latvia, and Croatia in 1941; that deportations were occurring simultaneously in many countries by the summer of 1942; that women, children, the sick, and the elderly were being transported along with the men; and that deported Jews were being murdered. If its origins with the pope were clear, such a message and protest would have been believed. It might not have altered Nazi policy toward the Jews or the behavior of most of those charged with enforcement, but it would have prompted more Jews to hide sooner, and saved lives. It would also have enabled more non-Jews of good will to understand that the dangers threatening Jews were different and greater than those affecting Christians. Especially in the German Reich and countries to its east, such as Poland, Lithuania, Latvia, and Ukraine, where levels of Nazi-imposed terror were extreme and where local people were usually not inclined to help the Jews, such a protest would have caused more Catholics of good conscience to provide assistance. Others would have agreed to look the other way while their neighbors helped.

Why did Pius XII decide against issuing such a protest? He was, after all, the spiritual leader of millions of Catholics, and a moral spokesman for the entire world. His associates have testified to his personal anguish over the suffering of war victims, and this book has shown that he knew about the Final Solution. Why, then, did he remain silent? Certainly his primary motivation was not the protection of his activities behind the scenes to help Jews, for we have seen that he did very little. Nor was he silent in order to protect the many Jews hiding in Church institutions in Italy after the autumn of 1943, for a protest against deportations should have been issued much earlier, preferably in the summer or autumn of 1942. Rather, the pope did not speak out against the Holocaust because he did not want to antagonize or challenge the Axis powers, for many reasons.

Pius XII believed, first of all, that a public description and denunciation of the Holocaust would make matters worse for many while helping no one. He wrote as much to his friend Bishop Konrad von Preysing in Berlin on April 30, 1943. Preysing had begged the pope in March to intercede in some way on behalf of Jews affected by a new wave of deportations from Germany. "Regarding pronouncements by the bishops," Pius answered, "we leave it to local senior clergymen to decide if, and to what degree, the danger of reprisals and oppression, as well as, perhaps, other circumstances caused by the length and psychological climate of the war may make restraint advisable—despite the reasons for intervention—in order to avoid greater evils. This is one of the reasons why We limit ourselves in Our proclamations." [24] The pope repeated the explanation in his address to the Sacred College of Cardinals on June 2, 1943, declaring, "Every word directed by Us to the competent authorities [to ease suffering], and every public reference, have to be seriously pondered and measured by Us in the interest of those who suffer, in order not to make, even unintentionally, their situation more grave and insupportable." [25]

The fact that some Jews would have benefited from a papal protest was addressed above. Who, however, might have suffered because of it? Among other considerations, the pope feared that his protest would intensify the mental anguish of German and Austrian Catholics by forcing them to choose between their Church and their country. The outcome of such a choice, furthermore, would not necessarily be favorable to the Church. Threats of excommunication might have been ignored, and those affected might have left the Church and founded their own. [26] Such objections seem trivial, given the possibility of saving lives, but in the eyes of the Church, the alienation of Catholics can lead not only to institutional chaos but to the eternal damnation of souls.

Equally serious, Pius XII feared that a protest would make matters worse by enraging the Nazis and provoking violent reprisals against Catholics throughout Europe. There is some truth to this concern. News of a papal protest could only have circulated within the German Reich and its occupied countries illegally. Allied and Vatican radio broadcasts were often jammed, illegal to listen to, and sometimes not believed. Foreign newspapers, including

Vatican publications, were also banned. The most effective way of circulating news of a papal statement and making it credible would have involved the distribution of clandestine tracts by bishops, priests, and Catholic laypersons—an activity that carried horrible risks. Vatican fears of violence against these Catholics were justified, as was the concern about intensified reprisals on observant Catholics in countries like Poland, where anti-Catholic measures were already severe. But fears of reprisals against Catholics in Western Europe were perhaps exaggerated. It is difficult to believe that the Nazis would have wanted to establish a direct and visible link between a papal reference to the extermination of the Jews and their own violence against Catholics, thus confirming the former—unless, of course, Catholics acted on the reference and helped Jews. The Nazis would have preferred to deny the reference as propaganda, vilify the pope as pro-British and pro-American, and sow doubts among the faithful.

Also to be considered was the effect of a papal protest of the Holocaust on certain limited categories of Jews. For most Jews the situation could hardly have been worse, but the position of Jews who were converts or in mixed families was sometimes unclear. Generally speaking, Jews who had been baptized but whose parents were both Jewish were not exempt from deportation, but Jewish spouses in mixed marriages, whether observant or converted, and their baptized children, were often spared. But the signals were mixed and difficult to interpret. There were, first of all, many group and individual exceptions to the general rule. In addition, in some countries Jews by religion or culture were sometimes arrested and deported before the converts, leaving the impression that the latter, even if fully Jewish by birth, might be spared. In Slovakia, for example, as seen, the predominantly Catholic government authorities stopped deportations of Jews in June 1942 and granted exemptions to some 30,000 people, many of whom were converts. Most of those exempted were deported in 1944. In Croatia, the predominantly Catholic Ustasha sometimes refrained in 1941 from murdering Jews and Orthodox Serbs who converted, only to deport the former a year or two later.

The most frequently cited story in this regard concerns the Netherlands. The Nazis and their Dutch collaborators began arresting Jews in the summer of 1942, including many of the country's thousands of Jews who had been baptized or who were in mixed marriages.[27] Many of those in mixed marriages were ultimately spared, but the fate of converts was more complicated. For a time they were held as a separate group in the camp at Westerbork. Dutch Protestant and Catholic leaders intervened privately with the German authorities on behalf of all Jews, and they threatened to make their objections public if the deportations did not stop. The Germans responded by implying that converts would remain in the Netherlands if the churches remained silent. When the Catholic bishop of Utrecht nevertheless made his protest public, Jews who had become Catholics were immediately deported. Jews who were Protestants stayed in the camp longer but were also ultimately deported.[28] But this was known only later. For Pius XII and officials at the Vatican Secretariat of State, the lesson from the Netherlands at the time, as from Slovakia and Croatia, was that Jews who had been baptized had a chance, as long as spokesmen for the Church remained silent. In fact, baptized Jews with two Jewish parents had no better chance than those who were Jews by religion or culture.

The situation for Jewish spouses in mixed marriages and their baptized children was somewhat clearer at the time. They were, as seen, often spared in Italy, the country about which the pope was best informed. Those who were arrested in Rome on October 16, 1943, were immediately released. Italian police order number five, issued on December 1, 1943, declared that all Jews in Italy were to be arrested and interned by Italian police, with the exception of the baptized children of mixed marriages, who were not, in any case, considered to be Jewish. But nine days later the order provided exceptions also for Jewish spouses in mixed marriages, as well as for sick and elderly Jews.[29] As the situation was radicalized, especially in the last months of the German occupation, more and more deportations of technically exempt individuals occurred, even without the provocation of a papal protest. It was nevertheless reasonable to fear that such a protest might make matters worse.

In the last analysis, then, the pope was probably correct that some Jews involved with Catholicism, as well as some Catholics, would suffer from a public protest.

Another reason why the pope decided against a public denunciation of the Holocaust involved his personal diplomatic priorities. From the very onset of the war Pius XII had hoped to be called on by all belligerents to offer his good offices to negotiate a resolution of the conflict. At first his objective was simply the restoration of peace. After the Germans began to falter on the Russian front, however, he hoped to negotiate a separate peace between the Western Allies and the Reich at the expense of the Soviet Union, to avoid the disaster of postwar Communist seizures of power in Central and Eastern Europe. For if the pope disliked National Socialism especially because of its persecution of the Church, he feared godless Communism, with which no compromises were possible, far more.[30]

The Allies' insistence on the unconditional surrender of the German Reich, announced at Casablanca in January 1943, and their constant rejection of any possibility of a separate peace, should have convinced Vatican officials of the hopelessness of negotiations. But the pope regarded the policy of unconditional surrender as a calamity that would draw the Russians still deeper into Europe.[31] He was also influenced by his fondness for the German people, the legacy of his service as papal nuncio in their country from 1917 to 1929. Encouraged by German moderates like Ambassador to the Holy See Ernst von Weizsäcker who were eager to avoid the destruction of their country, Pius XII continued to nurse his illusions to the end. But, he believed, the Germans would call on him only if he demonstrated neutrality and good will. He could not, then, denounce the Holocaust or any other Nazi atrocities.

This argument is somewhat weakened by the fact that Pius XII did *not* remain scrupulously neutral throughout the conflict. He could not claim neutrality when members of all the non-Communist political parties affiliated with the Italian *Comitato di Liberazione Nazionale* were sheltered in the extraterritorial Seminario Romano in the autumn of 1943 and allowed to come and go to attend political meetings, in violation of international laws concerning the right of asylum. Such laws were violated again in May 1944 when General Roberto Bencivenga, the head of the non-Communist Resistance, was accepted at the same Vatican property and allowed to maintain a radio and to direct military operations.[32]

In many other ways, Vatican officials did not necessarily violate international law regarding neutrals but showed distinct and sometimes shifting preferences in the conflict. For example, it was always official policy to refuse asylum behind the Vatican walls to political dissidents, escaped Allied prisoners of war, and, after September 8, 1943, Jews. As long as the Vatican City was surrounded by Italians, that policy was strictly enforced, in part because many Italian employees behind the walls, whether spies or just loyal patriots, would have reported violations to their own government on the outside. By the end of 1943 or early 1944, however, as general Italian hostility toward the Germans and the war increased dramatically and, perhaps, as it became apparent that the Allies would win the war, enforcement began to soften. As seen, about 160 political refugees and Jews were ultimately admitted, along with a few escaped Allied prisoners of war. They always entered unofficially, sponsored by individual priests quite apart from the Vatican authorities, but they nevertheless entered.[33] At the same time, the pope and officials at the Secretariat of State turned a blind eye to the activities of British Minister to the Holy See Sir d'Arcy Osborne, the Irish Monsignor Hugh O'Flaherty, and others who were helping thousands of escaped Allied prisoners hidden throughout Rome.[34] This was, strictly speaking, an expression of preference that risked angering the Germans and jeopardizing possibilities of being asked to negotiate a separate peace.

Other examples of Vatican preferences may be seen by examining the press in the period following the liberation of Rome. As long as they were in power, Mussolini, Badoglio, and the German occupiers censored *La Civiltà Cattolica* and prohibited *L'Osservatore Romano* from reporting war news if it wished to be distributed in Italy. Immediately after the Allies entered the city on June 4, 1944, however, war news reappeared in both publications, as did articles dealing enthusiastically with the liberators and the new Italian government headed by Ivanoe Bonomi. As early as June 9–10, *L'Osservatore Romano* referred to the pope's gratitude to God for the "salvation of the Eternal City" and reported papal audiences with important Allied officers and statesmen.[35] On July 1, 1944, *La Civiltà Cattolica* not only announced exultantly that "the Germans have been cleared out [*cacciati*] from south of the Pescara River" and "the Allies [have made] important progress all along the front," but it also referred to the "struggle against Nazism," the "liberated regions," and, still more startling, recently uncovered evidence of torture and massacres conducted by the Germans and their Fascist collaborators in and around Rome.[36] But the war would last another eleven months. Millions of Catholics and thousands of Jews in mixed marriages, all vulnerable to Nazi reprisals, still lived under German control. The Russians were not yet in Warsaw. Peace at the expense of the Soviet Union was still regarded by many to be desirable. Nevertheless, Pius XII no longer seemed so eager to avoid antagonizing the Axis powers.

Although the wish to conduct possible peace negotiations and fear of the effect on vulnerable Catholics and Jews were undoubtedly factors in the pope's decision to remain silent about the Holocaust, it seems likely that the primary explanation lay elsewhere. Above all else, Pius XII feared for the integrity of the Vatican itself. The Vatican City was surrounded by Italian belligerents from May 10, 1940, until September 8, 1943, and by the German occupiers of Rome from September 8 until June 4, 1944. The intentions of Fascist and Nazi extremists toward the Church have been long debated. Some historians have pointed to statements by men close to Hitler that the latter envisioned an invasion of the Holy See. Others have argued that Hitler would never have opted for so drastic a confrontation with Catholics, and that statements to the contrary were usually self-serving, made after the war by Germans who wished to show that they had helped change the Führer's mind.[37] There is little concrete evidence. The fact remains, however, that the Italians or Germans could have invaded the Vatican City at any time, searched archives, destroyed property, and even kidnapped the pope. Short of that, they could have cut off water, electricity, and food supplies; denied access to Vatican personnel who lived outside the walls, or had them arrested; prevented Allied diplomats from residing within the Vatican; and disrupted all communications with the outside world. As a demonstration of their power, they maintained continual harassment. Fascist thugs beat up newspaper vendors of *L'Osservatore Romano* in the streets of Rome in 1940, when the journal was still printing war reports that included news of Italian defeats. The Vatican Radio was regularly jammed. Italian and German censors consistently interrupted and read diplomatic communications of the Holy See.

The pope's sense of security was further affected by the fact that Italian agents bribed, blackmailed, or intimidated Vatican employees to act as spies, with much success. Those employees were, after all, mostly Italian citizens living outside the walls, dependent on their jobs and vulnerable to threats. Also, most of them were Italian patriots and, especially before the German occupation, sympathetic to their country at war and their relatives in military service. Some high-ranking prelates in the Vatican hierarchy, even including individuals who resided there and had relinquished their Italian citizenship to become citizens of the Holy See, shared that view. Such sympathies altered somewhat after Badoglio announced the armistice and tried to take his country out of the war. Lower-level Vatican employees and police were demonstrably less willing to meet the demands of the Germans than those of the Italians. But security leaks continued.[38]

Pius XII and his advisors were naturally anxious to avoid a military occupation that would prevent them from functioning. Their motives were not solely political, administrative, and practical. These were, after all, religious men, focused on God and convinced that life on earth was inevitably brutish and short. Suffering was regrettable but, compared with the vast expanse of eternity, insignificant, except insofar as it opened the gates of heaven for the faithful. The Church, however, had to be defended in all places at all costs, for individuals could attain salvation only through the sacraments it offered. It was a harsh doctrine with harsh consequences. The implication was that the

Church could accept any compromises as long as it was able to keep going, to administer the sacraments to those in need of them.

To keep the Vatican going, as they saw it, the pope and his officials at the Secretariat of State deferred to Italian and German demands on numerous occasions. In 1940, for example, they agreed that *L'Osservatore Romano* would no longer print war news, that Allied diplomats residing in the Vatican would not be allowed to go in and out, that fugitives would not be accepted behind Vatican walls, and much more. As tensions grew, they intervened diplomatically but always politely with Italian, Croatian, Slovakian, and other authorities but, as seen, rarely with the Germans. This deference should not be construed as cowardice. Other neutral nations and institutions, such as Sweden, Switzerland, and the International Red Cross, made similar compromises in order to continue to function. We may not like the compromises, but they were made for reasons of *réal politique* rather than cowardice.

For the pope and his advisors, réal politique in this period meant not only protecting the institution but also building bridges to a newly liberated Italy, the country within which the Vatican City State must function in the future and the country whose citizens were most carefully watching and judging it during the war. Thus, in 1944, Vatican officials endorsed causes of most concern to Italians. They complained bitterly to British and American diplomats about the Allies' destruction of the Benedictine monastery at Monte Cassino and refusal to declare Rome an open city.[39] They said little about the destruction of religious buildings and whole cities elsewhere. They allowed priests to shelter Italian politicians capable of forming a new, non-Communist government after the war. They permitted other priests to assist escaped Allied prisoners of war, for humanitarian reasons but also to assure good relations with the new occupiers of Italy.

Yet for all this, there was much that Pius XII did not do, even after the institution was freed from the danger of hostile invasion. Among those omissions was a public papal denunciation of the Holocaust. For if the pope remained silent to protect the Vatican, why did he not speak out after June 4, 1944, when it was safe?

A final and comprehensive explanation of the silence, therefore, must take into account the broad array of personal attitudes and conditions at the Vatican that have been touched on in this book, along with the unfolding chronology. Most prelates of the Church, first of all, were suspicious of those who were Jewish by religion or culture. They saw Jews as agents of the challenge of modernism, the enemies of an increasingly vulnerable and threatened Church. Consequently, they initially welcomed laws that would separate Jews from Catholics and possibly contribute to a partial restoration of an ancien régime. They did not approve of violence, but they preferred to overlook it at first as temporary, in the hope of achieving the objective of separation. With that bias and inclination, they were slow to perceive the significance of the Nazis' transition from the legal separation of Jews to their ghettoization, and from sporadic violence to systematic extermination. After all, many others were also suffering. Why would the torments of the Jews be any different?

In this book I have shown that Pius XII received ample and reliable information that the torments *were* different. With his pleasant personal memories of Germany and his attachment to such German friends as Fathers Robert Leiber and Monsignor Ludwig Kaas, however, the pope must have found the information difficult to absorb at first. Also, unlike parish priests who dealt with human frailty every day, the pope was sheltered not from political and diplomatic manueuvering but from the unpleasant realities of cruelty and suffering. He lived in an unreal world. British Minister Osborne understood this when he moved into the Vatican on June 14, 1940, and wrote in his diary, "The stupendous architecture of St. Peter's, which is pure Michelangelo on this side, is like a safety curtain that shuts out the world. The effect is a little like living in an embalmed world." [40] Under such conditions the pope's imagination may well have failed when confronted with the initial reports of mass exterminations.

When Pius XII and officials at the Vatican Secretariat of State finally understood, probably in the autumn of 1942, that extermination was threatening all Jews throughout German-occupied and German-allied Europe, it was embarrassingly late to protest. Why had the pope not spoken out earlier about the abuses and atrocities that he did know about? Why had he not denounced the anti-Jewish laws and growing persecution in many countries before the war, the ghettoization of Jews in Poland in 1940, the mass murders in the German-occupied Soviet Union in 1941, and deportations in the spring of 1942?

Still other personal attitudes influenced decisions about what to do. Pius XII and the officials of the Vatican Secretariat of State were conservative bureaucrats. Nothing could have been more alien to them than a loud radical act of direct public confrontation. As government officials, also, they defined their primary goals and responsibilities as focusing on Catholics, including converts, rather than on humanity in general. Their vision of their moral duty was as limited as their imagination of violence. They seem to have forgotten that the pope was not only the leader of a government and an institution, but also the spokesman of a Church whose moral and spiritual mission transcended practical considerations. This concept of a moral mission is not a twenty-first-century creation, imposed retroactively by those attempting to evaluate Pius XII's papacy. It was shared by many of the pope's contemporaries, if not by himself and his advisors. Bishop Preysing was just one of many Catholic prelates, priests, and laypersons who begged the pope to intercede to save the Jews. Scores of Jewish leaders sent appeals to the one spiritual figure whom they believed could help them. Moderate German diplomats in Rome greatly feared a papal protest at the time of the roundup, if not before. But the pope had other objectives and concerns.

Apart from a direct, specific, defiant public condemnation of the deportations and murders of European Jews between 1941 and 1944, what exactly could Pius XI and XII have done in Italy, where they were most involved, to ease the appalling tragedy of the Holocaust? How could they have made some difference without directly confronting Hitler?

As they witnessed the rising tide of anti-Judaism in Europe in the 1930s, Pius XI or Pius XII could have issued an encyclical condemning it. The declaration could have been clear and unambiguous, with a specific denunciation of the persecution of those who were Jewish in religion or culture. The terrible truth is that they did not issue such a document because they were not opposed to moderate measures separating Jews from Christian society. That attitude continued throughout the war and complicated every decision. With each week and month that passed it became more awkward and difficult to oppose measures that should have been denounced from the onset.

In addition, Pius XI could have raised his voice loudly and vehemently against the Italian anti-Jewish laws in 1938. His failure to object when Jews under his very windows were forced out of schools, jobs and businesses was a disgrace. It sent a bitter message around the world. The Catholic Church would protest against "exaggerated nationalism" and against racism that made no allowance for religion, but it would not protect the rights of individuals of different faiths. A papal statement against Fascist anti-Judaism would have enraged Mussolini and jeopardized Catholic Action, but it would not have prevented the Vatican from functioning or brought violence down upon Catholics in the German Reich. It would have constituted an unstated but unmistakable appeal for compassion toward Jews everywhere. It would have provided moral guidance to the faithful.

Vatican efforts to encourage Catholic countries, especially in Central and South America, to accept Jewish immigrants would also have provided such guidance. Instead, bureaucrats worked only for Jews who had become Catholics. As with the anti-Jewish laws, where objections were articulated only against measures affecting converts and Jews in mixed marriages, the preoccupation with Jews connected to Catholicism sent a fatal message. The Church hierarchy cared only about its own. Why should the Catholic masses act any differently?

With regard to internment camps in Italy during the early years of the war, the Vatican could have sent another kind of message throughout the world. Papal nuncios and other priests and prelates visiting the camps could have spoken openly about fair treatment, decent conditions, and human rights for all peoples. The pope could have called for tolerance and compassion for innocent civilians, not in arcane and obscure language, as he did in some of his speeches, but clearly and unequivocably, in the context of internment. Foreigners were interned in many countries at war, including the United States. How many people might have been reminded of the need for charity and the limits of nationalism? How many priests, at least, might have been reminded of their duty to guide their flocks?

It is difficult to criticize the interventions of Vatican diplomats on behalf of Jews in the Italian-occupied territories as timid and tardy, simply because more forceful measures proved to be unnecessary. Again, however, the pope had an opportunity to make a statement, criticize Italian Fascists rather than German Nazis, and convey a message without confronting Hitler. The same might be said for papal admonitions of Catholic governments in Vichy France, Slovakia, and Croatia. In the guise of instructing Catholics, Pius XII could have articulated principles and concepts applicable in Germany as well. Confrontation with the Nazis could have been avoided, while moral guidance was provided.

During the Badogio interregnum, the forty-five days between Mussolini's fall in July and the German occupation of Italy in September 1943, Pius XII had another opportunity to exercise moral leadership. He could immediately have urged the revocation of the anti-Jewish laws. Badoglio may well have ignored him, but the pope would have made his position clear without confronting Hitler. Catholics would have understood that their Church opposed the persecution of the Jews.

Throughout the world, most people accept the prejudices articulated for them by the elites of their society. Thus, after years of government propaganda, many Germans came to believe that the Jews were their enemies, and the cause of their troubles. The concept was often simply a given, unquestioned, taken for granted. Nor were only Germans guilty of such lack of skepticism and thought. African and native Americans were subject to legal discrimination in the United States for centuries, while most whites took the system for granted. After December 7, 1941, the government of the United States informed its citizens that Japanese Americans were dangerous enemies, and should be interned. How many Americans raised questions about the legality and justice of such measures? Women were excluded from many educational institutions and professional positions until very recently, and few asked whether that condition was just and reasonable.

If intolerance and segregation are to be challenged and destroyed, someone must raise the initial questions. The economic, political, and social elites of a nation have a vested interest in the preservation of the status quo. Religious leaders suffer from the same constraints, but they, at least, might be expected to rise above them. A papal challenge against resurgent anti-Judaism in Europe in the 1930s and early 1940s might have caused people to think twice about the phenomenon.

Also during the Badoglio period, Vatican officials could have brought pressure upon Italian bureaucrats in the Ministry of the Interior to facilitate the passing of Jews from southern France through Italy to North Africa. Most officials at the Foreign Ministry were well inclined toward the project, discussed in Chapter Ten, but some at the Interior resisted. Instead of acting promptly and positively to end that resistance, Vatican officials viewed the project as too difficult—complicated and thus impossible. A precious opportunity to save thousands of Jewish lives was lost.

When the Germans occupied Italy, the pope could have informed the directors of Church institutions in Rome that he would look favorably upon all help offered to fugitives, and would provide financing, supplies, and other support to sustain hospitality. No one, then, would have been turned away from fear of lack of space, food, or payment, as many were, especially in the early days of the occupation. He could have been in close communication with the Jewish Community of Rome, informing its leaders of even the slightest rumors or warnings of a possible roundup. He could, also, have warned the Germans, clearly and forcefully, at the very onset of the occupation, that he would protest the arrests and deportations of Jews from the Eternal City. Maglione could have said to Weizsäcker in September what he told him on October 16, but more forcefully, and with conviction. It is difficult to understand why these things were not done. Pius XII had every reason to oppose a massive roundup of Jews under his very windows—an event that would make him look helpless, weak, and irrelevant. Yet he did nothing to prevent it.

Outside Rome, the pope's options resembled those within Rome. He could have issued the very directive his defenders claim that he did issue, urging bishops and priests, monks and nuns, to do everything they could to help the Jews. He could have explained that the Jews were in greater danger than others—that their situation was dire and different. He could have provided funds and supplies. He could, at the very least, have answered the petitions of his bishops differently. Instead of simply assuring the patriarch of Venice that the Holy See was doing everything possible, he could have offered suggestions, guidance, and encouragement. Many prelates and priests, as seen, did not need such encouragement but were already deeply involved in rescue operations. Some, like Bishop Antonio Santin in Trieste, were attempting to guide the faithful by reminding them from the pulpit that "charity, goodness, [and] humanity" must be extended to the Jews.[41] But there could have been more. Had there been more papal guidance, Don Giuseppe Peaquin in the Valle d'Aosta would not have been scolded by his bishop for helping two Jewish families.[42] Don Leto Casini of Varlungo would not have been turned away by the archbishop of Perugia and obliged to spend a night in the open.[43] More men and women throughout Italy might have helped the Jews. Furthermore, the pope's directive and guidance could have been conveyed to other countries as well, where it was even more needed.

Finally, Pius XII could have intervened behind the scenes, quietly but strenuously, with political and police authorities at all levels in the new Italian Social Republic and even with certain German diplomats, on behalf of Jews in Italy. His token effort in August 1944 and the more ambitious attempt in October by the papal nuncio in Bern, Monsignor Filippo Bernardini, described in Chapter Twenty, suggest what could have been done earlier, more often, and more forcefully.

In addition to the option of a public protest, then, there were many other ways in which the pope and his officials could have helped the Jews of Italy. Why did they not do more? Much of the answer has already been given in the context of the general silence. It includes the anti-Jewish bias of those concerned, their actual preference for the separation of Jews from Christians, their intense personal conservatism and lack of imagination, their narrow focus on their own Catholic constituency, and their fear of antagonizing the Fascists and Germans if discovered in acts of even the slightest opposition. But there are still other explanations. As seen, only about fifty people worked at the Secretariat of State in 1944, including archival and clerical personnel.[44] Even that small figure represented an increase from thirty-one at the beginning of the war.[45] Among the fifty, the still fewer men who actually made decisions and formulated policy must have felt overwhelmed by reports of complex problems that arrived daily from throughout the world at war. They could hardly have had time to rise above mere acknowledgment or perfunctory responses. There was little time to anticipate issues or initiate policy.

The handful of decision-makers, furthermore, were diplomats who, without the distractions of wives and children, were single-mindedly devoted to their careers and their institutions, and unwilling to risk either. Most of them, also, believed that the "preponderant Jews," in the traditional phrase of *La Civiltà Cattolica,* were a well-organized and well-financed international force, able to take care of themselves. The Vatican must concentrate its resources and energies on the Catholic faithful, so threatened by the modern world.

Ultimately, of course, responsibility for the action or inaction of his officials rests with Pius XII. Ironically, given the fact that he is currently a candidate for sainthood, Pius XII was a man who placed a priority on political and diplomatic responses rather than moral teaching. And diplomatic responses entailed formality, correctness, courtesy, patience, and conciliation—the exact opposite of what was needed if people were to be rescued and hidden. The pope's preferences and example greatly influenced the behavior of those around him.

It bears repeating that the pope was the leader of millions of Catholics, who had been taught to look to him above all others for spiritual and moral guidance. He was also esteemed throughout the world as a symbol and spokesman of ethical principles. His obligations during the Second World War to guide and instruct the masses exceeded those of politicians, statesmen, diplomats, soldiers, philanthropists, and lower-level Christian pastors and priests. As 6 million Jews were being torn from their homes, crammed into trains, deported to unknown destinations, and shot before open ditches or gassed and burned in factories of death, men and women of all faiths and persuasions looked to him for a word, a sign, an indication of how to respond.

As some 6,746 Jews from Italy were being shipped north to share the fate of the others, the pope's own countrymen similarly looked to him for guidance.[46] They found little or nothing.

The content and emphasis in Church teaching with regard to the Jews have changed significantly since the Second World War. As early as the 1950s, Pius XII tried to alter the translation of the Latin word "perfideles" from its medieval sense of perfidious or treacherous to its original meaning of, roughly, not fully believing. The Good Friday prayer for the conversion of the "perfidious Jews" was thus changed in many missals to a prayer for the "unbelieving Jews." In 1965, the Second Vatican Council dropped the reference to conversion altogether, mandating a prayer that the Jews remain and increase in their faith in the revelation given them.[47] Vatican II also stated that the Church "deplores" anti-Semitism "in every time and on whoever's part." Still more significantly, it declared that "what was committed during the passion [of Christ] cannot be imputed either indiscriminately to all Jews then living or to the Jews of our time."[48] In other words, Jews in general, past and present, cannot be held responsible for the killing of Jesus.

The pace of change intensified after Vatican II. On June 7, 1979, Pope John Paul II visited Auschwitz and prayed there first for victims who were Jewish, and then for those who were not. On April 13, 1986, he visited the central synagogue on the banks of the Tiber in Rome, where he prayed together with Roman Jews. He was the first bishop to visit a synagogue since the time of St. Peter. Then in December 1993, the Holy See and Israel signed a Fundamental Agreement that paved the way for the exchange of ambassadors the following year.

With regard to Catholics and the Holocaust, the Holy See's Commission for Religious Relations with the Jews issued a statement entitled "We Remember: A Reflection on the *Shoah*" in March 1998. The document addressed several questions that have been discussed in this book. It pointed out the difference between anti-Semitism, "based on theories contrary to the constant teaching of the Church on the unity of the human race," and anti-Judaism, "of which, unfortunately, Christians also have been guilty." It asked, "Did anti-Jewish sentiment among Christians make them less sensitive or even indifferent to the persecutions launched against the Jews by National Socialism when it reached power?" It implied that the answer is affirmative. It went on, "Did Christians give every possible assistance to those being persecuted and in particular to the persecuted Jews?" It answered, fairly enough, "Many did, but others did not." It spoke of a "heavy burden of conscience" imposed on Christians by the events of the Holocaust, and declared, "We deeply regret the errors and failures of those sons and daughters of the Church." It concluded with an appeal to Catholics "to renew the awareness of the Hebrew roots of their faith" and to remember that "the Jews are our dearly beloved brothers."[49]

On several occasions since the publication of "We Remember," Pope John Paul II has returned to the theme of the mistreatment of Jews by Catholics. On Sunday, March 12, 2000, at a Lenten service at St. Peter's Basilica in Rome, he delivered a broad apology for the errors of the sons and daughters of the Church toward Jews and others since the birth of Jesus. In an unprecedented step, a specific confession regarding historic wrong-doing was woven into the papal liturgy, followed by a prayer for God's forgiveness and grace to avoid such offenses in the future.[50] At the same time, the Vatican released a long document entitled "Memory and Reconciliation: The Church and the Faults of the Past."[51] Then, in a moving speech at Yad Vashem in Israel eleven days later, the pope declared that "the Catholic Church . . . is deeply saddened by the hatred, acts of persecution and displays of anti-Semitism directed against the Jews by Christians at any time and in any place."[52]

These statements are commendable and welcome. For the most part, the words are balanced, reasonable, and fair, as far as they go. The texts from which they come, however, contain important errors and gaps. For example, the document "We Remember" never explains that the contrasting attitudes toward racial anti-Semitism and anti-Judaism based on religion and culture flourished even at, or especially at, the highest levels of the Vatican hierarchy. "By the end of the eighteenth century and the beginning of the nineteenth century," it declares, "Jews generally had achieved an equal standing with other citizens in most states." It does not add that they continued to suffer discrimination in papal Rome until that city was forcibly acquired by Italy in 1870. It tells us that Pius XI announced on September 6, 1938, that "anti-Semitism is unacceptable. Spiritually, we are all Semites." It does not admit that the official Vatican newspaper L'Osservatore Romano never printed his words. But still more seriously, nowhere in "We Remember" is there the faintest criticism of the wartime leadership of the Church. On the contrary, as seen, Pope Pius XII is mentioned incorrectly as having saved hundreds of thousands of Jews, personally or through his representatives. Postwar expressions of gratitude from Jewish leaders are evoked as ostensible proof of his activities.[53]

Pope John Paul II's more recent statements contain similar gaps. While he referred generally in his Lenten apology to sins against the people of Israel, he did not specifically mention the Holocaust. Nor did he state clearly that leaders of the Church may be included among its children who have committed errors against Jews and others since the birth of Jesus. Then in his speech in Israel, at the museum commemorating the murder of the 6 million, he again refrained from mentioning the responses of Pius XII to that horrendous crime.

The Church has not yet completed the process of dealing honestly with its history during the Holocaust. It has not yet made clear whether popes and high Vatican officials are to be included among its sons and daughters in every age who sometimes committed regrettable errors. It has not yet expressed sorrow and repentance for the failures of Popes Pius XI and Pius XII during the years of the persecution and extermination of European Jews. It seems to have apologized only for the failures of lesser clergymen and their flocks. Ironically, some, though certainly not all, of those men and women were less grievously at fault than their superiors in the Vatican. In Italy, at least, large numbers of priests, nuns, monks, and Catholic laypersons risked their lives to save Jews with little guidance from the pope.

Abbreviations

The following items are cited in the text or notes.

ARCHIVES

AAF	Archivio Arcivescovile di Firenze
ACIV	Archivio della Comunità Israelitica di Venezia
ACS	Archivio Centrale dello Stato, Rome
ACT	Archivio della Curia di Torino
ACVT	Archivio della Curia Vescovile di Trieste
ADG	Archivio Diocesano di Genova
AIRSML	Archivio dell'Istituto Regionale per la Storia del Movimento Liberazione nel Friuli-Venezia Giulia
ASDM	Archivio Storico della Diòcesi di Milano
ASL	Archivio del Seminario Lombardo, Rome
ASPV	Archivio Storico del Patriarcato di Venezia
AST	Archivio dello Stato, Turin
ASV	Archivio dello Stato, Venice
CDEC	Centro di documentazione ebraica contemporanea, Milan
CDJC	Centre de documentation juive contemporaine, Paris
ISRT	Istituto Storico della Resistenza in Toscano, Florence
NA	National Archives of the United States, College Park, Maryland
RL	Roosevelt Library, Hyde Park, New York

OTHER

ADSS	Actes et documents du Saint Siège relatifs à la seconde guerre mondiale
b.	busta, or large archival folder
CLN	Comitato di liberazione nazionale
CNS	Catholic News Service, Washington D.C.
Delasem	Delegazione per l'assistenza agli emigranti
EW	European War
f. and s.f.	fascicolo and sottofascicolo, subdivisions within a busta
GNR	Guardia nazionale repubblicana
ICR	Intergovernmental Committee on Refugees
OSCAR	Organizzazione Soccorsi Cattolici Antifascisti Ricercati
SD	State Department
UJA	United Jewish Appeal
WRB	War Refugee Board

Notes

INTRODUCTION

1. The speech was printed in *L'Osservatore Romano*, December 25, 1942, 1–3, 2; and *La Civiltà Cattolica*, anno 94, 1943, vol. I, quad. 2222, January 4, 1943, 65–78, 77. It is also quoted in *Actes et Documents du Saint Siège relatifs à la seconde guerre mondiale*, VII, doc. 71, December 24, 1942, 161–67, 166. *Actes et Documents* will henceforth be cited as ADSS. For description of the ADSS, see below. In her book *Into That Darkness* (1974; New York: Vintage, 1983), 331, Gitta Sereny points out that the speech was more than 5,000 words in length. By the time the pope came to his remarks about those doomed to death because of their nationality or descent, he would have been speaking for about forty-five minutes.

2. Printed in *L'Osservatore Romano*, June 3, 1943, 1; and *La Civiltà Cattolica*, anno 94, 1943, vol. II, quad 2232, June 19, 1943, 329–34, 331. See also ADSS, IX, Introduction, 40.

3. In his defense of Pius XII, Dr. Joseph L. Lichten misquoted or mistranslated the Christmas message of 1942 and used the word "race." See his "A Question of Judgment: Pius XII and the Jews," *Pius XII and the Holocaust: A Reader* (1963; repub. Milwaukee: Catholic League for Religious and Civil Rights, 1988), 94–137, 108. In discussion in French of the June 2, 1943, speech the editors of ADSS, IX, Introduction, 40, also translated the Italian word "stirpe" as "race," ignoring subtle differences between the two terms. Robert A. Graham, S.J., "How to Manufacture a Legend," *Pius XII and the Holocaust: A Reader*, 15–23, 21, also translated "stirpe" as "race" in English.

4. "La carità del Santo Padre," *L'Osservatore Romano*, October 25–26, 1943, 1.

5. The speech was printed in *L'Osservatore Romano*, June 3, 1944, 1; and *La Civiltà Cattolica*, anno 95, 1944, vol. II, quad. 2256, June 17, 1944, 337–45.

6. The articles were "Carità civile," December 3, 1943, 1; and "Motivazioni," December 4, 1943, 1. This matter is discussed in Chapter Fifteen.

7. Some of these explanations were already articulated during the war. See, for example, NA, SD, 740.00116 (EW) 1939/573 1/2, Chargé d'Affaires Harold Tittmann to American secretary of state, September 8, 1942; and diary of British Minister to the Holy See Sir d'Arcy Osborne, entries in 1942, quoted in Owen Chadwick, "The Pope and the Jews in 1942," in W. J. Sheils, ed., *Persecution and Toleration: Papers Read at the 22nd Summer Meeting and the 23rd Winter Meeting of the Ecclesiastical History Society* (Great Britain, no city: Basil Blackwell, 1984), 435–72, and same author, *Britain and the Vatican During the Second World War* (Cambridge: Cambridge University Press, 1986).

8. See, for example, John Cornwell, *Hitler's Pope* (New York: Viking, 1999); Carlo Falconi, *The Silence of Pius XII*, trans. Bernard Wall (1965 in France and Italy; Boston: Little, Brown, 1970); Guenter Lewy, *The Catholic Church and Nazi Germany* (New York: McGraw-Hill, 1964), 268–308; Giovanni Miccoli, *I dilemmi e i silenzi di Pio XII: Vaticano, Seconda guerra mondiale e Shoah* (Milan: Rizzoli, 2000), and "La Santa Sede e le deportazioni," *Spostamenti di popolazione e deportazioni in Europa, 1939–1945* (Bologna: Cappelli, 1987), 236–49; and Anthony Rhodes, *The Vatican in the Age of Dictators (1922–1945)* (New York: Holt, Rinehart and Winston, 1973), 337–58.

9. For this argument, made during the war, see ADSS, IX, doc. 127, notes of the Secretariat of State, April 1, 1943, 216. For the argument presented after the war, see ADSS, IX, Introduction, 37–43; Pierre Blet, S.J., *Pius XII and the Second World War: According to the Archives of the Vatican*, trans. from French by Lawrence J. Johnson (1997; New York: Paulist Press, 1999); Alberto Giovannetti, "Storia, teatro e storie," *L'Osservatore Romano*, April 5, 1963, 3; Robert A. Graham, S.J., "How to Manufacture a Legend" and "Pius XII's Defense of Jews and Others: 1944–45," in *Pius XII and the Holocaust: A Reader*, 15–89; and Angelo Martini, S.J., "La Vera storia e 'Il Vicario' di Rolf Hochhuth," *La Civiltà Cattolica*, anno 115, 1964, vol. II, quad. 2735, n. 11, June 6, 1964, 438–54. For enormously inflated statistics of Jews helped, see Pinchas E. Lapide, *The Last Three Popes and the Jews* (London: Souvenir, 1967) or *Three Popes and the Jews* (New York: Hawthorn, 1967), 133–35, 214–15, and 223; and Lichten, "Question of Judgment."

10. For a detailed and objective study of the Vatican's diplomatic interventions on behalf of the Jews in occupied Europe, see John F. Morley, *Vatican Diplomacy and the Jews During the Holocaust, 1939–1943* (New York: KTAV, 1980). For a briefer appraisal, see John S. Conway, "Records and Documents of the Holy See Relating to the Second World War," *Yad Vashem Studies* XV, 1983, 327–45.

11. For studies in English on Jewish and non-Jewish rescuers of Jews in Belgium and France, see Lucien Steinberg, "Jewish Rescue Activities in Belgium and France," *Rescue Attempts During the Holocaust* (Jerusalem: Yad Vashem, 1977), 603–15; and Susan Zuccotti, *The Holocaust, the French and the Jews* (New York: Basic Books, 1993).

12. For these claims about Italy, see Blet, *Pius XII and the Second World War;* Alberto Giovannetti, "Storia, teatro e storie," *L'Osservatore Romano,* April 5, 1963, 3; Robert A. Graham, S.J., "Relations of Pius XII and the Catholic Community with Jewish Organizations," in Ivo Herzer, ed., *The Italian Refuge: Rescue of Jews During the Holocaust* (Washington, D.C.: Catholic University of America Press, 1989), 231–53; Lapide, *Last Three Popes and the Jews,* 127–38 and 256–66; Robert Leiber, S.J., "Pio XII e gli ebrei di Roma, 1943–1944," *La Civiltà Cattolica,* anno 112, 1961, vol. I, quad. 2657, March 4, 1961, 449–58; Lichten, "Question of Judgment," 119–27; Margherita Marchione, *Yours Is a Precious Witness: Memoirs of Jews and Catholics in Wartime Italy* and *Pope Pius XII: Architect for Peace* Mahwah, N.J.: Paulist Press, 1997 and 2000); Meir Michaelis, *Mussolini and the Jews: German-Italian Relations and the Jewish Question in Italy, 1922–1945* (Oxford: Clarendon, 1978), 364; and Rhodes, *Vatican in the Age of the Dictators,* 340–41. Léon Poliakov, "The Vatican and the 'Jewish Question,' " *Commentary,* November 1950, 439–49, goes even further, alleging that instructions to help Jews went out from the Vatican to all national churches.

13. Michael Tagliacozzo, "Ebrei refugiati nelle zone extraterritoriali del Vaticano," memorandum to Meir Michaelis, June 16, 1975, cited in Michaelis, "Italy," in David S. Wyman, ed., *The World Reacts to the Holocaust* (Baltimore: Johns Hopkins University Press, 1996), 545.

14. For the statistic regarding Jews, see Liliana Picciotto Fargion, *Il Libro della memoria* (Milan: Mursia, 1991), 793 and 805–6. See also Chapter Eleven, footnote 10.

15. For more on the Lateran Accords, see Chapter One.

16. Chadwick, *Britain and the Vatican,* 187. Pius XII tried to bring more non-Italians into the bureaucracy, but in 1961, 76 percent of the officials at the Secretariat of State, 80 percent of the professional staff of all the congregations, including typists and technicians, and 91 percent of the cardinal prefects who headed the congregations were still Italians. Also Italians, as late as 1967, were 95 percent of the so-called secretaries who directed the operations of the congregations. Diversity has increased substantially since then. For statistics from the 1960s, see Thomas J. Reese, *Inside the Vatican: The Politics and Organization of the Catholic Church* (Cambridge: Harvard University Press, 1996), 141 and 147.

17. The play opened in Berlin on February 20, 1963, and in London, translated as *The Representative,* on September 25. With the title *The Deputy* it had its American premiere in New York on February 26, 1964. For responses to the play, see especially Eric Bentley, ed., *The Storm Over "The Deputy"* (New York: Grove, 1964); *Commonweal,* February 28, 1964, 647–62; Fritz J. Raddatz, ed., *Summa iniuria oder durfte der Papst schweigen?: Hochhuths "Stellvertreter" in der öffentlichen Kritik* (Reinbek bei Hamburg: Rowohlt, 1963); and *Der Streit um den Stellvertreter* (Basel: Basilius, 1963).

18. *Actes et Documents du Saint Siège relatifs à la seconde guerre mondiale* (ADSS), eds. Pierre Blet, Robert A. Graham, Angelo Martini, and Burkhart Schneider, 11 vols. (Vatican City: Libreria Editrice Vaticana, 1965–81). Father Graham is not listed

as an editor in the early volumes, and Fathers Martini and Schneider died before the project ended.

19. Montini also held the untranslatable title of "Sostituto." The two positions were roughly equal in importance. For details, see Morley, *Vatican Diplomacy and the Jews*, 1–17; Emile Poulat, *L'Eglise c'est un monde: L'Ecclésiosphère* (Paris: Cerf, 1986); Reese, *Inside the Vatican;* and Andrea Riccardi, *Il Potere del Papa da Pio XII a Paolo VI* (Rome: Laterza, 1988).

20. David Alvarez and Robert A. Graham, S.J., *Nothing Sacred: Nazi Espionage Against the Vatican, 1939–1945* (London: Frank Cass, 1997), 177.

CHAPTER ONE: THE VATICAN AND ANTI-SEMITISM

1. See "Cronaca contemporanea," *La Civiltà Cattolica*, anno 79, 1928, vol. II, April 21, 1928, 171–72, 171. The function of the Holy Office was the preservation of authentic Catholic teaching and the ferreting out of heresy and error. In 1965 it was renamed the Congregation for the Doctrine of the Faith, but its original purpose did not change.

2. Ibid.

3. "Il Pericolo Giudaico e gli 'Amici d'Israele,' " *La Civiltà Cattolica*, anno 79, 1928, vol. II, May 19, 1928, 335–44, 344. It will be recalled that until it was removed by the Second Vatican Council in 1965, the sacred liturgy included a reference to the "perfidious Jews." Offering a slightly different explanation for the dissolution of Friends of Israel, Antonio Spinosa suggested that the organization fell out of favor because it instituted a special Catholic rite in Hebrew. See his "Le Persecuzioni razziali in Italia," part 2: "L'Atteggiamento della chiesa," *Il Ponte* VIII (8), August 1952, 1078–96, 1081.

4. "Il Pericolo Giudaica e gli 'Amici d'Israele,' " 338–39.

5. Ibid., 339–40.

6. Ibid., 340.

7. Ibid., 343.

8. In almost the only significant exception, Spanish Jewish converts to Catholicism and their descendants for several generations in the sixteenth century were denied rights equal to those of Catholics with no Jewish lineage.

9. These distinctions are often made through the use of the terms racial anti-Semitism, religious anti-Semitism, and political, economic, or social anti-Semitism. Of course one type of anti-Semitism often feeds on the others.

10. Giovanni Miccoli, "Santa Sede e Chiesa italiana di fronte alle leggi antiebraiche del 1938," *La legislazione antiebraica in Italia e in Europa: Atti del Convegno nel cinquantenario delle leggi razziali (Roma, 17–18 ottobre 1988)* (Rome: Camera dei deputati, 1989), 163–274, 168.

11. Richard A. Webster, *The Cross and the Fasces: Christian Democracy and Fascism in Italy* (Stanford: Stanford University Press, 1960), 126.

12. Andrea Riccardi, *Il Potere del Papa da Pio XII a Paolo VI* (Rome: Laterza, 1988), 65.

13. Not all Jesuits in the 1930s shared the anti-Jewish views of the conservative

editors of *La Civiltà Cattolica*. On the contrary, many young Jesuit priests, especially in France and northern Italy, were exploring new channels of Catholic-Jewish dialogue and accommodation. Their efforts would bear fruit in the postwar period.

14. E. Rosa, " 'La questione giudaica' e l'antisemitismo nazionalsocialista," *La Civiltà Cattolica*, anno 85, 1934, vol. IV, quad. 2024, October 20, 1934, 126–36, 136.

15. Ibid., quad. 2025, November 3, 1934, 276–85.

16. "La questione giudaica," *La Civiltà Cattolica*, anno 87, 1936, vol. IV, quad. 2071, October 3, 1936, 37–46, 43. The book under review was Léon de Poncins, *La mystérieuse Internationale juive* (Paris: G. Beauchesne, 1936).

17. "La Questione giudaica e il sionismo," *La Civiltà Cattolica*, anno 88, 1937, vol. II, quad. 2087, June 5, 1937, 418–31, 418. Joseph Hilaire Pierre Belloc (1870–1953), a French-born Catholic, became a British citizen in 1902. The author of many histories and novels, he also sat in the House of Commons from 1906 to 1910. His 308-page book *The Jews* was originally published by Constable in London and Houghton Mifflin in Boston in 1922. Both publishing companies reissued the book in 1937.

18. Ibid.

19. Ibid., 419.

20. Ibid, 429–30. The book under review was published in Paris in 1937 by Perrin.

21. Ibid., 430–31.

22. "La questione guidaica e le conversioni," *La Civiltà Cattolica*, anno 88, 1937, vol. II, quad. 2088, June 1937, 497–510; and "La questione giudaica e l'apostolato cattolico," *La Civiltà Cattolica*, anno 88, 1937, vol. III, quad. 2089, July 3, 1937, 27–39.

23. "La questione giudaica e l'apostolato cattolico," 39.

24. Romagna, Umbria, and the Marches became part of the new Kingdom of Italy in 1860, but Rome was not acquired until 1870.

25. M. Barbera, "Mito razzista anticristiano," *La Civiltà Cattolica*, anno 85, 1934, vol. I, quad. 2007, February 3, 1934, 238–49, 249.

26. U. Lopez, "Difesa della razza ed etica cristiana," *La Civiltà Cattolica*, anno 85, 1934, vol. I, quad. 2010, March 17, 1934, 574–87.

27. Ibid., vol. II, quad. 2011, April 7, 1934, 27–42, 27.

28. M. Barbera, "Giustizia tra le 'razze,' " *La Civiltà Cattolica*, anno 88, 1937, vol. IV, quad. 2100, December 18, 1937, 531–38, 534.

29. By the 1930s and 1940s in Italy the term Don was used primarily to refer to a priest in the secular clergy. It could be attached familiarly to a first name or more formally to a last name, as, in this case, Don Minzoni. The term Padre usually designated a priest of the regular clergy, a member of a religious order who had been ordained. A member of a religious order who was not ordained was usually called a brother. I have translated "Padre," but "Don" is not translatable, and it remains. I have capitalized it according to English usage, but it is usually not capitalized in Italian.

30. Anthony Rhodes, *The Vatican in the Age of the Dictators (1922–1945)* (New York: Holt, Rinehart and Winston, 1973), 31.

31. For discussion of the demise of the Popolari, see Webster, *Cross and the Fasces*, 78–106.

32. For the text of the Lateran Accords, see Sidney Z. Ehler and John B. Morrall, eds., *Church and State Through the Centuries: A Collection of Historic Documents with Commentaries* (London: Burns and Oates, 1954), 382–407. See also D. A. Binchy, *Church and State in Fascist Italy* (1941; London: Oxford University Press, 1970); and Rhodes, *Vatican in the Age of Dictators*, 37–52.

33. The pope's Christmas message of 1930 is printed in full in *L'Osservatore Romano*, December 25, 1930, 1; and *La Civiltà Cattolica*, anno 82, 1931, vol. I, January 3, 1931, 3–9.

34. The encyclical is printed in full in *The Papal Encyclicals*, Claudia Carlen Ihm, ed., vol. III: 1903–1939 (Raleigh, N.C.: McGrath, 1981), 445–58. The quotations are from paragraphs numbered 11 and 62. According to Michael Glazier and Monika K. Hellwig, eds., *The Modern Catholic Encyclopedia* (Collegeville, Minn.: Liturgical Press, 1994), 279–80, "Encyclicals are circular letters written by the pope to convey timely teachings on matters of faith and morals. . . . Only if the pope clearly expresses that he is defining 'ex cathedra' is the encyclical an exercise of his solemn and infallible magisterium." Encyclicals can be doctrinal or social.

35. *Non abbiamo bisogno*, in *Papal Encyclicals*, 445–58. Quotations are from paragraphs 44 and 59.

36. For analysis of Vatican objectives and negotiations to secure a concordat with Germany, see John Cornwell, *Hitler's Pope: The Secret History of Pius XII* (New York: Viking, 1999); and Rhodes, *Vatican in the Age of the Dictators*, 173–83.

37. Daniel Carpi, "The Catholic Church and Italian Jewry Under the Fascists (To the Death of Pius XI)," *Yad Vashem Studies* IV, 1960, 54, referred to "this courageous stand by Pius XI against the principles of racialism." Rhodes, *Vatican in the Age of Dictators*, 204, called the encyclical "one of the greatest condemnations of a national regime ever pronounced by the Vatican."

38. *Mit brennender Sorge*, in *Papal Encyclicals*, 525–36, paragraph 5.

39. Ibid., paragraph 17.

40. Ibid.

41. Ibid., paragraph 15.

42. Ibid., paragraph 14.

43. *Divini Redemptoris*, in *Papal Encyclicals*, 537–54. Quotations are from paragraphs 4, 7, 8, and 20.

44. See "Lettera Enciclica di S.S. Pio XI 'del comunismo ateo,' " 3–18, and G. Ledit, "La nuova condanna del comunismo," 19–32, both in anno 88, 1937, vol. II, quad. 2083, April 3, 1937, and "Lettera Enciclica di S.S. Pio XI 'del comunismo ateo,' " 97–113, and A. Brucculeri, "Roma e Mosca nell'Enciclica *Divini redemptoris*," 114–25, in anno 88, 1937, vol. II, quad 2084, April 17, 1937. The encyclical itself mentioned (p. 538) that some aspect of Communism had been

condemned in five other encyclicals by Pius XI, three of his allocutions, and his Christmas message of 1936, as well as in two encyclicals by previous popes.

45. "Lettera Enciclica di SS Pio XI sulle condizioni della Chiesa cattolica nel Reich germanico," 193–216; and A. Messineo, "La via dolorosa della Chiesa in Germania," 217–30, in anno 88, vol. II, quad. 2085, May 1, 1937.

46. Messineo, "La via dolorosa," 217.

47. Michele Sarfatti, *Gli ebrei nell'Italia fascista: Vicende, identità, persecuzione* (Turin: Einaudi, 2000), 16. Actual marriage between Italian citizens and black African "subjects" in the colonies was not prohibited until November 1938, when the racial laws banned marriage between Italian "Aryans" and all other races. Sarfatti suggests that in 1937 the government was not yet prepared to rescind its agreement with the Holy See, as stated in the religious concordat of the Lateran Accords in 1929, to recognize and register all marriages performed in accordance with canon law. As will be seen, the Church endorsed interracial marriages as long as both parties were Catholics or certain other criteria were met.

48. E. Rosa, "Cattolicismo e Nazismo: Idee chiare e pericolosi equivoci," *L'Osservatore Romano*, June 10, 1938, 2. The emphasis is mine.

49. ADSS, I, doc. 315, note 1, 456; and Philip V. Cannistraro, "Press," entry in Cannistraro, ed., *Historical Dictionary of Fascist Italy* (Westport, Conn.: Greenwood, 1982), 440.

CHAPTER TWO: THE VATICAN AND ANTI-SEMITISM IN ITALY

1. Benito Mussolini, *Opera omnia,* Edoardo and Duilio Susmel, eds., vol. XXIX (Florence: La Fenice, 1959), 494–95. The statement was originally printed in *Informazione diplomatica,* n. 14, an official news bulletin intended to make government positions known in Italy and abroad. According to a special census in August 1938, there were 47,252 Italian Jews and 10,173 foreign Jews in the country. Jews represented about one-tenth of 1 percent of the general population. For the statistics, see Renzo De Felice, *Storia degli ebrei italiani sotto il fascismo* (1961; Turin:einaudi, 1988), 6–10.

2. Michele Sarfatti, *Mussolini contro gli ebrei: Cronaca dell'elaborazione delle leggi del 1938* (Milan: Silvio Zamorani, 1994), 17–18. For more on the evolution of an official anti-Jewish position in Italy prior to the racial laws, see Michele Sarfatti, *Gli ebrei nell'Italia fascista: Vicende, identità, persecuzione* (Turin: Einaudi, 2000), 120–37.

3. Sarfatti, *Mussolini contro gli ebrei,* 18–20. The authors were not originally identified. When their names were publicized several days later, they turned out to be, with one exception, little known. See Antonio Spinosa, "Le Persecuzioni razziali in Italia," part 2: "Atteggiamento della chiesa," *Il Ponte* VIII (8), August 1952, 1078–96, 1080; and Salvatore Jona, "Contributo allo studio degli ebrei in Italia durante il fascismo," *Gli Ebrei in Italia durante il fascismo: Quaderni del Centro di Documentazione Ebraica Contemporanea* II, March 1962, 7–31, 19.

4. From the text of the manifesto, in Sarfatti, *Mussolini contro gli ebrei,* 18–20.

5. Ibid., 19.

6. Ibid., 20.

7. *Opera omnia*, vol. XXIX, 497–98. The announcement, released in *L'Informazione diplomatica*, n. 18, was carried in major Italian newspapers the following day.

8. The speech is printed in *L'Osservatore Romano*, December 25, 1937, 1; and "Cronaca contemporanea," *La Civiltà Cattolica*, anno 89, 1938, vol. I, quad. 2102, January 15, 1938, 179–83.

9. The letter was published in full, but without comment, in "Cronaca contemporanea," *La Civiltà Cattolica*, anno 89, 1938, vol. III, quad. 2113, July 2, 1938, 83–84.

10. "Esemplificazioni di teorie razziste," *L'Osservatore Romano*, April 30, 1938, 2. Authorship was indicated only by the letter "V." The article addressed recent German racist publications alleging that the Nordic race excelled in specific characteristics, including discernment, energy, sincerity, responsibility, conscientiousness, and will power. The German publications distinguished between the Nordic and Mediterranean races and found the latter only partially distinct from the people of northern Africa. The Italian Manifesto of the Racial Scientists would refute these claims on July 14.

11. "Il Santo Padre a Castel Gandolfo," *L'Osservatore Romano*, May 2–3, 1938, 1. Pinchas E. Lapide, *The Last Three Popes and the Jews* (London: Souvenir, 1967), 113, erred when he wrote that this particular issue of *L'Osservatore Romano*, which appeared during Hitler's visit, published Pius XI's entire letter of April 13 against racism.

12. M. Barbera, "La Questione dei giudei in Ungheria," *La Civiltà Cattolica*, anno 89, 1938, vol. III, quad. 2114, July 16, 1938, 146–53.

13. Ibid., 149.

14. Ibid., 151.

15. Ibid., 152.

16. For more on the encyclical, see Michael Marrus, "The Vatican on Racism and Antisemitism, 1938–39: A New Look at a Might-Have-Been," *Holocaust and Genocide Studies* 11 (3), Winter 1997, 378–95; Giovanni Miccoli, "L'Enciclica mancata di Pio XI sul razzismo e l'antisemitismo," *Passato e presente* XV (40), 1997, 35–54; Georges Passelecq and Bernard Suchecky, *The Hidden Encyclical of Pius XI*, trans. from French by Steven Rendall (New York: Harcourt Brace, 1997); and Garry Wills, *Papal Sins: Structures of Deceit* (New York: Doubleday, 2000), 29–40. One of the Jesuits responsible for the first draft was Father John LaFarge, whose work on behalf of African Americans in the South had been praised in *La Civiltà Cattolica* in 1937. The other two were Gustav Gundlach, a German, and Gustave Desbuquois, French.

17. From one version of a draft of the encyclical, entitled *Humani generis unitas*, printed in full in Passelecq and Suchecky, *Hidden Encyclical*, 176–275.

18. Ibid., article by Johannes H. Nota, S.J., quoted on p. 12.

19. "Rapporti fra l'apostolato missionario e le vocazioni religiose—Errori e pericoli

del nazionalismo esagerato," in *L'Osservatore Romano*, July 17, 1938, 1. Printed also in "Cronaca contemporanea," *La Civiltà Cattolica*, anno 89, 1938, vol. III, quad. 2115, August 6, 1938, 269–70.

20. Lapide, *Last Three Popes and the Jews*, 95, not only described Pius XI's message incorrectly but also confused the assembly of July 15 with an audience on July 28. Lapide continually ignored differences between racism and anti-Judaism, as perceived by the Church. Passelecq and Suchecky, *Hidden Encyclical*, xix, also exaggerate when they refer to "a series of . . . attacks [by Pius XI] on the anti-Jewish laws, given to different groups in the summer of 1938."

21. *L'Osservatore Romano*, July 17, 1938, 1.

22. Ibid.

23. "Il fascismo e i problemi della razza," *L'Osservatore Romano*, July 16, 1938, 2.

24. A. Brucculeri, "Razzismo italiano," *L'Avvenire*, July 17, 1938, quoted in De Felice, *Storia degli ebrei italiani*, 293.

25. "La parola di Sua Santità agli Assistenti Ecclesiastici della Gioventù di Azione Cattolica," *L'Osservatore Romano*, July 23, 1938, 1. See also "Cronaca contemporanea," *La Civiltà Cattolica*, anno 89, 1938, vol. III, quad. 2115, August 6, 1938, 271.

26. "La parola del Sommo Pontefice Pio XI agli alunni del Collegio di Propaganda Fide," *L'Osservatore Romano*, July 30, 1938, 1. See also "Cronaca contemporanea," *La Civiltà Cattolica*, anno 89, 1938, vol. III, quad. 2116, August 20, 1938, 371–75.

27. *L'Osservatore Romano*, July 30, 1938, 1.

28. In a speech in Forlí on July 30, for example, he told his audience, "You and everyone else know that even in racial matters we will march straight ahead. To say that Fascism has imitated anyone or anything is simply absurd." In Trieste on September 18, he again referred to the "racial problem," and added, "Those who claim that we are adhering to imitations, or, worse, suggestions are poor defectives whom we don't know whether to disdain or pity." See *Opera omnia*, vol. XXIX, 126 and 146. For the response of Trieste's Bishop Antonio Santin, see Chapter Nineteen.

29. Angelo Martini, "L'Ultima battaglia di Pio XI," *La Civiltà Cattolica*, anno 110, vol. II, quad. 2626, June 20, 1959, 574–91, 580.

30. Galeazzo Ciano, *Diario 1937–1938* (Bologna: Cappelli, 1948), entry for July 30, 1938, 216. Ciano was Mussolini's son-in-law.

31. A. Messineo, "Gli elementi costitutivi della nazione e la razza," *La Civiltà Cattolica*, anno 89, 1938, vol. III, quad. 2115, August 6, 1938, 209–23, and "Intorno alla 'nazionalità,' " *L'Osservatore Romano*, August 13, 1938, 2.

32. "Cronaca contemporanea," *La Civiltà Cattolica*, anno 89, 1938, vol. III, quad. 2115, August 6, 1938, 275–78.

33. "Una precisazione sul 'razzismo italiano,' " *L'Osservatore Romano*, August 7, 1938, 6.

34. Ciano, *Diario*, August 8, 1938, 217.

35. Ibid., August 9, 1938, 217.

36. For Pius XI's determination to defend Catholic Action, see his speech to a group of its leaders in *L'Osservatore Romano*, September 25, 1938, 1.

37. ADSS, VI, appendix 3, notes of the Secretariat of State (summarizing steps taken since July), November 14, 1938, 532.

38. "Una citazione berlinese," *L'Osservatore Romano*, August 12, 1938, 1.

39. Father Francesco Capponi, "Gli Ebrei ed il Concilio Vaticano," *L'Osservatore Romano*, August 14, 1938, 2.

40. Ibid.

41. See David I. Kertzer, *The Kidnapping of Edgardo Mortara* (New York: Knopf, 1997).

42. This memorandum was first published in 1959 by Angelo Martini, a Jesuit priest, in his "L'Ultima battaglia di Pio XI," 582. It is reproduced and discussed in Sarfatti, *Mussolini contro gli ebrei*, 25–28; and Giovanni Miccoli, "Santa Sede e Chiesa italiana di fronte alle leggi antiebraiche del 1938," *Legislazione antiebraica in Italia e in Europa. Atti del Convegno nel cinquantenario delle leggi razziali: Roma: 17–18 ottobre 1988* (Rome: Camera dei deputati, 1989), 185–87.

43. "Una visita di Sua Santità al Collegio di Propaganda Fide," *L'Osservatore Romano*, August 22–23, 1938, 1. See also "Cronaca contemporanea," *La Civiltà Cattolica*, anno 89, 1938, vol. III, quad. 2117, September 3, 1938, 464–65. In his diary, August 22, p. 223, Ciano wrote, "It seems that the pope gave another unpleasant speech yesterday on exaggerated nationalism and racism." Spinosa, "Persecuzione razziale," 1084, also wrote that the pope had attacked racism. The pope's actual words, as print d in *L'Osservatore Romano*, do not show that to be the case.

44. "Cronaca contemporanea," *La Civiltà Cattolica*, anno 89, 1938, vol. III, quad. 2117, September 3, 1939, 464–65.

CHAPTER THREE: ITALIAN ANTI-JEWISH LAWS
DURING THE PAPACY OF PIUS XI

1. The decree was published in the *Gazzetta ufficiale del Regno d'Italia* on September 13. It is printed in full in Michele Sarfatti, *Mussolini contro gli ebrei: Cronaca dell'elaborazione delle leggi del 1938* (Turin: Silvio Zamorani, 1994), 186. A measure passed on November 15 required elementary schools with more than ten Jewish pupils to establish separate sections and facilities for them. Secondary schools had no such obligation, but individual Jewish Communities could organize their own schools if they wished. Jewish students could prepare for and take government examinations, but always separately from non-Jewish students. See Sarfatti, 195–97.

2. See, for example, Adriana Muncinelli, *Even: Pietruzza della memoria: Ebrei 1938–1945* (Turin: Abele, 1994). The author studied the responses of educational administrators in the province of Cuneo and found that they diligently listed for dismissal not only all people with Jewish-sounding names but also many with strange or unusual, and thus "suspect," names, without checking for religious affiliations.

3. The decree was published in the *Gazzetta ufficiale* on September 12. See Sarfatti, *Mussolini contro gli ebrei*, 185. On November 17, 1938, another measure declared that foreign Jews over the age of sixty-five or married to Italian citizens before October 1, 1938, could, upon immediate application, be allowed to remain in the country.

4. Ibid., 38–39, for quotations from Mussolini's speech referring to Jews.

5. Ibid., 187–89, for the text of the declaration.

6. The decrees were published in the *Gazzetta ufficiale* on November 19, 1938. They may be found in Sarfatti, *Mussolini contro gli ebrei*, 190–94; and Renzo De Felice, *Storia degli ebrei italiani sotto il fascismo* (1961; Turin: Einaudi, 1988), 576–80.

7. For details, see Michele Sarfatti, *Gli ebrei nell'Italia fascista: Vicende, identità, persecuzione* (Turin: Einaudi, 2000), 187–200 and 270–71; and Susan Zuccotti, "The Italian Racial Laws, 1938–1943: A Reevaluation," in Jonathan Frankel, ed., *The Fate of the European Jews, 1939–1945: Continuity or Contingency? Studies in Contemporary Jewry* XIII (New York: Oxford University Press, 1997), 133–52.

8. Subsequent measures permitted the baptism at birth of the children of mixed marriages born after the onset of the anti-Jewish laws. For details, see Sarfatti, *Gli ebrei nell'Italia fascista*, 154–64.

9. Michele Sarfatti, "Documenti della legislazione antiebraica: Le circolari," *La Rassegna mensile di Israel* LIV (1–2), 169–98.

10. From *La Libre Belgique*, September 14, 1938, quoted in Alberto Cavaglion and Gian Paolo Romagnani, *Le interdizioni del Duce: A cinquant'anni dalle leggi razziali in Italia (1938–1988)* (Turin: Albert Meynier, 1988), 130–31.

11. "Il paterno elogio di Sua Santità ai pellegrini della Gioventù Cattolica del Belgio," *L'Osservatore Romano*, September 9, 1938, 1.

12. The speech's publication history is described in Cavaglion and Romagnani, *Le interdizioni del Duce*, 127–31; and Giovanni Miccoli, "Santa Sede e Chiesa italiana di fronte alle leggi antiebraiche del 1938," *Legislazione antiebraica in Italia e in Europa; Atti del Convegno nel cinquantenario delle leggi razziali: Roma: 17–18 ottobre 1988* (Rome: Camera dei deputati, 1989), 211–12, and same author, "Santa Sede, questione ebraica e antisemitismo fra Otto e Novecento," *Gli Ebrei in Italia*, C. Vivanti, ed. (Turin: Einaudi, 1997), 1372–1574, 1570.

13. "Luminose parole del Santo Padre ad insegnanti di Azione Cattolica," *L'Osservatore Romano*, September 8, 1938, 1.

14. "Cronaca contemporanea," *La Civiltà Cattolica*, anno 89, 1938, vol. III, quad. 2118, September 17, 1938, 557–60.

15. "Un tremendo atto d'accusa," *Il Regime fascista*, August 30, 1938.

16. The three articles in *La Civiltà Cattolica* were "Della questione giudaica in Europa," anno 41, serie XIV, vol. VIII: "Le Cause," quad. 967, October 4, 1890, 5–20; "Gli Effetti," quad. 970, November 15, 1890, 385–407; and "I Rimedii," quad. 972, December 20, 1890, 641–55.

17. Article on December 20, 1890, 648.

18. Ibid., 646.

19. Ibid., 654.

20. "Sfogliando i giornali," *L'Osservatore Romano*, 2.

21. The responses in *La Civiltà Cattolica* were "Cronaca contemporanea," anno 89, 1938, vol. III, quad. 2118, September 17, 1938, 560–61; and E. Rosa, "La Questione giudaica e 'La Civiltà Cattolica,' " anno 89, 1938, vol. IV, quad, 2119, October 1, 1938, 3–16.

22. Articles on September 17, 1938, 561; and October 1, 1938, 10.

23. Article on December 20, 1890, 648, for the original claim; October 1, 1938, 8, for the confirmation.

24. Article on October 1, 1938, 9.

25. Ibid.

26. A. Messineo, "L'Ordine giuridico nella nuova Germania," *La Civiltà Cattolica*, anno 89, 1938, vol. III, quad. 2118, September 17, 1938, 506–19.

27. Ibid., 519.

28. Angelo Martini, "L'Ultima battaglia di Pio XI," *La Civiltà Cattolica*, anno 110, vol. II, quad. 2626, June 20, 1959, 574–91, 589.

29. Ciano quoted the ambassador at length in his own report to several Italian cabinet members on October 10, 1938. Ciano's report is printed in full in Renzo De Felice, *Storia degli ebrei italiani sotto il fascismo* (1961; Turin: Einaudi, 1988), 561–62.

30. "Cronache italiane: Le deliberazioni del Gran Consiglio," *L'Osservatore Romano*, October 8, 1938, 6. *La Civiltà Cattolica* also published the declaration in full but without comment in "Cronaca contemporanea," anno 89, 1938, vol. IV, quad. 2121, November 5, 1938, 269–71.

31. The few exceptions regarded individuals already married to others in civil ceremonies and cases of mental illness. The religious concordat also precluded the option of civil marriage for Catholics in Italy, in effect making religious marriages mandatory for them.

32. Parts of this document are printed in Martini, "L'Ultima battaglia di Pio XI," 588.

33. They had already become more difficult to obtain. As the Italian ambassador to the Holy See reported on October 7, "Instructions have recently been given to the bishops to make the principle prohibiting mixed marriages still more severe and to urge the bishops to use every possible means to avoid them." See Ciano's report to cabinet ministers, October 10, 1938, in De Felice, *Storia degli ebrei italiani*, 561–62.

34. Martini, "L'Ultima battaglia di Pio XI," 588.

35. ADSS, VI, Appendice 3, notes of the Secretariat of State, November 14, 1938, 532–36.

36. See drafts in Glauco Buffarini Guidi, *La vera verità: I documenti dell'archivio segreto del ministro degli Interni Guido Buffarini Guidi dal 1938 al 1945* (Milan: Sugar, 1970), 26–29, and analysis in Sarfatti, *Mussolini contro gli ebrei*, 48–53.

37. The letters are printed in full in De Felice, *Storia degli ebrei italiani*, 564–65.

38. Ibid., 566.

39. See the report in Ciano's report, October 10, 1938, in De Felice, *Storia degli ebrei italiani*, 561.

40. The memorandum is printed in full in Buffarini Guidi, *La vera verità*, 25–26.

41. Sarfatti, *Mussolini contro gli ebrei*, 50.

42. About 4,000 people disassociated themselves from the Jewish Community, but not all of that number became Catholics. See De Felice, *Storia degli ebrei in Italia*, 334.

43. Quoted in another report from Ciano to various cabinet ministers, October 13, 1938, printed in De Felice, *Storia degli ebrei italiani*, 563.

44. "A proposito di un nuovo Decreto Legge," *L'Osservatore Romano*, November 14–15, 1938, 1. This article was reprinted in "Cronaca contemporanea," *La Civiltà Cattolica*, anno 89, 1938, vol. IV, quad. 2123, December 3, 1938, 471–74. Like the Vatican newspaper, the Jesuit journal never printed the full content of the anti-Jewish laws or editorialized against them. It did publish a brief description of the November laws, in the same "Cronaca contemporanea" column, December 3, 1938, 474–75. It announced new property measures against Jews in anno 90, 1939, vol. I, quad. 2125, January 7, 1939, 91; and new measures against Jewish professionals in anno 90, 1939, vol. II, quad. 2135, June 3, 1939, 475–76.

45. "Ancora a proposito di un nuovo Decreto Legge," *L'Osservatore Romano*, November 16, 1938, 1.

46. See articles, for example, on November 17, 1938, 1; November 19, 1; November 20, 6; November 23, 1; November 24, 6; November 25, 2; and November 26, 2 and 6.

47. "Un'Omelia dell'Em.mo Cardinale Schuster nella prima domenica dell'Avvento ambrosiano," *L'Osservatore Romano*, November 18, 1938, 2.

48. For the text of the speech, see "Sollecitudini afflizioni speranze nella commossa parola del Padre," *L'Osservatore Romano*, 1; and "Allocuzione natalizia del Santo Padre," *La Civiltà Cattolica*, anno 90, 1939, vol. I, quad. 2125, January 7, 1939, 83–86.

49. "Ostracismi," *L'Osservatore Romano*, December 12–13, 1938, 6.

50. "Un'omelia del Vescovo di Cremona: La chiesa e gli ebrei," *L'Osservatore Romano*, January 15, 1939, 2.

51. Bérard's report is quoted in Léon Poliakov, *Harvest of Hate: The Nazi Program for the Destruction of the Jews of Europe* (Paris: Calmann-Lévy, 1951; rpt. New York: Holocaust Publications, 1986), 297–98. It was first published in *Le Monde juif*, n. 2, October 1946.

52. ADSS, VIII, doc. 165, papal nuncio in France to Maglione, September 30, 1941, 295–97; and doc. 189, Maglione to papal nuncio in France, October 31, 1941, 333–34.

53. Ibid., doc. 189, 334.

54. Ibid., doc. 165, attached note of Maglione, 297.

55. Ibid., IX, doc. 317, Tacchi Venturi to Maglione, August 29, 1943, 458–59, 459.

56. Ibid., VI, doc. 125, footnote 2, Sheil to directors of the United Jewish Appeal, December 29, 1938, 211–212. For how the money was used, see Chapter Five.

CHAPTER FOUR: ITALIAN ANTI-JEWISH LAWS DURING
THE PAPACY OF PIUS XII

1. Forty-two votes from a total of sixty-two were necessary to elect a pope. Pacelli
was not elected unanimously, as reported as the time. For description of the
secret conclave and the rumors that surrounded it, see Owen Chadwick, *Britain
and the Vatican During the Second World War* (Cambridge: Cambridge University
Press, 1986), 30–56; and François Charles-Roux, *Huit Ans au Vatican: 1932–1940*
(Paris: Flammarion, 1947).

2. John Cornwell, *Hitler's Pope: The Secret History of Pius XII* (New York: Viking,
1999), 9–14 and 114; and Anthony Rhodes, *The Vatican in the Age of Dictators
(1922–1945)* (New York: Holt, Rinehart and Winston, 1973), 219. Pacelli's
grandfather Eugenio was among the founders of *L'Osservatore Romano;* his
father Filippo was a canon lawyer who, among other things, served in the
Tribunal of the Sacred Rota and examined cases for beatification. His brother
Francesco, also a lawyer, helped the Vatican in the drafting and negotiation of
the Lateran Accords.

3. Notes of Monsignor Domenico Tardini, secretary of the Section for Extraordinary
Ecclesiastical Affairs since 1937, written on February 22, 1939, and quoted in
ADSS, I, Introduction, 5. Tardini claimed that Pius XI told him that Pacelli "will
be a fine pope!" See also Charles-Roux, *Huit Ans au Vatican*, 260; and Domenico
Tardini, *Pio XII* (Vatican City: Libreria Editrice Vaticano, 1960), 105.

4. The institutions included the Almo Collegio Capranica, the Università
Gregoriana, and the exclusive Accademia dei Nobili Ecclesiastici, which invited
only students from or closely associated with the papal nobility to attend. See
Andrea Riccardi, *Il Potere del Papa da Pio XII a Paolo VI* (Rome: Laterza, 1988),
31–61, 33.

5. Cardinal G. B. Montini, "Pius XII and the Jews," letter to *The Tablet,* received on
June 21, 1963, and published on July 6; reprinted in Eric Bentley, ed., *The Storm
Over "The Deputy"* (New York: Grove, 1964), 66–69; and *Commonweal*, February
28, 1964, 651–52.

6. Wladimir d'Ormesson, *De Saint-Pétersbourg à Rome* (Paris: Plon, 1969), 196.

7. Albrecht von Kessel, "The Pope and the Jews," originally published in *Die Welt,*
Hamburg, April 6, 1963; reprinted in Bentley, *Storm Over "The Deputy,"* 71–76.

8. Osborne, letter to *The Times,* London, May 20, 1963, 7.

9. Tardini, *Pio XII,* 39, 69, 79. Sister Pasqualina also described a pope who fasted
and wept for the suffering of humanity in her memoirs, *Ich durfte Ihm dienen:
Erinnerungen an Papst Pius XII* (Würzburg: Naumann, 1983).

10. Aryeh L. Kubovy, "The Silence of Pope Pius XII and the Beginnings of the 'Jewish
Document,' " *Yad Vashem Studies* VI, 1967, 7–25, 15. The words are Kubovy's,
who recorded in a memorandum on June 9, 1944, what Morleon had told him.

11. See the report of François Charles-Roux, quoted in Chadwick, *Britain and the
Vatican,* 43.

12. Ibid., 48, from a report from Sir Robert Vansittart of the British Foreign Office to
British Foreign Minister Lord Halifax.

13. Quoted in Owen Chadwick, "Weizsäcker, the Vatican, and the Jews of Rome," *Journal of Ecclesiastical History* 28 (2), April 1977, 179–99, 182.

14. Robert Leiber, S.J., "Pius XII," originally published in *Stimmen der Zeit*, November 1958; reprinted in Bentley, *Storm Over "The Deputy*,*"* 173–95.

15. Carlo Falconi, *The Silence of Pius XII*, trans. Bernard Wall (1965 in France and Italy; Boston: Little, Brown, 1970), 85.

16. For information about this work, see the introduction to this book.

17. Malachi Martin, *Three Popes and the Cardinal* (New York: Farrar, Straus and Giroux, 1972), 6 and 175.

18. Guenter Lewy, *The Catholic Church and Nazi Germany* (New York: McGraw-Hill, 1964), 297.

19. John S. Conway, "The Silence of Pope Pius XII," in Charles F. Delzell, ed., *The Papacy and Totalitarianism Between the Two World Wars* (New York: Wiley, 1974), 79–108, 83.

20. Riccardi, *Il Potere del Papa*, 40.

21. Chadwick, *Britain and the Vatican*, 50.

22. For a detailed description of Pius XII's efforts for peace in 1939, see especially ADSS, I, Introduction, 3–45; and, based on ADSS, Pierre Blet, S.J., *Pius XII and the Second World War: According to the Archives of the Vatican*, trans. from French by Lawrence J. Johnson (1997; New York: Paulist Press, 1999), 5–25.

23. Quoted phrases are from paragraphs numbered 19, 20, 38, 42, 43, and 44 of *Summi pontificatus*, in *The Papal Encyclicals*, Claudia Carlen Ihm, ed., vol. IV: 1939–1958 (Raleigh, N.C.: McGrath, 1981), 5–22.

24. Ibid., paragraphs 46 and 47.

25. ADSS VI, doc. 5, Tacchi Venturi to Maglione, March 28, 1939, 56–60. Regarding the first request, the anti-Jewish laws had decreed that "Aryan" status could be conferred upon the baptized children of mixed marriages only if the "Aryan" parent was an Italian citizen.

26. Ibid., doc. 13, Maglione to Borgongini Duca, April 11, 1939, 71–72.

27. Ibid.

28. Ibid., doc. 22, Maglione to Borgongini Duca, May 5, 1939, 85–86.

29. Ibid., doc. 25, Borgongini Duca to Maglione, May 19, 1939, 88; and doc. 32, Borgongini Duca to Maglione, June 14, 1939, 97.

30. Ibid., doc. 26, May 23, 1939, 89–90; and doc. 123, December 22, 1939, 208. Both documents are from Maglione to Tacchi Venturi.

31. Ibid., doc. 24, Borgongini Duca to Maglione, May 15, 1939, 87.

32. Ibid., doc. 157, Vatican Secretariat of State to the Italian Embassy to the Holy See, February 25, 1940, 247–48. The statistic itself was stated by Tacchi Venturi in a communication with Maglione, same vol., doc. 211, May 22, 1940, 316–17.

33. Ibid., doc. 157.

34. Ibid.

35. Ibid., doc. 211, May 22, 1940, 316–17; doc. 259, July 19, 1940, 366–67; and doc. 418, December 1940, 521–22; and VIII, doc. 77, footnote 4, May 25, 1941, 181. All

four reports are from Tacchi Venturi to Maglione. See also VIII, doc. 89, notes of Tardini and Maglione, May 30, 1941, and June 3, 1941, 198–200.

36. See ADSS, VIII, doc. 89, note by Tardini, May 30, 1941, attached note of Maglione, June 3, 1941, 200. On keeping the issues alive, see same vol., doc. 195, Maglione to Borgongini Duca, November 6, 1941, 340; doc. 331, Tacchi Venturi to Maglione, March 26, 1942, 483; and doc. 490, annex, Maglione to Tacchi Venturi, October 3, 1942, 662–63.

37. ADSS, VI, Introduction, 22.

38. Ibid., 23.

39. Ibid., 17.

40. ADSS, VIII, Introduction, 24.

41. Ibid., doc. 77, Tacchi Venturi to Maglione, May 5, 1941, 180.

42. For details, see Michele Sarfatti, *Gli ebrei nell'Italia fascista: Vicende, identità, persecuzione* (Turin: Einaudi, 2000), 159–60. See also Eucardio Momigliano, *Storia tragica e grottesca del razzismo fascista* (Verona: Arnoldo, 1946), 107; and Antonio Spinosa, "Le persecuzioni razziali in Italia," part 4: "La legislazione," *Il Ponte* IX (7), July 1953, 950–68, 959.

43. Joseph L. Lichten, "A Question of Judgment: Pius XII and the Jews," *Pius XII and the Holocaust: A Reader* (1963; repub. Milwaukee: Catholic League for Religious and Civil Rights, 1988), 94–137, 121.

44. Renzo De Felice, *Storia degli ebrei italiani sotto il fascismo* (1961; Turin: Einaudi, 1988), 373.

45. ADSS, VIII, doc. 394, Tittmann to Montini, June 10, 1942, 556–57.

46. Ibid., doc. 399, Tacchi Venturi to Maglione, June 17, 1942, 560–61; and attachment, footnote 2, Tacchi Venturi to Buffarini Guidi, n.d. but described as June 1, 1942.

47. Ibid., doc. 394, attached note of Maglione, June 11, 1942, 557. The published Vatican documents do not indicate whether the Italian ambassador did in fact intercede.

48. ADSS, VII, doc. 7, Borgongini Duca to Maglione, November 10, 1942, 80–83, 82. Buffarini Guidi replied that Italian laws were meant to "defend the race" but not to persecute, that he did not want to send Jewish professionals to perform hard manual labor, and that he disliked the hard anti-Jewish line of about twenty Fascist fanatics, of whom he named only Roberto Farinacci and Giovanni Preziosi.

49. Friedrich Heer, "The Need for Confession," *Commonweal*, February 28, 1964, 656–60, 658–59; reprinted in Bentley, *Storm Over "The Deputy,"* 166–73, 170.

50. For more on what Vatican officials knew, see Chapter Seven.

CHAPTER FIVE: REFUGEES AND EMIGRATION, 1939–1942

1. ADSS, IX, doc. 38, Borgongini Duca to Maglione, January 31, 1943, 109–13.

2. Klaus Voigt, letter to this author, February 15, 2000.

3. There is no mention of an intervention in ADSS, as there certainly would have been had it occurred. Klaus Voigt also found no evidence in his extensive

research. Interview with this author, Florence, May 8, 1998. See also his *Il Rifugio precario: Gli esuli in Italia dal 1933 al 1945*, 2 vols. (Florence: La Nuova Italia, 1996), II, 258–59; and "I Ragazzi di Villa Emma a Nonantola," *Le Comunità ebraiche a Modena e a Carpi: Dal medioevo all'età contemporanea*, Franco Bonilauri and Vincenza Maugeri, eds. (Florence: La Giuntina, 1999), 241–65. Both works were translated from German by Loredana Melissari.

4. For the story of the *Pentcho*, see John Bierman, *Odyssey* (New York: Simon and Schuster, 1984); Carlo Spartaco Capogreco, *Ferramonti: La vita e gli uomini del più grande campo d'internamento fascista (1940–1945)* (Florence: La Giuntina, 1987), 99–112; and Voigt, *Il Refugio precario*, II, 38–41.

5. See his *The Last Three Popes and the Jews* (London: Souvenir, 1967), 129. For one author who repeated it, see Anthony Rhodes, *The Vatican in the Age of Dictators: (1922-1945)* (New York: Holt, Rinehart and Winston, 1973), 340.

6. See Pierre Blet, S.J., *Pius XII and the Second World War: According to the Archives of the Vatican* (1997; New York: Paulist Press, 1999); and Robert A. Graham, S.J., "How to Manufacture a Legend" and "Pius XII's Defense of Jews and Others: 1944–45," in *Pius XII and the Holocaust: A Reader* (Milwaukee: Catholic League for Religious and Civil Rights, 1988), 15–89; and same author, "Relations of Pius XII and the Catholic Community with Jewish Organizations," in Ivo Herzer, ed., *The Italian Refuge: Rescue of Jews During the Holocaust* (Washington, D.C.: Catholic University of America Press, 1989), 231–53.

7. ADSS, VIII, doc. 140, bishop of Lubliana to Maglione, September 6, 1941, 263; doc. 147, Tacchi Venturi to Maglione, September 10, 1941, 274; and doc. 176, Tacchi Venturi to Maglione, October 18, 1941, 318.

8. Ibid., doc. 235, Tacchi Venturi to Maglione, December 17, 1941, 386–87.

9. Appeals from the cardinal archbishop of Munich, Michael von Faulhaber, and bishop of Osnabrück, Wilhelm Berning, both dated March 31, 1939, are in ADSS, VI, doc. 8 and 9, 62–67. According to the secretary general of the Opera di San Raffaele, there were 12,000 to 15,000 "non-Aryan Catholics" in Germany in 1940. See his report to Maglione in ADSS, VI, doc. 419, December 27, 1940, 524.

10. Ibid., doc. 11, Maglione to papal nuncio in Rio de Janeiro, April 5, 1939, 69–70.

11. Ibid., doc. 33, papal nuncio in Rio de Janeiro to Maglione, June 20, 1939, 98. For more on the Brazilian visa project, see especially Jeffrey Lesser, *Welcoming the Undesirables: Brazil and the Jewish Question* (Berkeley: University of California Press, 1995).

12. ADSS, VI, doc. 57, annex I, secretary general of the Opera di San Raffaele to the papal nuncio in Berlin, September 1, 1939, 130–32; forwarded to Maglione on September 2.

13. Ibid., doc. 57, annex III, notes of Montini, September 10, 1939, 134; doc. 61, papal nuncio in Berlin to Maglione, September 11, 1939, 138; and doc. 111, Secretariat of State to Brazilian Embassy, November 22, 1939, 194–96.

14. Ibid., doc. 129 and 275, papal nuncio in Rio de Janeiro to Maglione, January 6 and August 2, 1940, 217–18 and 380.

15. Ibid., doc. 184, Orsenigo to Maglione, April 6, 1940, 284–85.

16. Ibid., doc. 164, Brazilian ambassador to the Vatican Secretariat of State, March 4, 1940, 253–54. To help process applications, the Opera di San Raffaele set up an office in Rome at the monastery of the Palatine Order on Via Pettinari, near the Tiber.

17. Ibid.

18. Ibid., doc. 170, Secretariat of State to Brazilian ambassador, March 17, 1940, 264. The baptismal date was in fact updated to 1937 or 1938 for a time, and then backdated to 1934.

19. Ibid., doc. 357, Maglione to papal nuncio in France, October 29, 1940, 458–59; and ADSS, VIII, doc. 205, Brazilian ambassador to Maglione, November 20, 1941, footnote 2, note of an unidentified official at the Secretariat of State, 351–52.

20. Voigt, Il Refugio precario, II, 362–64.

21. ADSS, VI, doc. 285, annex, secretary general of the Opera di San Raffaele to Orsenigo, August 13, 1940, 390–91.

22. Ibid., doc. 299, notes of the Secretariat of State, 404–5.

23. ADSS, VIII, doc. 205, Brazilian ambassador to Maglione, November 20, 1941, 351.

24. Ibid., footnote 2, two notes by unidentified officials at the Secretariat of State, 351–52.

25. Ibid., doc. 429, Brazilian ambassador to the secretary of state, July 15, 1942, 600, in answer to a question on July 10 about reopening the special visa program. The answer was negative.

26. For more on what Vatican officials knew, see Chapter Seven.

27. Report by German SS statistician Richard Korherr, cited in Raul Hilberg, The Destruction of the European Jews, 3 vols. (New York: Holmes & Meier, 1985), II, 469. The statistics include the Sudetenland but not Austria or the Czech Protectorate.

28. Delasem was founded in December 1939. It replaced an organization known as the Comitato di assistenza agli ebrei in Italia, or Comasebit, which had been dissolved by the Italian government in August. Delasem was responsible to the Unione delle Comunità Israelitiche Italiane. A large portion of its funding came from the American Jewish Joint Distribution Committee.

29. Unione delle Comunità israelitiche italiane, Delegazione Assistenza Emigranti, Emigrazione dall'Italia di ebrei stranieri dal 1 Giugno al 30 Novembre 1940 (Genoa: n.p., n.d. but before September 1943), 11–30.

30. ADSS, X, doc. 316, Weber to Pius XII, September 2, 1944, 406–12, 409. In this same ADSS document, Weber claimed, improbably, that his organization gave help and advice to some 25,000 people. The statement of Sister Margherita Marchione, Yours Is a Precious Witness: Memoirs of Jews and Catholics in Wartime Italy (Mahwah, N.J.: Paulist Press, 1997), 169, that the organization helped 25,000 Jews to emigrate is based on a misreading of this claim and is wildly inaccurate.

31. See, for example, Voigt, Il Refugio precario, II, 364.

32. ADSS, VIII, doc. 34, Hecht to Pius XII, February 28, 1941, 120–23. Hecht also asked the pope to intervene with Italian officials to change the government's new policy of prohibiting the emigration of individuals carrying Italian passports or Nansen documents, issued for stateless persons, while allowing emigration of those with other passports. His concern, however, was again explicitly for "non-Aryan Catholics." Maglione asked Tacchi Venturi to intervene for these "non-Aryan Catholics," and he did so on April 1. He learned from Buffarini Guidi that some exceptions could be made. See ADSS, VIII, doc. 40, Maglione to Tacchi Venturi, March 7, 1941, 132–33, and footnote 2, Tacchi Venturi's response, April 17, 1941, 133.

33. Ibid., footnote 5, 123; and doc. 86, Delasem to Pius XII, May 16, 1941, 193–95.

34. Ibid., doc. 106, Weber to Pius XII, June 27, 1941, and footnote 6, 219–20.

35. ADSS, VI, doc. 419, annex, notes of the Secretariat of State, January 2, 1941, 525.

36. Voigt, Il Rifugio precario, 2 vols. (Florence: La Nuova Italia, 1993), I, 403.

37. ADSS, VI, doc. 52, notes of the Secretariat of State, August 26, 1939, 122–23.

38. Ibid., doc. 126, notes of the Secretariat of State, January 4, 1940, 213–14; doc. 159, Montini to his delegate at The Hague, February 28, 1940, 249; doc. 183, notes of the Secretariat of State, April 5, 1940, 282–83; and doc. 341, notes of the Secretariat of State, probably October 16, 1940, 437–39; and ADSS, VIII, doc. 315, Maglione to Apostolic Delegate Cicognani in Washington, D.C., March 20, 1942, 467–68.

39. ADSS, VI, doc. 183, notes of the Secretariat of State, April 5, 1940, 282–83.

40. Ibid., doc. 135, notes of Montini and Tardini, January 22 and 23, 1940, 223; and doc. 215, notes of the Secretariat of State, May 25, 1940, 322.

41. ADSS, VIII, doc. 315, Maglione to Apostolic Delegate Cicognani in Washington D.C., March 20, 1942, 467–68.

42. ADSS, IX, doc. 38, Borgongini Duca to Maglione, January 31, 1943, 109–13, 110.

43. Ibid., 110–11.

44. Voigt, Il Refugio precario, II, 355–56.

45. ADSS, VIII, doc. 119, Delasem to Borgongini Duca, July 25, 1941, 232–33.

46. Ibid., footnote 2, Borgongini Duca's reply to Delasem, August 6, 1941, 233.

47. Papal nuncio to Italy to Mussolini, October 21, 1938, printed in full in Glauco Buffarini Guidi, La vera verità: I documenti dell'archivio segreto del Ministro degli Interni Guido Buffarini Guidi dal 1938 al 1945 (Milan: Sugar, 1970), 25–26.

48. ADSS, VIII, doc. 246, Maglione to bishop of Osnabrück, December 27, 1941, 398–400, 398.

49. "Pius XII e gli ebrei di Roma, 1943–1944," La Civiltà Cattolica, anno 112, 1961, vol. I, quad. 2657, March 4, 1961, 449–58, 452.

50. Joseph L. Lichten, "A Question of Judgment: Pius XII and the Jews," in Pius XII and the Holocaust: A Reader (1963; repub. Milwaukee: Catholic League for Religious and Civil Rights, 1988), 95–137, 123–24.

51. Lapide, Last Three Popes and the Jews, 115–28.

52. For discussion of possible reasons for the errors and distortions of Lichten and Lapide, see the conclusion to this book.

CHAPTER SIX: FOREIGN JEWS IN ITALIAN INTERNMENT CAMPS, 1940–1943

1. Klaus Voigt, *Il Refugio precario: Gli esuli in Italia dal 1933 al 1945*, 2 vols., trans. from German by Loredana Melissari (Florence: La Nuova Italia, 1996), II, 2–3.

2. ACS, Min. Int., DGPS, Massime: M4, Mobilitazione civile, b. 104, f. 16 "N 16—Campi di concentramento," ins. 14/2—Visite del nunzio apostolico, list of 40 camps with inmates, March 1941. This series will hitherto be referred to as ACS, Massime.

3. Ibid.

4. ACS, Massime, b. 122, ins. Cosenza—Ferramonti—Affari generali, "Elenco internati nel campo di concentramento di Ferramonti," September 28, 1940, signed by Cav. Paolo Salvatore, director of the camp. For more on Ferramonti, see Carlo Spartaco Capogreco, *Ferramonti: La vita e gli uomini del più grande campo d'internamento fascista (1940–1945)* (Florence: La Giuntina, 1987); Francesco Folino, *Ferramonti: Un lager di Mussolini: Gli internati durante la guerra* (Cosenza: Brenner, 1985) and *Ebrei destinazione Calabria* (Palmero: Sellerio, 1988); Voigt, *Il Rifugio precario*, II; and Francesco Volpe, ed., *Ferramonti: Un lager nel Sud: Atti del convegno internazionale di studi 15/16 maggio 1987* (Cosenza: Orizzonti Meridionali, 1990).

5. ACS, Massime, b. 104, f. 16, ins. 14/2, list of 40 camps with inmates, March 1941.

6. ACS, Massime, b. 121, f. 16 "N 16—Campi di concentramento," sf. 2—Affari per provincia, ins. 13/6—Ferramonti VI, report from inspector general of police to Min. Int., September 16, 1942. Of these newcomers, 494 from the *Pentcho* arrived in February and March 1942, as mentioned in Chapter Five.

7. "Il Santo Padre per i prigionieri e per i profughi," *L'Osservatore Romano,* January 18, 1941, 1.

8. ACS, Massime, b. 104, f. 16, ins. 14/2, Prefect Sacchetti to Min. Int., December 27, 1940. Unless otherwise noted, subsequent statistics of internees during Borgongini Duca's camp visits in 1941 are all from the list of forty camps with inmates, March 1941, in b. 104.

9. Ibid., Prefect Ristagno to Min. Int., December 27, 1940.

10. Ibid., Apostolic Nunciature, itinerary, no date.

11. Ibid., inspector general of Public Security, Pescara, to Min. Int., April 9, 1941.

12. Ibid., inspector general of Public Security, Macerata, to Min. Int., April 9, 1941; and prefect of the province of Ancona to Min. Int., April 15, 1941.

13. Ibid., prefect of the province of Ancona to Min. Int., April 15, 1941.

14. Ibid., prefect of the province of Matera to Min. Int., May 22, 1941; and ADSS, VIII, doc. 104, footnote 1, note of Borgongini Duca, n.d. but late May 1941, 217.

15. See Callisto Lopinot, "Diario 1941–1944: Ferramonti-Tarsia," entry for July 28, 1941, in Volpe, *Ferramonti: Un lager nel Sud,* 157.

16. ACS, Massime, b. 104, f. 16, ins. 14/2, inspector general of Public Security, Pescara, to Min. Int., April 9, 1941. According to the existing reports, the only camp where Borgongini Duca was not well received was Istonio, in the province

of Chieti, where the 108 prisoners were all Italian non-Jews, presumably political dissidents. According to the inspector general of Public Security writing from Pescara, "The usual renouncers of God and the Country maintained a cynical and reproachful attitude when the nuncio . . . urged them to have faith in God and hope that peace comes soon so that they can return totally free to the bosoms of their families." Ibid., report to Min. Int., April 26, 1941.

17. See ADSS, VIII, doc. 75, Jews interned at Lama dei Peligni to Pius XII, April 1941, 178–79; and doc. 104, Borgongini Duca to Maglione, June 24, 1941, 217–18.

18. Ibid., doc. 104, Borgongini Duca to Maglione, June 24, 1941, 217–18.

19. See, for example, ACS, Massime, b. 104, f. 16, ins. 14/2, inspector general of Public Security, Pescara, to Min. Int., April 9, 1941; prefect of the province of Macerata to Min. Int., April 10, 1941; inspector general of Public Security, Pescara, April 26, 1941; and questore of the province of Foggia to Min. Int., May 20, 1941.

20. Ibid., inspector general, Macerata, to Min. Int., April 9, 1941.

21. Ibid., Borgongini Duca's letter to Min. Int., June 4, 1941.

22. Ibid., inspector general, Pescara, to Min. Int., April 12, 1943.

23. ADSS, VIII, Introduction, 24. This is the same allegation mentioned in Chapter Four, in which the editors claimed to have obtained some "exemptions from every restriction" of the anti-Jewish laws.

24. ACS, Massime, b. 121, f. 16, sf. 2, ins. 13/6, Lopinot to his superiors in Rome, January 22, 1942. See also Lopinot, "Diario," entries for November 30 and December 3, 1941.

25. ACS, Massime, b. 121, f. 16, sf. 2, ins. 13/6, Ferramonti official to Min. Int., November 7, 1940.

26. Ibid., unidentified Catholic pamphlet, n. 35, Pentecost 1941, 251–52. The emphasis is mine.

27. Ibid., b. 104, f. 16, ins. 14/2, reports of inspector general of Public Security, Pescara, to Min. Int., August 1, 1941, and May 23, 1942.

28. CDEC, Fondo Israel Kalk, VII-1, testimony of internee Mirko Haler, 15 pp., 8.

29. Fr. Callistus a Geispolsheim (Lopinot), "De Apostolatu inter Hebraeos in publicae custodiae loco cui nomen v. 'Campo di Concentramento Ferramonti-Tarsia (Cosenza),' " in *Analecta Ordinis Fratrum Minorum Capuccinorum* 60, 1944, 70–75, and 61, 1945, 40–47, 71.

30. Haler testimony, 8. For references to tensions, see Lopinot, "Diario," entries for October 16, 1941, and March 8, 1942.

31. Haler testimony, 7–8.

32. ACS, Massime, b. 121, sf. 2, ins. 13/6, Lopinot to minister of the interior, October 27, 1942.

33. Lopinot, "Diario," entry for June 23, 1942, 174.

34. Ibid., entry for December 19, 1941, 165.

35. Luigi Intrieri, "Assistenza religiosa e sociale nel campo di Ferramonti," in Volpe,

Ferramonti, 142–55, 146; and Lopinot, "Diario," entry for October 21–28, 1941, 163.

36. ADSS, VIII, doc. 335, Borgongini Duca to Maglione, April 2, 1942, 490; and doc. 348 and 371, two letters of thanks from internees, 505–7 and 532. See also Lopinot, "De Apostolatu inter Hebraeos," 1944, 73. Pinchas E. Lapide, *The Last Three Popes and the Jews* (London: Souvenir, 1967), 129, greatly exaggerated when he wrote that these Jews "had been not only saved by papal intervention, but also fed, clad and looked after at Vatican expense." For more on the Jews of the *Pentcho,* see Chapter Five.

37. Lopinot, "De Apostolatu inter Hebraeos," 1944, 74; and "Diario," entry for March 31, 1943, 181.

38. Lopinot, "De Apostolatu inter Hebraeos," 1944, 73.

39. Both Delasem and Israel Kalk's Milan-based Mensa dei bambini provided cash supplements for children, along with clothes, blankets, medicines, and funds for the establishment of a school. Aid was later allocated to pregnant women, sick adults, and refugees from the *Pentcho,* as well as to a library, theater, and professional training group. Chief Rabbi Riccardo Pacifici from Genoa was allowed to visit the camp three times, in March and October 1942 and July 1943. See CDEC, Fondo Israel Kalk, VI-4 and VII-2.

40. ADSS, VI, doc. 378, Bishop Besson to Pius XII, November 23, 1940, 477–79, 477.

41. Ibid., doc. 378, footnote 3, 479.

42. Ibid., doc. 378, attached note of Montini, December 1, 1940, 479.

43. Andrea Riccardi, *Il Potere del Papa da Pio XII a Paolo VI* (Rome: Laterza, 1988), 45.

44. ADSS, VIII, doc. 329, Lopinot to Borgongini Duca, March 25, 1942, 481–82.

45. Ibid., note attached to doc. 329, 482.

46. Ibid., doc. 471, Lopinot to Borgongini Duca, September 10, 1942, 642.

47. No document in ADSS refers to such an intervention at the end of 1942. Nor does Father Robert Graham, in his writings on Lopinot's report of September 10, 1942, ever indicate that the Vatican responded. See his "Relations of Pius XII and the Catholic Community with Jewish Organizations," in Ivo Herzer, ed., *The Italian Refuge: Rescue of Jews During the Holocaust* (Washington, D.C.: Catholic University of America Press, 1989), 231–53, 236; and "Il Vaticano e gli ebrei profughi in Italia durante la guerra," *La Civiltà Cattolica,* anno 138, vol. I, quad. 3281, March 7, 1987, 429–43, 431.

48. CDEC, Fondo Kalk, VII/4, Testimonianze e documentazione, "Sono scampato allo sterminio degli ebrei da parte dai tedeschi," testimony of Herzl Kawa, 24 pp.

49. CDEC, Fondo Israel Kalk, VII/2, "Memorandum about Emigration of Alien Jews from Italy."

CHAPTER SEVEN: WHAT THE POPE KNEW ABOUT THE HOLOCAUST

1. The article, "Der Papst und die Verfolgung der Juden," is printed in Fritz J. Raddatz, ed., *Summa iniuria oder durfte der Papst schweigen? Hochhuths*

"*Stellvertreter*" *in der öffentlichen Kritik* (Reinbek bei Hamburg: Rowohlt, 1963), 101–7, 106.

2. Alberto Giovannetti, "Storia, teatro e storie," *L'Osservatore Romano*, April 5, 1963, 3.

3. Angelo Martini, "La Vera storia e 'Il Vicario' di Rolf Hochhuth," *La Civiltà Cattolica*, anno 115, 1964, vol. II, quad. 2735, June 6, 1964, 437–54, 448–49.

4. ADSS, IX, Introduction, 38. See also Pierre Blet, S.J., *Pius XII and the Second World War: According to the Archives of the Vatican*, trans. from French by Lawrence J. Johnson (1997; New York: Paulist Press, 1999), 160–67. Blet was an editor of ADSS.

5. Walter Laqueur, *The Terrible Secret: Suppression of the Truth About Hitler's "Final Solution"* (Boston: Little, Brown, 1981), 55.

6. Gerhart M. Riegner, *Ne jamais désespérer: Soixante années au service du peuple juif et des droits de l'homme* (Paris: Cerf, 1998), 169. See also Carlo Falconi, *The Silence of Pius XII*, trans. Bernard Wall (1965 in Italy and France; Boston: Little, Brown, 1970); and Giovanni Miccoli, "La Santa Sede e le deportazioni," *Spostamenti di popolazione e deportazioni in Europa: 1939–1945* (Bologna: Cappelli, 1987), 236–49. Among those who disagree is Owen Chadwick, "The Pope and the Jews in 1942," in W. J. Sheils, ed., *Persecution and Toleration: Papers Read at the 22nd Summer Meeting and the 23rd Winter Meeting of the Ecclesiastical History Society* (Great Britain, no city: Basil Blackwell, 1984), 435–72, esp. 436; and same author, *Britain and the Vatican During the Second World War* (Cambridge: Cambridge University Press, 1986), esp. 201–2.

7. Laqueur, *Terrible Secret*, 57.

8. Blet, *Pius XII and the Second World War*, 71. See also Falconi, *Silence of Pius XII*, 109–256; Richard C. Lukas, *The Forgotten Holocaust: The Poles Under German Occupation, 1939–1944* (1986; New York: Hippocrene, 1997); and John F. Morley, *Vatican Diplomacy and the Jews During the Holocaust, 1939–1943* (New York: KTAV, 1980), 129–46.

9. ADSS, VIII, doc. 206, Scavizzi to Maglione, November 21, 1941, and footnote 2, 352.

10. ADSS, III, part 2, doc. 357, Sapieha to Pius XII, February 28, 1942, 539–40.

11. Falconi, *Silence of Pius XII*; Guenter Lewy, *The Catholic Church and Nazi Germany* (New York: McGraw-Hill, 1964), 227–46; and Morley, *Vatican Diplomacy and the Jews*. The pope also failed to condemn the murders of mental patients in the Third Reich, and Gypsies, Socialists, Communists, civilian hostages, homosexuals, Protestant pastors, Jehovah's Witnesses, Russian prisoners of war, and Orthodox Serbs in Croatia.

12. Blet, *Pius XII and the Second World War*, 69–92.

13. ADSS, VIII, doc. 184, Burzio to Maglione, October 27, 1941, 327–28.

14. See Thomas Dehler, "Sie zuckten mit der Achsel," in Raddatz, *Summa iniuria*, 231.

15. See Chapter Eight.

16. Raul Hilberg, *The Destruction of the European Jews*, 3 vols. (New York: Holmes &

Meier, 1985), I, 207. Administered as a separate unit by former Minister of Justice and Minister without Portfolio Hans Frank, the German-occupied General Government included the cities of Warsaw, Radom, Lublin, Cracow, and Lvov.

17. ADSS, VIII, doc. 5 and 14, Innitzer to Pius XII, January 20 and February 4, 1941, 78–79 and 90–92.

18. Ibid., doc. 235, Tacchi Venturi to Maglione, December 17, 1941, 386–87.

19. Ibid., doc. 261, Tacchi Venturi to Maglione, January 20, 1942, 416–17.

20. Ibid., doc. 263, notes of the Secretariat of State, January 25, 1942, 418.

21. Osborne diary, January 31, 1942, cited in Chadwick, "Pope and the Jews in 1942," 439–40; and same author, *Britain and the Vatican*, 205.

22. ADSS, VIII, doc. 298, Burzio to Maglione, March 9, 1942, 453.

23. Ibid., doc. 300, Bernardini to Maglione, March 10, 1942, 455.

24. Ibid., doc. 303, Rotta to Maglione, March 13, 1942.

25. Ibid., doc. 317, Rotta to Maglione, March 20, 1942, 470.

26. Ibid., doc. 314, Bernardini to Maglione, March 19, 1943, 466. The report had been delivered to Bernardini only the day before, by Gerhart Riegner of the World Jewish Congress and Richard Lichtheim of the Jewish Agency for Palestine. Copy of Riegner and Lichtheim's covering letter to Bernardini, in the possession of Riegner, March 18, 1942; and letter from Riegner to this author, July 2, 1999. See also Riegner, *Ne jamais désespérer*, 165.

27. The report is printed in Saul Friedländer, *Pius XII and the Third Reich: A Documentation*, trans. Charles Fullman (New York: Knopf, 1966), 105–10; and Morley, *Vatican Diplomacy and the Jews*, appendix B, 212–15.

28. ADSS, VIII, doc. 305, Secretariat of State to the Slovakian Legation, March 14, 1942, 459–60.

29. Ibid., doc. 322, notes of Montini, March 24, 1942, with attached note of Maglione, March 25, 1942, 475.

30. Ibid., doc. 334, Burzio to Maglione, March 31, 1942, 486–89.

31. Ibid., doc. 334, attached note of Tardini, April 10, 1943 [*sic*, but printing error; 1942 intended], 489.

32. Ibid., doc. 343, Burzio to Maglione, April 9, 1942, 501.

33. Ibid., doc. 346, notes of Maglione, April 11, 1942, 504.

34. Ibid., doc. 364, Rotta to Maglione, May 1, 1942; and attached annex, Pozdech to the Jewish Community of Budapest, April 20, 1942, 524–25.

35. The statistics of those deported and remaining are from a Slovakian deportation conference held on June 26, 1942, cited in Hilberg, *Destruction of the European Jews*, II, 734. On those who escaped, see p. 735.

36. For apologists, see Fiorello Cavalli, S.J., "La Santa Sede contro le deportazioni degli ebrei della Slovacchia durante la seconda guerra mondiale," *La Civiltà Cattolica*, anno 112, 1961, vol. III, quad. 2665, July 1, 1961, 3–18; Pinchas E. Lapide, *The Last Three Popes and the Jews* (London: Souvenir, 1967), 138–49; and Joseph L. Lichten, "A Question of Judgment: Pius XII and the Jews," *Pius XII and the Holocaust: A Reader* (1963; repub. Milwaukee: Catholic League for

Religious and Civil Rights, 1988), 94–137, 110. More surprisingly, Léon Poliakov, "The Vatican and the 'Jewish Question,' " *Commentary*, November 1950, 439–49, 441, shared this opinion. Significantly, Pierre Blet, S.J., an editor of the ADSS who had access to all documents, made no such claim for 1942 (*Pius XII and the Second World War*, 172–73).

37. ADSS, VIII, doc. 382, Burzio to Maglione, May 23, 1942, 541; and Hilberg, *Destruction of the European Jews*, II, 734 and 739.

38. For examples of Slovakian Catholics who helped Jews, see Morley, *Vatican Diplomacy and the Jews*, 85–86.

39. Ibid., 90–98.

40. ADSS, VIII, doc. 360, Burzio to Maglione, April 27, 1942, attached annex, 517–19, 519.

41. Ibid., Burzio to Maglione, 515–16, 516.

42. Morley, *Vatican Diplomacy and the Jews*, 101.

43. I refer simply to Auschwitz, the best-known name for what were in fact three adjacent camps. Birkenau, or Auschwitz II, was located about three kilometers from the smaller original camp, Auschwitz I. Most of the vast complex's killing facilities were at Birkenau. Monowitz, or Auschwitz III, also called Buna after IG Farben's huge synthetic rubber plant there, was an industrial work camp. At two other death camps, Treblinka and Majdanek (Lublin), the gassing of Jews began in July and September 1942, respectively.

44. ADSS, VIII, doc. 374, Scavizzi to Pius XII, May 12, 1942, 534.

45. Ibid., doc. 431, Marcone to Maglione, July 17, 1942, 601–2. For more on this report, see Chapters Eight and Nineteen. Blet, *Pius XII and the Second World War*, 160, suggests that Marcone did not believe that this information should be taken literally, but there is no evidence or indication that this was the case.

46. ADSS, VIII, doc. 438, Orsenigo to Montini, July 28, 1942, 607–8.

47. The meeting occurred on August 18 and was reported to Mussolini on August 21. The words "dispersion and elimination" are in the Foreign Ministry report, reproduced in full in Jonathan Steinberg, *All or Nothing: The Axis and the Holocaust, 1941–1943* (London: Routledge, 1990), 2.

48. ADSS, VIII, doc. 434, Valeri to Maglione, August 7, 1942, 613–14.

49. Ibid.

50. Ibid., doc. 460, vicar general to Bernardini, August 31, 1942, 632–33.

51. Ibid., footnote 3, 633; and doc. 477, Maglione to Valeri, September 17, 1942, 646.

52. For details, and for more on the Vatican's failure to protest to the highly Catholic Vichy regime about Jewish deportations, see especially Morley, *Vatican Diplomacy and the Jews*, 48–70.

53. ADSS, VIII, doc. 493, footnote 2, 665–66. Riegner, *Ne jamais désespérer*, 167, believes that Malvezzi was part of the Vatican secret service.

54. The memorandum from Geneva is in NA, SD, 740.00116 (EW) 1939/597A and 1939/756. It and Taylor's letter are in *Foreign Relations of the United States: Diplomatic Papers, 1942,* 7 vols., III (Europe) (Washington, D.C.: United States Government Printing Office, 1961), Taylor to Maglione, September 26, 1942,

775–76. Strangely, Taylor did not inform Maglione of a different report recently received from Gerhart Riegner of the World Jewish Congress in Geneva. In early August, Riegner learned from a prominent German businessman with high-level contacts that the Nazis were carrying out a carefully designed plan to exterminate all the Jews of Europe. Riegner's information was sent to the Foreign Office in London on August 10 and to the American State Department on August 11, 1942. For details, see Walter Laqueur and Richard Breitman, *Breaking the Silence* (1986; Hanover, N.H.: University Press of New England, 1994); and David S. Wyman, *The Abandonment of the Jews: America and the Holocaust, 1941–1945* (New York: Pantheon, 1984), 42–49.

55. ADSS, VIII, doc. 493, notes of Montini, September 27, 1942, and attached notes of Maglione and from his office, 665. Curiously, Blet, *Pius XII and the Second World War*, 160, declared that the "information from Malvezzi . . . did not correspond to the report from Geneva." This is incorrect. Both reports described the emptying of ghettos and systematic massacres of Jews. Malvezzi did not mention, and may not have known, that the murders occurred in special camps, but the content of his report was in no way inconsistent with the one from Geneva.

56. ADSS, VIII, doc. 497, notes of the ambassador of Poland, October 3, 1942, 670.

57. Ibid., doc. 496, footnote 4, report by Scavizzi, 669.

58. Peter Körfgen, "Das ist dir nicht erlaubt," in *Summa iniuria*, 107.

59. ADSS, VIII, doc. 507, Secretariat of State to Tittmann, October 10, 1942, 679. See also doc. 496, notes of Montini, October 1, 1942, 669.

60. Cited in Michael Balfour and Julian Frisby, *Helmut von Moltke: A Leader Against Hitler* (London: Macmillan, 1972), 203. Moltke was executed for anti-Nazi activities in January 1945.

61. See Helmuth James von Moltke, *Letters to Freya, 1939–1945*, trans. Beate Ruhm von Oppen (New York: Knopf, 1990), esp. 184–85.

62. ADSS, VII, doc. 7, Borgongini Duca to Maglione, November 10, 1942, 80–83, 82. This meeting is also mentioned in Chapter Four.

63. The document from the archives of the Foreign Ministry is reproduced in full in Steinberg, *All or Nothing*, 78. For more on the Pièche report, see Chapter Eight.

64. Alberto Pirelli, *Taccuini 1922/1943* (Bologna: Il Mulino, 1984), 365.

65. Diary of Luca Pietromarchi, entry for November 27, 1942, in Joseph Rochlitz, *The Righteous Enemy: Document Collection*, unpublished manuscript, Rome, 1988, 8.

66. NA, SD, 740.00116 (EW) 1939/726, Tittmann report.

67. Osborne diary, quoted at length in Chadwick, "The Pope and the Jews in 1942," 466–67; and same author, *Britain and the Vatican*, 216.

68. ADSS, VIII, doc. 573, Polish Embassy to Secretariat of State, December 19, 1942, 755.

69. Quoted in Gitta Sereny, *Into That Darkness* (1974; New York: Vintage, 1983), 159. From his waiting train, the soldier also witnessed the roundup in Siedlce and

even managed to take some photographs of it. His diary description confirms the report of the three escapees.

70. Saul Friedländer, *Kurt Gerstein ou l'ambiguïté du bien* (Tournai, Belgium: Casterman, 1967), 141; and Guenter Lewy, "Pius XII, the Jews, and the German Catholic Church," *Commentary*, February 1964, 23–35, 27, and same author, *The Catholic Church and Nazi Germany*, 288. See also Saul Friedländer, *Pius XII and the Third Reich*, 125–29; Rolf Hochhuth, "Sidelights on History," a well-documented essay published at the end of his play *The Deputy*, trans. Richard Winston and Clara Winston (New York: Grove, 1964), 288–95; and Pierre Joffroy, *L'Espion de Dieu: La Passion de Kurt Gerstein* (Paris: Grasset, 1969), 168–71.

71. Lewy, "Pius XII, the Jews, and the German Catholic Church," 28, and *Catholic Church and Nazi Germany*, 288. Lewy's information about Müller came from an interview with him on March 26, 1962.

72. These efforts did not materialize. For details, see Chadwick, *Britain and the Vatican*, 86, 109, 139, and 273–74.

73. Ministero degli Affari Esteri, Commissione per la pubblicazione dei documenti diplomatici, *I Documenti diplomatici italiani*, series 9: 1939–1943, vol. IX, Alfieri to Ciano, February 3, 1943, 580–83.

74. ADSS, IX, doc. 82, Preysing to Pius XII, March 6, 1943, 170.

75. Ibid., doc. 85, Burzio to Maglione, March 7, 1943, footnote 6, 178.

76. Ibid., doc. 152, Tacchi Venturi to Maglione, April 14, 1943, 254. For the context of this report, see Chapter Eight.

77. Ibid., doc. 174, notes of the Secretariat of State, May 5, 1943, 274. Emphasis mine.

78. ADSS, VII, doc. 282, Roncalli to Montini, July 8, 1943, 473–76, 474.

79. ADSS, X, doc. 204, Burzio to Maglione, May 22, 1944, 281.

80. Ibid., footnote 1, 281. Fathers Blet and Graham, both editors of the documents, declared separately that the delay resulted from the blockage of communications after the liberation of Rome on June 4, 1944. This is difficult to believe, since Burzio sent it almost two weeks before Rome was liberated, and since documents published in ADSS, X, show that the Vatican continued to receive reports. See Blet, *Pius XII and the Second World War*, 166; and Robert A. Graham, S.J., "Pius XII's Defense of Jews and Others: 1944–45," in *Pius XII and the Holocaust: A Reader* (Milwaukee: Catholic League for Religious and Civil Rights, 1988), 27–89, 63–64. For more on the Protocol, see Miroslav Karny, "The Vrba and Wetzler Report," in *Anatomy of the Auschwitz Death Camp*, Yisrael Gutman and Michael Berenbaum, eds. (Bloomington: Indiana University Press, 1994), 553–68; Henryk Swiebocki, ed., *London Has Been Informed: Reports by Auschwitz Escapees*, trans. from Polish by Michael Jacobs and Laurence Weinbaum (Oswiecim: Auschwitz-Birkenau State Museum, 1997), 169–274; and Wyman, *Abandonment of the Jews*, esp. 288–89.

81. Tisserant to Saul Friedländer, published in Friedländer, *Pius XII and the Third Reich*, n.p. but preface.

CHAPTER EIGHT: ITALIAN-OCCUPIED CROATIA, APRIL 1941–JULY 1943

1. At the same time, Macedonia fell to Bulgaria, and Vojvodina to Hungary. For the best description of these divisions, see Klaus Voigt, *Il Refugio precario: Gli esuli in Italia dal 1933 al 1945*, II, trans. from German by Loredana Melissari (1993; Florence: La Nuova Italia, 1996), 242.

2. Pavelic to Ciano, December 16, 1941, recorded in Malcolm Muggeridge, ed., *Ciano's Diplomatic Papers*, documents trans. by Stuart Hood (London: Odhams, 1948), 471.

3. For cases in which Italian military personnel failed to intervene to save Jews being murdered by the Ustasha, mostly in 1941, see Zvi Loker, "The Testimony of Dr. Edo Neufeld: The Italians and the Jews of Croatia," *Holocaust and Genocide Studies* 7 (1), Spring 1993, 67–76.

4. For description of this period, see Jonathan Steinberg, *All or Nothing: The Axis and the Holocaust, 1941–1943* (London: Routledge, 1990), 15–49.

5. ADSS, VIII, Marcone's report to Maglione, footnote 1 attached to doc. 139, August 23, 1941, 261.

6. See ADSS, VIII, covering documents relating to war victims from January 1, 1941, to December 1942.

7. Ibid., doc. 132, Alatri to Maglione, August 14, 1941, 250–52.

8. Ibid., doc. 139, Maglione to Marcone, September 3, 1941, 261-62.

9. Menachem Shelah, *Un Debito di gratitudine: Storia dei rapporti tra l'Esercito Italiano e gli Ebrei in Dalmazia (1941–1943)*, trans. from Hebrew by Gaio Sciloni (Rome: Stato Maggiore dell'Esercito, Ufficio Storico, 1991), 45–48.

10. Voigt, *Il Refugio precario*, II, 243.

11. Ibid., 255.

12. The quotations are from an Italian Foreign Ministry report of the meeting with Bismarck, prepared for Mussolini and dated August 21, 1942. It is reproduced in full in Steinberg, *All or Nothing*, 2.

13. Ibid.

14. See Mackensen's report of Mussolini's order, printed in full in Léon Poliakov and Jacques Sabille, *Jews Under the Italian Occupation* (Paris: Centre de Documentation Juive Contemporaine, 1954), doc. VIII, October 28, 1942, 174–75.

15. Shelah, *Un Debito di gratitudine*, 105–14, gives examples.

16. Diary of Luca Pietromarchi, entry for December 10, 1942, in Joseph Rochlitz, *The Righteous Enemy: Document Collection*, unpublished manuscript, Rome, 1988, 8.

17. For excellent detailed analysis of the Italian decision-making process, see especially Voigt, *Il Refugio precario*, II, 241–92; and Steinberg, *All or Nothing*, 50–84 and 130–34. See also Jacques Sabille, "Attitude of the Italians to the Persecuted Jews in Croatia," in Poliakov and Sabille, *Jews Under the Italian Occupation*, 131–50; Daniel Carpi, "The Rescue of Jews in the Italian Zone of

Occupied Croatia," in Yisrael Gutman and Efraim Zuroff, eds., *Rescue Attempts During the Holocaust: Proceedings of the Second Yad Vashem International Historical Conference* (Jerusalem: "Ahva" Cooperative Press, 1977), 465–525; and Menachem Shelah, "The Italian Rescue of Yugoslav Jews, 1941–1943," in Ivo Herzer, ed., *The Italian Refuge: Rescue of Jews During the Holocaust* (Washington, D.C.: Catholic University of America Press, 1989), 205–17, and *Un Debito di gratitudine.*

18. ADSS, VIII, doc. 431, Marcone to Maglione, July 17, 1942, 601–2.

19. See Owen Chadwick, *Britain and the Vatican During the Second World War* (Cambridge: Cambridge University Press, 1986), 201–2, from Osborne's diaries.

20. Examples of those with titles include Marchese Blasco Lanza d'Ajeta; Count Luca Pietromarchi; Count Leonardo Vitetti, director general of European and Mediterranean Affairs; Count Luigi Vidau, chief of the Department of Confidential Affairs; and Baron Michele Scamacca, Foreign Ministry liaison officer with the Supreme Military Command in Rome. Of course not all individuals with titles were practicing Catholics, but many were.

21. ADSS, VIII, doc. 450, Yugoslavian Legation to the Secretariat of State, August 14, 1942, 622–23.

22. Ibid., doc. 473, Borgongini Duca to Maglione, September 11, 1942, 643. The response of the apostolic visitor in Zagreb, who had also been notified, arrived a full two months later. He reported that he had been able to achieve very little for the Jews from the Croatian police. He added that the new police chief had informed him that "sooner or later all [Jews in Croatia] must be transported to Germany." See ADSS, VIII, doc. 537, apostolic visitor to Maglione, November 8, 1942, 709–10.

23. Ibid., doc. 461, notes of Tardini, September 4, 1942, 633–34.

24. The original document is reproduced in Carpi, "Rescue of Jews in Italian-Occupied Croatia," 521.

25. ADSS, VIII, footnote 1 attached to doc. 541, Morpurgo to Montini, November 6, 1942, 712.

26. Ibid., doc. 541, Maglione to Borgongini Duca, November 13, 1942, 712.

27. Ibid., footnote 2 attached to doc. 541, 712.

28. For description and analysis of their efforts, see Steinberg, *All or Nothing,* 50–84; and Shelah, *Un Debito di gratitudine.*

29. Pièche's report to Mussolini is quoted in Steinberg, *All or Nothing,* 77.

30. See report about Pièche's information, Italian Foreign Ministry to Mussolini, November 4, 1942, printed in full in Carpi, "Rescue of Jews in Italian-Occupied Croatia," 520; and in Steinberg, *All or Nothing,* 78. See Steinberg also on Pièche's change of attitude.

31. Diary of Pietromarchi, entry for March 1, 1943, in Rochlitz, *Righteous Enemy,* 9.

32. According to one source, Mussolini informed Robotti, probably in early March, that he had felt obliged to promise a consignment of Jews to Ribbentrop, but that Robotti could invent any excuses he liked to obstruct delivery. The report of this

conversation, related by Robotti to Colonel Vincenzo Carla, chief of the First Bureau of the Second Army, and recorded by Carla after the war, is quoted at length by Sabille in *Jews Under the Italian Occupation*, 147–48.

33. ADSS, IX, doc. 55, Maglione to Borgongini Duca, February 17, 1943, 131. Footnote 1 attached to doc. 55 explains that Maglione's information came from the Polish ambassador to the Holy See, in a communication on February 10.

34. Ibid., footnote 2 attached to doc. 55, Borgongini Duca to Maglione, February 27, 1943, 131.

35. Ibid., doc. 49, Maglione to Borgongini Duca, February 13, 1943, 124.

36. Ibid., footnote 2 attached to doc. 49, March 21, 1943, 124.

37. Ibid., doc. 79, Maglione to Borgongini Duca, March 5, 1943, 168–69. The document does not name the original source of the request. Nor does it mention that the Czechs in question were Jews, but the expressed fear of deportation to Poland suggests that they were.

38. Ibid., doc. 83, Cicognani to Maglione, March 6, 1943, 171. Rabbi Stephen Wise was the president of the American Jewish Congress. The source of the exaggerated statistic is unclear.

39. Ibid., doc. 108, British Legation at the Holy See to the secretary of state, March 20, 1943, 197–98.

40. Ibid., foonote 3 attached to doc. 79, no date, 169.

41. Ibid., note from Montini, attached to doc. 108, March 21, 1943, 198.

42. Ibid., doc. 146, Montini to Borgongini Duca, April 10, 1943, 245.

43. Ibid., footnote 2 attached to doc. 146, Borgongini Duca to Montini, April 13, 1943, 245.

44. Ibid., doc. 92, notes of Maglione, March 13, 1943, 183.

45. Ibid., doc. 104, Maglione to Tacchi Venturi, March 17, 1943, 195.

46. Ibid., footnote 3 attached to doc. 83, March 17, 1943, 171.

47. Ibid., doc. 152, Tacchi Venturi to Maglione, April 14, 1943, 254–56. Tacchi Venturi's delay was not from lack of trying. He had first tried to obtain a hearing at the Ministry of the Interior. On March 22 he was told that the issue of Jews in Croatia was not under the jurisdiction of the Interior, and that he should approach the Foreign Ministry. The meeting with Bastianini could not be arranged before April 14.

48. The decision is quoted in Shelah, *Un Debito di gratitudine*, 148.

49. ADSS, IX, doc. 152, Tacchi Venturi to Maglione, April 14, 1943, 254–56. For discussion, at the same meeting, of Jews in Italian-occupied France, see the next chapter.

50. Shelah, *Un Debito di gratitudine*, 150. Italian sources often claim that 2,600 or 2,700 Jews were gathered at Arbe, but according to Shelah, Yugoslavian sources maintain that there were 3,577 Jews on the island when anti-German partisans reached it in September 1943.

CHAPTER NINE: ITALY AND ITALIAN-OCCUPIED FRANCE,
NOVEMBER 1942–JULY 1943

1. For the most reliable population estimates, see Klaus Voigt, *Il Rifugio precario: Gli esuli in Italia dal 1933 al 1945*, II, trans. from German by Loredana Melissari (Florence: La Nuova Italia, 1996), 296 and 306.

2. For accounts of the Italian occupation of France, see Daniel Carpi, *Between Mussolini and Hitler: The Jews and the Italian Authorities in France and Tunisia* (Hanover: Brandeis University Press, 1994); Serge Klarsfeld, *Vichy Auschwitz: Le rôle de Vichy dans la solution finale de la question juive en France, 1943–1944* (Paris: Fayard, 1985); Michael R. Marrus and Robert O. Paxton, *Vichy France and the Jews* (New York: Basic Books, 1981); Léon Poliakov, "The Jews Under the Italian Occupation in France," in Léon Poliakov and Jacques Sabille, *Jews Under the Italian Occupation* (Paris: Centre de Documentation Juive Contemporaine, 1954), 17–44; Jonathan Steinberg, *All or Nothing: The Axis and the Holocaust, 1941–43* (London: Routledge, 1990), esp. 105–30; Voigt, *Il Refugio precario*, II, 293–334; and Susan Zuccotti, *The Holocaust, the French, and the Jews* (New York: Basic Books, 1993).

3. See Steinberg, *All or Nothing*, 117.

4. Mackensen's report is translated and printed in full in Poliakov and Sabille, *Jews Under the Italian Occupation*, doc. 8, 68–70.

5. Giuseppe Bastianini, *Uomini, Cose, Fatti: Memorie di un ambasciatore* (Milan: Vitagliano, 1959), 86–88; and Luca Pietromarchi, diary entry for March 31, 1943, in Joseph Rochlitz, *The Righteous Enemy: Document Collection*, unpublished manuscript, Rome, 1988, 10–11. In his memoirs *Quando ero Capo della Polizia: 1940–1943* (Rome: Ruffolo, 1946), 103, Carmine Senise also claimed credit for Mussolini's change of mind. Bastianini declared that the police chief was called in after the change had been made.

6. Mackensen's report to Berlin on the meeting with Bastianini is translated and printed in full in Poliakov and Sabille, *Jews Under the Italian Occupation*, 70–72. Mackensen dated the meeting March 20, while Bastianini, *Uomini, Cose, Fatti*, 88, claimed that it occurred on March 19.

7. See Lospinoso's account, written at the time of the trial of Adolf Eichmann in Jerusalem in 1961, and printed in Rochlitz, *Righteous Enemy*, 49–57; and Chief of the Gestapo Heinrich Müller's report from Berlin to the Commandant of the SIPO and SD, Paris, April 2, 1943, printed in full in Poliakov and Sabille, *Jews Under the Italian Occupation*, doc. 9, 73.

8. CDJC, CCXVIII-22, Exposé de Monsieur Donati, 5 pp., 3. For more on Donati, see Chapter Ten.

9. ADSS, IX, doc. 105, notes of Montini, March 18, 1943, 196.

10. Bastianini, *Uomini, Cose, Fatti*, 86–88. Pietromarchi also mentioned the second encounter in his diary, writing, "Shortly after the meeting [when Bastianini informed Mackensen of Mussolini's change of policy] the nuncio hastened to see the acting secretary [Bastianini]." See Pietromarchi diary, entry for March 31, 1943, in Rochlitz, *Righteous Enemy*, 11.

11. ADSS, IX, footnote 3 attached to doc. 105, 196. The note states that Borgongini Duca answered Montini on March 19, but it does not give the content of the message. Instead, it quotes Montini telling Borgongini Duca on March 24, "I have learned with lively satisfaction of the tranquillizing assurances that were given to you by Bastianini."

12. See, for example, Robert A. Graham, S.J., "Il Vaticano e gli ebrei profughi in Italia durante la guerra," *La Civiltà Cattolica*, anno 138, vol. I, quad. 3281, March 7, 1987, 429–43, 436.

13. ADSS, IX, doc. 152, Tacchi Venturi to Maglione, April 14, 1943, 254.

14. For details, see Daniel Carpi, *Italian Diplomatic Documents on the History of the Holocaust in Greece* (Tel Aviv: Diaspora Research Institute of Tel Aviv University, 1999); Jacques Sabille, "The Attitude of the Italians to the Jews in Occupied Greece," in Poliakov and Sabille, *Jews Under the Italian Occupation*, 151–60; and Steinberg, *All or Nothing*, 94–104.

15. See documents in ACS, Min. Int., DGPS, Uff. RG, 1942, b. 11.

16. Quoted in Voigt, *Il Rifugio precario*, II, 388.

17. Roosevelt Library (RL), Hyde Park, Taylor papers, box 11, telegraph, Barou-Easterman to Wise, London, June 19, 1943.

18. See Lospinoso report in Rochlitz, *Righteous Enemy*, 52; Michele Sarfatti, "Fascist Italy and German Jews in South-Eastern France in July 1943," *Journal of Modern Italian Studies* 3 (3), 1998, 318–28; and Carpi, *Between Mussolini and Hitler*, 183–85. Klaus Voigt points out that the extradition of German Jews from Italian-occupied France would have made it extremely difficult to continue to protect the Jews at Arbe. Letter to this author, February 15, 2000.

19. Quoted in Voigt, *Il Refugio precario*, II, 389. See also Michele Sarfatti, *Gli ebrei nell'Italia fascista: Vicende, identità, persecuzione* (Turin: Einaudi, 2000), 174–75.

20. ADSS, IX, doc. 228, Maglione to Borgongini Duca, June 13, 1943, 338.

21. Ibid., footnote 3 attached to doc. 228, Borgongini Duca to Maglione, June 14, 1943, 338.

22. Ibid., doc. 247, British chargé d'affaires to Maglione, June 29, 1943, 38.

23. Ibid., footnote 1 attached to doc. 247, British Legation to the Vatican Secretariat of State, July 1, 1943, 38.

24. Ibid., footnote 2 attached to doc. 247, Vatican Secretariat of State to British chargé d'affaires at Cairo, July 3, 1943, 368–69.

25. Quoted in Voigt, *Il Rifugio precario*, II, 394.

26. This exchange of letters may be seen in RL, Taylor papers, box 11.

27. Ibid., Cicognani to Taylor, July 3, 1943.

28. ADSS, IX, doc. 276, apostolic delegate to Maglione, July 23, 1943, 413.

29. Ibid., notes by Maglione and Tardini attached to doc. 276, 413.

30. Ibid., footnote 2 attached to doc. 276, 413.

31. ADSS, VIII, doc. 403, Borgongini Duca to Maglione, June 22, 1942, 565–66.

CHAPTER TEN: THE FORTY-FIVE DAYS:
THE VATICAN, BADOGLIO, AND THE JEWS

1. For the statistics for Italy, see Liliana Picciotto Fargion, *Il Libro della memoria* (Milan: Mursia, 1991), 793 and 806.

2. ADSS, IX, doc. 317, Tacchi Venturi to Maglione, August 29, 1943, 458–59.

3. Ibid., 459.

4. Ibid., doc. 289, Tacchi Venturi to Maglione, August 10, 1943, 423–24.

5. Ibid., doc. 296, Maglione to Tacchi Venturi, August 18, 1943, 433–34; and annex attached to doc. 317, Tacchi Venturi to Italian minister of the interior, August 24, 1943, 459–62.

6. Ibid., doc. 294, petition to Maglione from converted Jews, names deleted, August 15, 1943, 431–32.

7. Order to prefect of Cosenza, quoted in Klaus Voigt, *Il Refugio precario: Gli esuli in Italia dal 1933 al 1945*, II, trans. from German by Loredana Melissari (1993; Florence: La Nuova Italia, 1996), 208–9.

8. Menachem Shelah, *Un Debito di gratitudine: Storia dei rapporti tra l'Esercito Italiano e gli Ebrei in Dalmazia (1941–1943)*, trans. from Hebrew by Gaio Scilone (Rome: Stato Maggiore dell'Esercito, Ufficio Storico, 1991), 150; and Daniel Carpi, "The Rescue of Jews in the Italian Zone of Occupied Croatia," in Yisrael Gutman and Efraim Zuroff, eds., *Rescue Attempts During the Holocaust: Proceedings of the Second Yad Vashem International Historical Conference* (Jerusalem: "Ahva" Cooperative Press, 1977), 465–525, 502.

9. ADSS, IX, doc. 271, apostolic delegate to Maglione, July 20, 1943, 406.

10. Ibid., annex attached to doc. 271, Easterman to apostolic delegate, July 19, 1943, 407–8.

11. Ibid., doc. 282, Easterman to Pius XII, August 2, 1943, 417–18.

12. Ibid., annex attached to doc. 271, Easterman to apostolic delegate, July 19, 1943, 407–8.

13. Ibid., footnote attached to doc. 282, telegram to apostolic delegate, August 6, 1943, 418.

14. Ibid., doc. 291, Italian chargé d'affaires to Maglione, August 12, 1943, 427.

15. Ibid., doc. 346, Easterman to apostolic delegate, London, September 24, 1943.

16. For analysis of their efforts, see Daniel Carpi, *Between Mussolini and Hitler: The Jews and the Italian Authorities in France and Tunisia* (Hanover: Brandeis University Press, 1994), 164–92; and Voigt, *Il Refugio precario*, II, 293–334.

17. See his account at CDJC, CCXVIII-22, Exposé de Monsieur Donati, n.d. but probably soon after September 8, 1943, 5 pp., 3.

18. Interview with this author, Paris, April 25, 1988.

19. In his various testimonies, Father Benoît did not explain the reasons for this recall. He did state clearly that his Capuchin superiors in Rome knew exactly what he was doing in Marseilles to help Jews, and approved. See his *Livre d'Or des Congrégations françaises: 1939–1945* (Paris: DRAC, 1948), 308.

20. Father Benoît explained that before he left France, he and Donati met with Raoul Lambert, president of the Union Générale des Israélites de France; Edmond

Fleg, president of the Eclaireurs Israélites; Jacques Helbronner, president of the Consistoire central de France; and several important French rabbis. See ADSS, IX, doc. 264, Father Marie Benoît to Pope Pius XII, July 15, 1943, 393–97, 394–95; and Father Benoît, *Livre d'Or*, 309–10.

21. ADSS, IX, doc. 264, Tardini's note attached, 393.

22. Hérissé was identified in the *Annuario Pontificio*, 1943, 848, as Giuseppe (Joseph) Hérissé, from Le Mans. The only mention of his role at the Vatican involved his membership in an honorary society of more than two thousand priests called the Camerieri segreti soprannumerari di Sua Santità.

23. Testimony of Father Benoît, *Livre d'Or*, 305–31; and CDJC, CDXLVI, dossier Joseph Bass, letter of Father Benoît, February 26, 1946.

24. ADSS, IX, doc. 267, notes of Father Benoît, 401–2. The document apparently bore no date. The date provided by the editors, July 16, 1943, cannot be correct. Benoît referred to the ongoing gradual Italian army withdrawal from France and a German presence in the environs of Nice, which would date his document in August 1943.

25. Ibid., footnotes 5 and 6, 402.

26. CDJC, CDXLVI, dossier Joseph Bass, letter of Benoît, February 26, 1946, 2; and Benoît testimony, *Livre d'Or*, 312–14.

27. ADSS, IX, doc. 321, notes of Father Benoît, September 1943, no day provided, 465–67.

28. Robert A. Graham, S.J., "Relations of Pius XII and the Catholic Community with Jewish Organizations," in Ivo Herzer, ed., *The Italian Refuge: Rescue of Jews During the Holocaust* (Washington, D.C.: Catholic University of America Press, 1989), 231–53, 244. The chronology in Graham's account of Lospinoso's activities, 241, is incorrect.

29. Ibid., 244.

30. Carpi, *Between Mussolini and Hitler*, 302.

31. ADSS, IX, doc. 300, Cicognani to Maglione, August 20, 1943, 437.

32. Ibid., footnote 2, telegram to Cicognani, August 26, 1943, 437–38.

33. Klarsfeld, *Vichy-Auschwitz: 1943–1944*, 124. See also Jean-Louis Panicacci, "Les Juifs et la question juive dans les Alpes-Maritimes de 1939 à 1945," *Recherches regionales Côte d'Azur et contrées limitrophes: Bulletin trimestriel*, ed. Archives departementales des Alpes-Maritimes, n.d. but between 1983 and 1987, Appendix XVIII, 329.

34. See accounts by Klarsfeld, *Vichy-Auschwitz: 1943–1944*, 117–26; and Zuccotti, *The Holocaust, the French and the Jews*, 181–87.

35. CDEC, f. Delasem, s.f. Delasem: Padre Benedetto Maria, "Riassunto dell'attività di Padre Benedetto Maria OFM Cap. e dei suoi collaboratori," by St. Schwamm. Father Benoît was known as Father Maria Benedetto in Italy.

36. The statistic is from Picciotto Fargion, *Il Libro della memoria*, 805. For their story, see especially Alberto Cavaglion, *Nella Notte straniera: Gli ebrei di St.-Martin-Vésubie* (1981; Cuneo: L'Arciere, 1991).

37. Picciotto Fargion, *Il Libro della memoria*, 43.

CHAPTER ELEVEN: UNDER THE POPE'S VERY WINDOWS:
THE ROME ROUNDUP, OCTOBER 16, 1943

1. The Duce was confined on the islands of Ponza and La Maddalena before being moved to the resort at Campo Imperatore on the Gran Sasso.

2. Liliana Picciotto Fargion, *Il Libro della memoria: Gli Ebrei deportati dall'Italia (1943–1945)* (Milan: Mursia, 1991), 760–61 and 805–7. See also Marco Nozza, *Hotel Meina: La prima strage di ebrei in Italia* (Milan: Mondadori, 1993). On September 17, two Jews were also killed in Novara, fifty-six kilometers south of Stresa.

3. Picciotto Fargion, *Il Libro della memoria*, 42 and 805–7. These first deportees were sent to the transit camp of Reichenau in Austria, from which they went on to Auschwitz, probably on March 7, 1944.

4. Ibid., 43.

5. Ibid., 805–7.

6. For much of this information I am grateful to Harold H. Tittmann III, the son of the American chargé d'affaires, who remained in the Vatican City with his parents during the German occupation. Interview with this author, New York, May 17, 1999. See also David Alvarez and Robert A. Graham, S.J., *Nothing Sacred: Nazi Espionage Against the Vatican: 1939–1945* (London: Frank Cass, 1997); Owen Chadwick, *Britain and the Vatican During the Second World War* (Cambridge: Cambridge University Press, 1986); and Robert A. Graham, S.J., "Spie naziste attorno al Vaticano durante la seconda guerra mondiale," *La Civiltà Cattolica*, anno 121, quad. 2869, January 3, 1970, 21–31.

7. For one explanation, see Michele Sarfatti, *Gli ebrei nell'Italia fascista: Vicende, identità, persecuzione* (Turin: Einaudi, 2000), 239.

8. Picciotto Fargion, *Il Libro della memoria*, 54 and 867. See also Gemma Volli, "Trieste 1938–1945," *Gli Ebrei in Italia durante il fascismo: Quaderni del Centro di Documentazione Ebraica Contemporanea*, III, November 1963, 38–51, 47; and Silva Bon Gherardi, *La Persecuzione antiebraica a Trieste (1938–1945)* (Udine: Del Bianco, 1972), 48.

9. Until the anti-Jewish laws in 1938, Ettore Ovazza believed that Jews would not be persecuted if they supported Mussolini and opposed Zionism with sufficient fervor. In 1934 he founded a newspaper, *La Nostra Bandiera*, to present his views. At the same time, he maneuvered successfully to oust the leadership of his local Jewish Community of Turin and replace it with himself and his friends. See especially Alexander Stille, *Benevolence and Betrayal: Five Italian Jewish Families Under Fascism* (New York: Summit, 1991), 42–89.

10. For the statistic, see Picciotto Fargion, *Il Libro della memoria*, 805–6. The author estimates that there were 40,157 Jews in Italy at the time of Mussolini's fall; 1,200 to 1,300 arrived from France in September 1943; 6,000 escaped to Switzerland or the Allied zone, mostly in September and October; and 2,000 to 2,100 internees were freed in the first two months of the occupation as the Allies moved north.

11. Sarfatti, *Gli ebrei nell'Italia fascista*, 240–41. The message went to national and

regional offices of the RSHA and the Ministry of Foreign Affairs concerned with Jewish issues. (For explanation of RSHA, see note 20.) Sarfatti suggests that those directly responsible for arresting Jews in Italy were probably informed separately, in a document as yet undiscovered.

12. Michael Tagliacozzo, "La Comunità di Roma sotto l'incubo della svastica: La grande razzia del 16 ottobre 1943," *Gli Ebrei in Italia durante il fascismo: Quaderni del Centro di Documentazione Ebraica Contemporanea* III, November 1963, 8–37, 9–10; and Robert Katz, *Black Sabbath: A Journey Through a Crime Against Humanity* (Toronto: Macmillan, 1969) 48 and 54.

13. Ugo Foà, "Relazione del Presidente della Comunità Israelitica di Roma Foà Ugo circa le misure razziali adottate in Roma dopo l'8 settembre a diretta opera delle Autorità tedesche di occupazione," written November 15, 1943, to be saved in case he did not survive. The report is in *Ottobre 1943: Cronaca di una infamia*, Comunità Israelitica di Roma, ed., pamphlet printed in 1961, 9–29, 13.

14. For other accounts of the gold extortion, the subsequent pillaging of Jewish Community offices, and the Roman roundup itself, see Fausto Coen, *16 ottobre 1943: La grande razzia degli ebrei di Roma* (Florence: La Giuntina, 1993); Giacomo Debenedetti, *16 ottobre 1943* (Rome: OET, 1945); Katz, *Black Sabbath;* Picciotto Fargion, *Il Libro della memoria*, 811–18; and Michael Tagliacozzo, "La Comunità di Roma sotto l'incubo della svastica," 8–15, and same author, "La Persecuzione degli ebrei a Roma," *L'Occupazione tedesca e gli ebrei di Roma: Documenti e fatti*, Liliana Picciotto Fargion, ed. (Rome: Carucci, 1979), 149–71. Tagliacozzo was in Rome on October 16, 1943.

15. A rumor to that effect apparently circulated at the time. See diary entry, September 29, 1943, in M. De Wyss, *Rome Under the Terror* (London: Robert Hale, 1945), 139–40. See also Robert Leiber, S.J., "Pio XII e gli ebrei di Roma, 1943–1944," *La Civiltà Cattolica*, anno 112, 1961, vol. I, quad. 2657, March 4, 1961, 449–58, 450; and Domenico Tardini, *Pio XII* (Vatican City: Libreria Editrice Vaticana, 1960), 39. Monsignor Antonino Arata of the Congregation for the Eastern Church provided Vatican officials with information about the gold extortion on September 27. See ADSS, IX, doc. 349, notes of the Secretariat of State, September 27, 1943, 491. It is not clear if this was the first notice received.

16. Oscar Halecki and James F. Murray, Jr., *Pius XII: Eugenio Pacelli, Pope of Peace* (n.p.: Farrar, Straus and Young, 1951), 192; Leonidas E. Hill III, "The Vatican Embassy of Ernst von Weizsäcker, 1943–1945," *Journal of Modern History* 39 (1), March 1967, 138–59, 147; Pinchas E. Lapide, *The Last Three Popes and the Jews* (London: Souvenir, 1967), 259; Joseph L. Lichten, "Pius XII and the Jews," *Catholic Mind* LVII (1142), March–April 1959, 159–62, 161; and Léon Poliakov, "The Vatican and the 'Jewish Question,' " *Commentary*, November 1950, 439–449, 441.

17. Foà, "Relazione," 14.

18. ADSS, IX, doc. 353, Chief of Special Administration of the Holy See Nogara to Maglione, September 29, 1943, 494. Nogara reported that Chief Rabbi Israele Zolli had informed him at 2:00 P.M. on September 28 that fifteen kilograms of

gold had been "found within the Catholic community." A Vatican contribution would therefore not be necessary. The editors of ADSS declared in footnote 2 that they did not know which Catholic communities had contributed. Contributions from non-Jews actually came from individuals rather than organized groups.

19. Katz, *Black Sabbath*, 87, from an interview with Renzo Levi. This version was also accepted as accurate by Renzo De Felice in his *Storia degli ebrei italiani sotto il fascismo* (1961; Turin: Einaudi, 1988), 468. In his book *Before the Dawn: Autobiographical Reflections* (New York: Sheed and Ward, 1954), 160–61, the controversial Chief Rabbi Israele (later Eugenio) Zolli said that it was he who sought and received a promise of a Vatican loan. He claimed that he advised Foà of that fact, but that Foà denied it after liberation. For more on Zolli, see Chapter Twelve.

20. Katz, *Black Sabbath*, 102. The Reichssicherheitshauptamt (RSHA) was one of twelve departments in Heinrich Himmler's SS. It fused the security police of the German state (the Secret State Police, or Geheime Staatspolizei [Gestapo] and the Criminal Police [Kripo]) with the Nazi party intelligence system (the Security Service, or Sicherheitsdienst [SD]). SS Lieutenant General Reinhard Heydrich headed the agency until his assassination by Czech resistants in May 1942. He was replaced by Kaltenbrunner. Reich Marshal Hermann Göring charged Heydrich with making "all necessary . . . preparations for a complete solution of the Jewish question in the German sphere of influence in Europe" on July 31, 1941. Within the RSHA, Adolf Eichmann's section IV-B-4 had the job.

21. On these incidents, see especially excerpts from the diary of Rosina Sorani, an employee of the Jewish Community of Rome, in *Ottobre 1943*, 35–38.

22. Kappler report to SS Lieutenant General Karl Wolff, commander of the SS in Italy, evening of October 16, 1943, printed in full in Meir Michaelis, *Mussolini and the Jews: German-Italian Relations and the Jewish Question in Italy, 1922–1945* (Oxford: Clarendon, 1978), 367–68.

23. ADSS, IX, doc. 370, notes of the Secretariat of State, October 1943 (n.d. but probably October 17), 507. The report admitted that Vatican efforts had been "especially [for] cases of baptized non-Aryans, who were not liberated, like others in their condition, after their arrest." The wording suggests that the initial screening had already taken place. The author erred, however, if he believed that other "baptized non-Aryans" had been released earlier. Only those connected with mixed families were spared. See also ADSS, IX, doc. 374, notes of Secretariat of State, October 17, 1943, in which a Vatican official reported his visit to the Military College that morning, during which he learned for the first time that some of the prisoners were baptized. British Minister to the Holy See Sir d'Arcy Osborne was misinformed when he told his government on October 31 that many Jews were released when Maglione protested to Weizsäcker about the roundup. Osborne's report is quoted in Chadwick, *Britain and the Vatican*, 289; and ADSS, IX, footnote 3, 506, and VII, Introduction, 62.

24. Although the number of people arrested is clear from Kappler's report, accounts

of the exact number actually deported differ slightly. Explaining small discrepancies, infants may not have been counted consistently, one woman joined the deportees at the train station, several people died before arrival at Auschwitz, and at least one man escaped. CDEC in Milan has identified 1,023 deportees, of the 1,259 arrested. Accounts of the number of detainees released before deportation on October 18 also vary slightly. The number 236, cited here, is calculated from the difference between the 1,259 arrested, according to Kappler, and the 1,023 deportees identified by CDEC. See Picciotto Fargion, *Il Libro della memoria*.

25. Picciotto Fargion, *Il Libro della memoria*, 42.
26. After the war, Möllhausen, in his memoirs *La Carta perdente* (Rome: Sestante, 1948), 111–12, wrote that General Rainer Stahel, German army commander of Rome, called him to his office and told him. Stahel, fearing disorder in his area of command, opposed the deportations.
27. Möllhausen's telegrams to Foreign Minister Joachim von Ribbentrop on October 6 and 7, 1943, are printed in Saul Friedländer, *Pius XII and the Third Reich: A Documentation*, trans. from French and German by Charles Fullman (New York: Knopf, 1966), 204–5. Originals are in the archives of the German Ministry of Foreign Affairs.
28. Ibid., 205, for the text of the telegram. Original in German archives. For one possible reason why the telegram mentioned Mauthausen, see below.
29. For Weizsäcker's motives and some evidence that he and his aide Albrecht von Kessel tried in September to send a message to Jewish leaders, advising them to tell Roman Jews to hide, see Kessel's testimony in Eric Bentley, ed., *The Storm Over "The Deputy"* (New York: Grove, 1964), 73–75. See also Owen Chadwick, "Weizsäcker, the Vatican, and the Jews of Rome," *Journal of Ecclesiastical History* 28 (2), April 1977, 179–99, 186–88; and Hill, "The Vatican Embassy of Ernst von Weizsäcker," 147–51.
30. Katz, *Black Sabbath*, 139, from a personal interview with Möllhausen. Other historians who believe that the pope received an early warning from Möllhausen and Weizsäcker include Michaelis, *Mussolini and the Jews*, 364; and Picciotto Fargion, *Il Libro della memoria*, 817 and 894. Michaelis is always scrupulous in his defense of the pope, while Picciotto Fargion, though more critical, is invariably balanced and fair.
31. ADSS, IX, doc. 363, notes of the Secretariat of State, October 11, 1943, 501.
32. ADSS, IX, doc. 388, notes of the Secretariat of State, October 25, 1943, 524.
33. Hans Kirchhoff, "SS-Gruppenführer Werner Best and the Action Against the Danish Jews—October 1943," *Yad Vashem Studies* XXIV, 1994, 195–222, and letter to this author, November 29, 1999; Mordecai Paldiel, *The Path of the Righteous: Gentile Rescuers of Jews During the Holocaust* (Hoboken, N.J.: KTAV, 1993), 369–70; and Leni Yahil, *The Rescue of Danish Jewry: Test of a Democracy* (Philadelphia: Jewish Publication Society of America, 1969), and same author, *The Holocaust: The Fate of European Jewry* (New York: Oxford University Press, 1990), 575.

34. Katz, *Black Sabbath*, 40–42, is most critical of Almansi and Foà. Defenders of the two men include Renato J. Almansi, "Mio padre, Dante Almansi," *La Rassegna Mensile di Israel*, XLII, May–June 1976, 251–52; and Augusto Segre, *Memorie di vita ebraica: Casale Monferrato-Roma-Gerusalemme, 1918–1960* (Rome: Bonacci, 1979), 235–36.

35. Zolli, *Before the Dawn*, 141–42, claimed that he tried to persuade Jewish Community leaders to close the synagogue and warn Jews to hide, but they ignored him.

36. Robert A. Graham, S. J., "La Strana condotta di E. von Weizsäcker ambasciatore del Reich in Vaticano," *La Civiltà Cattolica*, anno 121, quad. 2879, June 6, 1970, 455–71. Graham heard the story from Princess Pignatelli herself. He received written confirmation from Wollenweber in August 1969.

37. ADSS, IX, doc. 368, notes of Cardinal Maglione, October 16, 1943, 505–6. The punctuation in the report was uneven. It is recorded here as written. For a complete distortion of this meeting, see Jean Chélini, *L'Eglise sous Pie XII: La Tourmente, 1939–1945* (Paris: Fayard, 1983), 284–85.

38. For one example of an alarming report at this time, see ADSS, IX, doc. 355, notes of the Secretariat of State, October 1, 1943, 495–96. The author wrote of rumors that General Rainer Stahel intended to invade the Vatican City and remove the pope to a destination as yet undecided. For more on the plot to kidnap the pope, see Alvarez and Graham, *Nothing Sacred*, 85–88.

39. Tittmann interview. See also Chadwick, *Britain and the Vatican*, 268 and 272.

40. Ribbentrop to Weizsäcker, declaration for delivery to Maglione, October 7, 1943, printed in Friedländer, *Pius XII and the Third Reich*, 202.

41. "Nostre Informazioni," *L'Osservatore Romano*, October 30, 1943, 1.

42. For one such rumor, see ADSS, IX, doc. 474, notes of the Secretariat of State, December 20, 1943, 612. This incident is discussed in Chapter Fifteen.

43. From Gumpert's testimony at Weizsäcker's trial at Nuremberg, cited by Graham, "La Strana condotta di E. von Weizsäcker," 468; and Rolf Hochhuth, "Reply to Cardinal Montini," in Bentley, *Storm Over "The Deputy,"* 69–71, 69. Weizsäcker was tried after the war for his activities as state secretary under Foreign Minister Joachim von Ribbentrop from April 1938 to April 1943, before he became the German ambassador to the Holy See. He was sentenced in April 1948 to seven years for, among other things, not having hindered the deportation of French Jews. He served two and a half years, was amnestied, and died in 1951. For discussion of his career as state secretary, see Lewis Namier, *In the Nazi Era* (London: Macmillan, 1952), 63–83.

44. The document is quoted fully in Friedländer, *Pius XII and the Third Reich*, 205–6, from the original incorporated in a telegram to Berlin and preserved at the German Foreign Ministry. Hudal must have sent a copy to the Holy See, for it is included in ADSS, IX, doc. 373, Hudal to Stahel, October 16, 1943, 509–10. The letter was delivered to General Stahel by Father Pancrazio Pfeiffer, the superior general of the Order of the Salvatorians and Pius XII's personal liaison

with Stahel. Gumpert, officially with the German Embassy to Italy, was working for Stahel at this time because his own office had been transferred to the north.

45. Chadwick, "Weizsäcker, the Vatican, and the Jews of Rome," 191–93; Graham, "La Strana condotta di E. von Weizsäcker," 468–70; and Hill, "Vatican Embassy of Ernst von Weizsäcker," 148.

46. Gumpert to Robert Katz. See Katz, *Black Sabbath*, 198–203 and 212–15.

47. Graham, "La Strana condotta di E. von Weizsäcker," footnote 22, 470.

48. Claims that the pope caused Hudal to write the letter may be found, with no evidence offered, in Pierre Blet, S.J., *Pius XII and the Second World War: According to the Archives of the Vatican*, trans. from French by Lawrence J. Johnson (1997; New York: Paulist Press, 1999), 216; Lapide, *Last Three Popes and the Jews*, 259; and Angelo Martini, S.J., "La Vera Storia e 'Il Vicario' di Rolf Hochhuth," *La Civiltà Cattolica*, anno 115, vol. II, quad. 2735, n. 11, June 6, 1964, 438–54, 444.

49. Weizsäcker's report is printed in Friedländer, *Pius XII and the Third Reich*, 206–7, from the original in the archives of the German Foreign Ministry.

50. "La strage degli innocenti," *L'Osservatore Romano*, October 25–26, 1943, 1.

51. "La carità del Santo Padre," *L'Osservatore Romano*, October 25–26, 1943, 1.

52. Printed in Friedländer, *Pius XII and the Third Reich*, 207–8, from the original report preserved at the German Foreign Ministry.

53. Ibid.

54. Graham, "La Strana condotta di E. von Weizsäcker," 455–71.

55. Ibid., 456.

56. Kirchhoff letter, November 29, 1999; and Raul Hilberg, *The Destruction of the European Jews*, 3 vols. (New York: Holmes & Meier, 1985), II, 564–65; and Yahil, *Rescue of Danish Jewry*.

57. ADSS, IX, doc. 370, notes of the Secretariat of State, October 1943 (no day), 507. See also doc. 375, 376, 377, 381, 385, 397, 404, 407, 416, 426, and 449.

58. Ibid., doc. 390, Tacchi Venturi to Maglione, October 25, 1943, 525–26; and attached note from Dell'Acqua, October 27, 1943, 526.

59. Ibid., doc. 405, notes of Montini, November 1, 1943, 538–39.

60. These incidents will be discussed in subsequent chapters.

61. Giovanni Battista Montini, "Pius XII and the Jews," letter to the British Catholic periodical *The Tablet*, reproduced in Eric Bentley, *Storm Over "The Deputy*,*" 67–68.

62. Hudal is quoted in ADSS, IX, doc. 373, footnote 4, 510. The claim is repeated in Blet, *Pius XII and the Second World War*, 216; Paul Duclos, *Le Vatican et la seconde guerre mondiale: Action doctrinale et diplomatique en faveur de la paix* (Paris: Pedone, 1955), 190; and Lapide, *Last Three Popes and the Jews*, 260.

63. Kappler's report is printed in Michaelis, *Mussolini and the Jews*, 367–68.

64. Graham, "La Strana condotta di E. von Weizsäcker," 470. Blet, *Pius XII and the Second World War*, 217; and Chadwick, "Weizsäcker, the Vatican, and the Jews of Rome," 199, share this view.

65. Picciotto Fargion, *Il Libro della memoria*, 29.

66. Ibid., 56–62.

67. Ibid. On two occasions, trains originating in Manua and Verona merged with trains from Fossoli.

68. ADSS, IX, doc. 389, bishop of Padua to Maglione, October 25, 1943, 525.

1. Sources disagree on the numbers involved. The number 200 is given by Stefan Schwamm, in CDEC, b. 13-B, f. Roma, "Riassunto dell'attività di Padre Benedetto Maria OFM CAP. e dei suo [sic] collaboratori," December 20, 1945, 6 pp., 1. According to CDEC, b. 8-Opera di soccorso e di assistenza ai perseguitati e superstiti, f. Delasem, s.f. Attività generale-Genova, "Attività della Delasem dopo l'8 settembre 1943," Sorani report, May 16, 1944, 12 pp., 7, there were only 110 persons involved.

2. ADSS, IX, doc. 338, notes of the Secretariat of State, September 18, 1943, 482–83. Footnote 1, 482, identifies the author of this document as Monsignor Di Meglio and declares that the Jewish lawyer was probably Foà.

3. Ibid., doc. 336, note of the Secretariat of State, September 17, 1943, 480–81.

4. Regarding Di Meglio's note, Monsignor Domenico Tardini wrote ambiguously that the pope had already alluded to the matter twice with the German ambassador. Documents referred to in ADSS as confirmation of the claim do not address the issue. Monsignor Giovanni Battista Montini added that the possibility of making such a recommendation should be studied. See ADSS, IX, doc. 336, note of the Secretariat of State, September 17, 1943, attached notes of Tardini and Montini, 481.

5. On Foà, see the diary of Rosina Sorani, an employee of the Jewish Community of Rome, in *Ottobre 1943: Cronaca di una infamia*, Comunità Israelitica di Roma, ed., 1961, entry for November 16, 1943, 39. The information about Almansi is from family letters in the possession of his son Renato Almansi, who was in New York at the time. My own statement in *The Italians and the Holocaust: Persecution, Rescue, and Survival* (New York: Basic Books, 1987), 114, that Almansi quietly went into hiding during the first week of October was an error.

6. Settimio Sorani, *L'Assistenza ai profughi ebrei in Italia (1933–1947): Contributo alla storia della "Delasem"* (Rome: Carucci, 1983), 148. Sorani refers to her as Rina Cavalieri, but she is identified as Alina in Liliana Picciotto Fargion, *Il Libro della memoria: Gli Ebrei deportati dall'Italia 1943–1945* (Milan: Mursia, 1991), 177. The latter book lists all known deportees from Italy.

7. Sorani, *L'Assistenza ai profughi ebrei in Italia*, 138 and 147.

8. Paolo Dezza, S.J., "Eugenio Zolli: Da gran rabbino a testimone de Cristo (1881–1956)," *La Civiltà Cattolica*, anno 132, vol. I, quad. 3136, February 21, 1981, 340–49, 342. See also Eugenio (formerly Israele) Zolli, *Before the Dawn: Autobiographical Reflections* (New York: Sheed and Ward, 1954); Robert Katz, *Black Sabbath: A Journey Through a Crime Against Humanity* (Toronto: Macmillan, 1969), 19–24 and 43; Louis I. Newman, *A "Chief Rabbi" of Rome*

Becomes a Catholic: A Study in Fright and Spite (New York: Renascence, 1945); and Robert G. Weisbord and Wallace P. Sillanpoa, *The Chief Rabbi, the Pope, and the Holocaust: An Era in Vatican-Jewish Relations* (New Brunswick, N.J.: Transaction, 1992). After the liberation of Rome, Roman Jews accused Zolli of abandoning his post, and dismissed him. In February 1945, Zolli converted to Catholicism, taking the name Eugenio after Pope Pius XII. He claimed to have had mystical visions of Jesus long before the dispute with the Jewish Community, but Roman Jews accused him of deliberately wishing to embarrass and hurt them.

9. The joke is related by Piero Modigliani, who survived the war in Rome, in his memoirs *I Nazisti a Roma: Dal diario di un ebreo* (Rome: Città Nuova, 1984), 17.

10. Luciano Morpurgo, *Caccia all'uomo!* (Rome: Dalmatia, 1946), 87–106.

11. Modigliani, *I Nazisti a Roma*, 18–23.

12. Testimony of Finzi in Marco Impagliazzo, ed., *La Resistenza silenziosa: Leggi razziali e occupazione nazista nella memoria degli ebrei di Roma* (Milan: Angelo Guerini, 1997), 74.

13. Ibid., testimony of David (no last name given), 26.

14. Arminio Wachsberger, "Testimonianza di un deportato da Roma," *L'Occupazione tedesca e gli ebrei di Roma*, Liliana Picciotto Fargion, ed. (Rome: Carucci, 1979), 175–207, 175.

15. Interview with this author, Rome, October 24, 1996. Lea Di Nola also recorded her memoirs in an article, "Anni difficili," unpublished manuscript, copy in possession of this author.

16. Interview with this author, Rome, November 4, 1996. See also Lia Levi, *Una Bambina e basta* (Rome: Edizioni e/o, 1994).

17. CDEC, Milan, 5-H-b: *Vicissitudini dei singoli—particolare*, f. A, s.f. Ascarelli Castelnuovo Silvana di Roma.

18. Lea Di Nola, for example, thinks there was a request to open convents to Jews about a week before October 16 because she was herself turned away at first but accepted later. Interview with this author.

19. ADSS, IX, doc. 356, notes of Montini, October 1, 1943, 496. The vicar of Rome during the German occupation was seventy-four-year-old Cardinal Francesco Marchetti-Selvaggiani. He was often ill, and in any case did not usually deal with day-to-day issues of popular charity and assistance. He left such matters to Traglia.

20. "Relazione sull'attività della DELASEM di Padre Benedetto," printed in full in Renzo De Felice, *Storia degli ebrei italiani sotto il fascismo* (1961; Turin: Einaudi, 1988), 633–34.

21. Testimony of Father Maria Benedetto (Marie Benoît), *Livre d'Or des Congrégations françaises, 1939–1945* (Paris: DRAC, 1948), 305–31, 314.

22. Sorani, *L'Assistenza ai profughi ebrei in Italia*, 145. Benedetto and Sorani spelled "Lungotevere" differently.

23. "Relazione . . . di Padre Benedetto," in De Felice, *Storia degli ebrei italiani*, 633–34.

24. Sorani, *L'Assistenza ai profughi ebrei in Italia*, 142.

25. "Relazione . . . di Padre Benedetto," in De Felice, *Storia degli ebrei italiani*, 634.

26. CDEC, b. 13-B, f. Roma, Sorani report, July 19, 1966, 5 pp., 4.

27. Sorani, *L'Assistenza ai profughi ebrei in Italia*, 146.

28. "Relazione . . . di Padre Benedetto," in De Felice, *Storia degli ebrei italiani*, 633. The editors of ADSS erred when they stated, in vol. IX, footnote 2, 431, that Benedetto administered the funds of Delasem during the occupation; De Felice, *Storia degli ebrei italiani*, 482, exaggerated when he wrote that the entire assistance operation was concentrated in Benedetto's hands.

29. Delasem's funds in Genoa had been entrusted to Cardinal Archbishop Pietro Boetto, as will be described in Chapter Sixteen. For Boetto's consignment of 1.2 million lire to Delasem in Rome, see CDEC, b. 13-B, f. Roma, Sorani report, July 19, 1966, 4. Father Robert Leiber, Pius XII's private secretary during most of his papacy, erred when he wrote that the money from Genoa was consigned first to the office of the papal nuncio to Italy, who then distributed it among the Jews. See his "Pio XII e gli ebrei di Roma, 1943–1944," *La Civiltà Cattolica*, 1961, vol. I, quad. 2657, March 4, 1961, 449–58, 452.

30. Father Maria Benedetto, "Alcune precisazioni di Padre Benedetto," *Israel* XLVI (36), July 6, 1961, 5.

31. "Relazione . . . di Padre Benedetto," in De Felice, *Storia degli ebrei italiani*, 634.

32. ADSS, X, note of Maglione attached to doc. 103, notes of the Secretariat of State, March 16, 1944, 177–79, 179. British Foreign Office documents indicate that at this same time, the Vatican Bank was extending credit in the amount of 5 million lire to Osborne, to assist escaped Allied prisoners of war in Rome, on a British guarantee of repayment. See Owen Chadwick, *Britain and the Vatican During the Second World War* (Cambridge: Cambridge University Press, 1986), 295.

33. Benedetto, "Alcune precisazioni," 5. In his previous reports on his wartime activities, Benedetto never claimed or denied Vatican funding. He wrote this frank article in July 1961 to correct errors in Father Leiber's article, "Pio XII e gli ebrei di Roma," printed in *La Civiltà Cattolica* four months earlier. Leiber implied, 452, that the pope had provided Benedetto's Jewish rescue group with substantial financial aid.

34. Benedetto, "Alcune precisazioni," 5.

35. Sorani, *L'Assistenza ai profughi ebrei in Italia*, 146.

36. CDEC, b. 8, Sorani report, May 16, 1944, 10. The CDEC report is unsigned, but the copy printed in Sorani, *L'Assistenza ai profughi ebrei in Italia*, appendix 43, "Attività della Delasem dopo l'8 Settembre 1943," May 16, 1944, 291–98, indicates that he wrote it.

37. ADSS, IX, note of the Secretariat of State, January 9, 1944, attached to doc. 412, 544–45.

38. Sorani, *L'Assistenza ai profughi ebrei in Italia*, 146.

39. ADSS, IX, doc. 433, notes of Don Salvatore Asta, an official at the Secretariat of State, November 19, 1943, 568–69, with attached note of Dell'Acqua, November 20, 1943, 569.

40. Ibid., doc. 487, notes of the Secretariat of State, December 29, 1943, footnote 4, annotation by Dell'Acqua, 631–32.

41. Ibid., doc. 412, Benedetto (Benoît) to Montini, November 5, 1943, 544; and doc. 415, notes of the Secretariat of State, November 6, 1943, 549.

42. Ibid., doc. 415, notes of the Secretariat of State, November 6, 1943, 549.

43. "Relazione . . . di Padre Benedetto," in De Felice, *Storia degli ebrei italiani*, 634. See also Benedetto, *Livre d'Or*, 317. For Hérissé's help in July, see Chapter Ten.

44. CDEC, b. 13-B, f. Roma, Sorani report, July 19, 1966, 4. See also Sorani, *L'Assistenza ai profughi ebrei in Italia*, 152. Benedetto, Sorani, and others often spelled the name Hérissé differently.

45. CDEC, b. 13-B, f. Roma, Schwamm report, December 20, 1945, 5; and Benedetto, *Livre d'Or*, 320. Monsignor Dionisi is not mentioned in the *Annuario Pontificio* for 1943.

46. Benedetto, *Livre d'Or*, 316.

47. De Felice, "Elenco delle case religiose in Roma che ospitarono ebrei," *Storia degli ebrei italiani*, 628–632, listed under "Opera di assistenza—Opera Delasem assunto dal Reverendo Padre Benedetto," 632. For analysis of this list, see Chapter Thirteen.

48. Benedetto, *Livre d'Or*, 323; and CDEC b. 13-B, f. Roma, Schwamm report, December 20, 1945, 6.

CHAPTER THIRTEEN: HIDING AFTER THE ROUNDUP: ROMAN CONVENTS, MONASTERIES, CATHOLIC HOSPITALS AND SCHOOLS

1. Federica Barozzi, " 'I Percorsi della sopravvivenza,' (8 settembre '43–4 giugno '44): Gli aiuti agli ebrei romani nella memoria di salvatori e salvati," unpublished thesis, Università degli studi di Roma "La Sapienza," Facoltà di lettere e filosofia, 1995–96, 153–64. Barozzi reached the number 67 by counting all Jewish-sounding names on preserved lists of "patients" at the hospital during the occupation. She acknowledged that others might have been there with false names.

2. Interview with three nuns by this author, Convent of the Sisters of Our Lady of Sion, Rome, October 22, 1996. See also Barozzi, "I Percorsi della sopravvivenza," 121.

3. Renzo De Felice, *Storia degli ebrei italiani sotto fascismo* (1961; Turin: Einaudi, 1988), 628. For discussion of the source of De Felice's statistics, see the end of this chapter.

4. Barozzi, "I Percorsi della sopravvivenza," 121.

5. Finzi testimony in Marco Impagliazzo, *La Resistenza silenziosa: Leggi razziali e occupazione nazista nella memoria degli ebrei di Roma* (Milan: Angelo Guerini, 1997), 73–84.

6. Ibid., 23–32, for David's testimony.

7. One priest who did claim to have seen a written papal directive, Don Aldo Brunacci in Assisi, will be discussed in Chapter Seventeen.

8. Frate Maurizio to Barozzi, "I Percorsi della sopravvivenza," 156.

9. Monsignor Elio Venier, interview with this author, Rome, November 13, 1996.

10. Francesco Motto, "L'Istituto salesiano Pio XI durante l'occupazione nazifascista di Roma: 'Asilo, appoggio, famiglia, tutto' per orfani, sfollati, ebrei," *Ricerche storiche salesiane: Rivista semestrale di storia religiosa e civile* XIII (2), July–December 1994, 315–59.

11. Ibid., 334.

12. Ibid., list of Jews at the Istituto, 339–44.

13. Ibid., 320.

14. Ibid., 344.

15. Ibid., 356. The emphasis is mine.

16. Interview with this author.

17. An original placard may be found in the archives of the Seminario Lombardo (henceforth cited as ASL), b. 7.A.83, *1943: Ricordi di guerra.*

18. Ibid., for a copy of the letter.

19. Interview with this author.

20. Filmed testimony, "Memoria Presenta: Ebrei e Città di Roma durante l'occupazione nazista," Centro di Cultura Ebraica della Comunità Ebraica di Roma, 1983; and Alatri Fiorentino's interview with Barozzi, "I Percorsi della sopravvivenza," 129–30.

21. Terracina's interview with Barozzi, "I Percorsi della sopravvivenza," 130–31.

22. Filmed testimony, "Memoria Presenta"; and Raganella interview with Nicola Caracciolo, printed in the latter's *Uncertain Refuge: Italy and the Jews During the Holocaust,* trans. Florette Rechnitz Koffler and Richard Koffler (1986; Urbana: University of Illinois Press, 1995), 46. Raganella related that he informed the Vicariate the next morning of what he had pressured the nuns to do, and that he was praised for his efforts. Presumably, the fugitives were moved elsewhere as soon as the coast was clear.

23. Filmed testimony, "Memoria Presenta."

24. Interview with this author, Rome, November 4, 1996.

25. For one reference to "the persecutors of yesterday" sheltered after the war, see Pietro Palazzini, *Il Clero e l'occupazione tedesca di Roma: Il ruolo del Seminario Romano Maggiore* (Rome: Apes, 1995), 5. Palazzini was an assistant to the rector of the Seminario during and after the war. Bishop Alois Hudal and Father Anton Weber, discussed elsewhere in this book, also helped many Germans flee from Italy after the war. It is not clear how much they knew about their pasts. See Gitta Sereny, *Into That Darkness* (1974; New York: Vintage, 1983), 275 and 317–23.

26. Margherita Marchione, *Yours Is a Precious Witness: Memoirs of Jews and Catholics in Wartime Italy* (Mahwah, N.J.: Paulist Press, 1997), 109. Sister Margherita is a member of the Filippini.

27. Interview with this author. For more on the Vatican Information Service, see Chapter Six.

28. CDEC, b. 13-B, f. Roma, report by Settimio Sorani, July 19, 1966, 5 pp., 3.

29. Carlo Badala, "Il Coraggio di accogliere," *Sursum Cordo,* anno LXXVII, n. 1, 1994, 43–46, 46. This case involved placement in an extraterritorial Vatican property and will be discussed in the next chapter.

30. ADSS, IX, doc. 398, Montini to Father Pasquini, October 29, 1943, 533.

31. Ibid., doc. 434, Mme. X [name withheld] to Pope Pius XII, November 20, 1943, and attached notes, November 21 and 22, 1943, 570–71.

32. De Felice, *Storia degli ebrei italiani*, 628–32.

33. Robert Leiber, "Pio XII e gli ebrei di Roma: 1943–1944," *La Civiltà Cattolica*, anno 112, vol. I, quad. 2657, March 4, 1961, 449–58. Among other statistics cited also by De Felice, Leiber stated, 451, that 100 convents sheltered 2,775 Jews; 55 monasteries and parish churches sheltered 992; 680 Jews received hospitality for just a few days; the convent of Our Lady of Sion accepted 187; and the Franciscans of San Bartolomeo all'Isola accepted 400. Leiber did not publish the complete list that named every institution along with the number of its guests.

34. Ibid., 451. De Felice, *Storia degli ebrei italiani sotto il fascismo*, 632, mentioned Father Ambord's charitable work.

35. See the reference to Fatebenefratelli at the beginning of this chapter.

36. *Annuario Pontificio*, 1943, 532–80 and 891–923.

CHAPTER FOURTEEN: HIDING AFTER THE ROUNDUP:
VATICAN PROPERTIES, OCTOBER 16–DECEMBER 1943

1. Testimony of Michael Tagliacozzo, letter to this author, March 30, 1999.

2. Testimony of Michael Tagliacozzo, Tagliacozzo archives, Israel; and letter to this author, October 16, 1998.

3. From the Lateran Accords, printed in Sidney Z. Ehler and John B. Morrall, trans. and eds., *Church and State Through the Centuries: A Collection of Historic Documents with Commentaries* (London: Burns and Oates, 1954), 386–407, 390. There are in Rome both a Pontificio Seminario Romano Maggiore al Laterano and a Pontificio Seminario Romano Minore al Vaticano. References to the Seminario Romano will henceforth always be to the Pontificio Seminario Romano Maggiore.

4. Lateran Accords in Ehler and Morrall, *Church and State*, 392.

5. Ivanoe Bonomi, *Diario di un anno: 2 giugno 1943–10 giugno 1944* (Cernusco sul Naviglio: Garzanti, 1947), 135.

6. For the names and brief descriptions of 135 guests, see Pietro Palazzini, *Il Clero e l'occupazione tedesca di Roma: Il ruolo del Seminario Romano Maggiore* (Rome: Apes, 1995), 21–35, and appendix A, 59–65. The list is incomplete. Don Palazzini was Ronca's assistant at the seminary during the occupation. He became an archbishop in 1962 and a cardinal in 1973. See also Elio Venier, *Il Clero Romano durante la Resistenza* (Rome: Colombo, 1969), 10. Venier's book was also published in *Rivista Diocesana di Roma*, n. 11–13, 1969, 1320–27, and n. 1–2, 1970, 142–56. Monsignor Venier was a young priest in Rome during the German occupation. Most of his account of the Seminario Romano came from interviews with Ronca and Palazzini.

7. ADSS, X, doc. 86, Senator Bergamini to the Vatican Secretariat of State, March 1, 1944, 163. The letter expressed Bergamini's gratitude to the pope, whom he credited with saving him. Bergamini referred to two former Fascist senators

whose rooms at the Seminario Romano were next to his as examples of the unbiased generosity of the Holy Father.

8. Palazzini, *Il Clero e l'occupazione tedesca di Roma*, 35.

9. Ibid., 35. According to Palazzini, the family members were Badoglio's daughter and her husband. According to ADSS, X, doc. 174, notes of the Secretariat of State, April 30, 1944, with an attached note dated May 27, 251, they were Badoglio's sister and two other women, accepted at the end of May.

10. Palazzini, *Il Clero e l'occupazione tedesca di Roma*, 6 and 33–34.

11. Ibid., 27–28, for the total of 200. See also Andrea Riccardi, "La Chiesa a Roma durante la Resistenza: L'ospitalità negli ambienti ecclesiastici," *Quaderni della resistenza laziale*, Rome, n. 2, 1977, 89–150, 121. For the number of Jews present, see Michael Tagliacozzo, "Perseguitati razziali rifugiati nella Zona extraterritoriale lateranense durante l'occupazione tedesca di Roma (1943–1944)," Tagliacozzo archives, Israel. Tagliacozzo provides the name and a brief description of each Jewish guest. Some of the names are not included on Palazzini's list.

12. Tagliacozzo, "Perseguitati razziali."

13. Letter to this author, October 16, 1998.

14. Palazzini, *Il Clero e l'occupazione tedesca di Roma*, appendix B, 67–72, provides a list of the dates of entry of 131 guests.

15. Ibid. The police order will be discussed in the next chapter.

16. Letter to this author, October 16, 1998.

17. Ibid.

18. Ibid.

19. Andrea Riccardi, *Roma "città sacra"? Dalla Conciliazione all'operazione Sturzo* (Milan: Vita e Pensiero, 1979), 259.

20. Venier, *Il Clero Romano durante la Resistenza*, 19.

21. Palazzini, *Il Clero e l'occupazione tedesca*, 40.

22. Bonomi, *Diario*, entries for January 18 and 31, 1944, 141.

23. Carlo Badala, "Il Coraggio di accogliere," *Sursum Cordo*, anno LXXVII, n. 1, 1994, 43–46, 43. Don Badala, a parish priest in Rome and a skilled historian, based his research on existing documents and records at the Seminario Romano.

24. Palazzini, *Il Clero e l'occupazione tedesca di Roma*, appendix B, 67–72, 71.

25. ADSS, IX, doc. 382, notes of the Secretariat of State, October 23, 1943, 518.

26. The document is printed in Badala, "Il Coraggio di accogliere," 43. Badala explains that the typed report was neither dated nor signed, but that it was certainly written by Ronca and his assistants.

27. The document, handwritten, signed, and dated, is reproduced in Badala, "Il Coraggio di accogliere," 44.

28. Clarizio to Badala, in Badala, "Il Coraggio di accogliere," 43.

29. Palazzini, *Il Clero e l'occupazione tedesca di Roma*, 19.

30. Ibid., 29.

31. Ibid., 35.

32. Ibid., 5.

33. Ibid., 17.

34. Finzi testimony in Marco Impagliazzo, *La Resistenza silenziosa: Leggi razziali e occupazione nazista nella memoria degli ebrei di Roma* (Milan: Angelo Guerini, 1997), 77.

35. ASL, b. 7.A.77, *1943: Periodo clandestino,* list of 110 outsiders sheltered at the Seminario Lombardo in December 1943, with names, addresses, dates of birth, professions, and dates of entry.

36. Ibid. See also b. 7.A.73, *1941–1944: Diario,* entry for September 29–30, 1943. The diary, handwritten but bound, covers the period from December 19, 1941, to August 29, 1944. Several priests contributed to it, for the handwriting changes over time.

37. Ibid., b. 7.A.77, list of 110 fugitives, and "Nominativi di ebrei ospiti nel Seminario Lombardo nell'anno 1943 (Elenco da completare)," which admits to being incomplete.

38. Ibid., b. 7.A.77, list of 110 fugitives.

39. ADSS, IX, editors' note 10 attached to doc. 482, 625.

40. ASL, b. 7.A.73, *Diario,* "Appendice: il 21 dicembre 1943," written shortly after the war, 4 and 10. The author of the appendix did not contribute to the original diary.

41. Ibid., b. 7.A.77, list of 110 fugitives.

42. Ibid., b. 7.A.73, *Diario,* "Appendice," 6.

43. Ibid., b. 7.A.77, "Dal Seminario Lombardo iscritti alla P. Univ. Gregoriana negli anni scolastici 1943–1944–1945."

44. Ibid., identification cards.

45. Ibid., b. 7.A.73, *Diario,* entry for November 1, 1943.

46. Ibid., entries in November and December 1943.

47. Ibid., exact date unclear.

48. Ibid., entry for November 27, 1943.

49. See ADSS, IX, doc. 387, notes of Montini, October 25, 1943, 524, and editors' footnote 2.

50. ADSS, X, doc. 53, Anichini to Pius XII, February 13, 1944, 127–29.

51. Although such soldiers tried to avoid attracting attention and did not roam freely about the Vatican City, Harold H. Tittmann, son of the American chargé d'affaires confined there during the entire German occupation of Rome, remembers seeing them. It was a sight that a young American boy was not likely to forget. Interview with this author, New York, May 17, 1999. The situation, however, must not be exaggerated. Most Allied military escapees remained outside the Vatican City. They were hidden throughout Rome with help from, among others, British minister to the Holy See d'Arcy Osborne and Irish Monsignor Hugh O'Flaherty. The pope was only vaguely aware of these activities. Furthermore, on several occasions before the German occupation and at least one case during it, Vatican gendarmes delivered escaped British prisoners of war who had managed to get into the Vatican City to the Italian police on the outside. See Owen Chadwick, *Britain and the Vatican During*

the *Second World War* (Cambridge: Cambridge University Press, 1986), 292.

52. ADSS, X, doc. 219, notes of the Secretariat of State, June 2, 1944, 300–301.

CHAPTER FIFTEEN: RAIDS AND RECONSIDERATION,
DECEMBER 1943–JUNE 1944

1. Liliana Picciotto Fargion, *Il Libro della memoria: Gli Ebrei deportati dall'Italia (1943–1945)* (Milan: Mursia, 1991), 825.
2. Ibid., 825–26.
3. Ibid., 829–31. See also Michele Sarfatti, *Gli ebrei nell'Italia fascista: Vicende, identità, persecuzione* (Turin: Einaudi, 2000), 245–62.
4. "Carità civile," *L'Osservatore Romano*, December 3, 1943, 1.
5. "Motivazioni," *L'Osservatore Romano*, December 4, 1943, 1.
6. ADSS, IX, doc. 469, notes of the Secretariat of State, December 17, 1943, 606–7.
7. Ibid., doc. 472, Maglione to Tacchi Venturi, December 19, 1943, 610–11.
8. Ibid., footnote 1 attached to doc. 473, p. 611. The editors quote only Tacchi Venturi's opening sentences and do not describe the rest of the note.
9. Ibid., doc. 473, notes of Maglione, December 20, 1943, 611.
10. Ibid., doc. 453, Foligno to Maglione, December 2, 1943, and attached note of Montini, 589–90.
11. Ibid., doc. 474, notes of the Secretariat of State, December 20, 1943, 612.
12. Ibid., notes of the Secretariat of State, December 23, 1943, attached to doc. 482, 627–28; and ASL, b.7.A.73, *Diario*, "Appendice: il 21 dicembre 1943," 8. Koch, the son of a former German naval officer, had a wine business in Avellino before the war. After the liberation of Rome he led his increasingly bloodthirsty band north, torturing and murdering hundreds of victims. Thirty-seven years old when the war ended, he was tried in Rome in a single session and executed the following day, June 5, 1945.
13. This account is taken from ASL, b.7.A.73, *Diario*, "Appendice," 7–17.
14. Ibid., 15.
15. The number twelve is from ADSS, IX, doc. 482, Father Herman to Maglione, December 22, 1943, 623–28, 625; the number fifteen is from the colonel's report to the Secretariat of State, December 23, 1943, attached to doc. 482, 627.
16. ASL, b.7.A.73, *Diario*, "Appendice," 15.
17. Ibid., 10.
18. Enrico Ravenna is included in the list of all known Italian Jewish deportees to Auschwitz and other camps, in Picciotto Fargion, *Il Libro della memoria*, 493. The citation errs in the date of his arrest.
19. ASL, b.7.A.73, *Diario*, "Appendice," 15.
20. Ibid., 17.
21. A vivid account of the raids on the Istituto Orientale and the Collegio Russo, written by a priest who was there, is printed in ADSS, IX, doc. 482, 623–25. In his article "Pio XII e gli ebrei di Roma 1943–1944," *La Civiltà Cattolica*, anno 112,

vol. I, quad. 2657, March 4, 1961, 449–58, 454, Father Robert Leiber dates the
raid in the spring of 1944—one of many major errors in this postwar article by
Pius XII's closest personal aide.

22. Picciotto Fargion, *Il Libro della memoria*, 613. Vatican officials apparently tried to
learn about the fate of Warschauer, for the bishop of Carpi reported to
Monsignor Montini on April 17, 1944, that he was not at Fossoli. See ADSS, X,
doc. 148, 219–20.

23. ADSS, IX, notes from officials at the Vatican Secretariat of State, December 23,
24, and 26, 1943, attached to doc. 482, 626.

24. Ibid., December 22, 1943, 626.

25. Ibid., note of Cardinal Maglione, December 23, 1943, 626.

26. ADSS, X, doc. 32, note of the Secretariat of State, January 31, 1944, 105.

27. Archivio del monastero di San Paolo fuori le Mura, "Cronaca del Ven. Monastero
di San Paolo in Roma, dall'anno 1907 al 1958," unpublished manuscript, entry
for February 4, 1944, by a monk present at the time, 169.

28. Ibid., 171. The monk wrote that one of the principal agents was "a certain Kock";
a Vatican investigation also stated that Koch was the chief of operations,
although Police Chief Pietro Caruso was the organizer. See ADSS, XI, doc. 24,
notes of the Secretariat of State, February 4, 1944, but written after that date,
110–17, 113 and 116. Forty-four-year-old Caruso, a veteran of the Fascists' march
on Rome in 1922, was caught, tried, and executed in September 1944.

29. "Cronaca del Monastero," 170.

30. Ibid., 171.

31. All five are listed as deportees to Auschwitz who did not survive in Picciotto
Fargion, *Il Libro della memoria*, 273 and 561, with the dates of their arrests,
February 3 and 4, 1944. Settimio Sorani, *L'Assistenza ai profughi ebrei in Italia
(1933–1947): Contributo alla storia della "Delasem"* (Rome: Carucci, 1983), 154,
states that Carlo Fiorentini and Leonardo and Aurelio Spagnoletto were arrested
at the monastery of San Paolo.

32. ADSS, XI, doc. 25, notes of Tardini, February 4, 1944, 117–18; and *L'Osservatore
Romano*, February 7–8, 1944, 1.

33. Article 22, diplomatic treaty, Lateran Accords, published in Sidney Z. Ehler and
John B. Morrall, trans. and eds., *Church and State Through the Centuries: A
Collection of Historic Documents with Commentaries* (London: Burns and Oates,
1954), 392.

34. ADSS, XI, doc. 30, notes of Maglione, February 6, 1944, 126.

35. ASL, b.7.A.73, *Diario*, "Appendice," 17–18.

36. Pietro Palazzini, *Il Clero e l'occupazione tedesca di Roma: Il ruolo del Seminario
Romano Maggiore* (Rome: Apes, 1995), 42.

37. Bonomi, *Diario*, 146–47.

38. Ibid., entry for February 9, 1944, 147.

39. Bergamini remained with the Augustinians. On March 2, 1944, he wrote to the
Vatican secretary of state, declaring that "what the Holy See is doing now, aiding
people without distinction of class, religion or party, is raising the Church to a

position of extraordinary prestige." He concluded, "I am certain that for a hundred years there can be no anti-clericalism in Italy; it will be impossible to forget what the clergy has done." See his letter in ADSS, X, doc. 86, March 1, 1944, 163.

40. Bonomi, *Diario,* entries for February 15 and 21, and March 3, 6, 22, 23, and 24, 1944, 147–63.

41. Letter to this author, March 30, 1999.

42. Ibid.; and written testimony, August 18, 1998, Tagliacozzo archives, Israel.

43. ASL, b.7.A.73, *Diario,* "Appendice," 18.

44. ADSS, X, doc. 37, notes of Ronca, February 6, 1944, 109.

45. Ibid., doc. 48, notes of Ronca, February 11, 1944, 123–24.

46. Ibid., doc. 92, notes of Vigano, March 6, 1944, 170. The exact day of the note is not certain.

47. Ibid., doc. 53, Anichini to Pius XII, February 13, 1944, 127–29.

48. Ibid., note by Tardini attached to doc. 53, 129.

49. Information about Canali is from Owen Chadwick, *Britain and the Vatican During the Second World War* (Cambridge: Cambridge University Press, 1986), 125, 131, 172–73, and 292.

50. ASL, b.7.A.73, *Diario,* "Appendice," 18.

51. Ibid.

52. Ibid.

53. ADSS, X, doc. 93, notes of the Secretariat of State, March 7, 1944, 171.

54. Ibid., doc. 219, notes of the Secretariat of State, June 2, 1944, 300–301.

CHAPTER SIXTEEN: THE VATICAN AND RESCUE IN THE NORTH: GENOA, TURIN, AND MILAN

1. Renzo Segre, *Venti mesi* (Palermo: Sellerio, 1995).

2. Francesco Repetto, "La Consegna della Medaglia dei Giusti fra le Nazioni," *Liguria,* anno XLIX, n. 3, May–June 1982, 27–30, 29.

3. Archivio Diocesano di Genova (ADG), Carte Boetto, f. 10: Lettere per ebrei. Many of those who received help were converts or members of mixed families. See also Carlo Brizzolari, *Gli Ebrei nella storia di Genova* (Savona: Sbatelli, 1971), 289.

4. Such claims by actual participants are rare. As will be seen in the next chapter, Don Aldo Brunacci of Assisi later stated that he saw a written directive from the pope in his bishop's hand in 1943, but he seems to be unique. No bishop or archbishop during the war made such a claim then or later. For examples of later claims from secondary sources, see Gianfranco Bianchi, "I Cattolici," in Leo Valiani, Gianfranco Bianchi, and Ernesto Ragioneri, *Azionisti cattolici e comunisti nella Resistenza* (Milan: Franco Angeli, 1971), 211–24, 211; Sergio Minerbi, *Raffaele Cantoni, un ebreo anticonformista* (Assisi: Beniamino Carucci, 1978), 118; and the introduction to this book, note 10.

5. For discussion of how Teglio became involved with Delasem, see Alexander Stille, *Benevolence and Betrayal: Five Italian Jewish Families Under Fascism* (New York: Summit, 1991), 223–78; and testimony of Teglio in Nicola Caracciolo,

Uncertain Refuge: Italy and the Jews During the Holocaust, trans. Florette Rechnitz Koffler and Richard Koffler (1986; Urbana: University of Illinois Press, 1995), 131–33.

6. Chiara Bricarelli, ed., *Una Gioventù offesa: Ebrei genovesi ricordano* (Florence: La Giuntina, 1995), 39–53.

7. CDEC, b. 13-B—Comunità Ebraiche in Italia dal 1922 al 1945, f. Genova, "Conversazione con il Sig. Massimo Teglio, Genova, 19 gennaio 1965, presenti Rav. Aldo Luzzatto, Delia Sdraffa, Pupa Dello Strologo," 6 pp., 1. See also Brizzolari, *Gli Ebrei nella storia di Genova,* 310; and Stille, *Benevolence and Betrayal,* 245.

8. Stille, *Benevolence and Betrayal,* 272.

9. Repetto, "La Consegna della Medaglia dei Giusti," 28.

10. Massa and Rotondi were released after the intervention of Cardinal Ildefonso Schuster, archbishop of Milan, and Monsignor Giuseppe Bicchierai, Schuster's regular liaison with the Germans. In November 1944, Monsignor Bicchierai wrote that he had obtained the liberation of 42 priests and monks from German custody. Most, he claimed, had been arrested for helping Jews. See Archivio della Curia di Torino (ACT), b. 14.14.107.VI, f. II—Correspondenza, Mons. Barale, Carte concernenti periodo bellico, sf. 1944, "Relazione riassuntiva dei rapporti avuti con l'autorità tedesca dal 20 dicembre 1943 ad oggi novembre 1944," typed report.

11. For more on Genoa, see Brizzolari, *Gli Ebrei nella storia di Genova,* 285–325; Aldo Luzzatto, "La Deportazione degli ebrei di Genova," *Quaderni del Centro di Studi sulla Deportazione e l'Internamento,* n. 8, 1969–71, 83–85; Emanuele Pacifici, "Testimonianza sulla deportazione di Riccardo Pacifici," *Quaderno del Centro di Studi sulla Deportazione e l'Internamento,* n. 4, 1967; Stille, *Benevolence and Betrayal,* 223–78; Giovanni Battista Varnier, "Un Vescovo per la guerra: L'Azione pastorale del Cardinale Boetto, Arcivescovo di Genova (1936–1946)," in Bartolo Gariglio, ed., *Cattolici e Resistenza nell'Italia settentrionale* (Bologna: Mulino, 1997), 33–57; and Susan Zuccotti, *The Italians and the Holocaust: Persecution, Rescue, and Survival* (New York: Basic Books, 1987), 162–64.

12. Repetto, "La Consegna della Medaglia dei Giusti," 30.

13. ASL, b.7.A.73, *Diario,* entries for December 9 and 13, 1943.

14. ACT, b. 14.14.107.X, f. II—Guerra: Ricerche, raccomandazioni, assistenza, "Offerte pro Ebrei profughi," in Barale's handwriting, receipts and disbursements from October 5, 1943, to January 10, 1944.

15. Ibid., for all letters.

16. Valobra later testified that when he fled to Switzerland, at the end of November 1943, he left 3 million lire with Delasem in Genoa and sent 27 million more there between January and June 1944, plus smaller amounts in the autumn of 1944 and the winter of 1944–45. The amounts seem high, but some went to Sorani and Father Benedetto in Rome, while other funds were distributed throughout northern Italy by the CLN. See Michele Sarfatti, "Raffaele Jona ed il

soccorso agli ebrei del Piemonte durante la Repubblica Sociale Italiana,"
Questioni di storia della Valle d'Aosta contemporanea, n. 3, 1990, 76–95, 79. See
also CDEC, Fondo Valobra.

17. ACT, b. 14.14.107.X, f. II, Repetto to Barale, October 18, 1943.

18. Ibid., Repetto to Barale, October 31, 1943.

19. Ibid., Repetto to Barale, November 3, 1943.

20. Ibid., "Offerte pro Ebrei profughi," entries for October 23, November 18,
December 13 and 31, 1943, and January 7, 1944. See also Walter E. Crivellin, *I
Sacramentini a Torino: Momenti e figure*, Fondazione Carlo Donat-Cattin
(Racconigi: Tipolitografia Boston, 1996).

21. ACT, b. 14.14.107.IX, f. IV, original bill from the Ospizio poveri convalescenti
alla Crocetta, April 1944. Barale recorded his payments in the name of a Signora
Vittoria Necco, who delivered them.

22. ACT, b. 14.14.107.X, f. II, December 10, 1943.

23. Ibid., Barale to Suor Assistente, November 6 and 12, 1943.

24. Ibid., "Offerte pro Ebrei profughi," entry for November 13, 1943.

25. CDEC, Milan, 9/1—Riconoscimento benemeriti nell'opera di soccorso, f. Biella,
statement of Davide Nissim, December 13, 1954. Don Giuseppe Peaquin ignored
parishioners and bishop alike and continued to help. He eventually had to save
himself by taking refuge with the partisans.

26. ACT, b. 14.14.107.X, f. II, handwritten report on Delasem stationery, Turin,
without date but from autumn of 1943.

27. Giorgina Levi, "Gli ebrei jugoslavi internati nella Provincia di Aosta
(1941–1945)," in *Questioni di storia della Valle d'Aosta contemporanea: Quaderno di
ricerca e documentazione a cura dell'Istituto Storico della Resistenza in Valle d'Aosta*,
n. 3, 1990, 9–53, 39.

28. ACT, b. 14.14.107.X, f. II, list of disbursements, Barale's handwriting.

29. Archivio dello Stato, Torino (AST), mazzo 509, f. 29—"Barale, Monsignor
Vincenzo, Torino," report, capo della provincia to Ministero dell'Interno, August
7, 1944. Included also are copies of several letters from Barale to directors of the
Sacramentini, recommending Jews, sending money for their maintenance, and
thanking priests and monks for their help.

30. Giuseppe Garneri, *Tra Rischi e pericoli: Fatti e testimonianze nel periodo della
Resistenza, della Liberazione e della persecuzione contro gli Ebrei*, 2nd ed. (Pinerolo:
Alzani, 1985), 118–21.

31. For a fuller account than is possible here, see Alberto Cavaglion, "La
Deportazione degli ebrei piemontesi: Appunti per una storia," in Federico Cereja
and Bruno Mantelli, eds., *La Deportazione nei campi di sterminio nazisti: Studi e
testimonianze* (Milan: Franco Angeli, 1986), 107–26; Bartolo Gariglio, "I Cattolici
piemontesi nella guerra e nella Resistenza," in Gariglio, *Cattolici e Resistenza
nell'Italia settentrionale*, 15–32; Riccardo Marchis, "Le Relazioni dei parroci su
guerra e resistenza nella diocesi di Torino," in Marchis, ed., *Cattolici, Guerra e
Resistenza in Piemonte: Le fonti e gli archivi* (Turin: Franco Angeli, 1987), 103–23;

and Giuseppe Tuninetti, *Clero, Guerra e Resistenza nella diocesi di Torino (1940–1945): Nelle relazioni dei parroci del 1945* (Casale Monferrato: Piemme, 1996).

32. Aldo Giraudo, "Salesiani in Piemonte nel periodo bellico: Percezione degli eventi e scelte operative," in Bartolo Gariglio and Riccardo Marchis, eds., *Cattolici, ebrei, ed evangelici nella provincia di Torino: Vita religiosa e società* (Milan: Franco Angeli, 1999), 165–218.

33. ACT, b. 14.14.108/bis, typed report on stationery of the Convento San Domenico, no date and no signature.

34. AST, mazzo 509, copy of *L'Angelo della famiglia*, anno XXXIX, n. 4, April 11, 1944, article "L'Opera del Papa in Questi Penosi Momenti," in files of prefect of Turin.

35. These figures, from a 1938 census, are for the entire provinces of Milan, Turin, and Genoa. See Renzo De Felice, *Storia degli ebrei italiani sotto il fascismo* (1961; Turin: Einaudi, 1988), 10.

36. Testimony of Sala, cited in full in Paolino Beltrame-Quattrocchi, *Al di sopra dei gagliardetti: L'arcivescovo Schuster: Un asceta benedettino nella Milano dell' "era fascista"* (Casale Monferrato: Marietti, 1985), 325–26.

37. CDEC, b. 13-B—Comunità Ebraiche in Italia dal 1922 al 1945, f. Milano, "Notizie dalla Comunità di Milano sul periodo 1938–1945," 2 pp., 1.

38. On Schuster's speech, see Chapter Three.

39. Teglio testimony in Caracciolo, *Uncertain Refuge*, 133.

40. Ildefonso Schuster, *Gli Ultimi tempi di un regime* (Milan: Pontificia Editrice Arcivescovile Daverio, 1960). An earlier version of the book appeared in 1946.

41. Bianchi, "I Cattolici," 211.

42. Dorina Di Vita, "Gli Ebrei di Milano sotto l'occupazione nazista," *Quaderni del Centro di Studi sulla deportazione e l'internamento*, n. 6, 1969–71, 22–72.

43. CDEC, b. 9/2—Medaglie d'oro: Riconoscimento ai benemeriti, f. Riconoscimenti, Benemeriti nell'opera di soccorso, Giuseppe Sala, acceptance speech, April 17, 1955.

44. Archivio Storico della Diocesi di Milano (ASDM), Sezione Resistenza, f. Ghetti don Andrea, copy of a GNR report to GNR superiors, the Muti Legion, and the Decima Mas (all fanatic Fascist organizations), February 31, 1945.

45. ACT, b. 14.14.107.VI, f. II, sf. 1944, "Relazione riassuntiva dei rapporti avuti con l'autorità tedesca dal 20 dicembre 1943 ad oggi novembre 1944," report by Bicchierai probably for Schuster or Montini, typed copy in Barale's files.

46. ASDM, Sezione Resistenza, f. Bicchierai Mons. Giuseppe, "Testimonianza e documentazione inviata da Mons. Giuseppe Bicchierai," 6 pp. See also Giovanni Barbareschi, *Memoria di Sacerdoti: "Ribelli per amore"* (Milan: Centro Ambrosiano di Documentazione e Studi Religiosi, 1986), 44–47.

47. For more on Milan, see Giorgio Vecchio, "L'Episcopato e il clero lombardo nella guerra e nella Resistenza (1940–1945)," in Bartolo Gariglio, *Cattolici e Resistenza nell'Italia settentrionale*, 59–136.

48. The priests included Giovanni Barbareschi, Enrico Bigatti, Andrea Ghetti, Aurelio Giussani, Carlo Gnocchi, Natale Motto, and Luigi Re.

49. Ghetti's testimony in Barbareschi, *Memoria di Sacerdoti*, 199–203. See also Di Vita, "Gli Ebrei di Milano," 32–36.

50. CDEC, b. 8/B—Opera di assistenza e di socorrso ai perseguitati e superstiti, f. Testimonianza di Don Paolo Liggeri, December 3, 1968. This testimony is also printed in full in Di Vita, "Gli Ebrei di Milano," appendix, 63–66, 63.

51. Barbareschi, *Memoria di Sacerdoti*, 236–39; Di Vita, "Gli Ebrei di Milano," 38–39; and Don Paolo Liggeri, *Triangolo rosso* (Milan: La Casa, 1946).

52. Barbareschi, *Memoria di Sacerdoti*, 19–21; Di Vita, "Gli Ebrei di Milano," 39; P. Fedele Merelli, *Momenti di vita di P. Giannantonio Agosti*, pamphlet, 1997; and Giannantonio Agosti, *Nei lager vinse la bontà* (Milan: Missioni estere dei Padre Cappuccini, 1960).

53. ASDM, Sezione Resistenza, f. Varischi, letter signed by Varischi, July 20, 1945.

54. Ibid.

55. Repetto, "La Consegna della Medaglia dei Giusti fra le Nazioni," 28.

56. CDEC, b.8/B, f. Liggeri, testimony of Liggeri, December 3, 1968.

57. ASDM, Sezione Resistenza, f. Varischi, letter signed by Varischi, July 20, 1945.

58. For details, see Chapter Twelve.

CHAPTER SEVENTEEN: THE VATICAN AND RESCUE IN
CENTRAL ITALY: FLORENCE AND ASSISI

1. CDEC, b. 13-B—Comunità ebraiche in Italia, f. Firenze, "Consiglio di amministrazione della Comunità israelitica di Firenze," signed by Eugenio Artom, a Community official, May 10, 1945, 8 pp., 1.

2. For Cassuto and Cantoni's role, see CDEC, b 8-A-I, f. Materiale per una storia della Delasem, "Testimonianza del Sig. Giorgio Nissim," Pisa, March 2, 1969, 2 pp. Nissim was a Delasem representative in Pisa.

3. CDEC, b. 13-B, f. Firenze, Artom report, 1. The population statistic is from Paola Pandolfi, *Ebrei a Firenze nel 1943: Persecuzione e Deportazione* (Florence: Università di Firenze—Facoltà di Magistero, 1980), 11. According to Renzo De Felice, *Storia degli ebrei italiani sotto il fascismo* (1961; Turin: Einaudi, 1988), 10, there had been 2,326 Jews in Florence in 1938. About 700, then, had emigrated or otherwise disguised themselves.

4. CDEC, Artom report, 2.

5. Ibid., 3.

6. Pandolfi, *Ebrei a Firenze nel 1943*, 36; Bruna Bocchini Camaiani, "Ricostruzione concordataria e processi di secolarizzazione: L'azione pastorale di Elio Dalla Costa," in *La Chiesa del Concordato*, II (Bologna: Il Mulino, 1983), 170; and Bruna Bocchini Camaiani, interview with this author, Florence, May 6, 1998. On La Pira and Cassin, see Sergio Minerbi, *Raffaele Cantoni, un ebreo anticonformista* (Assisi: Beniamino Carucci, 1978), 118. La Pira became a popular mayor of Florence after the war.

7. Louis Goldman, *Amici per la vita* (Florence: SP 44, 1993), 59–60.

8. Archivio Arcivescovile di Firenze (AAF), Fondo Dalla Costa, b. 8—Israeliti, 1944–1945, doc. 31, "Assistenza prestata agli ebrei in Firenze nel momento più cruciale della discriminazione razziale," testimony of Leto Casini, signed and dated March 1972, 2 pp. A copy of this testimony is at the Istituto Storico della Resistenza in Toscano (ISRT), Florence, Fondo Il Clero toscano nella Resistenza, Archivio del Card. Elia Dalla Costa, Carteggio Ebrei, f. VI, doc. 9.

9. From 1936 until German and Italian police came looking for him there on September 29, 1943, La Pira often stayed on retreat at the convent. See Cipriano Ricotti, *La Chiesa che io ho amato* (Florence: Domenicani di San Marco, n.d. but after 1988).

10. Leto Casini, *Ricordi di un vecchio prete* (Florence: La Giuntina, 1986), 49–50. See also ISRT, Casini testimony. Both Don Casini and Father Ricotti were later honored by Yad Vashem as Righteous Among the Nations.

11. Report of Madre Sandra to Dalla Costa, printed in full in Emanuele Pacifici, *Non Ti Voltare: Autobiografia di un ebreo* (Florence: La Giuntina, 1993), 103–9.

12. Pandolfi, *Ebrei a Firenze*, 36–37. Pandolfi stated, p. 77, that she "collected direct testimony" from both Ricotti and Casini in 1974.

13. Archivio della Curia di Torino (ACT), b. 14.14.107.X, f. II—Guerra: Ricerche, raccomandazioni, assistenza, Repetto to Barale, October 18, 1943.

14. AAF, Casini testimony.

15. Casini, *Ricordi di un vecchio prete*, 50.

16. Minerbi, *Raffaele Cantoni*, 119.

17. AAF, Fondo Dalla Costa, b. 8—Israeliti, 1944–45, doc. 29, "Istituti e Conventi e Parrocchie che hanno ospitati o aiutati Israeliti su preghiera dell'arcivescovado e con suoi contributo—denaro"; and doc. 49, "Qualche memoria sulla protezione e assistenza ad Ebrei in Firenze nel periodo di spietata persecuzione 1943–1945," 3 pp., 3.

18. AAF, Fondo Dalla Costa, b. 8, doc. 117, "Pio Istituto delle Suore Serve di Maria SS Addolorata, via Faentina 195," bill submitted to the archbishop's office. Mother Sandra wrote that the women and girls sheltered at the Franciscan convent at the Piazza del Carmine were subsidized "by the synagogue." Report in Pacifici, *Non Ti Voltare*, 103.

19. Bruna Bocchini Camaiani, "Per un profilo storico del card. Elia Dalla Costa," in Comitato regionale toscano per il trentennale della Resistenza e della Liberazione, eds., *Il Clero toscano nella Resistenza: Atti del Convegno Lucca 4–5-6/4/75* (Florence: La Nuova Europa, 1975), 93–108.

20. Most of the false documents were provided by Mario Finzi, a young Delasem worker from Bologna who was later arrested and deported to die at Auschwitz. Ironically, Finzi was not caught because of his clandestine work, but because he was recognized by chance as a Jew by a former acquaintance during a routine document check. See Casini, *Ricordi di un vecchio prete*, 50–52; and Susan Zuccotti, *The Italians and the Holocaust: Persecution, Rescue, and Survival* (New York: Basic Books, 1987), 66–67.

21. Casini, *Ricordi di un vecchio prete*, 65; and AAF, Casini testimony.

22. AAF, Fondo Dalla Costa, b. 8, doc. 17, 18, 38, 39, 41–46, and 52; and CDEC, b. 13-B, f. Firenze, Artom report.

23. In his report (CDEC, b. 13-B, f. Firenze), Artom claimed that the archbishop's office contributed half of the funds to support poor Florentine Jews, and the Jewish Community provided the other half. However, the archbishop's office drew on Ziegler's contribution and Delasem funds entrusted to it. Artom, a leader of the Community, would not have known that.

24. Goldman, *Amici per la vita,* 59; and Pandolfi, *Ebrei a Firenze,* 40.

25. Casini, *Ricordi di un vecchio prete,* 50. Cantoni told Father Ricotti that the money he distributed came from Genoa, and that he traveled to Genoa to get it. Ricotti to Pandolfi, in Pandolfi, *Ebrei a Firenze,* 79.

26. AAF, Fondo Dalla Costa, b. 8, doc. 52/11, Meneghello to M. Rev.do Signore (later noted on document—"probably Repetto"), January 15, 1946.

27. Pandolfi, *Ebrei a Firenze,* 48–50. Pandolfi put the number at 200.

28. CDEC, b. 13-B, f. Firenze, Artom report, 3. Artom estimated that about 300 Jews were arrested, including those caught at the synagogue.

29. See Liliana Picciotto Fargion, *Il Libro della memoria: Gli Ebrei deportati dall'Italia (1943–1945)* (Milan: Mursia, 1991), list of all known Jewish deportees from Italy, 175, 343, and 364.

30. Ibid., 630–31. Rabbi Cassuto's wife, Anna Di Gioacchino Cassuto, was caught two or three days after her husband, along with Raffaele Cantoni and her brother-in-law Saul Campagnano. Anna had left the Convento della Calza, where she was hiding, in the hope that she and the two men could learn about Nathan. They too were duped by Ischia. Cantoni and Campagnano were deported to Auschwitz on December 6. Cantoni escaped from the train and made his way to Genoa to warn Valobra and Cardinal Boetto that the net was tightening. Campagnano died at Auschwitz. Anna was deported with her husband on January 30. She survived Auschwitz to be killed on April 13, 1948, with seventy other people, in an attack on a bus in Arab-held territory in Jerusalem during the Arab-Israeli War. She and Campagnano are also listed in Picciotto Fargion, *Il Libro della memoria,* 170–71 and 227. For more on Ischia, see especially Pandolfi, *Ebrei a Firenze,* 57. The Seminary Minore was requisitioned in February 1944 to serve as a German hospital. Still later, it became an SS headquarters.

31. For a list of the women arrested and information about where remaining family members were, see AAF, Fondo Dalla Costa, b. 8, doc. 48, "Ebrei presi a Piazza del Carmine e portati a Verona il 30 nov. 1943."

32. Emanuele Pacifici, interview with this author, Rome, October 29, 1996. See also Emanuele Pacifici, "Testimonianza sulla deportazione di Riccardo Pacifici," in *Quaderno del Centro di Studi sulla Deportazione e l'Internamento,* 1967, n. 4; and Mother Sandra's description of the raid in her report, printed in Pacifici, *Non Ti Voltare,* 103–9.

33. Riccardo Pacifici and his wife, Wanda Abenaim, are listed in Picciotto Fargion, *Il Libro della memoria,* 95 and 458.

34. Pandolfi, *Ebrei a Firenze,* 55–56.

35. ADSS, IX, doc. 444, Maglione to Borgongini Duca, November 27, 1943, 580.

36. Ibid., doc. 457, Borgongini Duca to Maglione, December 7, 1943, 593–94.

37. CDEC, b. 8-A-I, f. Materiale per una storia della Delasem, "Testimonianza del Sig. Giorgio Nissim Via Santamarta 90, Pisa," March 2, 1969, 2 pp.; and b. 13-B, f. Pisa, testimony, January 10, 1956, unsigned but by the Sacerdoti Oblati, 3 pp.

38. ISRT, b. 4, f. V-Ebrei, "Nazismo, clero cattolico ed ebrei," relazione di Settimio Sorani, n.d. For an account of the men and women of the Church in Tuscany during the war, see Giulio Villani and Fabrizio Poli, *Chiese Toscane: Cronache di Guerra, 1940–1945* (Florence: Libreria Editrice Fiorentina, 1995). For a more general account, see Carlo Francovich, *La Resistenza a Firenze* (Florence: La Nuova Italia, 1975).

39. CDEC, b. 8-A-I, Nissim testimony.

40. *Corriere della Sera*, "Sui margini del breviario scrisse l'addio alla vita," April 31, 1949.

41. Casini, *Ricordi di un vecchio prete*, 60.

42. AAF, doc. 62, unnamed Jewish writer from Rome to Dalla Costa, May 30, 1944. The writer was attempting to send a package to Fossoli with help from the bishop of Carpi. See also ADSS, X, doc. 148, bishop of Carpi to Montini, April 17, 1944, 219.

43. Klaus Voigt, interview with this author, Florence, May 8, 1998.

44. Report from British Minister to the Holy See Sir d'Arcy Osborne to Foreign Secretary Anthony Eden, "Partiti e movimenti politici in Italia," printed in full in Lamberto Mercuri, "La Situazione dei partiti italiani vista dal Foreign Office (dicembre 1943)," *Storia Contemporanea*, anno XI, n. 6, December 1980, 1049–60, 1057.

45. Casini, *Ricordi di un vecchio prete*, 61.

46. The number 100 was provided by Graziella Viterbi, herself an Italian Jewish refugee hidden in Assisi, in an interview with this author, Rome, October 17, 1996. Don Aldo Brunacci, involved in hiding Jews, thought that the number might have reached 200, but explained that the entire group was not present the whole time. Brunacci, interview with this author, Assisi, November 2, 1996.

47. Brunacci interview.

48. Francesco Santucci, *Assisi, 1943–1944: Documenti per una storia* (Assisi: Accademia Properziana del Subasio, 1994), 121.

49. Viterbi interview. Vacations in hotels were prohibited to Jews under the racial laws, unless they secured special permissions, which this family had done.

50. Brunacci interview.

51. Ibid. Alexander Ramati, *The Assisi Underground: The Priests Who Rescued Jews* (New York: Stein and Day, 1978), also mentions Brizi frequently.

52. Brunacci interview.

53. Ibid.

54. See a report written by one of the Colettine after the war, reprinted in Santucci, *Assisi, 1943–1944*, 131–33. Don Aldo Brunacci also spoke of the incident in his interview with this author. The Finzis apparently represented a mixed marriage.

The husband converted to Catholicism during his stay with the Colettine, and their child was baptized.

55. Viterbi interview. Ramati, *Assisi Underground*, is based primarily on interviews with Father Rufino Nicacci. Both Don Aldo Brunacci and Father Rufino Nicacci received the Medal of Righteous Among the Nations from Yad Vashem.

56. Brunacci interview. See also Don Aldo Brunacci, "Giornata degli ebrei d'Italia: Ricordi di un protagonista," public lecture, Assisi, March 15, 1982, printed in full in Brunacci, *Ebrei in Assisi durante la guerra: Ricordi di un protagonista*, Assisi, January 27, 1985, 7–15, 9.

57. Graziella Viterbi, "Una tranquilla casa in collina," *Shalom*, n. 3, March 1982, 18.

CHAPTER EIGHTEEN: THE VATICAN, THE PATRIARCH, AND THE JEWS IN VENICE

1. Paolo Sereni, "Della Comunità ebraica a Venezia durante il fascismo," in Giannantonio Paladini and Maurice Reberschak, eds., *La Resistenza nel Veneziano: La società tra fascismo, resistenza, repubblica*, 2 vols. (Venice: Stamperia di Venezia, 1985), I, 503–39, 512–13.

2. Reports for 1938 and 1940 are quoted by Sereni, "Della Comunità ebraica a Venezia," 521.

3. Francesco Feltrin, "La persecuzione degli ebrei nel Veneto," in Associazione degli ex-consiglieri Regione Veneto, *Il Veneto nella Resistenza: Contributi per la storia della lotta di liberazione* (Vittorio Veneto: Grafiche De Bastiani, 1997), 339–60, 340.

4. Sereni, "Della Comunità ebraica a Venezia," 529.

5. See a copy of the police chief's telegram to the Ministry of the Interior, December 6, 1943, from the Archivio dello Stato, Venezia (ASV), in Renata Segre, ed., *Gli Ebrei a Venezia: 1938–1945: Una Comunità tra persecuzione e rinascita* (Venice: Il Cardo, 1995), 154.

6. Liliana Picciotto Fargion, *Il Libro della memoria: Gli Ebrei deportati dall'Italia (1943–1945)* (Milan: Mursia, 1991), 832–33.

7. Police report to prefect, December 31, 1943, from ASV, quoted in Segre, *Gli Ebrei a Venezia*, 155.

8. Police report to director of Fossoli, quoted in Segre, *Gli Ebrei a Venezia*, 155.

9. Picciotto Fargion, *Il Libro della memoria*, 46; and Archivio della Comunità Israelitica di Venezia (ACIV), b. 76—Deportazione, f. Certificati.

10. Segre, *Gli Ebrei a Venezia*, 160.

11. Ibid. See also documents at the Archivio dell'Istituto Regionale per la Storia del Movimento Liberazione nel Friuli-Venezia Giulia (AIRSML), Trieste, Fondo Processo Risiera, b. 87, f. II—Ricerche, citazioni verbali, esame testi.

12. Picciotto Fargion, *Il Libro della memoria*, 54.

13. Ibid., 454.

14. Carlo Schiffrer, "La Risiera," *Trieste: Rivista politica della regione* VII (44), July–August 1961, 21–24.

15. For an excellent and forthright analysis of Cardinal Piazza's ideas, see especially Bruno Bertoli, "Indirizzi pastorali del Patriarca Piazza," in Bruno Bertoli, ed., *La Chiesa di Venezia dalla Seconda Guerra Mondiale al Concilio* (Venice: Edizioni studium cattolico veneziano, 1997), 15–68, esp. 33–38. Don Bruno Bertoli is the director of the Archivio Storico del Patriarcato di Venezia (ASPV). Also useful are two works by Silvio Tramontin: "La Chiesa Veneziana dal 1938 al 1948," in Paladini and Reberschak, *La Resistenza nel Veneziano*, I, 451–501, 458, and "La notificazione dell'episcopato triveneto dell'aprile 1944," in *Humanitas*, n. 10, 1975, 889–908; and Giovanni Vian, "Fedeltà alla chiesa e servizio alla patria nella tragedia di due amici fra Resistenza e RSI: Guido Bellemo e Gino Pizzolotto," in Bruno Bertoli, ed., *La Resistenza e i cattolici veneziani* (Venice: Edizioni studium cattolico veneziano, 1996), 57–100, 59.

16. ADSS, IX, doc. 455, footnote 3, 591–92. The exact date of Piazza's letter is not given.

17. Ibid., doc. 455, Rossi to Maglione, December 6, 1943, 591.

18. Ibid., doc. 455, footnote 4, 592. Rossi forwarded Maglione's actual letter to Piazza. It is preserved at ASPV, Sezione moderna 1801–1935, b. Guerra 1940–45, f. Aiuti ad Ebrei.

19. ADSS, X, doc. 357, notes of Tardini, October 1944, 446. Regarding a reply to be sent to the American representative to the Vatican regarding an inquiry about Jews, Tardini wrote, with supreme cynicism, "The answer from the Holy See must be ample and warm. To say simply 'we will do everything possible' seems like bureaucratic coldness. The less one can obtain, the more necessary it is to show the concern of the Holy See."

20. In fact, the original Italian anti-Jewish laws of 1938 already resembled the Nuremberg laws. In both Germany and Italy, Jews who had been baptized were always considered Jews if both parents were Jews. The chief difference was that in Italy, an individual with one Jewish parent was declared a full "Aryan" if he or she was baptized, but Jewish if not. An individual with one Jewish grandparent was "Aryan." In Germany, an individual with one Jewish parent or grandparent was declared a *Mischling*, first or second degree, regardless of baptism, as long as he or she did not practice Judaism or was not married to a Jew. Most German Mischling were not deported.

21. Koester's report is translated into English from the original and printed in Saul Friedländer, *Pius XII and the Third Reich: A Documentation*, trans. Charles Fullman (New York: Knopf, 1966), 209–11.

22. Ibid., 210–11.

23. On September 28, 1943, for example, a local Nazi sympathizer sent a letter to Koester, describing the Italian Catholic Church as profoundly anti-Semitic, anti-Bolshevik, and blindly devoted to the pope. The writer portrayed Piazza as a convinced Fascist. See ASPV, Sezione moderna, b. Guerra 1940–45, f. Carteggio con Comando tedesco. Koester must have given the letter to the patriarch, for the archives' copy is the original.

24. Ibid., f. Azione Card. Piazza, Allied Command to prefect of Venice, n.d.

25. Ibid., report from patriarch's office, August 29, 1945.
26. Ibid., f. Aiuti ad Ebrei, Urbani to police chief, December 14, 1943.
27. Of about 106 descriptions by survivors from Venice of non-Jews who helped them, none mentioned Piazza and just one mentioned Urbani. That one declared, without details, that Urbani, along with another priest, provided "moral comfort and food" to Jews arrested on December 5–6. See ACIV, b. 76— Deportazione, f. Aiuti di non ebrei a ebrei, doc. XIII, testimony of Girolamo Segre.
28. Correspondence regarding Sister Lidia Cressin is in ASPV, Sezione moderna, b. Guerra 1940–45, f. Aiuti ad Ebrei and f. Salvezza suor Lidia Cressin cenossiana di origine ebraica.
29. ASPV, Sezione moderna, b. Guerra 1940–45, f. Azione Card. Piazza, "A Difesa degli Ebrei."
30. Ibid.
31. See a photograph of the police chief of Venice's original handwritten order to his police agents, December 5, 1943, from ASV, printed in Segre, *Gli Ebrei a Venezia*, doc. 211, 153.
32. ASPV, Sezione moderna, b. Guerra 1940–45, f. Azione Card. Piazza, "A Difesa degli Ebrei."
33. Ibid.
34. These census figures are cited in Renzo De Felice, *Storia degli ebrei italiani sotto il fascismo* (1961; Turin: Einaudi, 1988), 10.

CHAPTER NINETEEN: THE VATICAN, THE BISHOP,
AND THE JEWS IN TRIESTE

1. Renzo De Felice, *Storia degli ebrei italiani sotto il fascismo* (1961; Turin: Einaudi, 1988), 10.
2. CDEC, b. 13-B, f. Trieste, 12 pp., 1.
3. Ibid.
4. Gemma Zolli, "Trieste 1938–1945," *Gli Ebrei in Italia durante il fascismo: Quaderni del Centro di Documentazione Ebraica Contemporanea* III, November 1963, 38–50, 46–47.
5. Liliana Picciotto Fargion, *Il Libro della memoria* (Milan: Mursia, 1991), 866; and Silva Bon Gherardi, *La Persecuzione antiebraica a Trieste (1938–1945)* (Udine: Del Bianco, 1972), 213–20.
6. Picciotto Fargion, *Il Libro della memoria*, 54 and 867; and Bon Gherardi, *La Persecuzione antiebraica a Trieste*, 48.
7. Fargion, *Il Libro della memoria*, lists of trains from Trieste, 60–63, and list of Jews deported from Italy, 94–632.
8. CDEC, b. 13-B, f. Trieste, 12.
9. For details on the pope's charge and Mussolini's response, see Chapter Two.
10. Santin's handwritten account of the incident is in the Archivio della Curia Vescovile di Trieste (ACVT), archivio mons. Antonio Santin, n. 23, "Miei contatti con Mussolini," n.d. See also Paolo Blasina, "Mussolini, mons. Santin e il

problema razziale (settembre 1938)," *Qualestoria*, n. 2–3, August–December 1991, 189–95.

11. ACVT, archivio mons. Antonio Santin, n. 23. Unfortunately, there is no other verification of the content of the meeting.

12. On the meeting with Buffarini Guidi, see Pietro Zovatto, *Il Vescovo Antonio Santin e il razzismo nazifascista a Trieste (1938–1945)* (Quart d'Altino, Venezia: Pier Luigi Rebellato, 1977), 33–36.

13. Giuseppe Fano, "Cenni sulla Costituzione del Comitato Italiano di Assistenza agli Emigranti Ebrei," *La Rassegna Mensile di Israel* XXXI (10–11), October–November 1965, 495–530, 517. Fano was the director of the Trieste section of Delasem before the German occupation. His report for the years 1938 to 1943 included reprints of correspondence in 1942 between Morpurgo and Santin and between Santin and Roatta. Originals of the correspondence may be found in ACVT, archivio mons. Santin, n. 37–44. Zovatto, *Il Vescovo Antonio Santin*, 48, distorted Fano's report, stating that he, Fano, credited Santin and the Holy See with getting 3,000 Jewish refugees in Lubliana admitted to Italy in 1941. Fano never mentioned interventions by churchmen in 1941, and he clearly showed that Santin's efforts were in 1942. Those efforts did not lead to admissions of Jews into Italy. Nor did Fano mention interventions by the Holy See.

14. Letter quoted in Zovatto, *Il Vescovo Antonio Santin*, 47. It does not appear in ADSS, VIII, covering the period from January 1941 to December 1942.

15. ACVT, archivio mons. Santin, Maglione to Santin, October 6, 1942. There is no copy in ADSS, VIII.

16. ADSS, VIII, doc. 502, Maglione to Marcone, October 6, 1942, 675.

17. Ibid., doc. 430, Marcone to Maglione, July 17, 1942, 601–2. This report was also cited in Chapters Seven and Eight.

18. Ibid.

19. John F. Morley, *Vatican Diplomacy and the Jews During the Holocaust, 1939–1943* (New York: KTAV, 1980), 164–65.

20. ACVT, archivio mons. Santin, Santin to Wolsegger, handwritten draft. The letter is reprinted in Antonio Santin, *Trieste, 1943–1945: Scritti, discorsi, appunti, lettere presentate, raccolte e commentate*, Guido Botteri, ed. (Udine: Del Bianco, 1963), 28.

21. See Santin, *Trieste, 1943–1945*, 29–31, for the full text of the speech, November 3, 1943.

22. ACVT, archivio mons. Antonio Santin, doc. 36, Santin to Pius XII, handwritten draft. The letter is reprinted in Santin, *Trieste, 1943–1945*, 31–32. It does not appear in ADSS, IX, which covers the year 1943.

23. Ibid.

24. ADSS, IX, doc. 441, Maglione to Weizsäcker, November 26, 1943, 578.

25. Santin, *Trieste: 1943–1945*, letter to his clergymen, December 2, 1943, 32.

26. ADSS, IX, doc. 448, notes of Santin, November 30, 1943, 585.

27. Adolfo Scalpelli, ed., *San Sabba: Istruttoria e processo per il Lager della Risiera*, 2 vols., ANED (Milan: Mondadori, 1988), I, 39.

28. Santin, *Trieste 1943–1945*, letter to Coceani, March 29, 1944, 40.

29. Ibid., editor's note 2, 40.

30. See ADSS, X, doc. 165, Santin to Maglione, April 24, 1944, 239–42, 239, for Santin's description of the meeting.

31. ACVT, archivio mons. Antonio Santin, Santin to Wolsegger, typed copy, April 23, 1944.

32. ADSS, X, doc. 165, Santin to Maglione, April 24, 1944, 239–42, 240.

33. ACVT, archivio mons. Antonio Santin, Santin to Globocnik, typed copy, July 2, 1944.

34. Picciotto Fargion, *Il Libro della memoria,* list of Jews deported from Italy, 94–632, 504.

35. Santin, *Trieste 1943–1945*, editor's note 2, 52.

36. ACVT, archivio mons. Antonio Santin, SS report to Santin, July 26, 1944.

37. Ibid., Sicherheitspolizei u. des SD to Curia, "Pia Marangoni-Rivalta," September 17, 1944.

38. Ibid.

39. Botteri, *Antonio Santin,* 39–40; and Zovatto, *Il Vescovo Antonio Santin,* 61–63.

40. See a letter from the president of the Jewish Community of Trieste to Santin, August 28, 1945, thanking him for the return of the documents, in ACVT, archivio mons. Antonio Santin.

41. Botteri, *Antonio Santin,* 39.

42. Ibid., 42–52; and Scalpelli, *San Sabba,* 88–89.

43. Bon Gherardi, *La Persecuzione antiebraica a Trieste,* 243.

44. Quoted in Zovatto, *Il Vescovo Antonio Santin,* 54.

45. Ibid., 56. Zovatto cited another case that draws us closer to Santin. He claimed that his uncle, Monsignor Paolo Lino Zovatto, was asked by the bishop of Portogruaro to hide a Jewish woman from Trieste and her son. The bishop had been asked to act by Santin. Unfortunately, there is no independent verification of the story.

46. For details, see Bon Gherardi, *La Persecuzione antiebraica a Trieste,* 244–47.

CHAPTER TWENTY: THE VATICAN AND JEWS ARRESTED IN ITALY, DECEMBER 1943–MAY 1945

1. Liliana Picciotto Fargion, *Il Libro della memoria: Gli Ebrei deportati dall'Italia (1943–1945)* (Milan: Mursia, 1991), 56–59 on statistics of the first four convoys to leave Italy, and 835–41 on intentions regarding deportation.

2. Ibid., 841–42; and Michele Sarfatti, *Gli ebrei nell'Italia fascista: Vicende, identità, persecuzione* (Turin: Einaudi, 2000), 262–63.

3. In the case of some convoys, the exact number of deportees is not certain. The numbers cited here are of individuals who have been positively identified from existing lists. Also, some trains from Milan, Verona, and Fossoli picked up

prisoners coming from Trieste and elsewhere. For descriptions of each convoy, see Picciotto Fargion, *Il Libro della memoria*, 42–55.

4. Ibid., 32.

5. Sarfatti, *Gli ebrei nell'Italia fascista*, 267.

6. For deportation statistics, see Picciotto Fargion, *Il Libro della memoria*, 42–62.

7. See Chapter Seven.

8. Founded in January 1944, the WRB represented the American government's long-overdue committment "to rescue the victims of enemy oppression who are in imminent danger of death," as stated in the executive order that created it. See David S. Wyman, *The Abandonment of the Jews* (New York: Pantheon, 1984), especially 204–87.

9. See Wyman, *Abandonment of the Jews*, 238–42.

10. For that explanation at the time, see below. For the claim later, see especially ADSS, IX, Introduction, 59, where the editors wrote, "How could the Holy See have protested to the government of the Republic of Salò [RSI] that it did not recognize?"

11. Giovanni Miccoli, *I Dilemmi e i silenzi di Pio XII: Vaticano, Seconda guerra mondiale e Shoah* (Milan: Rizzoli, 2000), 327.

12. For Weizsäcker, see Leonidas E. Hill, *Die Weizsäcker Papiere* (Frankfurt: Allstein, 1974). I am grateful to historian Michael Phayer for pointing this out to me. See his *The Catholic Church and the Holocaust, 1930–1965* (Bloomington: Indiana University Press, 2000), 60.

13. ADSS, X, notes of Maglione, January 6, 1944, 68.

14. See ADSS, X, docs. 2, 13, 43, 111, 145, and 148.

15. Founded after the Evian Conference on refugees in 1938, the ICR took on new life after the Bermuda Conference in April 1943. It originally represented twenty-nine nations but expanded to thirty-six by 1945. The ICR and the WRB cooperated and exchanged information to avoid duplicating their efforts. See Wyman, *Abandonment of the Jews*, 137–42.

16. Foreign Relations of the United States: Diplomatic Papers, 1944, 7 vols., vol. I (General) (Washington, D.C.: U.S. Government Printing Office, 1966), British Ambassador Winant to American Secretary of State, August 14, 1944, 1123–24. Henceforth cited as FR, 1944. See also Roosevelt Library, Morgenthau Diary, book 767 (reel 222), "Report of the War Refugee Board for the Week of August 14 to 19, 1944," 42–43.

17. ADSS, X, doc. 290, Secretariat of State to Weizsäcker, August 7, 1944, 373. In July 1944, Weizsäcker had moved into the same Santa Marta residence in the Vatican City where the American and British representatives to the Holy See had lived during the German occupation of Rome. Unlike them, however, he kept a secret radio transmitter with which he communicated with his government. See Owen Chadwick, *Britain and the Vatican During the Second World War* (Cambridge: Cambridge University Press, 1986), 309.

18. ADSS, X, note of Tardini attached to doc. 290, August 7, 1944, 373.

19. Ibid., footnote 3 attached to doc. 290, 373.

20. Ibid., doc. 319, undersecretary of the Section of Extraordinary Ecclesiastical Affairs to Taylor, September 8, 1944, 414; and FR, 1944, vol. I, American representative on the Advisory Council for Italy to the American secretary of state, September 8, 1944, 1149.

21. On August 7, for example, the day that Tardini spoke with Weizsäcker about the Jews in Italy, an American diplomat met with the pope to discuss the rescue plan for northern Italy. The diplomat reported that the pope assured him that "at the earliest moment he would make such an approach." But Pius did not tell him what Tardini was doing that very day. See Roosevelt Library, Morgenthau Diary, book 761 (reel 220), 133. At the end of August, a full month after Taylor's first contact with the pope on this matter, Allied diplomats still had no idea whether he had acted. See FR, 1944, vol. I, American secretary of state to political advisor Murphy, August 30, 1944, 1140–41.

22. More general Vatican appeals to the Germans on behalf of Jews continued, however. See ADSS, X, docs. 378, 388, 392, 394, 438, 439, 445, 456, and 462.

23. Ibid., XI, doc. 216, Maglione to Bernardini, June 7, 1944, 366; and doc. 248, Bernardini to Maglione, June 15, 1944, 401–402.

24. Ibid., X, doc. 284, Maglione to Bernardini, August 1, 1944, 368.

25. Ibid., footnote 2 attached to doc. 284, 368.

26. Ibid., doc. 379, notes of the Secretariat of State, end of October 1944, 463, also makes a vague reference to an effort by the papal nuncio to Italy, Monsignor Francesco Borgongini Duca, to help Jews in internment. If a meaningful effort was made, it is hard to understand why a document providing details was not published.

27. RL, WRB Box 59, folder on northern Italy, Heathcote-Smith to acting resident representative of the ICR in London, October 27, 1944, 4 pp. Roswell D. McClelland of the WRB later learned that Kiniger had been what he called a "commercial representative of the Neo-Fascist Gov. [sic] at Zürich" who had sought political asylum in Switzerland in August or September 1944, been refused, and subsequently offered his services to Bernardini. See RL, WRB, same box and folder, McClelland report, January 3, 1945.

28. Ibid., reports of Bruno Kiniger, Bern, November 12, 1944, 4 pp., and Klosters, January 5, 1945, 4 pp.

29. Ibid., Heathcote-Smith report, October 27, 1944, 1.

30. Ibid., Heathcote-Smith to McClelland, October 27, 1944.

31. Ibid. Heathcote-Smith to McClelland, January 19, 1945.

32. Ibid., McClelland to Heathcote-Smith, telegram, November 22, 1944.

33. Ibid., commissario of the Istituto nazionale fascista per l'assicurazione contro gli infortuni sul lavoro to Kiniger, December 18, 1944.

34. Ibid., Kiniger report, January 5, 1945, 1.

35. In one of the rare cases in which he defied German wishes, Mussolini dismissed Buffarini Guidi in February 1945. The former minister of the interior was caught while trying to flee to Switzerland at the end of April, and later executed in Milan.

36. Report of Raffaele Jona, March 1945, printed in full in Sarfatti, *Gli ebrei nell'Italia fascista*, 347–57, 357.

CONCLUSION

1. Letter cited in Robert Graham, "Relations of Pius XII and the Catholic Community with Jewish Organizations," in Ivo Herzer, ed., *The Italian Refuge: Rescue of Jews During the Holocaust* (Washington, D.C.: Catholic University of America Press, 1989), 231–53, 231. The rabbi added that he had also thanked the pope personally during a private audience on June 6.
2. Ibid., 232.
3. ADSS, X, doc. 288, unnamed Roman Jew to Pius XII, August 5, 1944, 371.
4. Graham, "Relations of Pius XII and the Catholic Community with Jewish Organizations," 232.
5. Aryeh L. Kubovy, "The Silence of Pope Pius XII and the Beginnings of the 'Jewish Document,' " *Yad Vashem Studies* VI, 1967, 7–25.
6. Robert Leiber, "Pio XII e gli ebrei di Roma, 1943–1944," *La Civiltà Cattolica*, 1961, vol. I, quad. 2657, March 4, 1961, 449–58, 458.
7. Published in *Catholics Remember the Holocaust* (Washington, D.C.: U.S. Catholic Conference, 1998), 47–56, 53. The estimate that the pope and his representatives saved hundreds of thousands of Jews came from Pinchas Lapide, who explained clearly that he came to that conclusion first by subtracting the 6 million Jewish dead from the total of 8.3 million Jews in German-controlled Europe before the war, then by subtracting roughly 1 million who fled into the free world from the total of 2.3 million who escaped death, and finally by subtracting "all reasonable claims" of rescues made by Protestants and non-Christians. He thus calculated that "the Catholic Church had been instrumental" in saving at least 700,000 Jews, and more probably 860,000. Such methodology was obviously flawed, and the results were unreliable. Also, Lapide did not say that the 700,000 to 860,000 Jews were all saved by the pope and his representatives. He included Catholics in general among the rescuers. See his *The Last Three Popes and the Jews* (London: Souvenir, 1967), 212 and 215. The book was published by Hawthorn in New York the same year, under the title *Three Popes and the Jews*.
8. Kubovy, "Silence of Pope Pius XII," 19.
9. Ibid., 18.
10. See *Pius XII and the Holocaust: A Reader* (Milwaukee: Catholic League for Religious and Civil Rights, 1988), 94–137.
11. CDEC, b. 13-B, f. Roma, Sorani report, July 19, 1966, 5 pp., 3.
12. See Chapter Ten.
13. See Chapter Eleven.
14. Ibid.
15. See Chapter Fifteen.
16. See Chapter Thirteen.
17. See Chapter Twelve.

18. See Chapter Fourteen.

19. See Chapter Fifteen.

20. See Chapter Seventeen.

21. For details, see the introduction.

22. ADSS, IX, doc. 274, Cassulo to Maglione, July 21, 1943, 410–11.

23. Ibid., doc. 298, Maglione to Cassulo, August 20, 1943, 436.

24. ADSS, II, doc. 105, Pius XII to Preysing, April 30, 1943, 318–27, 324.

25. Printed in *L'Osservatore Romano*, June 3, 1943, 1; and *La Civiltà Cattolica*, anno 94, 1943, vol. II, quad. 2232, June 19, 1943, 329–34, 331. This explanation occurred in one of the two speeches, mentioned above and in the introduction, in which the pope stated that some people were dying because of their nationality or "descent."

26. These issues are discussed by Guenter Lewy, *The Catholic Church and Nazi Germany* (New York: McGraw-Hill, 1964), 303–4.

27. Raul Hilberg, *The Destruction of the European Jews*, 3 vols. (New York: Holmes & Meier, 1985), II, 586–87.

28. Leon Poliakov, *Harvest of Hate: The Nazi Program for the Destruction of the Jews of Europe* (1951 in France; 1954 in the United States; New York: Holocaust Library, 1986), 296. Among the deported Jews who had become Catholics was a nun named Edith Stein, who was gassed at Auschwitz on August 9, 1942. She has since been beatified.

29. See Chapter Fifteen.

30. See Father Robert Leiber's testimony to that effect in his article "Der Papst und die Verfolgung der Juden," in Fritz J. Raddatz, ed., *Summa iniuria oder durfte der Papst schweigen? Hochhuths 'Stellvertreter" in der öffentlichen Kritik* (Reinbek bei Hamburg: Rowohlt, 1963), 101–7, 104. See also documents published in Saul Friedländer, *Pius XII and the Third Reich: A Documentation*, trans. Charles Fullman (New York: Knopf, 1966), 183–96 and 211–16; and Lewy, *Catholic Church and Nazi Germany*, 305.

31. Leiber, "Der Papst und die Verfolgung der Juden," 103.

32. See Chapter Fourteen.

33. Ibid.

34. On these activities, see Owen Chadwick, *Britain and the Vatican During the Second World War* (Cambridge: Cambridge University Press, 1986), 291–300; and J. P. Gallagher, *Scarlet Pimpernel of the Vatican* (London: Souvenir, 1967). Contrary to what is sometimes claimed, Monsignor O'Flaherty's protégés rarely included Jews.

35. "Il dovere più arduo e più alto," and information column, *L'Osservatore Romano*, June 9–10, 1944, 1.

36. "Cronaca Contemporanea," *La Civiltà Cattolica*, anno 95, vol. III, quad. 2257, July 1, 1944, 56–59.

37. The arguments are well summarized in David Alvarez and Robert A. Graham, S.J., *Nothing Sacred: Nazi Espionage Against the Vatican, 1939–1945* (London: Frank Cass, 1997), 85–88; and Robert A. Graham, S.J., "Voleva Hitler

allontanare da Roma Pio XII?," *La Civiltà Cattolica,* anno 123, vol. I, quad. 2920, February 19, 1972, 319–27, and quad. 2921, March 4, 1972, 454–61.

38. Chadwick, *Britain and the Vatican,* 150–80.

39. Ibid., 222–45 and 278–86.

40. Ibid., 122.

41. See Chapter Nineteen.

42. See Chapter Sixteen.

43. See Chapter Seventeen.

44. See Chapter Six. The Secretariat of State was diminished even further by the death of Cardinal Maglione on August 22, 1944. The pope did not appoint a successor, and the burden on Montini and Tardini grew even heavier.

45. Alvarez and Graham, *Nothing Sacred,* 93.

46. Fargion, *Il Libro della memoria,* 26–27. Of the 6,749 deportees, 5,916 did not return. Another 303 Jews were murdered within the country. Approximately 4,159 of those deported and 192 of those murdered within the country had been born in Italy. The others were refugees.

47. I am grateful to Dr. Eugene J. Fisher of the National Conference of Catholic Bishops for this information.

48. Declaration of the Second Vatican Council, "Nostra Aetate," October 28, 1965, n.4.

49. "We Remember," 47–55.

50. The Lenten apology is described in *New York Times,* March 13, 2000, 1.

51. The document, prepared under the pope's direction by a special committee of theologians and signed by Cardinal Joseph Ratzinger of the Congregation for the Doctrine of the Faith, the former Holy Office, may be found at www.vatican.va/roman_curia/congregations (doctrine-of-the-faith). For detailed analysis, see Garry Wills, "The Vatican Regrets," *New York Review of Books,* May 25, 2000, 19–20; and *Papal Sins: Structures of Deceit* (New York: Doubleday, 2000), 13–19.

52. Official Vatican text of Pope John Paul's speech, *New York Times,* March 24, 2000, 6.

53. "We Remember," 47–55.

Index